Mesopotamian Religious Architecture

MESOPOTAMIAN

RELIGIOUS ARCHITECTURE

Alexander through the Parthians

SUSAN B. DOWNEY

PRINCETON UNIVERSITY PRESS

PRINCETON, NEW JERSEY

Copyright © 1988 by Princeton University Press
Published by Princeton University Press, 41 William Street,
Princeton, New Jersey 08540
In the United Kingdom: Princeton University Press, Guildford, Surrey

Library of Congress Cataloging in Publication Data will be
found on the last printed page of this book

ISBN 0-691-03589-X

This book has been composed in Linotron Bembo

Clothbound editions of Princeton University Press books
are printed on acid-free paper, and binding materials are
chosen for strength and durability. Paperbacks, although satisfactory
for personal collections, are not usually suitable for library rebinding

Printed in the United States of America by Princeton University Press,
Princeton, New Jersey

DESIGNED BY LAURY A. EGAN

TO EDWARD

CONTENTS

LIST OF ILLUSTRATIONS

LIST OF ABBREVIATIONS

Books and Articles

Andrae, *Partherstadt Assur* = Walter Andrae and Heinz Lenzen, *Die Partherstadt Assur* (57. *WVDOG*) (Leipzig, 1933; reprint Osnabrück, 1967).

Andrae, *Wiedererstandene Assur* = Walter Andrae, *Das Wiedererstandene Assur* (Leipzig, 1938; 2d ed., Barthel Hrouda, ed., Munich, 1977).

Aymard, "Une ville" = André Aymard, "Une ville de la Babylonie séleucide d'après les contrats cunéiformes," *Revue des études anciennes* XL (1938), 5-42.

Bernard, *Fouilles d'Aï Khanoum* I = Paul Bernard, et al., *Fouilles d'Aï Khanoum* I (*Mémoires de la délégation archéologique française en Afghanistan* XXI) (Paris, 1973).

Bernard, "Problèmes d'histoire coloniale grecque" = Paul Bernard, "Problèmes d'histoire coloniale grecque à travers l'urbanisme d'une cité hellénistique d'Asie centrale," *150 Jahre Deutsches archäologisches Institut 1829-1979* (Mainz, 1981).

Bernard, "Traditions orientales" = Paul Bernard, "Les traditions orientales dans l'architecture gréco-bactrienne," *Journal Asiatique* CCLXIV (1976), 245-75.

Bickerman, *Der Gott der Makkabäer* = Elias Bickerman, *Der Gott der Makkabäer* (Berlin, 1937).

Bickerman, *Institutions des Séleucides* = Elias Bikerman [Bickerman], *Institutions des Séleucides* (Haut-Commissariat de la République française en Syrie et au Liban, *Bibliothèque Archéologique et Historique* XXVI) (Paris, 1938).

Bowman, "Anu-uballit-Kephalon" = Raymond A. Bowman, "Anu-uballit-Kephalon," *American Journal of Semitic Languages and Literatures* LVI (1939), 231-43.

Colledge, *Parthian Art* = Malcolm A. R. Colledge, *Parthian Art* (Ithaca, N.Y., 1977).

Cumont, *Fouilles* = Franz Cumont, *Fouilles de Doura-Europos* (1922/23) (Haut-Commissariat de la Republique française en Syrie et au Liban, *Bi-bliothèque Archéologique et Historique* IX) (Paris, 1925).

Doty, *Cuneiform Archives* = Lawrence Timothy Doty, *Cuneiform Archives from Hellenistic Uruk* (dissertation, Yale University, 1977; University Microfilms, Ann Arbor, Mich.).

Downey, "Temples" = Susan B. Downey, " 'Temples à escaliers': The Dura Evidence," *California Studies in Classical Antiquity* IX (1976), 21-39.

Downey, *Heracles Sculpture* = Susan B. Downey, *The Excavations at Dura-Europos, Final Report* III, part I, fascicle 1: *The Heracles Sculpture* (New Haven, 1969).

Downey, *Stone and Plaster Sculpture* = Susan B. Downey, *The Stone and Plaster Sculpture: Excavations at Dura-Europos* (*Monumenta Archaeologica* 5) (Los Angeles, 1977).

Dura Report I [etc.] = *The Excavations at Dura-Europos, Preliminary Report on the First [etc.] Season of Work* (New Haven, 1929-1952).

Eissfeldt, *Tempel und Kulte* = Otto Eissfeldt, *Tempel und Kulte syrischer Städte in hellenistisch-römischer Zeit* (*Der alte Orient* 40) (Leipzig, 1941).

Falkenstein, *Topographie* = Adam Falkenstein, *Topographie von Uruk* I: *Uruk zur Seleukidenzeit* (*Ausgrabungen der Deutschen Forschungsgemeinschaft in Uruk-Warka* 3) (Leipzig, 1941).

Final Report = *The Excavations at Dura-Europos, Final Report*.

Francfort, *Fouilles d'Aï Khanoum* III = Henri-Paul Francfort, *Fouilles d'Aï Khanoum* III: *Le Sanctuaire du temple à niches indentées* 2: *Les trouvailles* (*Mémoires de la délégation archéologique française en Afghanistan* XXVII) (Paris, 1984).

Ghirshman, *Persian Art* = Roman Ghirshman, *Persian Art*, 249 B.C.-A.D. 651 (New York, 1962).

Ghirshman, *Terrasses sacrées* = Roman Ghirshman, *Terrasses sacrées de Bard-è Néchandeh et Masjid-i Solaiman* (*Mémoires de la délégation archéologique en Iran* XLV) (Paris, 1976).

Goossens, "Au déclin" = Godefroid Goossens,

"Au déclin de la civilisation babylonienne: Uruk sous les Séleucides," *Académie royale de Belgique, Bulletin de la classe des lettres et sciences morales et politiques*, 5th series, XXVII (1941), 222-44.

Grayson, *Chronicles* = A. K. Grayson, *Assyrian and Babylonian Chronicles* (Locust Valley, N.Y., 1975).

Gullini, *Architettura iranica* = Giorgio Gullini, *Architettura iranica dagli Achemenidi agli Sasanidi* (Torino, 1964).

Haller, *Heiligtümer* = Arndt Haller and Walter Andrae, *Die Heiligtümer des Gottes Assur und der Sin-Šamaš-Tempel in Assur* (67. *WVDOG*) (Berlin, 1955).

Heinrich, *Tempel und Heiligtümer* = Ernst Heinrich, *Die Tempel und Heiligtümer in alten Mesopotamien. Typologie, Morphologie und Geschichte* (Deutsches archäologisches Institut, *Denkmäler antiker Architektur* 14) (Berlin, 1982).

Hopkins, *Topography* = Clark Hopkins, *Topography and Architecture of Seleucia on the Tigris* (Ann Arbor, Mich., 1972).

Jordan, *Uruk-Warka* = Julius Jordan, *Uruk-Warka. Nach den Ausgrabungen durch die Deutsche Orient-Gesellschaft* (51. *WVDOG*) (Leipzig, 1928; reprint, Osnabrück, 1969).

Keall, *Late Parthian Nippur* = Edward John Keall, *The Significance of Late Parthian Nippur* (dissertation, University of Michigan, 1970; University Microfilms, Ann Arbor, Mich.).

Köhler and Ungnad, *Hundert ausgewählte Rechtsurkunden* = J. Köhler and A. Ungnad, *Hundert ausgewählte Rechtsurkunden aus der Spätzeit des babylonischen Schrifttums von Xerxes bis zum Mithradates II* (Leipzig, 1911).

Koldewey, *Die Tempel von Babylon und Borsippa* = Robert Koldewey, *Die Tempel von Babylon und Borsippa* (*Ausgrabungen der Deutschen Orient-Gesellschaft in Babylon* I) (15. *WVDOG*) (Leipzig, 1911).

Koldewey, *Wieder erstehende Babylon* = Robert Koldeway, *Das wieder erstehende Babylon* (Leipzig, 1913).

Lenzen, "Ausgrabungen in Hatra" = H. Lenzen, "Ausgrabungen in Hatra," *AA* LXX (1955), 334-75.

Lenzen, *MDOG* 87 = H. Lenzen, "Bericht über die vom Deutschen archäologischen Institut und der Deutschen Orient-Gesellschaft in Uruk-Warka am Anfang des Jahres 1954 unternommenen Ausgrabungen," *MDOG* 87 (Feb. 1955), 26-68.

Lenzen, *Neue Deutsche Ausgrabungen* = Heinrich

Lenzen, "Die deutschen Ausgrabungen in Uruk von 1954-1957," in Deutsches archäologisches Institut, *Neue deutsche Ausgrabungen in Mittelmeergebiet und im vorderen Orient* (Berlin, 1959), 12-30.

Lucian, *DDS* = Lucian, *De Dea Syria* (Περὶ τῆς Συρίης θεοῦ), Loeb Classical Library, vol. IV, A. M. Harmon, trans. (Cambridge, Mass., and London, 1961).

McEwan, *Priest and Temple* = Gilbert J. P. McEwan, *Priest and Temple in Hellenistic Babylonia* (*Freiburger altorientalische Studien* 4) (Wiesbaden, 1981).

Milik, *Dédicaces* = J. T. Milik, *Dédicaces faites par des dieux* (Institut français d'archéologie de Beyrouth, *Bibliothèque Archéologique et Historique* XCII) (Paris, 1972).

Oates, *Studies* = David Oates, *Studies in the Ancient History of Northern Iraq* (London, 1968).

Oelsner, "Kontinuität und Wandel" = Joachim Oelsner, "Kontinuität und Wandel in Gesellschaft und Kultur Babyloniens in hellenisticher Zeit," *Klio* LX (1978), 101-116.

Perkins, *Art* = Ann Perkins, *The Art of Dura-Europos* (Oxford, 1973).

Pliny, *NH* = Gaius Plinius Secundus, *Naturalis Historia (Natural History)*, Loeb Classical Library, H. Rackham, ed. (Cambridge, Mass., and London, 1942).

Pritchard, *ANET*, 3rd ed. = James Pritchard, *Ancient Near Eastern Texts Relating to the Old Testament*, 3rd ed. with supplement (Princeton, 1969).

Rostovtzeff, *Dura-Europos* = M. I. Rostovtzeff, *Dura-Europos and its Art* (Oxford, 1938).

Rostovtzeff, "Parthian Art" = M. I. Rostovtzeff, "Dura and the Problem of Parthian Art," *YCS* V (1935), 155-304.

Rostovtzeff, *SEHHW* = M. I. Rostovtzeff, *The Social and Economic History of the Hellenistic World* (Oxford, 1941).

Rostovtzeff, "Seleucid Babylonia" = M. I. Rostovtzeff, "Seleucid Babylonia," *YCS* III (1932), 1-114.

Rutten, *Contrats* = M. Rutten, *Contrats de l'époque Séleucide conservés au Musée du Louvre* (*Babyloniaca* XV) (Paris, 1935).

Safar and Mustapha, *Hatra* = Fuad Safar and Mohammed Ali Mustapha, *Hatra: The City of the Sun God* (Baghdad, 1974).

Sarkisian, "Self-governing Cities" = G. Ch. Sarkisian, "Samoupravlja juščijsja gorod Seluvkidskoj Babilonii," *Vestnik Drevnii Istorii* XXXIX (1952.1), 63-83.

Sarkisian, "Social Role" = G. Ch. Sarkisian, "Social'naja rol' klinopisnoj notarial'no-pravovoj sistemy v ellinističeskoj Vavilonii,"*Eos* XLVIII.2 (1956), 29-44.

Schippmann, *Feuerheiligtümer* = Klaus Schippmann, *Die iranischen Feuerheiligtümer* (Berlin and New York, 1971).

Schlumberger, *L'Orient hellénisé* = Daniel Schlumberger, *L'Orient hellénisé* (Paris, 1970).

E. Schmidt, "Die Griechen in Babylon" = Erich Schmidt, "Die Griechen in Babylon und das Weiterleben ihrer Kultur," *AA* LVI (1941), 786-844.

J. Schmidt, *BaM* V (1970) = Jürgen Schmidt, "Uruk-Warka, Zusammenfassender Bericht über die 27. Kampagne 1969," *BaM* V (1970), 51-96.

Smith, *Babylonian Historical Texts* = Sidney Smith, *Babylonian Historical Texts Relating to the Capture and Downfall of Babylon* (London, 1924).

Thureau-Dangin, *Rituels accadiens* = F. Thureau-Dangin, *Rituels accadiens* (Paris, 1921).

Tscherikower, *Hellenistischen Städtegründungen* = V. Tscherikower, *Die Hellenistischen Städtegründungen von Alexander dem Grossen bis auf die Römerzeit* (*Philologus*, suppl. XIX.1) (Leipzig, 1927).

Unger, *Babylon* = Eckhard Unger, *Babylon* (reprint Berlin, 1970, after the 1931 edition).

Welles, "Gods" = C. B. Welles, "The Gods of Dura-Europos," in *Beiträge zur alten Geschichte und deren Nachleben, Festschrift für Franz Altheim* II (Berlin, 1970), 50-65.

Welles, "Inscriptions" = R. N. Frye, J. F. Gilliam, H. Ingholt, and C. B. Welles, "Inscriptions from Dura-Europos," *YCS* XIV (1955), 127-213.

Wetzel, *Das Babylon der Spätzeit* = Friedrich Wetzel, Erich Schmidt, and Alfred Mallwitz, *Das Babylon der Spätzeit* (62. *WVDOG*) (Berlin, 1957).

Wetzel, *Hauptheiligtum* = Friedrich Wetzel and

F. H. Weissbach, *Das Hauptheiligtum des Marduk in Babylon, Esagila und Etemenanki* (59.*WVDOG*) (Leipzig, 1938; reprint, Osnabrück, 1967).

Will, *Histoire* II = Edouard Will, *Histoire politique du monde hellénistique* II: *Des Avènements d'Antiochos III et de Philippe V à la fin des Lagides* (*Annales de l'Est*, Mémoire no. 32) (Nancy, 1967).

PERIODICALS AND SERIES

AA = *Archäologischer Anzeiger.*

AJSemL = *American Journal of Semitic Languages and Literatures.*

BaM = *Mitteilungen des deutschen archäologischen Institut,* Abteilung Baghdad.

BCH = *Bulletin de correspondance hellénique.*

BEFEO = *Bulletin de l'École Française d'Extrême-Orient.*

CRAI = *Comptes rendus de l'Académie des inscriptions et belles lettres.*

EPRO = *Études préliminaires aux religions orientales dans l'Empire romain.*

JAOS = *Journal of the American Oriental Society.*

JCS = *Journal of Cuneiform Studies.*

JHS = *Journal of Hellenic Studies.*

JNES = *Journal of Near Eastern Studies.*

MDOG = *Mitteilungen der deutschen Orient-Gesellschaft.*

MélUSJ = *Mélanges de l'Université Saint-Joseph, Beyrouth.*

OGIS = *Orientis Graeci Inscriptiones Selectae.*

REA = *Revue des études anciennes.*

UVB = *Vorläufiger Bericht über die von der Notgemeinschaft der deutschen Wissenschaft in Uruk-Warka unternommenen Ausgrabungen* (issued under slightly varying titles from 1932 to the present).

WVDOG = *Wissenschaftliche Veröffentlichen der deutschen Orient-Gesellschaft.*

ZAssyr = *Zeitschrift für Assyrologie,* Berlin.

PREFACE

THE SUBJECT of this book overlaps the boundaries between Classical and Near Eastern studies. Though I have confined my discussion largely to the period after the arrival of Alexander the Great in the Near East, architectural and cultural developments after the Greek conquest are not comprehensible without reference to earlier periods. This is especially true of cities that had been prominent for centuries beforehand, e.g., Uruk and Babylon. My study is based primarily on the physical remains of the buildings and of cult installations. Any discussion of the possible functions of rooms within the temples and of rites that may have taken place there is, of necessity, based also—in some cases primarily—on textual and epigraphical evidence. Epigraphical evidence is likewise the foundation of what little can be said about the people who built and worshipped in these temples and about the place of each temple in the social and religious life of the city. Akkadian cuneiform texts provide considerable evidence about the temples of Uruk and, to a lesser extent, of Babylon; and Aramaic inscriptions are important for the understanding of Hatra and Assur. As a classicist, I am dependent on those texts which have been translated. For Uruk and Babylon, I have used especially Falkenstein, *Topographie von Uruk* (Leipzig, 1941), Thureau-Dangin, *Rituels accadiens* (Paris, 1921), and the recent book by Gilbert J. P. McEwan, *Priest and Temple in Hellenistic Babylonia* (Wiesbaden, 1981). In cases where the interpretation of a text is controversial, I have limited my discussion to reporting the controversies. Giorgio Buccellati of UCLA has assisted me in the interpretation of Akkadian texts. In the absence of a full excavation report, much of the information about the temples of Hatra is derived from Fuad Safar and Mohammed Ali Mustapha, *Hatra: The City of the Sun God* (Baghdad, 1974) (in Arabic). Portions of the text were translated for me by Yassin al-Khalesi of Arabico. Susan Matheson, curator of the Dura-Europos collection in the Yale University Art Gallery, kindly granted me access to the unpublished manuscripts by Frank E. Brown on the first Temple of Zeus Megistos at Dura-Europos, and by Henry Pearson on the Temples of Bel and Atargatis.

The research for this book was begun during a stay in Iran, Afghanistan, Iraq, and Syria in the difficult days of 1978/79. This trip was financed in part through a Grant-in-Aid from the American Council of Learned Societies. Though travel in the Middle East was somewhat restricted during that period, I was able to visit a number of the sites that figure prominently in this work, notably Uruk, Hatra, and Assur in Iraq and Dura-Europos in Syria. I wish to thank the State Organization of Antiquities of the Republic of Iraq and the Directorate General of Antiquities of Syria for facilitating my travel to these sites, and the State Organization of Antiquities of the Republic of Iraq for hospitality at Assur and Hatra.

During my stays in Tehran and Baghdad, I profited from discussion with other scholars. I would like to cite especially David Stronach, at that time director of the British Institute of Persian Studies; Peter Calmeyer and Hubertus von Gall of the Deutsches Archäologisches Institut, Abteilung Tehran; and Antonio Invernizzi of the University of Torino. In a field as complex and controversial as that covered by this study, differences of opinion are inevitable. The manuscript underwent a final revision in September/October 1986. Literature that appears after that date cannot be taken into account. Responsibility for opinions expressed, as well as for any errors, remains my own.

Credits for the photographs are given in the captions. I wish, however, to thank especially Paul Bernard for generously supplying photographs of Aï Khanoum. Grants from the Academic Senate at UCLA and a grant from the UCLA Arts Council aided in the purchase of photographs. Tim Seymour redrew the map and the following illustrations: figures 3, 5, 6, 8-13, 20, 26-28, 30-31, 39, 41, 45, 52-53, 55, 62, 65-66, 68, 71-88.

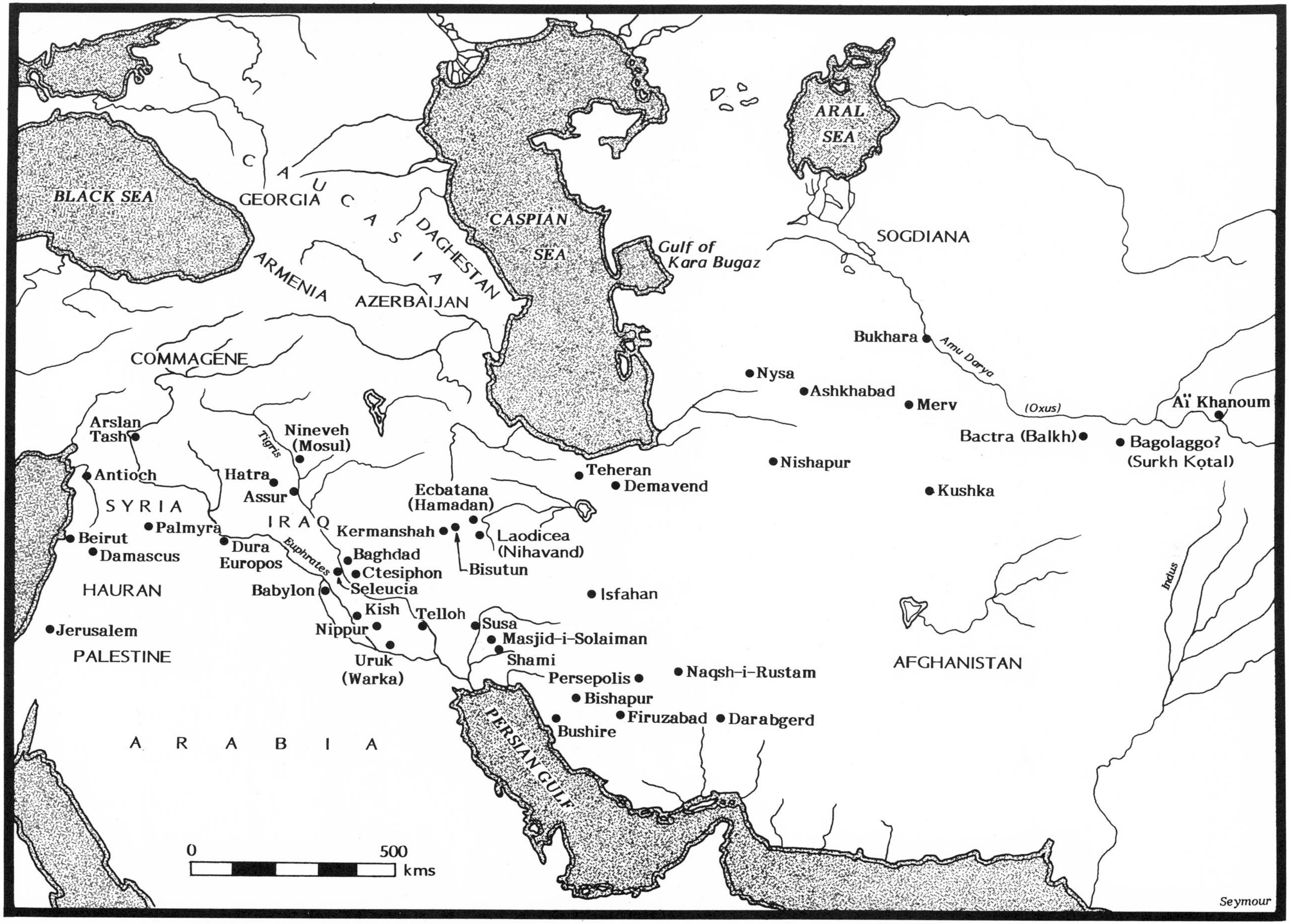

Aï Khanoum

Bagolaggo?
(Surkh Kotal)

Bactra (Balkh)

(Oxus)

Indus

Bukhara Amu Darya

SOGDIANA

Ashkhabad Merv Kushka

Nysa

AFGHANISTAN

ARAL
SEA

Nishapur

Gulf of
Kara Bugaz

Naqsh-i-Rustam

Demavend Darabgerd

Teheran Firuzabad

Bishapur

CASPIAN
SEA Isfahan Persepolis

Bushire

Masjid-i-Solaiman

Shami

Laodicea Susa

(Nihavand) PERSIAN GULF

Ecbatana Bisutun

(Hamadan)

Telloh

Kermanshah Kish

CAUCASIA Baghdad Ctesiphon Uruk

GEORGIA Seleucia Nippur (Warka)

DAGHESTAN

Nineveh Babylon

AZERBAIJAN (Mosul)

ARMENIA Euphrates

Tigris

Hatra Assur

COMMAGENE Dura

Europos ARABIA

Antioch Palmyra

Arslan Damascus

Tash S Y R I A

Beirut HAURAN

BLACK SEA

Jerusalem PALESTINE

I R A Q

500 kms

0

Map of the Near East

Seymour

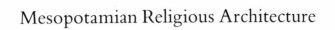

Mesopotamian Religious Architecture

INTRODUCTION

THE SUBJECT of this study, the survival and re-working of traditional Mesopotamian temple forms in the Near East during the Seleucid and Parthian periods, was suggested by the appearance in two widely separated cities of the Seleucid empire—Uruk in Mesopotamia and Aï Khanoum in Afghanistan—of temples that utilize traditional Mesopotamian forms to some degree. This is all the more striking because Uruk is an old city, an important center of Mesopotamian civilization, whereas Aï Khanoum is a Greek colony near the eastern limits of the Seleucid realm. The phenomenon might suggest a deliberate policy on the part of the Seleucid rulers of fostering traditional religious forms and practices in the old cities, while creating in the newly established colonies original types of religious architecture based on forms derived from Mesopotamian and other oriental traditions.

Royal support for the rebuilding of old shrines is clearly demonstrated at Babylon. Alexander the Great intended to rebuild the ziggurat of Marduk, Etemenanki (Strabo XVI.I.5; Arrian, *Anabasis* III.16.4; VII.17.1-4), and the archaeological record supports the statements in the sources that the task was begun.[1] In the years following Alexander's death, cuneiform texts record the clearing of debris from Esagila, the temple of Marduk; and Antiochos I at least made preparations for work on Esagila and on Ezida, the temple of Nabu in Borsippa. (These texts are discussed in the section on Babylon.) The Seleucid royal cult was apparently established in the temples of Babylon and Uruk. Uruk provides the most dramatic evidence for the revival of traditional religious architecture in Seleucid Mesopotamia, with the construction of two enormous sanctuaries, the Bit rēš and the Irigal, as well as work on one of the old sanctuaries, E-anna. The

Bit rēš and the Irigal were built by members of an old family, and there is only indirect evidence for royal support.[2]

The public architecture of Aï Khanoum shows a complex and apparently deliberate mixture of elements derived from a variety of traditions—Greek, Achaemenid, Mesopotamian. Although some of the civic buildings, notably the theater, gymnasium, and fountain, follow the norms of Greek architecture, the palace combines Greek and Achaemenid elements in an intricate fashion. The two temples so far discovered, on the other hand, are largely Mesopotamian in type, though raised on high podia probably derived from Achaemenid architecture. This combination of forms in the architecture of a distant colony argues for a considered attempt to create new styles of architecture based on an amalgamation of varied traditions.[3] The architecture of two Seleucid colonies in Mesopotamia, Dura-Europos and Seleucia on the Tigris, though poorly known, supports this idea to some extent.

The vast area from Mesopotamia through Iran and Afghanistan that was controlled at times by the Seleucids varies greatly, both culturally and geographically. Especially in the western part of this area, in Mesopotamia, Alexander and his successors found old cities with well-established, traditional cultures. Some of these cities, notably Babylon and Uruk, continued to exist under the Seleucids, and even to flourish, in the case of Uruk. Others, such as Nippur, Sippar, and Assur, fell into obscurity. The Seleucid kings, at the same time that they supported the rebuilding of temples in Babylon and probably in Uruk, also founded Greek colonies in Mesopotamia. The sources state explicitly that Seleukos I founded Seleucia on the Tigris for the purpose of drawing off the population of Bab-

---

[1] Mallwitz, in Wetzel, *Das Babylon der Spätzeit*, 2-22.
[2] McEwan, *Priest and Temple*, 161 f., 193-96; see the section on Uruk.

[3] Bernard, "Traditions orientales," 245-75.

3

ylon (Pausanias I.16.3; Pliny, *NH* VI.30.121f.). The colony of Dura-Europos on the Euphrates, founded about 300 B.C. by one Nicanor, possibly a general of Seleukos Nicator,[4] constitutes the westernmost point of this study.

Seleucid rulers also founded Greek colonies in Iran. Inscriptions show that two of these, Seleucia on the Eulaios, on the site of the venerable city of Susa, and Laodicea (Nihawand), had Greek political institutions. Antiochos III established the cult of his sister Laodice at Laodicea.[5] At the same time, as the sources demonstrate, some of the old temples not only survived the Greek conquest but remained wealthy and powerful. Inscriptions from Seleucia on the Eulaios, mostly enfranchisements of slaves, illustrate the complexity of the situation. They are texts in Greek, largely recording the freeing by Greeks of slaves according to Greek law, by consecration to the goddess Nanaia, but also for the life of the king.[6] These texts perhaps suggest that, as at Uruk, the traditional temples in Iran could be used for some administrative purposes. The wealth of the temples was tempting to some of the Greek rulers, hard-pressed for funds with which to wage war. Antiochos III was killed in 187 B.C. after plundering the Temple of Bel in Elam, for instance. According to Polybius (XXXI.9[11]), Antiochos IV wanted a contribution from the wealthy Temple of Artemis (Nanaia) in Elymais, presumably the temple at Susa. Polybius implies that Antiochos went away disappointed, but Appian (*Syr.* 66) states that he sacked the temple.[7] These attempts to take the temple treasure contrast with the situation in Babylon, where no such attempts are recorded. It is not clear whether the Seleucid rulers applied different policies in Iran than in Babylonia. Perhaps the riches of the temples in Elymais were more portable than the wealth of the temples in Babylonia, where much of the temple income was derived from property, especially land.[8] In Babylonia it appears that Antiochos tried to raise money by establishing or increasing taxes[9] rather than by plundering temples.

Few remains of architecture, either religious or civil, that can be attributed to the period of Greek

rule have been discovered in Iran. The open-air precinct at Shami might be a temple of Antiochos IV Epiphanes,[10] but could be of Parthian date.[11] In any case, this shrine does not follow a Mesopotamian scheme. Only the site of Masjid-i Solaiman in Elymais might have remains of a temple of Babylonian form going back to the Seleucid period, if Ghirshman's dating is correct.[12]

After the Parthian conquest of Mesopotamia, some of the old cities declined, whereas others, notably Assur, rose again to prominence. Temples based on Mesopotamian principles continued to be built in some cities, along with temples of other forms. But in the two cities with fairly well documented remains of both the Seleucid and the Parthian periods—Uruk and Dura-Europos—the temple forms change radically. Evidence from Iran is again sparse; temples that borrow from Mesopotamian forms are so far attested only at Masjid-i Solaiman and Bard-è Néchandeh. Aï Khanoum was apparently destroyed about the middle of the second century B.C.[13]

Study of the architectural remains and of textual evidence reveals considerable variation from one city to another. In this volume, I shall present and discuss the evidence city by city in the hope of revealing some patterns—or perhaps the lack of pattern. I shall consider not only the architectural form of the temples but also the available information about the people who built and used them. The study will be confined to temples that in some way follow or reflect Mesopotamian traditions, though in some cases I shall discuss other buildings in order to place the temples of Mesopotamian type in the context of the city's architecture as a whole. The evidence is unfortunately very uneven, due largely to a combination of the hazards of survival and the amount of excavation in the late levels of some of the old cities. For example, excavations have provided a great deal of information, both textual and archaeological, about Seleucid Uruk and a lesser amount about Babylon, but very little about other cities of southern Mesopotamia after the Greek conquest. Seleucia is very poorly preserved and only partially excavated. Dura-Europos, carefully

[4] Cumont, *Fouilles*, xv-xviii; Rostovtzeff, *Dura-Europos*, 10.

[5] Louis Robert, "Inscriptions séleucides de Phrygie et d'Iran," *Hellenica* VII (1949), 5-29.

[6] Louis Robert, "Études d'épigraphie grecque," *Revue de Philologie*, 3rd series, X (62)(1936), 137-48.

[7] Rostovtzeff, *SEHHW* II, 695 f.; Bickerman, *Institutions des Séleucides*, 121; W. W. Tarn, *The Greeks in Bactria and India* (Cambridge, 1938), 436-66, app. 7.

[8] McEwan, *Priest and Temple*, 121-24.

[9] Rostovtzeff, "Seleucid Babylonia," 69; Doty, *Cuneiform Archives*, 330.

[10] Ghirshman, *Iran* (London, 1954), 278 f.; idem, *Persian Art*, 21.

[11] Schippmann, *Feuerheiligtümer*, 227-33.

[12] Ghirshman, *Terrasses sacrées*, 71-91. The dating is discussed in the section on Masjid-i Solaiman.

[13] Bernard and Rapin, "Le Palais. La Trésorerie," *BEFEO* LXVIII (1980), 23-27.

excavated but incompletely published, provides our best evidence for the Parthian period; but little remains of the Seleucid city. The buildings of Parthian Assur are well known, but few inscriptions were found, and the excavations of Hatra have been published only in a summary form.

The evidence suggests that the traditions of Mesopotamian religious architecture remained strong but that the manifestations of this tradition were different from one city to another. It will be the object of this study to point out these differences and, where possible, to explain them.

1

OLD MESOPOTAMIAN CITIES
IN THE SELEUCID PERIOD

BABYLON

When Alexander the Great entered Babylon (fig. 1), he found the ziggurat of Marduk, Etemenanki, in ruins, probably as a result of neglect rather than of deliberate destruction. Both the written sources and the archaeological remains leave some doubt about Achaemenid policy and building activities in Babylon. The Nabonidus chronicle represents Cyrus as respecting the religion of the Babylonians. It reports that Ugbaru, governor of the Guti, and the troops of Cyrus entered Babylon without a fight: "The shield- (bearing troops) of the Guti entered Babylon without a fight. (But) there was no interruption (of rites) in Esagil or the (other) temples and no date (for a performance) was missed."[1] Cyrus was received with joy in Babylon: "There was peace in the city while Cyrus (II) spoke his greeting to all of Babylon." Furthermore, the gods of Akkad, whom Nabonidus had brought up to Babylon, were returned to their own cities. At the end of this section of the chronicle there is a mention of "Nabu to Esagil" and of Bel.[2] Likewise, the Cyrus cylinder represents Cyrus as restoring the old sanctuaries of Babylonia that had been violated or neglected by Nabonidus.[3] On baked bricks found in Uruk Cyrus is described as the "builder" or "caretaker" of Esagila and Ezida, the temples of Babylon and Borsippa.[4] Under Darius I (522/21-486 B.C.) the delivery of 410 baked bricks for the Temple of Marbiti (a part of Esagila) is recorded, and a further delivery of bricks for the cult niche of the Temple of the god Marbiti is recorded under Xerxes I (486-465 B.C.).[5] Both Strabo (XVI.I.5) and Arrian (III.16.4; VII.17.2) state that Xerxes destroyed the tomb or temple of Bel (the ziggurat). Weissbach, however, notes that the fact that Herodotos (I.181-83) says nothing about this destruction casts doubt on the truth of these statements. It seems more likely that the ziggurat had simply decayed through neglect.[6]

In any case, it is clear that when Alexander arrived in Babylon, the ziggurat needed to be rebuilt. According to Strabo (XVI.I.5), Alexander intended to rebuild the "Tomb of Belos" but was unable to finish this enormous task due to his illness

[1] Grayson, *Chronicles* 109 f., chron. 7.iii.15-18; Smith, *Babylonian Historical Texts*, 117, lines 15-18 (the discussion, transcription, and translation of the text are on pp. 98-123); Pritchard, *ANET*, 3rd ed., 305-307. Cf. also the "Verse Account of Nabonidus" (Smith, *Babylonian Historical Texts*, 90 f.; Pritchard, *ANET*, 3rd ed., 312-15).

[2] Grayson, *Chronicles*, 22, 110, chron. 7.iii.19-22, 111, line 28; Smith, *Babylonian Historical Texts*, 118, lines 19-22.

[3] Pritchard, *ANET*, 3rd ed., 315 f.; cf. the reports in the Nabonidus chronicle of the omission of the New Year's festival under Nabonidus: Grayson, *Chronicles*, 21, 106-108, chron. 7.ii.5 f., 10 f., 19 f., 23 f.; Smith, *Babylonian Historical Texts*, 115 f.

[4] M.E.L. Mallowan, "Cyrus the Great (558-529 B.C.)" *Iran* X (1972), 12, n. 56; F.H. Weissbach, *Die Keilinschriften der Achämeniden* (Leipzig, 1911), 8 f.; Horst Klengel, "Babylon zur Zeit der Perser, Griechen, und Parther," Staatliche Museen zu Berlin, *Forschungen und Berichte* V (Berlin, 1962), 43.

[5] Wetzel, *Das Babylon der Spätzeit*, 70, nos. 8, 9.

[6] Wetzel, *Haupttheiligtum*, 79 f.

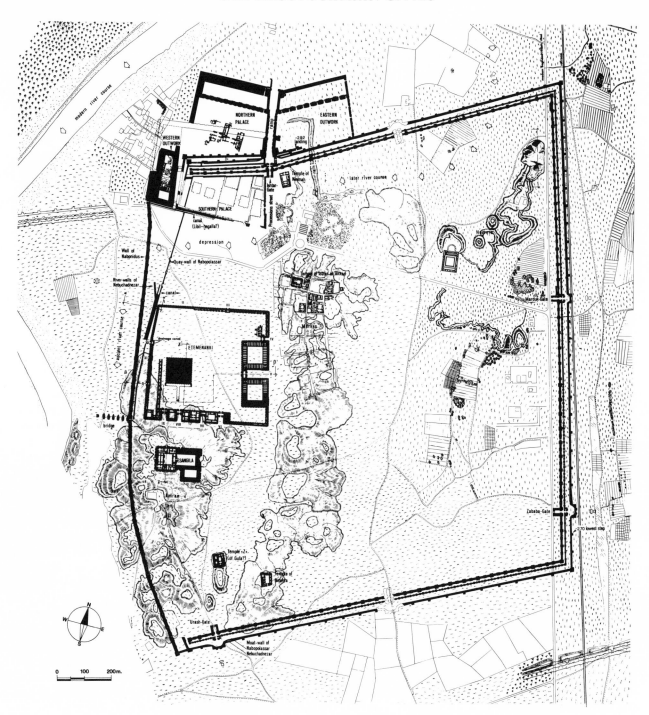

1. Babylon, city plan, after the survey in autumn 1974.

and subsequent death. Arrian (*Anabasis* III.16.4; VII.17.1-4) also records Alexander's desire to rebuild the ziggurat and states that while the conqueror was away in the east, the work of clearing the site proceeded so slowly that on his return he decided to set his troops to work on the task. According to Arrian, Alexander suspected the "Chaldaeans" of not wanting him to enter the city on his return so that they could continue to have the use of the temple revenues.[7] Strabo (XVI.I.5)) goes on to say that none of Alexander's successors cared to complete the task and that even what was left of the city was allowed to fall into ruins, particularly after Seleukos Nicator founded Seleucia on the Tigris.

Cuneiform sources suggest that Strabo may have been at least partly wrong; though no work on Etemenanki is recorded after Alexander's death, clearing of the ruins of Esagila, the "low temple" connected with the ziggurat, is recorded, and Antiochos I began to mold the bricks for the rebuilding of Esagila and Ezida, the temple of Nabu in Borsippa. These documents will be discussed below. The archaeological record demonstrates that during the period of Greek rule, debris was hauled away from Etemenanki, and possible traces of Seleucid work remain on the enclosure wall. It appears that Esagila remained standing, at least as a ruin, into the Seleucid period. Thus the archaeological and the literary and inscriptional evidence complement one another to some extent, but it is not possible to correlate the two at all closely.

The scanty remains of the Greek period and the literary sources demonstrate that after the founding of Seleucia on the Tigris, Babylon lost its importance as a city. According to Pausanias (I.16.3), Seleukos I took the population of Babylon to Seleucia, and only "Chaldaeans" remained around the "Temple of Bel."[8] Pliny (*NH* VI.30.121f.) also reports that Seleukos Nicator founded Seleucia for the purpose of reducing Babylon to insignificance and that only the "Temple of Jupiter Bel" now stands: "Durat adhuc ibi Iovis Beli templum . . . cetero ad solitudinem rediit exhausta vicinitate Se-

leuciae ob id conditae a Nicatore." That the Seleucids felt the city still had some importance even after the founding of Seleucia is perhaps indicated by an inscription of 166 B.C., which was probably found between Babylon-Dschumdschuma and Borsippa and which speaks of Antiochos as σωτῆρος τῆς Ἀσίας καὶ κτίσ[του/ τῆς πόλεως ("Savior of Asia and Founder of the City"). Although the city is unspecified, scholars agree that it refers to Babylon on the basis of its probable finding place.[9]

Strabo's statement that Alexander intended to rebuild the ziggurat but was unable to finish the task, since even the clearing required that ten thousand men work for two months, is supplemented by cuneiform tablets recording, among other things, the clearing of dust from Esagila in the years 321, 317/16, and 315/14, according to Smith's dating.[10] In some of these passages, however, much of the name Esagila is wholly or partially restored. For example, in a chronicle concerning the Diadochs, which narrates events beginning at least as early as 320/19 and continuing at least as late as 308/307, removal of dust from Esagila is mentioned three times. The first mention in the fourth regnal year of Philip III reads: "In that same year the dust [of Esagil (. . .) was removed]."[11] Again in the sixth and eighth years of Alexander IV "the dust of Es[ag]i[l (. . .) was removed]," and "The dust of E[sagil (. . .) was removed]."[12] In a fragmentary chronicle concerning Antiochos the crown prince, tentatively identified by Grayson as Antiochos, son of Seleukos I, who was made co-regent in 294/93, removal of dust from Esagila is again mentioned: "In that same year the dust of Esagi[l (. . .) was removed]."[13] Assuming that the restorations to the texts are correct, the importance attributed by the Seleucids to the work in Esagila is shown by the fact that during some of these years the rulers were occupied with fighting. In addition, some of these same texts show that there were economic problems in Babylon.

The interpretation of this evidence appears to de-

[7] Mark A. Brandes, "Alexander der Grosse in Babylon," *Antike Kunst* XXII.2 (1979), 91-95, 97, discusses Alexander's intentions of rebuilding the temples in Babylon.

[8] Bickerman, *Institutions des Séleucides*, 176.

[9] Wetzel, *Das Babylon der Spätzeit*, 29, 72, no. 30; Schmidt, "Die Griechen in Babylon," 815, no. 2; Klengel, Staatliche Museen zu Berlin, *Forschungen und Berichte* V (1962), 50. Ulrich Köhler in the original publication doubted the reliability of the information about the finding place of the inscription and suggested that the city referred to was Antioch on the Orontes. "Zwei Inschriften aus der Zeit Antiochos' IV. Epiphanes," (*Sitzungsberichte der königlich preuss-*

ischen Akademie der Wissenschaften zu Berlin LI [1900], 1100-1106). This inscription is often used as evidence for the policies of Antiochos IV; the implications of this assumption will be discussed in the section on Antiochos IV.

[10] Smith, *Babylonian Historical Texts*, 130, 135 f., 142 obv. line 5, 144 rev. line 33.

[11] Grayson, *Chronicles*, 25, 116, chron. 10, obv. line 6.

[12] Ibid., 117 f., chron. 10, rev. lines 13, 33. The date is discussed on pp. 25 f.

[13] Ibid., 26, 120, chron. 11, obv. line 2.

pend on whether Esagila is considered as part of the complex of Etemenanki. Smith sees these clearing operations as a continuation of Alexander's efforts,[14] whereas Wetzel takes the absence of later references to the removal of debris from Etemenanki as confirmation of Strabo's statement that Alexander's successors abandoned his plan of rebuilding the ziggurat.[15]

The removal of debris from Esagila was apparently financed in part by tithes from private citizens, in a continuation of earlier practices, though the evidence for this is very slight. A text dated to the sixth year of Alexander, either Alexander II or III, records that one Baraqa, the slave of Nabarzanu, gave one mina of silver to Bel and Beltia as a tithe for the clearance of debris from Esagila.[16]

Texts of the Seleucid period also mention Esagila in contexts that are not always clear but that make at least its existence and apparently also its continued use after the Greek conquest certain. In some cases, Esagila may be used only as a topographical reference point. This is true of a passage in the chronicle concerning the Diadochs that relates events of the seventh year of Alexander II: "[. . . Ant]igonos rebelled . . . [. . .]/[. . .] between Esagil and E . . .[. . .]." The same chronicle records that in the ninth year, ". . . Esagil (or "of Esagil") he entrusted."[17] More significant are two passages in a chronicle of uncertain date, probably at the earliest from the second half of the second century B.C. The first, "[. . . in Es]agil to the office of lamentation priest/[he appointed . . .]," if correctly restored, suggests that Esagila still functioned as a temple. This is confirmed by the second passage, which mentions the setting up of something, either an offering or plunder, in Esagila.[18] Other texts demonstrate that Antiochos I at least made preparations for work in Esagila. One, a historical account of part of his reign, states that "in that year (37, Seleucid era, 275/74 B.C.) a quantity of bricks

for rebuilding E.SAG.ILA were made above and below Babylon."[19] The other text, a cylinder now in London, records preparations for work on Esagila and Ezida, the latter in Borsippa. The general purport of the text is clear. The passage reads, in Pritchard's translation: "When I conceived the idea of (re)constructing Esagila and Ezida, I formed with my august hands (when I was still) in the country Hatti the (first) brick for Esagila and Ezida with the finest oil and brought (it with me) for the laying of the foundation of Esagila and Ezida. And in the month of Addaru, the 20th day, the 43rd year (of the Seleucid era) (= 28 March, 268 B.C.), I did lay the foundation of Ezida, the (only) true temple of Nabu which is in Borsippa . . . may I personally conquer (all) the countries from sunrise to sunset, gather their tribute, and bring it (home) for the perfection of Esagila and Ezida."[20] The interpretation of this inscription varies. Wetzel takes it, along with other inscriptions, as evidence that the temple in Babylon was rebuilt by Seleucid rulers.[21] Klengel takes it to mean that the foundation of Esagila was laid in the same year as that of Ezida.[22] Schmidt also states that the temple was rebuilt under Antiochos I; his opinion is based in part on archaeological evidence.[23] Rostovtzeff, on the other hand, takes the fact that the inscription mentions laying the foundations for Ezida in Borsippa but no actual work on Esagila as an indication that Antiochos' actual building activity was confined to Ezida.[24] Rostovtzeff's interpretation is surely the logical one.

Other textual mentions of Esagila include a chronicle of the year 185 of the Seleucid era (126 B.C.) naming a gate of Esagila, and fragments of an offering calender of an uncertain year (ca. 146 B.C.) naming deities of Etemenanki and Esagila.[25] The calendar especially suggests that the temple and ziggurat were still in use. Weissbach in fact argues from the calendar that the high temple on the ziggurat still functioned.[26] A text dating to 127 B.C., in

---

[14] Smith, *Babylonian Historical Texts*, 130.

[15] Wetzel, *Das Babylon der Spätzeit*, 19.

[16] McEwan, *Priest and Temple*, 58 f.; a slightly different spelling of the names is given by Köhler and Ungnad, *Hundert ausgewählte Rechtsurkunden*, 61, no. 89; Unger, *Babylon*, 318, no. 56. N. Pigulevskaja interprets this text to mean that slaves were offered to the temple (*Les villes de l'état iranien aux époques parthe et sassanide* [Paris, 1963], 37), but the records studied by McEwan show that hired labor was used at Babylon (*Priest and Temple*, 58-60). According to McEwan, the practice of tithes did not long survive the Greek conquest; contributions or entrance fees replaced tithing (124-28).

[17] Grayson, *Chronicles*, 118 f., chron. 10, rev. lines 21-22, 37; Smith, *Babylonian Historical Texts*, 144.

[18] Grayson, *Chronicles*, 27 f., 123, chron. 13, obv. lines 10-11; rev. lines 3-4.

[19] Smith, *Babylonian Historical Texts*, 157, line 19.

[20] Pritchard, *ANET*, 3rd ed., 317; cf. Weissbach, *Die Keilinschriften der Achämeniden*, 132-35, col. I, lines 7-15; col. II, lines 19-21; Wetzel, *Das Babylon der Spätzeit*, 29.

[21] Wetzel, *Das Babylon der Spätzeit*, 20, 72.

[22] Klengel, "Babylon zur Zeit der Perser, Griechen, und Parther," Staatliche Museen zu Berlin, *Forschungen und Berichte* V (1962), 47.

[23] Schmidt, "Die Griechen in Babylon," 811 f. The archaeological evidence is discussed below.

[24] Rostovtzeff, *SEHHW* I, 435 and n. 234.

[25] Wetzel, *Das Babylon der Spätzeit*, 29, 72, no. 29.

[26] Wetzel, *Haupttheiligtum*, 84.

the reign of Hyspaosines of Charax, records a decision of the assembly of Esagila; the mention of priests suggests that the temple still functioned as such at this date.[27] A tablet found in Babylon but written by Bel-aḫ-iddin in Borsippa in 175 of the Seleucid era/111 Arsacid era (138 B.C.) is an extract from an early textbook on astronomy from Borsippa. It records a ritual celebrated in Esagila and Ezida, in which the "Daughters of Esagila" go to Ezida in the month Duzu (June) and the "Daughters of Ezida" come to Esagila in the month Tebet (December), because Ezida is the "House of Night" and Esagila is the "House of Day."[28] The latest meaningful archival reference to Esagila known to Unger in 1931 is dated to the year 219 of the Seleucid era (93 B.C.).[29] An Arsacid text of the year 219 (of the Arsacid era(?), 28/27 B.C.) records repairs of a gate in the north wall of Esagila, and repairs to this gate are also mentioned in another text.[30] Thus the archival and textual evidence strongly suggests that at least Esagila and probably also Etemenanki remained in use during the Seleucid period and perhaps even down into the period of Arsacid rule.

The importance of Esagila for Seleucid rulers is also shown by the chronicle texts. One such text mentions that the king, apparently unnamed, made a *nindabu* offering to Bel and Beltia in Esagila. Although the *nindabu* was originally a bread and cereal offering, this king gave a large number of cattle, sheep, and geese. An "additional offering of the king" is also mentioned. Antiochos I made an offering of sheep to Egišnugal, the temple of Sin in Babylon, and Seleukos I gave offerings to Bel and Beltia in Esagila. A chronicle text mentioning the "ritual of Seleucus and his offspring" in Esagila provides the only explicit evidence for the royal ancestral cult in Babylonian temples. According to McEwan, this cult appears to have had much the same status as cult activities in honor of Bel and Beltia.[31]

The continued respect of the Seleucid rulers for the people and especially for the temples of Babylon, as well as for those of its neighbors, Borsippa

and Cutha, is also shown by other texts. For example, Antiochos I in 279 B.C. gave land to Babylon, though that gift was withdrawn five years later. A cuneiform text of the year 139 of the Seleucid era (173/72 B.C.) is a copy made during the reign of Antiochos IV Epiphanes from a record on stone dating to 75 of the Seleucid era (233/32 B.C.), in the reign of Seleukos II Kallinikos. It reports a gift of land and valuables by Antiochos II Theos to his wife Laodice, which was then given back to the people of Babylon, Borsippa, and Cutha, and finally ceded "for all time" to the temples of Babylon.[32] Sarkisian interprets this text as an indication of the existence of a temple-city community at Babylon.[33] An unusual text records that the temple provided a governor of Babylon with the purchase of an offering sheep,[34] a further indication of friendly relations between the temple and the government.

Textual evidence suggests that the administrative practices at Babylon, unlike those at Uruk, continued the old form. The assembly of Esagila continued to function, though largely confined to temple affairs. The traditional practice of temple slavery, which remained at Uruk, was apparently not continued at Babylon, where work seems to have been done by hired labor.[35] The temple income at Babylon seems to have been distributed entirely in the form of rations, which may have been subject to government tax, as is suggested by the notation that a copy of the record was made in Greek.[36]

The relative abundance of textual evidence for the activity of Alexander and his successors in the sanctuaries of Babylon contrasts with the paucity of the archaeological material, but the archaeological record does appear to confirm Strabo's statement that Alexander began to clear away the debris from the ziggurat. The hill called Homera, in the northeastern part of the city, consists largely of debris of the Neo-Babylonian period, with no remains of buildings of this date. In the debris were found bricks with stamps of Nebuchadnezzar and part of a cylinder of Nebuchadnezzar recording the building of Etemenanki. The heaping of the debris

[27] Unger, *Babylon*, 319-23, no. 57.

[28] Jos. Epping and J. N. Strassmaier, "Neue Babylonische Planeten-Tafeln," *ZAssyr* VI (1891), 228; Unger, *Babylon*, 271, no. 14 (with slightly different dating); Wetzel, *Das Babylon der Spätzeit*, 73, no. 32.

[29] Unger, *Babylon*, 168; Köhler and Ungnad, *Hundert ausgewählte Rechtsurkunden*, 65, no. 99.

[30] Gilbert J. P. McEwan, "Arsacid Temple Records," *Iraq* XLIII (1981), 138-40, AB 246, lines 11 f., with commentary.

[31] McEwan, *Priest and Temple*, 161, 168 f., 193 f.

[32] Rostovtzeff, *SEHHW* I, 435; cf. C.F. Lehmann, "Noch einmal Kassû: Κίσσιοι, nicht Κισσαῖοι," *ZAssyr* VII (1892), 330-34.

[33] Sarkisian, "City Land in Seleucid Babylonia," in I. M. Diakonov, ed., *Ancient Mesopotamia* (Moscow, 1969), 320-27.

[34] McEwan, *Priest and Temple*, 147 f.

[35] Ibid., 154-58, 192 f.; Sarkisian, "Self-governing Cities," 76 f. Idem, "Social Role," 40 f., argues for a slightly greater civic importance for the assembly of Esagila.

[36] McEwan, *Priest and Temple*, 136-42, 149-51.

in this place can be dated to the Greek period on the basis of the fact that the artificial mound thus created was used as the foundation for a Greek theater, which probably belongs, according to its architectural form, to the late fourth or early third century B.C. That the debris came from Etemenanki is suggested not only by the discovery of Nebuchadnezzar's cylinder but also by the fact that on the site of Etemenanki the excavators found the remains of a monumental building but no building debris.[37]

It is not clear from the excavation report to what height the core building of Etemenanki remained. Remains of a core of unbaked bricks belonging to an early building and the surrounding mantle of baked bricks of the later reconstruction were found, but the upper surface of the core area was not cleared. The lengths of the sides of the remains are given, but not the height.[38] The section (33) on plate 16 of Wetzel's *Haupttheiligtum* shows the height of the core of the ziggurat as ca. 8.50 meters above the level of Kasr (their zero point), whereas the clay bed that serves as its foundation lies at −3.82 meters.

Information about the form of the ziggurat after the work begun by Alexander is perhaps given by a tablet dated to "the month Kislimmu, 26th day, year 83 of King Seleukos" (II) (December 12, 229 B.C.). This tablet, written and verified after a tablet in Borsippa by one Anubēlšunu, a member of a traditional scribal family of Uruk, gives the measurements of Esagila and Etemenanki, including the high temple on Etemenanki. It uses the traditional system of measurement. The text states that the height is the same as the length and gives the measurements of six strongly stepped stories topped by a high temple, which is counted as the seventh story.[39] Koldewey states that the tablet describes not the original state of the ziggurat, but rather the state of the ruins after Alexander's work. He suggests that discrepancies between the measurements

of the high temple and those of the base (section 7, line 37; section 8, lines 1-6, in his edition) arise from the fact that the writer used authorities from several different periods.[40] If Koldewey is correct, the stories listed in the Esagila tablet must be the result of Alexander's removal of the debris and perhaps of trimming back the core, and the ziggurat must have survived to a considerable height. Weissbach uses the Esagila tablet as an aid to reconstructing Etemenanki and the high temple, but does not seem to deal with the question of whether the tablet describes the state of Etemenanki after Alexander.[41] Erich Schmidt has suggested that the tablet describes the Seleucid rebuilding and that the archaic system of measurements is the result of the attempt of the Seleucids to continue as much as possible traditional practices.[42] Jürgen Schmidt, on the other hand, argues that the Esagila tablet describes the ziggurat according to the plan of Nabupolassar.[43]

The enclosure walls of Etemenanki do show traces of Seleucid building. The front edge of the new walls corresponds to the building of Nabupolassar, though the corners do not. E. Schmidt had earlier stated that two periods of Seleucid work were visible on the enclosure, and he suggested that this construction was connected with a raising of the level of the processional street. He tentatively dates the work to the reigns of Antiochos I and Antiochos IV.[44] No Hellenistic work on the processional street is mentioned in *Das Babylon der Spätzeit*, but a Hellenistic level between gates IV and V is shown in the section on plate 18b there. Wetzel feels that it is extremely unlikely that the Seleucid walls were, like the earlier ones, enclosure walls for the ziggurat Etemenanki. His doubts that the ziggurat still served as part of a sanctuary in the Seleucid period are based in part on the opinion that in Nippur and Uruk, as well as in Assur, the ziggurats during the late period served as citadels.[45] Since it is now know that E-anna in Uruk continued to have

[37] Mallwitz, in Wetzel, *Das Babylon der Spätzeit*, 2-22; Koldewey, *Wieder erstehende Babylon*, 299-301; H. Schmid, "Ergebnisse einer Grabung am Kern-Zikkurat in Babylon," *BaM* XII (1981), 136 f.

[38] Wetzel, *Haupttheiligtum*, 31-33. Cf. Heinrich, *Tempel und Heiligtümer*, 307-310.

[39] Weissbach, in Wetzel, *Haupttheiligtum*, 52-56; the dating and signature are given in the colophon (lines 48-50); the information that it was copied after a tablet in Borsippa is included in section 8; the measurements are given in sections 4-7. Koldewey, "Der Babylonische Turm nach der Tontafel des Anubelschunu," *MDOG* 59 (May 1918), 4-7, sections 5-8.

[40] Koldewey, *MDOG* 59 (May 1918), 16-19.

[41] Wetzel, *Haupttheiligtum*, 80-84. Cf. Heinrich, *Tempel und Heiligtümer*, 307, who states that this tablet, as a copy of an older one,

gives particularly important information for the reconstruction of Etemenanki. Cf. also Koldewey, *Wieder erstehende Babylon*, 189-93, written when the Esagila tablet was poorly known. M. A. Powell in a recent article seems to assume that the text reflects the state of the ziggurat before Alexander ("Metrological Notes on the Esagila Tablet and Related Matters," *ZAssyr* LXXII [1982], 106-23).

[42] E. Schmidt, "Die Griechen in Babylon," 811.

[43] Schmid, "Ergebnisse einer Grabung am Kern-Zikkurat in Babylon," *BaM* XII (1981), 128-30.

[44] E. Schmidt, "Die Griechen in Babylon," 811.

[45] Wetzel, *Das Babylon der Spätzeit*, 27-31; cf. p. 76, where he lists as one of the desiderata for new excavations an attempt to locate a Hellenistic or Parthian level of the street.

a religious function during the Seleucid period and since it seems possible that this was true also of the Assur ziggurat in Assur during the Parthian period (see below), part of this argument falls. Furthermore, the mention of Etemenanki in an offering calender of approximately 146 B.C.[46] makes the survival of the sanctuary, at least in some form, probable. Obviously, Etemenanki could have continued to function as a ziggurat only if the core survived to a reasonable height. That it might have done so is suggested not only by the drawing on plate 16 of *Das Hauptheiligtum des Marduk in Babylon, Esagila und Etemenanki*, but also by the statements of both Pliny (*NH* VI.30.121f.) and Pausanias (I.16.3) that the "Temple of Bel" still stood in their time.

The extent of Seleucid work on Esagila is hard to determine, at least in part because of the incomplete excavations. Most of the work was done by tunnelling along the walls, and only one cella, attributed to Ea, was completely excavated.[47] Koldewey states that the small finds on the floor of the sanctuary show that it must have stood during the Seleucid period.[48] The excavations in this cella show that the temple was erected in the Assyrian period and restored in Neo-Babylonian times. No certain traces of Seleucid work were found in the room, but in the main court were the remains of a floor located above the floor level of the time of Nebuchadnezzar, which might possibly be attributed to the Seleucid period. The temple appears to have been neglected after the reign of Nebuchadnezzar; and both in the excavated chapel and in the court in front of it, a layer of courses of mud without small finds overlays the floor of his time. Wetzel states that it is possible that a floor, now disappeared, lay over these layers of mud. The inscription mentioning Antiochos' intention of working in Esagila leads him to date Seleucid activity in the temple to Antiochos' reign, though the excavations provided no evidence for dating. At some point, the outer walls received an additional coating of baked bricks. Since none of the bricks bear stamps, which would have been unusual in the period of Nebuchadnezzar, this *kisu* might possibly be Seleucid

work,[49] and E. Schmidt tentatively attributed it to Antiochos IV. Schmidt in 1941 suggested that not only was there a floor of the Seleucid period above the floor of Nebuchadnezzar, but that also part of the wall of one of the courts was rebuilt in the Seleucid period, using the traditional Babylonian system of projections and recesses.[50] He also suggested that the eastern annex might have been built in the Seleucid period. It appears, however, that Wetzel does not accept Schmidt's ideas.

As seen above, the wording of Antiochos' inscription is ambiguous about whether he actually did any building in Esagila, but since other texts suggest that the sanctuary continued in use, it is highly probable that there was work on it during the Seleucid period. According to Wetzel, it is improbable that the sanctuary continued in use during the Parthian period, since Babylon had declined by the second and first centuries B.C. The excavations were not sufficiently extensive to determine whether a residential quarter grew up in the ruins of the sanctuary, as in the Anu and Irigal precincts in Uruk, but Wetzel states that the very thick strata with small finds of the Hellenistic and Parthian periods suggest the debris of a residential quarter.[51]

Cuneiform texts from the Arsacid period recording the income and expenditures of temples show that at least some of the temples of Babylon survived into this period. A group of texts analyzed by Gilbert J. P. McEwan is dated in the years 219 and 218 of the Arsacid era (28/27 and 29/28 B.C.). Esabad, one of the temples of the goddess Gula, figures prominently in this archive, and two other temples of Gula, Eḫursagskila and Eḫursagkuga, and a temple of Nabu are mentioned as well. The mention of the offering of a sheep in the Akitu temple is especially significant, since this text implies that the Akitu festival was still celebrated, though there is no information about the form of the ceremony.[52]

Literary sources provide additional evidence of Alexander's interest in the traditional religion of the people of Babylon. During his final illness, he made daily sacrifices to the gods, presumably the local deities. In addition, his generals spent the night before his death in the "temple of Serapis" to

---

[46] Ibid., 72, no. 29.

[47] Wetzel, *Das Babylon der Spätzeit*, 29 f. Heinrich, *Tempel und Heiligtümer*, 287, feels that the attribution of this cella to Ea is based on insufficient evidence. For his description of the temple, which in its essential form he attributes with some hesitation to Nebuchadnezzar, see pp. 310-12.

[48] Koldewey, *Wieder erstehende Babylon*, 208.

[49] Wetzel, *Das Babylon der Spätzeit*, 30. Heinrich, *Tempel und Hei-*

ligtümer, 311, argues that Nebuchadnezzar cannot be ruled out as the builder of the *kisu*, since he did not use stamped bricks in his palace.

[50] E. Schmidt, "Die Griechen in Babylon," 811 f., fig. 13.

[51] Wetzel, *Das Babylon der Spätzeit*, 30.

[52] McEwan, "Arsacid Temple Records," *Iraq* XLIII (1981), 132-35, AB 244, lines 3, 13-15, with commentary; 136 f., AB 245, line 5, with commentary; 141 f., AB 248, lines 2, 7-8.

ask the god if it would be better for him to be carried into the temple (Arrian, VII.25-26).[53] Koldewey apparently interprets this last statement as a reference to the cella of Ea in the temple of Marduk (Esagila).[54] Alexander also established himself as a successor to the earlier kings of Babylon by taking up residence in the summer palace of Nebuchadnezzar II (the Südberg). Small alterations, done either under Alexander or soon after his death, gave the palace a partly Greek character. Finds of roof tiles of Greek type suggest that a peristyle court might have been added, though no traces of the footing for columns survive. Small fragments of wall plaster bearing decorations of Greek type show that the interior of the palace was refurbished. The palace was damaged, however, perhaps under the Diadochs, and the Parthians or Sasanians seem to have turned it into a fortress.[55] Schmidt suggests that this fortification might date to the period of the Diadochs.[56]

While he respected the traditional religion, Alexander also altered the character of the city to some extent. He built a funeral pyre for Hephaistion, for example. Some burnt remains on the middle hill of Homera might mark its site,[57] though Schmidt suggests that they are instead the ruins of the agora.[58] Also, a Greek community, with Greek cultural institutions, was established at Babylon either during Alexander's lifetime or soon after his death, and this community survived, at least to some degree, as late as the second century A.D. The earliest purely Greek structure is the theater that was built into the artificial mound created by heaping up the debris from the clearing of the ziggurat. This theater was probably constructed originally in the late fourth or early third century B.C. It was rebuilt several times. The dates of the phases of the theater are hard to establish, but Mallwitz connects the building of the proskēnion with the reign of Antiochos IV Epiphanes, stating that the inscription calling him the founder of the city ($\kappa\tau\iota\sigma[\tau o\upsilon/\ \tau\tilde{\eta}\varsigma\ \pi\acute{o}\lambda\epsilon\omega\varsigma$)

suggests that the city had been neglected. The latest rebuilding, recorded in a Greek inscription, was due to the generosity of one Dioscurides; the inscription can be dated to the second century A.D. on palaeographical grounds.[59]

A Greek inscription of 109 B.C. giving a victory list of ephebes and youths in gymnastic contests shows, as do other inscriptions, that some Greek institutions survived the Arsacid conquest.[60] The peristyle court behind the theater had been identified as a palaestra by some scholars, though at least in its surviving form it was not built at the time of the contests recorded in the inscription. The identification of the court as a palaestra is doubted by some scholars on the basis of differences in architectural form between the building in Babylon and palaestras that are definitely identified as such.[61]

If an inscription said to have been found between Dschumdschuma and Borsippa refers to Babylon, as Schmidt suggests, Greek magistracies may have been established in that city during the period of Seleucid rule. The inscription records that a city, possibly Babylon, commends one Democrates, son of Buttakos, *stratēgos* and *epistatēs* of the city, who was in charge of the $\dot{\alpha}\kappa\rho o\phi\upsilon\lambda\alpha\kappa\acute{\iota}\omega\nu$, perhaps a treasury on the citadel. Schmidt dates the inscription to the reign of Tiberius or later on the basis of the letter forms.[62] Köhler, on the other hand, suggests that the Buttakos of the inscription might be the one who fought in the battle of Raphia under Antiochos IV, since Buttakos is a rare name. He also speculates that the city of the inscription is Antioch on the Orontes.[63]

In sum, although Greek rulers respected and indeed supported the traditional temples at Babylon, a Greek form of government appears to have been established, and the assembly of Esagila probably retained control only over temple affairs. At least some Greek institutions survived the Parthian conquest, and some of the old temples remained active at least into the later first century B.C.

[53] Fritz Schachermeyr, *Alexander in Babylon und die Reichsordnung nach seinem Tode* (Österreichische Akademie der Wissenschaft, Philosophisch-Historische Klasse, *Sitzungsberichte*, 268, Proceeding 3) (Vienna, 1970), 65-71.

[54] Koldewey, *Wieder erstehende Babylon*, 200; idem, *Die Tempel von Babylon und Borsippa*, 43.

[55] Schachermeyr, *Alexander in Babylon und die Reichsordnung nach seinem Tode* (Vienna 1970), 63-71; Brandes, "Alexander der Grosse in Babylon," *Antike Kunst* XXII.2 (1979), 95.

[56] E. Schmidt, "Die Griechen in Babylon," 821 f., fig. 17. He discusses the palace on pp. 821-27.

[57] Koldewey, *Wieder erstehende Babylon*, 301 f.

[58] E. Schmidt, "Die Griechen in Babylon," 832 f.

[59] Mallwitz, in Wetzel, *Das Babylon der Spätzeit*, 3-22, 49 f., pls.

8-11b, 20-22; E. Schmidt, "Die Griechen in Babylon," 819, no. 8, 833-41.

[60] Bernard Haussouillier, "Inscriptions grecques de Babylone," *Klio* IX (1909), 352 f., 355-62; E. Schmidt, "Die Griechen in Babylon," 814, 816-19, no. 5.

[61] Mallwitz, in Wetzel, *Das Babylon der Spätzeit*, 16 f., 21; G. E. Kirk, "Gymnasium or Khan? A Hellenistic Building at Babylon," *Iraq* II (1935), 223-31.

[62] E. Schmidt, "Die Griechen in Babylon," 819 f., no. 6; W. Dittenberger, *OGIS* I, 414 f., no. 254, gives the finding place as Babylon.

[63] Köhler, "Zwei Inschriften aus der Zeit Antiochos' IV. Epiphanes," *Sitzungsberichte der königlich preussischen Akademie der Wissenschaften zu Berlin* LI (1900), 1107 f.

BORSIPPA

THE SITE of Borsippa, to the south of Babylon, has been excavated only very partially. The remains were apparently heavily eroded, and at least some of the upper levels were removed in the excavations of Rassam.[64] A combination of poor preservation and incomplete excavation makes it impossible to assess the extent and character of Seleucid work at Borsippa, though textual evidence indicates that Antiochus I laid the foundations for Ezida, the temple of Nabu. Inscribed bricks found in the base under the floor of the cella in Ezida, dating to the reign of Nebuchadnezzar, refer to the building of Ezida and the surrounding *kisu*. A rebuilding dating to the reign either of Nebuchadnezzar or of one of his close successors raised the floor of the temple to a level that was completely removed by Rassam's excavations. Excavations under the south corner of the ziggurat, E-ur-imin-an-ki, revealed three cylinders of Nebuchadnezzar, and the bricks bear stamps of Nebuchadnezzar.[65] The ziggurat was violently destroyed by a fire that was apparently started by igniting oil poured into channels that had contained reed ropes designed to hold the mud bricks in place. This destruction probably dates to the Achaemenid period, perhaps specifically to the campaign of Xerxes I against the Babylonians.[66]

Though there is no archaeological evidence for work at Borsippa during the Seleucid period, a cuneiform inscription already discussed in connection with Babylon shows that Antiochos I laid the foundations for Ezida: "and in the month of Addaru, the 20th day, the 43rd year (of the Seleucid era), I did lay the foundation of Ezida, the [only] true temple of Nabu which is in Borsippa."[67] The date is March 28, 268 B.C.[68]

Further evidence that suggests at least some activity in Borsippa during the Seleucid period is provided by the so-called Esagila tablet, which gives measurements for Esagila and Etemenanki in Babylon. This tablet was copied on the 26th day of the month Kislimmu, in the year 83 of the Seleucid era (December 12, 229 B.C.), by Anubēlšunu of a learned scribal family of Uruk, after an exemplar from Borsippa.[69] This suggests that an archive was maintained in Borsippa. Additional evidence for scribal activity at Borsippa is provided by a tablet found in Babylon but written by Bel-aḫ-iddin in Borsippa in 175 of the Seleucid era/111 Arsacid era (138 B.C.). This text, already discussed in the section on Babylon, records a ritual celebrated in Esagila and Ezida,[70] which might imply that Ezida still functioned as a temple. Another text records payment to Borsippeans for participation in a procession.[71] Strabo (XVI.1.6) calls Borsippa a city sacred to Artemis and Apollo (probably Nabu) and cites Borsippeans as Chaldaean astronomers.

Scribal activity continued at Borsippa, and Ezida probably continued to function, at least in connection with festivals celebrated at Babylon. The three cities of Babylon, Borsippa, and Cutha were closely united in this period.[72]

URUK

URUK, modern Warka (fig. 2), provides the most important evidence in Mesopotamia for the continuation, or perhaps more accurately the revival, of Babylonian religious architecture and the rituals associated with it during the Seleucid period. The buildings of the Neo-Babylonian period were destroyed soon after the beginning of Achaemenid rule, probably under Darius I. This destruction was apparently followed by a gap in building activity until the period of Seleucid rule. Major Seleucid building activity is visible in the Bit rēš and Irigal sanctuaries, as well as outside the city wall, in the Bit Akitu.[73] The ziggurat in the E-anna precinct was also rebuilt in a new form.

Although the buildings of the Seleucid period

[64] Koldewey, *Die Tempel von Babylon und Borsippa*, 50-59. Cf. Unger, "Barsippa," in E. Ebling and B. Meissner, eds., *Reallexicon der Assyriologie* I (Berlin, 1928), 402-429; Hormuzd Rassam, *Asshur and the Land of Nimrod* (Cincinnati and New York, 1897), 268-71, 396. J. E. Reade has now published some of the main results of Rassam's excavations at Borsippa, which do not reveal any new information about the Seleucid levels: "Rassam's Excavations at Borsippa and Kutha, 1879-82" *Iraq* 48 (1986), 105-111, Pl. XI.

[65] Koldewey, *Die Tempel von Babylon und Borsippa*, 54-58. Heinrich, *Tempel und Heiligtümer*, 312 f.

[66] Rainer Michael Boehmer with Jann-Berend Kaufman, "Zur Zerstörung der Zikkurat von Borsippa," *BaM* XI (1980), 88 f.; cf. Koldewey, *Die Tempel von Babylon und Borsippa*, 58; Rassam, *Asshur and the Land of Nimrod*, 268 f. Reade disagrees with Boehmer's

conclusions about the date of the conflagration; *Iraq* 48 (1986), 111.

[67] Pritchard, *ANET*, 3rd ed., 317; Weissbach, *Die Keilinschriften der Achämeniden*, 132 f., col. I, lines 13-15.

[68] Wetzel, *Das Babylon der Spätzeit*, 72, no. 25, gives the year as 269 B.C.

[69] Weissbach, in Wetzel, *Hauptheiligtum*, 49 f., 54 f., section 8; colophon.

[70] Epping and Strassmaier, "Neue Babylonische Planeten-Tafeln," *ZAssyr* VI (1891), 228 (transcription only); Unger, *Babylon*, 271, no. 14; Wetzel, *Das Babylon der Spätzeit*, 73, no. 32.

[71] McEwan, *Priest and Temple*, 145.

[72] Ibid., 62 and n. 196; G. Sarkisian in I. M. Diakonoff, ed., *Ancient Mesopotamia*, (Moscow, 1969), 325 f.

[73] J. Schmidt, *BaM* V (1970), 75 f.

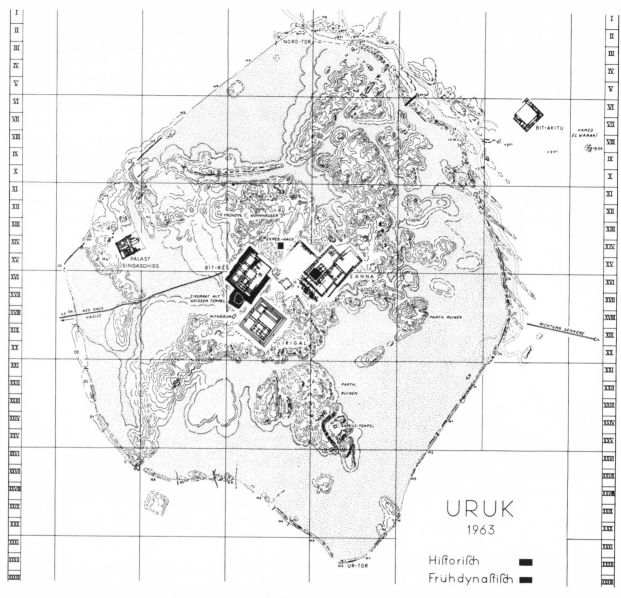

2. Uruk, city plan.

follow the traditions of Babylonian architecture, they do not represent merely a restoration of earlier temples; rather, they are either new creations or radical redesignings of the earlier structures. The Anu-Antum complex, built in part on the very badly destroyed Assyrian remains, follows a plan of Babylonian type with some modifications, and its architectural decoration is also Babylonian in character. No traces of Greek influence are discern-

ible. This is true also of the Irigal, built on a site where there are few remains of earlier structures.[74]

The Seleucid buildings were particularly monumental. For example, the Anu ziggurat, the sides of which are approximately 100 meters long, is the biggest ziggurat in Mesopotamia. The Bit rēš precinct measures 210 by 162 meters, the Irigal at least 198 by 205.[75] The Bit Akitu measures about 140 meters on a side.[76]

[74] Lenzen, *Neue Deutsche Ausgrabungen*, 24-26; J. Schmidt, *BaM* V (1970), 75 f.; Falkenstein, *Topographie*, 2 f., 30 f.; Lenzen, *UVB* XII/XIII, 8.

[75] Lenzen, *UVB* XII/XIII, 11; Heinrich, *UVB* V, 28; J. Schmidt, *UVB* XXVI/XXVII, 11.

[76] Lenzen, *MDOG* 87, 57; idem, *UVB* XII/XIII, 35 f.

A number of religious texts attest to the continuation or revival of Babylonian religious rites in the Seleucid period. These texts include a hymn to the sky god Anu and a text describing the route from the cella of Anu in the Anu-Antum temple to the Bit Akitu; both texts are dated to the year 61 of the Seleucid era.[77] McEwan points out that the fact that the same professions are mentioned in both religious and secular texts shows that the Seleucid copies of rituals and hymns reflect contemporary cult practices.[78]

Thus both the architecture of the temples and the texts suggest that during the Seleucid period there was a renaissance of Babylonian religion in Uruk. The continuation of Babylonian religious practices and the erection of religious buildings of Babylonian form on a grandiose scale must have had at least the tacit support of the Seleucid rulers; probably this revival of Babylonian religion represents a deliberate royal policy. This renaissance, however, apparently lasted only about one hundred years.[79] The Seleucid buildings were destroyed by fire, perhaps soon after the Parthian conquest of Babylonia in 141 B.C., and all three of the major sanctuaries lost their sacred character. During the Parthian period, residential quarters, apparently inhabited by non-local people, grew up on the ruins of the sanctuaries within fortification walls.[80]

The exact dates and circumstances of the burning and subsequent desacralization of each sanctuary are unknown. The Irigal may have gone out of use, at least as a repository for archives, earlier than the Bit rēš, since the latest dated tablets found there belong to the reign of Demetrios I Soter (162-150 B.C.). Until recently, the latest known mention of the Bit rēš occurred in a tablet dated to the year 109 of the Arsacid era (139 B.C.).[81] A destruction of the sanctuary shortly after this date, postulated by some scholars, would appear to suggest a connection with the Parthian conquest of Babylonia.[82] Oelsner, citing two unpublished texts from Uruk, would place the destruction slightly later. One of these is dated to 115 of the Arsacid era (133/32 B.C.), and the other bears a double dating to the Ar-

sacid and Seleucid eras: 120 Arsacid era/185 Seleucid era (128/27 B.C.). On the basis of these dates, Oelsner tentatively connects the end of the life of the sanctuaries either with the brief conquest of Babylon by Hyspaosines of Charax in 127/26 B.C. or with the period of unrest following the partially successful attempt of Antiochos VII Sidetes (138-129 B.C.?) to retake the eastern Seleucid kingdom from the Parthians.[83] Nissen accepts a date of approximately 140 B.C. for the destruction of the sanctuaries and further hypothesizes that a lack of sufficient water in the main channel of the Euphrates might explain the decline of Uruk and southern Babylonia. On the basis of coin evidence, he postulates a gap of approximately 130 years between the latest activity in the Seleucid sanctuaries and the resurgence of the town in the last years of the first century B.C.[84] A recently published text found in debris in the north section of E-anna suggests that this picture may have to be modified. The text, which deals with a butcher's prebend, mentions the "Irigal, Bit rēš, and all the gods' houses in Uruk," as if they were still functioning. It is dated to 139 of the Arsacid era (probably a mistake for 138, which is mentioned in the body of the text) the equivalent of 203 of the Seleucid era (108 B.C.). This text, if correctly interpreted, would imply that the sanctuaries continued to function into the reign of Mithradates II (123-88 B.C.). Kessler cites surface finds of coins from the early first century B.C. as further evidence for continued life at Uruk.[85]

BIT RĒŠ

Both the textual evidence and the archaeological remains show that the Anu-Antum temple with its associated ziggurat was the most important religious structure in Uruk during the Seleucid period, although in earlier times E-anna, the shrine of the goddess Inanna, had greatly overshadowed it in importance. The sky god Anu thus replaced Inanna as the most important deity of Uruk.[86]

The temple of Anu and his consort Antum ap-

[77] Falkenstein, *Topographie*, 8, 45-49. Cf. also Thureau-Dangin, *Rituels accadiens*. These and other texts will be discussed below as they affect the interpretation of the monuments.

[78] McEwan, *Priest and Temple*, 65 f.

[79] Falkenstein, *Topographie*, 3; J. Schmidt, *BaM* V (1970), 75 f.

[80] Lenzen, *UVB* XII/XIII, 19, 31; idem, *UVB* XV, 24; H. Schmid, *UVB* XVI, 20-22.

[81] Falkenstein, *Topographie*, 9, 34; Kessler, *BaM* XV (1984), 276.

[82] H. Schmid, *UVB* XVI, 19-22.

[83] Oelsner, "Randbemerkungen zur arsakidischen Geschichte

abhand von babylonischen Keilinschrifttexten," *Altorientalische Forschungen* III (1975), 32-35 and n. 22; idem, "Kontinuität und Wandel," 115, n. 62.

[84] H.J. Nissen, "Südbabylonien in parthischer und sasanidischer Zeit," *BaM* VI (1973), 82 f.; Robert McC. Adams and Hans J. Nissen, *The Uruk Countryside* (Chicago and London, 1973), 57 f.

[85] K. Kessler, "Eine arsakidenzeitliche Urkunde aus Warka," *BaM* XV (1984), 275-81.

[86] Falkenstein, *Topographie*, 2 f., 35.

pears in late inscriptions as *ʿréš* and *ʿre-éš*. According to Falkenstein, the use of an Akkadian word in an area where most temple names are Sumerian makes it likely that the name is a relatively late creation. Nonetheless, textual evidence indicates that already in the Neo-Babylonian period there was a shrine of Anu somewhere outside the E-anna precinct; Falkenstein suggests that this temple lay somewhere in the area of the later Anu sanctuary. Furthermore, the Neo-Babylonian archives of E-anna name a goddess ᵈbēltušarēš, mistress of the réš sanctuary; in Seleucid times this goddess had a cella in the réš sanctuary, and it is possible that this continued an earlier practice. Falkenstein also suggests that the *parak šimāti*, the "high seat of fate," which is mentioned in one text as early as the eighth century B.C. and which in Seleucid times was located in the réš sanctuary, might earlier have been in the precinct of Anu also. Thus it appears that the cult in the Anu precinct during the Seleucid period continued earlier practices to some extent. Falkenstein also states that some texts appear to be attempts to justify the Seleucid cult by using copies of earlier ritual texts.[87] Van Dijk states that not only does the building inscription place the origins of the sanctuary in mythological times, but also the second-century builder might have given himself a genealogy going back into the distant past.[88]

Architecturally, the Anu-Antum temple and the associated ziggurat represent a new conception that does not copy earlier forms, though the location of the complex is clearly connected with the position of the earlier remains. In the area both of the ziggurat and of the Bit réš precinct there was a hiatus of about one thousand years before signs of renewed building activity occurred under Esarhaddon. This hiatus suggests that the area had lost much of its cult significance; still, the fact that Esarhaddon built there demonstrates that it had not lost its religious meaning entirely. After the Assyrian rebuilding, there is again a hiatus until the Seleucid period, and in some places the Seleucid structure rests directly on Assyrian remains. The Anu ziggurat of the Seleucid period is both the largest ziggurat in Iraq and the only one certainly dedicated to the god of the heavens, Anu. The textual evidence for the ritual use of the ziggurat and the Bit réš sanctuary can be coordinated with the archaeolog-

ical evidence to allow a fairly certain reconstruction of physical form and religious functioning of the complex during the period of Seleucid rule.

THE ZIGGURAT

Julius Jordan believed that the Anu ziggurat stood within the Bit réš complex,[89] but Falkenstein argued on the basis of ritual texts that it could only have been located in front of the southwest part of the Bit réš, in a mound where traces of Seleucid building activity had already been found.[90] The latter location has now been confirmed, and it is evident that the Seleucid Anu ziggurat was built around the remains of a much earlier ziggurat, which had a long and complex building history, with renewed activity after long periods of neglect. According to Schmidt, the early structure must have had the aspect of a tell when Esarhaddon began work after a hiatus of about one thousand years. He apparently enclosed and roofed over the whole surface of the ruins of the earlier structure. Esarhaddon's building was so badly destroyed— whether by nature or by violence is uncertain—that discussion of its form and size is impossible.[91] After this destruction, the site was again left as a ruin until the Seleucid period. Traces of the Seleucid building that have been found in various places, including points where the ziggurat meets the Bit réš, allow a reasonably secure reconstruction of its form, though uncertainties remain (fig. 3). The Seleucid construction is careless in comparison to the Assyrian core around which it is built. The bricks are laid fairly far apart and the interstices filled with mortar. Thick layers of mortar also separate the courses of brick. J. Schmidt suggests that this technique was adopted to save time and that perhaps only by this method could such a large ziggurat have been constructed.[92] The facade has a series of rectangular projections and recesses, a decorative scheme that is similar in principle to that of the ziggurat at Babylon. The southwest corner could not be located, for the area where it ought to be is covered with a mound of ruins that prevented further excavations. The fact that no further remains attributable to the ziggurat are visible in the direction of the Irigal, however, suggests that the outer wall turned toward the northeast, in the direction of the

[87] Ibid., 4, 8 f.; cf. also Lenzen, *UVB* XII/XIII, 12.

[88] J. van Dijk, *UVB* XVIII, 43-52. He mistakenly cites the inscription of Anu-uballit-Nikarchos rather than that of Anu-uballit-Kephalon.

[89] Jordan, *Uruk-Warka*, 23 f., 43, figs. 2, 3.

[90] Falkenstein, *Topographie*, 27-29.

[91] J. Schmidt, *BaM* V (1970), 55-57; idem, *UVB* XXVI/XXVII, 13.

[92] J. Schmidt, *UVB* XXVI/XXVII, 10 f.

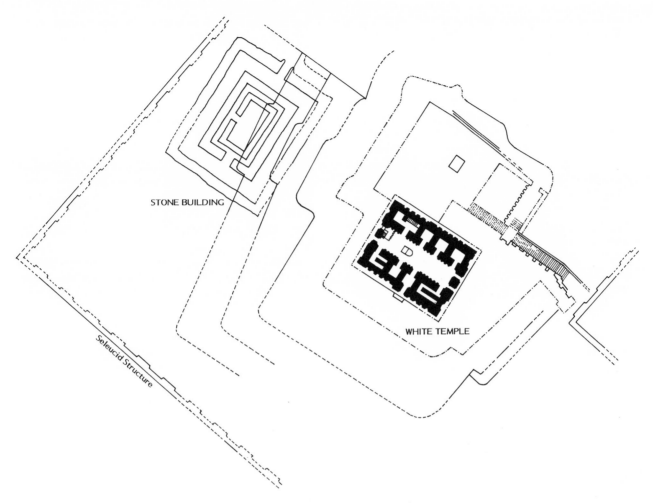

STONE BUILDING

Seleucid Structure

WHITE TEMPLE

3. Uruk, Anu ziggurat, schematic plan.

Anu-Antum temple. The ziggurat would then have occupied a square or roughly square area ca. 110 meters on a side. A zone on the southwest side of the ziggurat was kept free of buildings. A paved area six meters wide runs beside and parallel to the base of the ziggurat. This paving is in turn bounded by a water channel, which is connected to a further water channel in the court of a house. This house must have stood within the temple precinct, just as houses lay inside the temenos of Etemenanki in Babylon.[93]

The height of the Seleucid ziggurat can be calculated roughly. The texts speak of a high temple on the Anu ziggurat and of a "holy door which lies behind the [Anu] cella."[94] Lenzen had conjectured

that the "holy door" must have lain in the badly destroyed mud-brick wall behind the southwest side of the core building,[95] and Schmidt, using levels taken by Jordan, calculates that the "holy door" must have stood at a level of about +21.70 meters above the Uruk zero point. The ziggurat, with its high temple, must have towered over the Anu-Antum temple. Since the texts speak of coming down through the holy door into the cella, Schmidt conjectures that the platform of the ziggurat would have been between +45 and +60 meters above the Uruk zero point. The height cannot be calculated exactly, since it is not known whether the height was proportionate to the length of the sides, as at Babylon.[96] According to Schmidt, the stratigraphy

[93] J. Schmidt, *UVB* XXVI/XXVII, 11 f.; Heinrich, *Tempel und Heiligtümer*, 331. In *BaM* V (1970), 57, Schmidt suggests that a zone nine meters wide was kept free of constructions, so that the residential quarter was separated from the precinct.

[94] Falkenstein, *Topographie*, 27-29.

[95] Lenzen, *UVB* XII/XIII, 12.

[96] J. Schmidt, *BaM* V (1970), 56-59, pls. I, II; idem, *UVB* XXVI/XXVII, 10-12, pls. 1, 2.

shows that the ziggurat must have been the oldest of the Seleucid buildings in the area, and the buildings and rebuildings suggest that it remained in use until the end of the Seleucid era. His suggested date of the middle of the third quarter of the third century B.C. for the beginning of work on the ziggurat seems a bit late, for the Anu-uballit-Nikarchos temple is dated to 244.[97]

Inscriptions call the ziggurat the "ziggurat of Anu," the "ziggurat of the rēš (sanctuary)," or simply "the ziggurat." The high temple is referred to as the é-šár-ra, "the house of the all," or as para-maḫḫu, the "high seat." A text describing a night ritual that took place on the roof of the high temple indicates that in the Seleucid period Anu and Antum were worshipped in their astral manifestations.[98] Further rituals involving the ziggurat and the high temple will be discussed in relation to the rēš sanctuary as a whole.

THE ANU–ANTUM TEMPLE PRECINCT

The dates of the Seleucid phases of the Bit rēš can be established quite accurately by inscriptional evidence. The earlier of the two dated building inscriptions refers to the erection of the rēš sanctuary for Anu and Antum by one Anu-uballit-Nikarchos, a city official, for the lives of the kings Antiochos and Seleukos in the year 68 of the Seleucid era (244 B.C.). Anu-uballit-Nikarchos enumerates the doors and courts included in the sanctuary, as well as some details of its ornamentation. Lines 18f. of the inscription apparently allude to an earlier structure, and it is possible that an earlier building is also referred to in the inscription of Anu-uballit-Kephalon, whose temple replaced that offered by Nikarchos. Confirmation of the existence of an earlier Seleucid shrine to Anu is found in a hymn to Anu and a ritual text, both dated to the year 61 of the Seleucid era (251 B.C.). The ritual text records the stages in the procession from Enamenna, Anu's cella in the Bit rēš, to the Bit Akitu, the new year's house. The second building inscription states that one Anu-uballit-Kephalon, possibly a member of the same family as Anu-uballit-Nikarchos, rebuilt the cellae of Anu and Antum on a larger scale, providing wooden roofs and doors, for the life of King Antiochos. The inscription is dated to 110 of the Seleucid era (201 B.C.).[99]

The archaeological remains can in fact be correlated quite well with the work recorded in the inscriptions. The temple built by Anu-uballit-Kephalon must be the baked-brick "core building"; this building has effectively obliterated the traces of earlier work in the area. In other parts of the sanctuary (fig. 4), especially the northeast outer wall, there are more extensive remains of Anu-uballit-Nikarchos' sanctuary, later worked on by Anu-uballit-Kephalon. Jordan originally suggested that the structures in unbaked brick should be dated to the Neo-Babylonian period,[100] but according to Falkenstein,[101] he later abandoned that idea, and the remains are now considered to be those of the building of Anu-uballit-Nikarchos. A few traces of buildings that may belong to an earlier Seleucid period remain, especially in and just outside the eastern part of the precinct.[102] Alterations later in the Seleucid period gave the sanctuary a fortress-like character. It is notable that new outer layers of brick covered up the projections and recesses of the original precinct wall on the northeast, a decorative motif that continued the traditions of Babylonian sacred architecture.[103] The date of the destruction of the sanctuary is discussed in the introduction to this section.

The buildings of Anu-uballit-Nikarchos and Anu-uballit-Kephalon have largely destroyed the earlier Seleucid work, so that only small traces remain; this fact, combined with the incomplete state of the excavations, makes it difficult to determine the extent of earlier Seleucid building activity. The archaic terrace was rebuilt in the Assyrian period and again in the Seleucid period in order to create a uniform level for the building of the temple. The Assyrian terrace was so damaged in parts that it had to be levelled for the construction of the Seleucid terrace.[104] This terrace, however, did not extend to the eastern part of the area occupied by the Seleucid sanctuary; rather, in this area there are ruins and sherds from potters' workshops of the Jemdet Nasr and Early Dynastic periods, as well as traces of Assyrian walls. Most of the Assyrian walls seem to have belonged to houses, but a massive wall, remains of which were found under the northeast

---

[97] J. Schmidt, *BaM* V (1970), 60, where the date of the Anu-uballit-Nikarchos temple is given incorrectly as 224; idem, *UVB* XXVI/XXVII, 13. Cf. the description in Heinrich, *Tempel und Heiligtümer*, 331, fig. 417.

[98] Falkenstein, *Topographie*, 27-29.

[99] Ibid., 6-9, 45-49; H. Schmid, *UVB* XVI, 21.

[100] Jordan, *Uruk-Warka*, 10.

[101] Falkenstein, *Topographie*, 9.

[102] H. Schmid, *UVB* XVI, 13-16, 21 f.

[103] Lenzen, *UVB* XV, 25 f.; H. Schmid, *UVB* XVI, 17-21.

[104] Lenzen, *UVB* XII/XIII, 11 f.; H. Schmid, *UVB* XVI, 13-15.

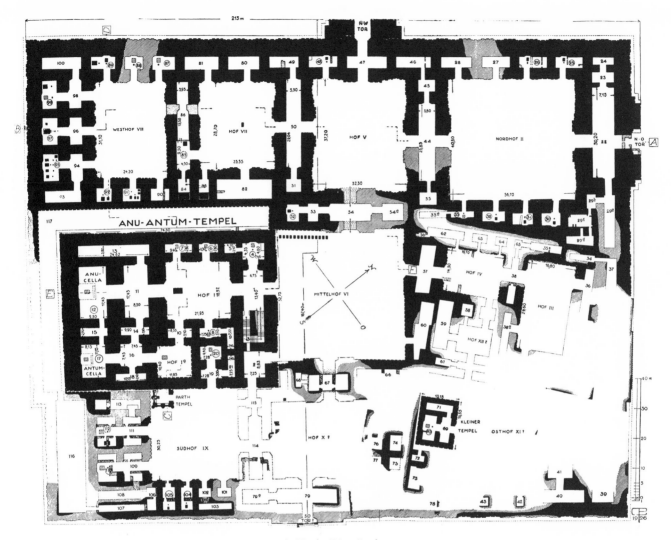

4. Uruk, Bit rēš, plan.

gate of the Bit rēš, probably belonged to the Assyrian reinforcement of the earlier terrace wall.[105]

In the northeast corner of the Bit rēš, an area that is not completely excavated and therefore not fully understood, there lie a number of rooms (fig. 4, nos. 39-41, 42, 43, 78) with an orientation that differs from that of the precinct as a whole. Schmid, following Jordan, suggests that these rooms may be the remains of an early Seleucid sanctuary that was later included in the new planning of the precinct.[106] Lenzen, on the other hand, attributed three of these rooms (42, 43, 78) to the period when the Bit rēš was no longer a sanctuary.[107] This part of the

complex also includes a small, self-contained temple consisting of an antecella, a cella, and a perpendicular corridor (69-70-71). The orientation of these rooms also differs strongly from that of the complex as a whole. This independent temple might well predate the buildings of Anu-uballit-Nikarchos and Anu-aballit-Kephalon, but it was probably later incorporated into the sanctuary.[108]

In front of the northeast wall of the Bit rēš are the remains of a Seleucid paving with an orientation that differs from that of the outer wall of the Seleucid sanctuary but is like that of the facade of east court XI (see fig. 4). This paving was in turn cut,

105 Lenzen, *UVB* XV, 25; H. Schmid, *UVB* XVI, 13 f.
106 Jordan, *Uruk-Warka*, 38; H. Schmid, *UVB* XVI, 15 f.
107 Lenzen, *UVB* XV, 24 f., pl. 43.

108 Jordan, *Uruk-Warka*, 35 f., 38 f.; H. Schmid, *UVB* XVI, 15 f. Heinrich, *Tempel und Heiligtümer*, 328, 330, attributes this temple to the same period as the rooms around courts IV and XII(?).

within the Seleucid period, and the water-borne debris in the fill within the cutting includes Seleucid bricks. Schmid suggests that the wall belongs to the early Seleucid sanctuary, while the later cutting is contemporary with or slightly later than the pavings outside the Bit rēš. He hypothesizes that the way taken by the god from his cella to the "high seat" and the "god's road" mentioned in the text of 251 B.C. may refer to the remains in the east corner of the precinct. He also suggests the possibility that an earlier Seleucid temple, all traces of which have vanished, might have stood on the terrace occupied by the buildings of Anu-uballit-Nikarchos and Anu-uballit-Kephalon. In that case, he suggests, the east building would have belonged to a deity other than Anu, perhaps the *Bēltušarēš* (mistress of the *rēš* [sanctuary]) who is often mentioned in Neo-Babylonian texts.[109]

I shall begin the discussion of the sanctuary as built by Anu-uballit-Nikarchos and rebuilt by Anu-uballit-Kephalon with a description of the baked-brick temple of Anu-uballit-Kephalon, which presumably replaced the building of Anu-uballit-Nikarchos. This earlier building was so thoroughly destroyed that no discussion of its form is possible.[110]

The temple proper as built by Anu-uballit-Kephalon is set at the back of a large complex (213 x 167.4 meters) that includes a number of courts, chapels, and passages (fig. 4). The temple itself is quite large (74.60 x 52.75 meters). It is set off from the rest of the complex as a closed whole and is distinguished from the other parts by the quality of the building material (baked brick set in mortar), by its decoration, and probably also by greater height. The heavy outer walls, even thicker than is usual in earlier Babylonian temples, are decorated with an elaborate system of projections, niches, and groups of shallow projecting flutes. A series of narrow vertical projections containing one or two shallow half-round flutes sets the rhythm of the facades. Their placement on the facades varies according to the position of the doors. The broader zones between these projections contain either one or two groups of decorative elements, consisting of

bands of half-round projecting flutes on the lower part of the walls and a series of wider and narrower stepped niches above, arranged according to a complicated rhythm. This system is based on the traditions of Babylonian religious architecture. Traces of color show that the verticality of the narrow niches was emphasized by yellow stripes on their walls.[111] Baked bricks with relief decoration and covered with glaze were found at a level within the ruins that suggests that they must have fallen from a high position. The surviving remains of the decoration include bits of animal bodies in white and yellow, as well as designs like stars and palmettes, presumably a later version of Neo-Babylonian decoration like that on the Ishtar Gate at Babylon. The original position of these glazed bricks is not certain. Jordan conjectures that the bricks might have formed part of the decoration of the lower part of the wall, perhaps in the niches, perhaps as a crowning for the zone of fluted decoration. The restored drawing, however, shows a frieze along the top of the wall.[112] Lenzen states that since the lower part of the wall is preserved, the frieze must have crowned the wall, as in Greek temples.[113]

The temple is built on the Babylonian court plan. The main entrance lies on the northeast side, and two smaller entrances on the east corner lead into a corner room (see figs. 4 and 5). A fourth entrance, on the southeast side, leads into a group of rooms that form a small self-contained temple: an antecella (19), a cella with a niche in the back wall (20), and an additional room to the northeast of the antecella (21). The main entrance room on the northeast side (1) is flanked on the west by a chapel (4) with a narrow niche in its rear wall; a door leads south from this room into another small room (5). On the other side of the entrance room is a staircase leading to the roof. The entrance room gives access to the main court (I), the walls of which are decorated with a system of projections and recesses like those on the outer walls of the temple. On the northwest side are two cellae (6 and 7), each with a small niche in the rear wall. On the opposite side is another cella (8), with a subsidiary room (9), and to its west is a room (10) that serves as a passage to

[109] H. Schmid, *UVB* XVI, 13-15, 21.

[110] Ibid.; Lenzen, *UVB* XII/XIII, 12. Heinrich states that the baked-brick core building of Anu-uballit-Nikarchos must have stood in the area later occupied by court VI, in the place where Jordan had located the ziggurat (*Tempel und Heiligtümer*, 328).

[111] Jordan, *Uruk-Warka*, 11, 15, 18 f., pl. 18. According to Heinrich, the use of baked brick for the core building runs counter to the

earlier practice of using baked brick only for particular purposes or for palaces (*Tempel und Heiligtümer*, 328 f.).

[112] Jordan, *Uruk-Warka*, 17-19, pls. 29, 31, 32, 40-42, 44, 48-52.

[113] Lenzen, *UVB* XXV, 23. Heinrich, *Tempel und Heiligtümer*, 329, also places the frieze at the top of the wall and states that it must have continued around the pillars and niches.

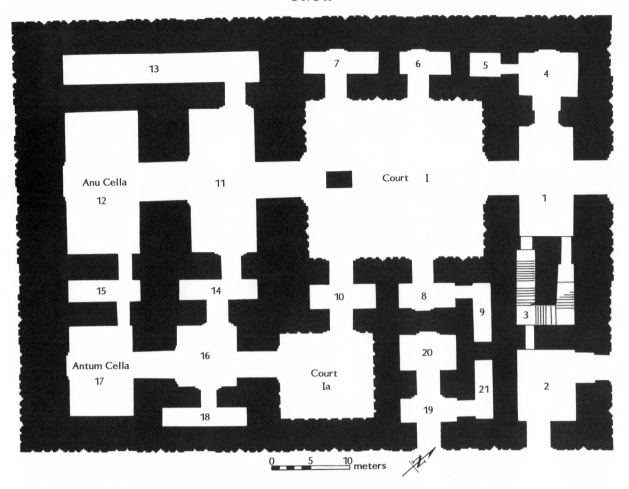

5. Uruk, Anu-Antum temple (core building of the Bit rēš), plan.

court Ia, in front of the Antum cella. Court I has not been completely excavated, but a small sounding has revealed a baked brick base on the axis of the entrance door and the doors to the antecella and cella of Anu. The fact that it is not bonded to the pavement of the court led Jordan to suggest that it is an altar belonging to a relatively late phase. Remains of a water channel also found in the court might be connected either with the sacrificial altar or with the drainage of the court.

The rear part of the structure, distinguished from the rest of the core building by its richly decorated facade, includes two antecella-cella complexes. The larger of the these complexes (rooms 11, 12), which lies on the axis of court I, can be identified as that of Anu by its large size and important position; the slightly smaller group to the southeast (16, 17) presumably belonged to Antum.

The doors of the antecella and cella of Anu lie on the same axis as the entrance doors into court I

(figs. 4, 5), so that a view to the cella was possible from the court in front of the complex (VI). A long narrow corridor (13) that runs the length of the two rooms is accessible only from the antecella. The court wall of the antecella, the wall between the antecella and the cella, and the rear wall of this part of the complex are unusually thick (6.45 meters, 6.26 meters, and 6.48 meters, respectively). Jordan notes that the great thickness of the walls might suggest that these rooms were vaulted, but since no remains of vaulting were found, he concludes that the roofs were probably flat. The walls of the cella still stand more than seven meters high, suggesting perhaps that this group of rooms towered over others in the complex. These rooms are larger than others in the temple; the antecella measures 17.45 x 8.30 meters, the cella 17.45 x 9.30 meters. They are, thus, larger than those of most Babylonian temples. In the rear wall of the cella, opposite the door and a few centimeters to the north of the main axis, is a niche 4.75 meters wide and one brick deep. The statue base that should stand in front of the niche is missing, but a hole four meters deep shows its position.

The antecella and cella of Antum (rooms 16, 17) are accessible though court Ia, on the axis of which they lie, and through two small rooms (14 and 15) opening from the antecella and cella of Anu, respectively. As in the Anu group, a corridor (18) runs along the outside wall, but in this case only beside the antecella, so that the cella is wider than the antecella. The smaller size of the rooms—the antecella (16) is 7.45 x 7.45 meters, the cella (17) 11.5 x 8.15 meters—and of the niche in the rear of the cella wall (3.55 meters wide) show the lesser importance of the deity. The walls of court Ia are decorated with stepped niches. In addition to the cellae for Anu and Antum, the core building contains five chapels, as mentioned above (4, 6, 7, 8, 20).[114]

The complex of which the Anu-Antum temple forms a part consists of a series of courtyards surrounded by rooms, some of which are cellae, while others are passages, storerooms, service rooms, and the like. Much of the complex is built in unbaked brick, in contrast to the baked-brick core building. The complex is divided into three parts: a northwest section; a central section at the back of which the Anu-Antum temple stands; and a southeast section that has been less completely excavated than the rest of the complex. The plan of the southeast section is therefore less well understood than that of the rest of the sanctuary, and some of the rooms in this area follow a different orientation from the Anu-Antum temple and the northwest sector of the sanctuary. A row of four courts (fig. 4, II, V, VII, VIII) with their surrounding rooms occupies the northwest section; at least one large court (VI) stands in the central section in front of the Anu-Antum temple; and at least three courts must have been located in the southeast sector.

The main entrance to the complex is through a gate in the northeast facade. The door is flanked by two towers decorated in the Babylonian fashion with a series of relatively shallow rounded projections. A frieze in glazed bricks with designs of animals and stars probably ran above this zone of molded decoration.[115] Schmid suggests that this tower facade, constructed of baked brick, represents an addition by Anu-uballit-Kephalon to the original facade in unbaked brick, which would have been the work of Anu-uballit-Nikarchos.[116] This entrance leads into the north court II, which is lined on the northwest and southeast sides with four chapels. This court, like all those in the complex, is decorated with niches and narrow, semicircular projecting flutes, and the gates are flanked by greater projections, also decorated with fluting. The chapels are identified as such by shallow niches in the rear walls. In front of each niche stands a base for the cult statue, and in front of each statue base is a small altar. A door on the same axis as the entrance gate gives access, across a passage, to another court (V) with doors on all four sides, the one on the northwest giving direct access to the outside. This gate was originally built with shallow projecting towers on each side. Soon, however, new, strongly projecting towers with decoration like that of the main gate were added. Both its relatively small size and the fact that no remains of decoration in glazed brick were found suggest that this was a subsidiary entrance. Heinrich, however, characterizes it as a principal entrance for traffic but not for liturgical purposes.[117] Presumably, the original door was built by Anu-uballit-Nikarchos, the addition by Anu-uballit-Kephalon. This door was walled up in the Parthian period. One cella (48) lies on the northwest side of this court, and a small antecella-cella complex occupies the southeast corner (52-53). The other rooms are passages, with one unexcavated side chamber.[118]

Courts II and V serve as forecourts to the Anu-Antum temple, which cannot be entered without passing through them, and at the same time as forecourts to a self-contained complex in the southwest corner of the sanctuary, centered around court VIII. A passage (50) on the south side of court V gives access to court VII. The door between these two courts lies not on the axis of the main northeast gate and of the passage between courts II and V, but a few meters to the northwest. Court VII appears to be a service court. Since none of the surrounding rooms had cult niches, they may have served for temple business. Heinrich suggests that the food brought into the temple may have been stored here. He quarrels with Jordan's identification of a large room on the southeast (82) as a storeroom on the grounds of its size and decoration with engaged pillars and suggests instead that it might have been a

[114] Jordan, *Uruk-Warka*, 1-19, pls. 18, 21, 22, 34-39. Cf. also Heinrich, *Tempel und Heiligtümer*, 328 f.

[115] Jordan, *Uruk-Warka*, 24 f., pl. 59a.

[116] H. Schmid, *UVB* XVI, 21 f.

[117] Heinrich, *Tempel und Heiligtümer*, 329.

[118] Jordan, *Uruk-Warka*, 24-28, pls. 9, 53, 59-62.

reception room.[119] Water channels run through the court, and Jordan interprets a base in the middle of this court and a similar one in room 84 as supports for water basins.[120]

Court VIII, on the other hand, is lined with chapels on the northwest and northeast sides. The room in the northeast corner (90) housed civic archives, since bullae, including one with the stamp Χρεοφυλακικός Ὄρχων (*chreophylax*, or registrar, of Orchoi), were found there. The southwest side of this court is occupied by three independent chapels, marked as such by niches in the rear walls of the cellae and by statue bases and altars in the cellae. The central chapel consists simply of an antecella and a cella (96, 97), the two side ones of an antecella, a cella, and a corridor accessible from the antecella and running the entire length of the antecella-cella group (98-99-100; 93-94-95). The cella in the southeast corner (95) differs from the other two in having four bases along the rear wall, each fronted by a small altar; a fifth base, with its altar, stands in the northwest corner.[121] These three chapels probably formed a self-contained temple, possibly dedicated to Enlil, Ea, and Hadad, who are among the most important gods mentioned in the economic texts.[122] Heinrich notes that the fact that one cella (91) lacks a cult niche shows that other rooms without a niche might also have been cult chambers. He states that sixteen cult centers have been found in the rooms around court VIII, that eight more are to be restored with certainty, and there could have been seven or eight more.[123] Court VIII with its chapels is separated from the Anu-Antum temple by a covered passageway 7.75 meters wide.

Court V also gives access to the central court VI, which serves as the forecourt for the Anu-Antum temple. The fact that there were apparently stairs between courts V and VI indicates a considerable difference in level.[124] The walls of court VI are decorated with simple flutes. A low bench was built in front of the northeast facade of the Anu-Antum temple and along the northwest wall of the court. A row of thirteen bases, probably originally fourteen, was set along the northwest wall of the court, next to the Anu-Antum temple. These bases were probably designed to hold divine symbols, either placed there permanently or put in position on the occasion of festivals.[125]

The section of the precinct to the north of court VI has been only partially explored, but it appears to contain courts and surrounding rooms whose orientation differs from that of the Anu-Antum temple, court VI, and the northern sector of the sanctuary complex. The orientation of this section, however, appears to correspond to that of some of the rooms in the southeastern part of the sanctuary. Heinrich interprets the rooms around court III and the so-called small temple in the southeastern part of the precinct as belonging to the earliest Seleucid phase of construction. He suggests that in the rebuilding of Anu-uballit-Kephalon, this area was reshaped to create an entrance into court VI. The rooms around courts IV and XII(?) would no longer have been a temple after this rebuilding. Heinrich suggests that administrative quarters and workshops may have been located in this area in the late Seleucid period.[126] The plan of the southern part of the precinct, especially its eastern section, is more uncertain than that of the rest of the complex. This uncertainty is due partly to the incomplete excavation of the area but partly also to its building history, which is apparently more complicated than that of the rest of the sanctuary. Jordan restores the southern section as containing three courts (IX, X, and XI), but the limits of these are conjectural. Court IX lies to the southeast of the core temple and follows the same orientation. Along its southwest side is a double temple consisting of two cellae, each with an antecella (109-110; 111-112). A number of rooms on the southeast side (101, 102, 104, 105) were used at least partly for cult purposes. During the Seleucid period the court must have remained free of obstacles so as to allow access to the self-contained group of cult rooms (19-20-21) on the southeast side of the Anu-Antum temple. Jordan further argues that there must have been an entrance somewhere in the middle of the southeast side of the Bit rēš. At some point, probably during the Parthian period, a small, self-contained temple of non-Babylonian form was built against the southeast wall of the core building;[127] this temple will be discussed in the section on Parthian Uruk.

It is to a great extent possible to identify the features found in the excavations with the doors, courts, cellae, and so on mentioned in the building

[119] Heinrich, *Tempel und Heiligtümer*, 329.
[120] Jordan, *Uruk-Warka*, 29-31, pls. 63a and b, 64.
[121] Ibid., 31-34, pls. 65c, 66-70; Lenzen, *UVB* XII/XIII, 11 f.
[122] Falkenstein, *Topographie*, 16.
[123] Heinrich, *Tempel und Heiligtümer*, 330.

[124] Ibid., 329.
[125] Jordan, *Uruk-Warka*, 39 f., pls. 74b, 75b.
[126] Heinrich, *Tempel und Heiligtümer*, 328, 330.
[127] Jordan, *Uruk-Warka*, 35-38.

inscriptions and the ritual texts. Some ambiguities remain, however, due largely to the incomplete excavation of the complex but partly also to ambiguities in the texts. For example, the Nikarchos inscription gives the names of four doors but states that there are three doors in all (line 8), while the building itself certainly had four large outer doors.

Falkenstein was able to identify some of the doors named in the texts with those revealed by excavations. Thus, the ká-maḫ, the "high gate" opening toward the northeast mentioned in the Nikarchos inscription (lines 4-6), must be the prominent gate near the west end of the northeast wall. This gate, which opens into a series of large courts, was distinguished by decoration in glazed brick. Falkenstein further conjectured that the second northeast gate, the ká-gal, the "great gate," must have stood in the unexcavated portion of the northeast wall, near its east corner.[128] This door has now been located.[129] The Nikarchos inscription names two more doors, the ká-ḫengalla, the "door of abundance," and the bābu mušēri ḫiṣib šadî, the "door, which allows the products of the mountains to be brought in." The location of neither of these doors is given. Since the text gives the total number of the doors as three, either these two gates must be identical, or the number three is an error. Heinrich has suggested that the terms "door of abundance" and "door, which allows the products of the mountains to be brought in" both designate the opening into court V from the northwest.[130] A ritual text names the ká-sag, the "main gate," through which the god Usmû enters the Bit rēš from outside. Falkenstein identified this door with the outer door in either the northwest or southwest wall and suggested that the ká-sag was either the fourth outer door known from the excavations but not named in the Nikarchos inscription, or that it might be identical with the bābu mušēri ḫiṣib šadî. The "holy door," the ká-sikilla, is located by another text "behind the cella" (papaḫa), which, according to Falkenstein, must have been the cella of Anu. Falkenstein thus believed that the holy door must have lain to the southwest of the Anu cella, in an area that had not then been investigated.[131] The outer wall, located about seven meters behind the core building, has now been excavated but has proved to be badly damaged by water. Lenzen suggested, as Falkenstein had, that the holy door must have lain in this wall, and he

speculated that its presence might even have been the cause of the damage by providing a channel for the water.[132] The suggested location of the door is not affected by Van Dijk's argument that a new text necessitates interpreting papaḫ not as "cella," but as a large complex.[133]

The Nikarchos inscription (lines 8f.) states that there are "seven courts around the court in which the parak šīmāti, 'the high seat of fate' lies." Falkenstein notes that a problem is raised by the fact that the number of courts is given for the building of Nikarchos, whereas the building of Kephalon, which alone survives at all clearly, enlarged and expanded on that of Nikarchos. Four large courts were found in the northwest section of the building (north court II, courts V and VII, west court VIII) and two in the southeast area (south court IX, court X); he suggests that there might have been one more in the east corner, thus arriving at the requisite number of seven. There are, however, several smaller courts in this area (courts III and IV, and a restored court XII), which Falkenstein feels might not have been included in the Nikarchos inscription. In any case, the excavation is still so incomplete that it is difficult to determine how many courts there actually were.

The parak šīmāti named in Nikarchos' inscription is also mentioned in several ritual texts, as are two courts, the ubšukkinakku and the kisalmaḫḫu ("main court," translated by Thureau-Dangin as "sublime cour"). The texts show that the main court must have lain in front of the Anu and Antum cellae; thus it should be identified with court I of the core building (fig. 4). The "door of Anu and Antum" can be identified with the entrance into this court. The ubšukkinakku and the parak šīmāti that is associated with it in at least one text raise slightly more complex problems. The importance of this court in temple ritual is shown by its Sumerian title, which originally referred to the assembly place of the deities for council and for giving judgment but was later transferred to its earthly counterpart. Various ritual texts make it clear that the ubšukkinakku in the Anu-Antum complex must have lain outside the core building. In a ritual occuring at night (AO 6460), after a ceremony taking place in front of the ziggurat, a torch is brought up into the main court (kisalmaḫḫu), then placed facing Anu. The priest and various deities, after entering the sanctuary of

---

[128] Falkenstein, *Topographie*, 10-26.

[129] Schmid, *UVB* XVI, 16 f. Cf. Heinrich, *Tempel und Heiligtümer*, 330.

[130] Heinrich, *Tempel und Heiligtümer*, 329. He accepts also a third designation for this door, *Ká-sag*, "main gate."

[131] Falkenstein, *Topographie*, 12. Cf. Heinrich, *Tempel und Heiligtümer*, 331.

[132] Lenzen, *UVB* XII/XIII, 12.

[133] Van Dijk, *UVB* XVIII, 60 f.

Antu, exit into the *ubšukkinakku*; after this, an ox is immolated for them near the *parak šīmāti*. That the court lay near the temple proper is, however, implied by another text (AO 6459, rev., lines 10f.) in which on the tenth day (of Tišri) the gods were awakened in the *ubšukkinakku*; when it was light, the door of the temple was opened. Thus it seems likely that the court lay in front of the door. The size and placement of court VI, directly in front of the main temple, as well as the presence in it of thirteen (originally fourteen) bases, make its importance clear. It seems probable, then, that court VI was the *ubšukkinakku*.[134] The text of AO 6460, summarized above, would seem to imply that the *parak šīmāti* was located in the *ubšukkinakku*; and Weissbach in his summary of the evidence for these features in various temples in Babylonia and Assyria accepts this location.[135] Falkenstein states that another text (VAT 7479 I-III) suggests that the "high seat of fate" lay close to the cellae of Anu and Antum, however, and that therefore a location in the court of the core building would be preferable. He suggests that possibly in the building of Nikarchos the "high seat of fate" might have stood in the forecourt before the main building.[136] Weissbach's interpretation of the texts, that the *parak šīmāti* lay in the *ubšukkinakku*, seems the more natural, but Falkenstein's is possible. No base that seems suitable for such a feature was found in either the main court of the core building (court I) or in court VI; therefore, the question cannot be resolved. The texts also indicate that seats for deities were placed in the main court; none were found in excavations.[137]

The excavations have revealed twenty-two cellae around the courts of the outer building, and there may in fact have been more. It is difficult to assign cellae to specific deities. According to the ritual for the Akitu of the month of Nisan (VAT 7849), more than fifty deities assembled in the temple of Anu. Some of these had seats elsewhere, e.g., in the Irigal, and others came from unknown shrines to participate in the festival. Still, there is room in the Anu complex for fifty divinities, since some cellae contain more than one base. Falkenstein suggests possible placements for a number of deities.[138]

The two large cellae placed against the rear (south) wall of the core building must have be-

longed to Anu and Antum. The Kephalon inscription gives the name of the sanctuary of Anu as *é-nam-en-na*, the "house of lordship" (lines 4f.), whereas in the Nikarchos inscription the same title is applied to the sanctuary of Anu and Antum together (lines 16-18). The texts name a number of pedestals belonging to Anu; these must have been located in his cella or in court I in front of it. The most important of these is the "high seat of royal rule." Other texts name the "high seat of Anu," which might be another name for the "high seat of royal rule," but which according to Thureau-Dangin should be equated with the *parak šīmāti*, the "high seat of fate." If Falkenstein's interpretation is accepted, the "high seat of royal rule" ought to lie within the cella of Anu, whereas if Thureau-Dangin is correct, it could be placed in the main court of the core building. The ritual for the Akitu of Nisan (VAT 7849) names two bases to the sides of the "high seat of royal rule," the "place of the right tiara" and the "place of the holy tiara to the left of Anu," where Enlil and Ea sat during the festival. A text for the Akitu festival of Tišrit names a base at which the door guardian Papsukal halted or on which he sat, after which he took the hand of Anu (AO 6459, lines 26f.). None of these bases can be identified with actual remains, since the main base in the cella of Anu has been destroyed and the rest of the cella floor could not be cleared; only one base remains in court I.[139]

The rooms of Antum are named in the texts less frequently than those of Anu. As already stated, in the Nikarchos inscription the term *é-nam-en-na*, "house of lordship," refers to the sanctuaries of both Anu and Antum. In the Kephalon inscription, on the other hand, the cult room of Antum is given its own name, *é-gašan-an-na*, the "house of the queen of heaven." A foreroom of Antum that is mentioned in several texts could be either the antecella (room 16) or court Ia, which lies in front of the antecella-cella complex. Another room within the Antum complex, the "room of the golden bed of Antum," could be the room used for the ritual marriage of Anu and Antum.[140] Somewhere in the temple was a storeroom for ornaments and garments of the gods, the *bīt pirištu*.[141]

Texts recording the sale of prebends provide some evidence for the existence of cult furniture.

---

[134] Thureau-Dangin, *Rituels accadiens*, 123, obv. lines 33 f.; rev. lines 1-7. Falkenstein, *Topographie*, 12-14.

[135] Weissbach, in Wetzel, *Hauptheiligtum*, 59.

[136] Falkenstein, *Topographie*, 22 f. Heinrich, *Tempel und Heiligtümer*, 328, identifies court I as the *kisalmaḫḫu* and locates the *parak šīmāti* within it.

[137] Falkenstein, *Topographie*, 23 f.

[138] Ibid., 15-17.

[139] Ibid., 18-24; Thureau-Dangin, *Rituels accadiens*, 95.

[140] Falkenstein, *Topographie*, 24-26.

[141] Doty, *Cuneiform Archives*, 126 f.; McEwan, *Priest and Temple*, 81 f.

For example, one text records the sale of a share "in the linens of the cultic stands, the curtains and the baldachins . . . the strips of carded wool, the sashes, the . . . garments and the strips of carded wool for the thrones of the temples." Another contract deals with the right to part of the "(linen of) the baldachins and cultic stands (and) curtains . . ." as part of a prebend of Anu, Enlil, Nana, and the mistress of rēš.[142]

IRIGAL

The second great sanctuary of Uruk in the Seleucid period has been identified with the building called in some texts "Irigal," the "great dwelling" (the so-called Südbau) (fig. 6).[143] It is closely linked, both physically and in ritual use, with the Bit rēš sanctuary. The texts clearly show that in the late period Ishtar was the chief goddess of the Irigal, where she was worshipped in association with Nana and ten other goddesses. This marks an important cult shift, since previously Ishtar and Nana had been honored in E-anna.[144] The material in the fill on which the Seleucid buildings rest suggests that the first remains on the site are Neo-Babylonian at the earliest.[145] The first datable textual mention of the Irigal occurs in the Anu hymn of the year 61 of the Seleucid era (251 B.C.).[146] The baked-brick building that constitutes the most substantial remains of the Seleucid period can be dated to roughly 200 B.C. on the basis of an Aramaic inscription in the niche behind the cult statue. This inscription, in glazed brick, names "Anu-uballit whose other name [is] Kephalon," clearly the same person as the builder of the Bit rēš.[147] The temple is not named. The fact that the language of the inscription is Aramaean, whereas the building inscriptions of the Bit rēš are written in Akkadian, may indicate that Aramaean was the current language during the third and second centuries B.C., whereas Akkadian was only a learned language.[148]

In the Irigal, as in the Bit rēš , the baked-brick building of Anu-uballit-Kephalon replaces one of unbaked brick of which little remains; presumably this earlier temple is the one referred to in the Anu hymn of 251 B.C.[149] According to Falkenstein, the fact that no remains predating the Neo-Babylonian period have survived does not necessarily mean that there were no earlier structures on the site. Indeed, he argues that the site of Irigal must have been holy ground, since the cults of Ishtar and Nana—transferred there from E-anna—continue a tradition that was millennia old.[150] As stated in my introduction to the section on Uruk, the latest texts found in the sanctuary are dated to the reign of Demetrios I Soter (162-150 B.C.), but the fact that the Irigal is mentioned in a text of 108 B.C. may suggest a later date for its destruction by fire.[151] Heinrich states that the blocking of the entrance door to the sanctuary at some unknown date marks the end of the cult use of the building. A period of decline followed, during which perhaps the outer walls of the sanctuary—the door of which was again walled up at a higher level—might have been used for a fortress. The rooms of the temple were reused, and the partially burnt debris of a roof was found above the debris belonging to the first period of collapse. The remains of the walls of the court and of the outer walls were in turn reused to build poor huts apparently for a particular stratum of the population.[152] Thus, the Irigal, like the Bit rēš, apparently ceased to function as a temple during the Parthian period.

Like the Bit rēš, the Seleucid Irigal sanctuary was built on a Babylonian court plan. The temple proper is set in a precinct enclosed by a thick double wall; the thickness on the southwest side is 17.40 meters, on the southeast, 19.80 meters. This wall enclosed an area of at least 198 x 205 meters. The lower edge of this precinct wall lay four meters below the deepest course of the core building so that the baked-brick temple stood on a high terrace that was built over and around an earlier temple. According to Heinrich, the facts that the baked-brick building rests on a levelling course rather than di-

---

[142] McEwan, *Priest and Temple*, 82 f., 130.

[143] Doty, *Cuneiform Archives*, 28, notes that no building inscriptions have been found that positively identify the Südbau as the Irigal.

[144] Falkenstein, *Topographie*, 30-35; Heinrich, *UVB* V, 31-34. Falkenstein has demonstrated that Irigal is the correct reading of the sign group read as Ešgal by Heinrich and Jordan (*Uruk-Warka*, 8).

[145] Heinrich, *UVB* V, 29 f.; idem, *UVB* VI, 30; Falkenstein, *Topographie*, 30 f.

[146] Falkenstein, *Topographie*, 34.

[147] v. Haller, *UVB* VII, 36 f., citing Kruckman; Falkenstein, *Topographie*, 31; Bowman, "Anu-uballit-Kephalon," 231-34.

[148] Goossens, "Au déclin," 224-42; Sarkisian, "Self-governing Cities," 70; Heinrich, *Tempel und Heiligtümer*, 302.

[149] Heinrich, *UVB* V, 29 f.; Falkenstein, *Topographie*, 30 f., 34; Heinrich, *Tempel und Heiligtümer*, 332.

[150] Falkenstein, *Topographie*, 31-35. Cf. Heinrich, *Tempel und Heiligtümer*, 332.

[151] Falkenstein, *Topographie*, 34; v. Haller, *UVB* VIII, 56 f. For the text of 108 B.C., see Kessler, "Eine arsakidenzeitliche Urkunde aus Warka," *BaM* XV (1984), 275-81.

[152] Heinrich, *UVB* V, 30 f.; idem, *UVB* VIII, 56 f.; Falkenstein, *Topographie*, 34.

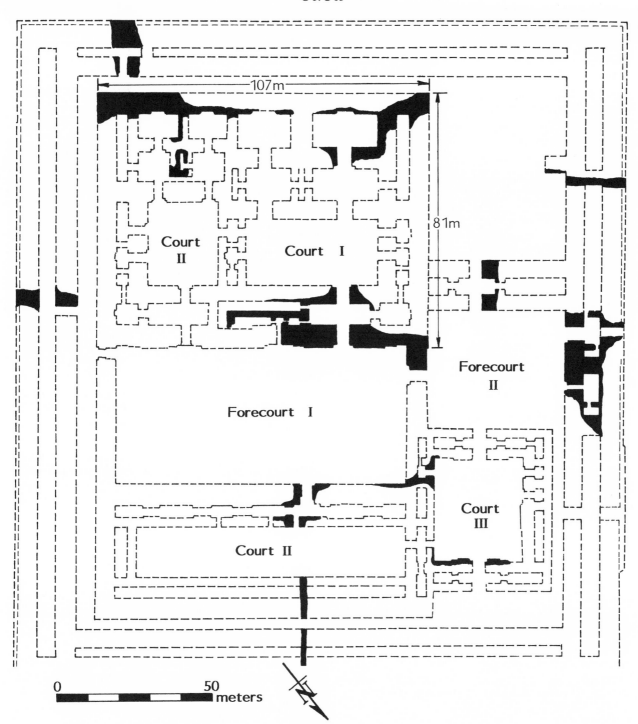

6. Uruk, Irigal, plan.

rectly on the terrace and that the niche decoration of the terrace differs from that of the core building raises the possibility that the terrace was originally designed to support an earlier temple, now lost. The relationship between the terrace and the precinct wall is not clear, and it is possible that the outer wall was built at the same time as the earlier temple. The maximum preserved height of the precinct wall is about 24 meters, and it is unlikely to have been much higher.[153] Two doors have been found in the northwest side of the precinct wall, but the placement of the main entrance is uncertain. As Falkenstein says, the main gate must be the "Ishtar Gate" mentioned in some economic texts; he suggests, plausibly, that it lay on the northeast side, the side on which the main entrance to the core building is placed.[154]

The excavations of the precinct wall were directed mainly toward finding its outer perimeter. Within the main temple, only the most important rooms were cleared, the other excavations being limited to test trenches to determine the plan. Therefore, many details remain uncertain, but the general outline is clear (fig. 6). The complex is divided into two unequal parts, the temple proper and the two courts that front it occupying the larger southeastern portion of the precinct, and the northwestern portion apparently containing three courts. A gate on the northwest side of the sanctuary opens into a forecourt (II); to the north of this is a smaller court (III) surrounded by a number of narrow rooms (as restored). Two small rooms on the northwest side of court III can be identified as cellae on the basis of the cult niches in their rear walls. The southwest corner of the precinct has hardly been explored.[155] A small room near the east end of the south precinct wall, with an entrance from the surrounding corridor, can be identified as a cult room for a minor deity or deities by the presence of two brick bases, one on the axis of the door and the other, smaller one to the southeast.[156]

As restored, the temple proper (core building) is fronted by two courts equal in length to the width of the temple (court IV and forecourt I). Falkenstein, following Heinrich, suggested that it is possible that forecourt I was divided into two courts, though, as Heinrich has commented in his recent book, such a division would make the court in front of Ishtar's cella rather small for the assembly of deities on the occasion of festivals.[157] The baked-brick core building, placed in the southeast corner of the temple precinct, forms a block 104 x 87 meters in size.[158] It is divided into two unequal parts, each with an entrance into a court behind which lie two antecella-cella complexes, for a total of four cellae at the rear of the building. The larger western portion presumably included the cellae of Ishtar and Nana. The main entrance into the core building does not lie in the center of the complex, but rather near its north corner, on the line of the doors into the larger antecella-cella complex. The gate in the precinct wall on the northeast side of the building has not been found, but the entrance from court IV into forecourt I lies on a different axis from that of the main entrance into the temple proper; thus the principle of an off-axis entrance, which is encountered frequently in Babylonian temples and is used in the Bit rēš, is maintained also here.

The two sections of the temple complex are similar in plan, though not identical. A major difference is the presence of the staircase leading to the roof at the left of the entrance into the larger western portion. The outer walls of the temple complex have been only partially explored, but they have been restored as containing a number of narrow rooms, including seven cellae, by analogy with the Bit rēš. A door between the inner courts I and II apparently connected the two parts of the complex. Court II, in the smaller eastern half, is deeper than court I, and the entrance to this court does not lie on the axis of either of the two cellae in that section of the building.

The temple was roofed in wood, as is shown by the abundant debris of burnt palm logs found in the entrance room and the main cella.[159] The outer walls of the temple proper were articulated with projections and niches in the traditional Babylonian fashion. The towers flanking the main door into the complex were decorated with small double niches, between which were set seven half-round flutes.

---

[153] Heinrich, *UVB* V, 28-30. Cf. also Heinrich's description in *Tempel und Heiligtümer*, 331-33.

[154] Falkenstein, *Topographie*, 37 f.

[155] Ibid., 30.

[156] Heinrich, *UVB* V, 29.

[157] Heinrich, *UVB* VI, 28; Falkenstein, *Topographie*, 36. Heinrich, *Tempel und Heiligtümer*, 332.

[158] These are the figures given by Heinrich in *UVB* V, 26, and

UVB VI, 27. On the plan in *UVB* VI (pl. 10), which is reproduced in Falkenstein, *Topographie*, pl. 3, the dimensions are given as 107 x 81 meters. Heinrich, *Tempel und Heiligtümer*, 332, gives 104 x 87. The core building is discussed by Heinrich in *UVB* V, 26-28, and *UVB* VI, 26-29, and by von Haller in *UVB* VII, 36-39. Citations for specific details will be given where appropriate.

[159] v. Haller, *UVB* VII, 37; Heinrich, *UVB* VI, 28; idem, *Tempel und Heiligtümer*, 332.

This system stopped about 4.50 meters above the floor of the court, to be replaced by a scheme of small stepped niches. Similar decoration was found on the east, west, and south corners of the building, as well as on the court walls near the gate. On the outer walls of the building, this decoration began above the fifth course of bricks, whereas on the court the articulation continued down to the pavement; this recalls the system in the Bit rēš. All of these surfaces were covered with gypsum plaster. Extensive remains of decoration in glazed bricks were also found; these will be discussed below.

The main cella, in the western half of the complex, is distinguished as such by its placement on the axis of the entrance from the forecourt into the inner court and by its large size—20.70 meters wide, 10.60 meters deep. The second cult room in the western half of the complex is also unusually broad—17.50 meters—whereas the two smaller cellae in the eastern portion are 12.50 meters wide. In the main cella the base for the cult statue lies on the axis of the door and the cult niche, 1.55 meters in front of the rear wall. The base, made of limestone and covered with gypsum plaster, is 2.28 meters long, 1.52 wide, and ca. 0.80 high. Parts remain of the cult statue, which is made of a number of pieces of wood held together with wooden clamps and wedges. Enough survives to show that it represented a female figure clad in a thin, rippled garment with a triangular opening at the back of the neck.[160] The cella also contained two other bases, both standing on the limestone pavement, which belongs to the period of Anu-uballit-Kephalon and is the fourth and uppermost level in the room. In the north corner of the room stood a sizeable base (1.00 x 1.00 x 0.22 meters) made of mud bricks held together with gypsum mortar. West of the niche and ca. 0.60 meters in front of the southwest wall is a second base, 0.90 x 0.90 x 0.50 meters. A trench dug around the cult base in an effort to determine periods of use disclosed an earlier floor, probably belonging to the cult room of a predecessor of the temple built by Anu-uballit-Kephalon. Two intermediate levels with which no floor could be associated were also found. Part of the altar in the main cella was broken through in an unsuccessful attempt to find a foundation document; this altar proved to be bonded to the remaining lowest courses of an altar that belonged to the cella of the preceding mud-brick building.[161]

The baked-brick temple built by Anu-uballit-Kephalon was extensively decorated with glazed brick. The pillars to the sides of the main entrance door were covered in blue brick. Heinrich suggested that these sections of blue brick continued to the top of the wall, so that the door would have been framed in a blue rectangle that stood out against the gray gypsum plastered walls.[162] Glazed bricks with blue or white grounds, as well as with designs in relief—e.g., yellow, star-shaped flowers and parts of lions and other animals—were found throughout the excavations around the walls of the core building. A particularly rich group was found around the main door. Heinrich suggests that perhaps in the Irigal, as in the Anu-Antum temple, a figured frieze ran around the walls of the temple proper. Blue tile beginning 1.40 or 1.80 meters above the floor also covers the two-stepped frame of the door into the main cella, as well as strips of the wall 0.95 meters wide to either side. In the two largest cellae, the cult niches, like the doors, have two recesses on either side. The niches are faced with blue-glazed tiles, and decoration in blue tiles also covers the walls to either side of the niches for a width of 0.95 meters, beginning 1.40 or 1.80 meters above the floor. The cult niches were thus treated like doors.[163]

The Aramaic building inscription, in white lettering, runs along the lowest row of glazed bricks in the cult niche. Such a location for a building inscription, behind the cult statue and therefore essentially invisible, is not known in earlier Babylonian architecture. Furthermore, the inscription is unusually laconic, since it does not give the name of the deity to whom the temple is dedicated.[164]

As stated above, ritual texts clearly show that the Irigal was the shrine of Ishtar and Nana. One text names "Anu, Antum, Ishtar, Nana, and the gods who dwell in the rēš, Irigal, and Ésárra, the 'high seat' of the Anu ziggurat" (AO 6451, rev., lines 1-2). Since the rēš and the high temple on the Anu ziggurat belong to Anu and Antum, only the Irigal is left for Ishtar and Nana. Another text (VAT 7849 I, lines 23ff.) records a ritual in which Ishtar goes to the rēš sanctuary accompanied by eleven other goddesses, of whom Nana takes the first place; this

---

[160] v. Haller, *UVB* VII, 37, pls. 32a, b, 39a.

[161] Ibid., 36-39, pls. 10, 33. The earlier floor level is at +15.87 meters, that of Anu-uballit-Kephalon's building at +22 meters (Lenzen, *UVB* XXV, 23).

[162] Heinrich, *UVB* V, 27 f.; idem, *UVB* VI, 28 f. Cf. Lenzen,

UVB XXV, 23, pl. 21c; Heinrich, *Tempel und Heiligtümer*, 333.

[163] Heinrich, *UVB* VI, 28 f., gives 1.40 meters; v. Haller, *UVB* VII, 36, pl. 31a, gives 1.80 meters. Heinrich, *UVB* V, 27 f.

[164] v. Haller, *UVB* VII, 36 f.

text shows that Ishtar shared a sanctuary with these goddesses. Some are unknown otherwise, whereas others appear in the canonical god lists as belonging to the court of Ishtar. Falkenstein argues that the fact that Anu is called "Lord of Irigal" in a hymn does not demonstrate that he had a cella there, but is merely an indication of his important position, since he is also called "Lord of E-anna," where there is no place for him.[165]

Coordination between the physical remains and the texts is less easy in the Irigal than in the Bit rēš because of the incomplete state of the excavations. It is clear, however, that the chief cella must be that of Ishtar-Inanna, which is called ᵉpapaḫa ᵈištar, according to Falkenstein.[166] Van Dijk has argued that the measurements of the papaḫ in the rēš and Irigal sanctuaries, as given in a newly discovered text from the Bit rēš archives, invalidate the translation of papaḫ as "cella." Instead, the measurements suggest a large building or a building complex.[167] Falkenstein has also proposed that the "seat of Anu in the cella of Ishtar" mentioned in a text (VAT 7849 I, 25) might be the small base next to the central base for the cult statue in the main cella of the Irigal. The "great house of heaven and earth" mentioned in the Anu hymn as dedicated to Anu in the Irigal might also be connected with this "seat of Anu." The cella next to the main cella must belong to Nana, the goddess next in importance to Ishtar, but the name of Nana's cella is not given in ritual texts. In addition to these, two other cellae are placed against the rear wall in the eastern part of the temple, behind court II, and seven more have been restored by analogy with the Bit rēš. It is obviously possible that other, unexcavated rooms remain. Falkenstein attributes the other cellae to the ten attendants of Ishtar, some whom could have been accommodated more than one to a cella. A ritual text (AO 7439) in which Ishtar was accompanied by other deities to the Bit Akitu is associated by Falkenstein with the Irigal. At sunrise the deities, assembled in the kisal-šà-ba (inner court), rise to face Ishtar (lines 15-16); from this Falkenstein identifies the kisal-šà-ba as the court in front of Ishtar's cella.[168]

Economic texts also name other places in the Irigal. Four gates are mentioned: the Anu gate, the Ishtar gate, the northwest gate, and the bāb sikkat.

The incomplete state of the excavation hinders identification. It seems clear, however, that the Ishtar gate must have been the principal one; Falkenstein suggests that both it and the bāb sikkat might have been on the northeast side. The Anu gate, along with the northwest gate, was probably located on the northwest side, the side facing the Anu ziggurat and part of the rēš sanctuary. It is interesting that although most of the men mentioned in these economic texts have Akkadian names, one text lists the bīt qāt of Nikolaos, son of Apollonides.[169]

Between the outer wall of the Irigal and the southeast corner of the Bit rēš runs a late wall, either Seleucid or Parthian, with a tower at about its midpoint. This wall runs approximately parallel to the so-called Seleucid wall (perhaps rather Parthian) at the northeast corner of the rēš. According to Heinrich, these walls appear to have closed off a space between the sanctuaries and parallel to them.[170]

E-ANNA

E-anna, the shrine of Innin, was one of the major sanctuaries of Uruk from the late fourth millennium B.C. through the Neo-Babylonian period (fig. 7), during which time the sanctuary underwent a number of rebuildings. Parts of E-anna had fallen into disrepair after the Kassite period and apparently remained in a ruined state until Marduk-apal-iddina II (721-710 B.C.) undertook to rebuild it. His rebuilding is documented by a cylinder found in Nimrud and is also evident in the archaeological record. Marduk-apal-iddina's work was incomplete when Sargon II (709-705 B.C.) conquered Uruk; and Sargon apparently intended to wipe out all traces of Marduk-apal-iddina's building activity and to replace these incomplete buildings with his own constructions. Apparently both Marduk-apal-iddina and Sargon largely followed the plan of E-anna as it existed during the Third Dynasty of Ur.[171] The sanctuary constructed by Sargon was burnt, and Nebuchadnezzar II (605-562 B.C.) reused Sargon's walls as foundations in his rebuilding. Nebuchadnezzar's structures were in turn destroyed by a major fire; in some places on the northeast casement wall, up to half a meter of

---

[165] Falkenstein, *Topographie*, 34 f.
[166] Ibid., 35; VAT 7849 I, 25.
[167] Van Dijk, *UVB* XVIII, 60 f., 108, W20030.
[168] Falkenstein, *Topographie*, 35 f.

[169] Ibid., 36-39. The text mentioning Nikolaos is no. 3, BRM II, 48, lines 8-9.
[170] Heinrich, *Tempel und Heiligtümer*, 333.
[171] Lenzen, *UVB* XII/XIII, 28-31; idem, *Neue Deutsche Ausgrabungen*, 21-26. Heinrich, *Tempel und Heiligtümer*, 260.

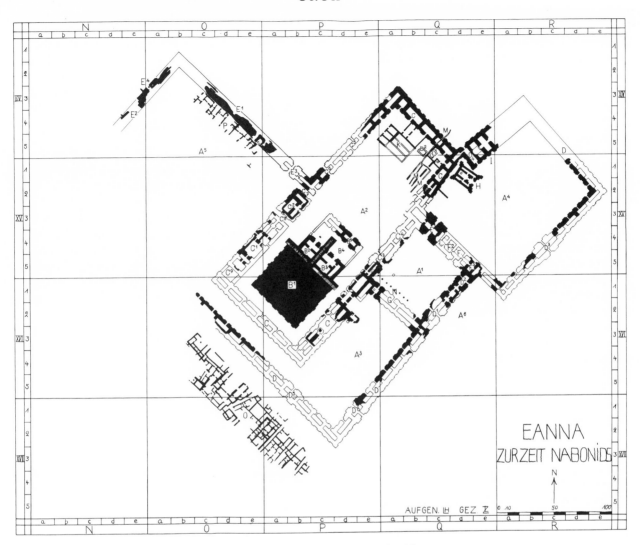

7. Uruk, E-anna in the time of Nabonidus.

burnt debris separates the level of Nebuchadnezzar's building from that of Nabonidus (555-539
B.C.), who rebuilt the sanctuary in a considerably
altered form.[172] There are considerable remains of
building activity under Cyrus, most of which consisted of improvements rather than major rebuildings. Work done under the early Achaemenids includes the construction of a room that housed
economic texts; the room was built probably under
Cambyses or Darius, but the texts mostly date
from the reign of Sargon II. The latest tablets in this
archive date to the reign of Darius I. Thus, E-anna
must have been destroyed anew after the accession
of Darius in 522 B.C.[173]

At one time it was thought that E-anna had lost
its religious function during the Seleucid period.
Though the building of a new outer covering for
the ziggurat during the Seleucid period was noted,
some of the excavators did not consider this an indication that the ziggurat continued to function as
such. Jordan had suggested that the ruins of the ziggurat were used as a watch tower.[174] Falkenstein
noted the traces of Seleucid building activity in
E-anna, but stated that it was impossible to determine whether the ziggurat retained its cult function.[175] Heinrich stated in his 1982 book that excavations had revealed no meaningful remains from
the Seleucid period.[176] Recent work has shown,

[172] Lenzen, *UVB* XII/XIII, 16.
[173] Ibid., 16-18, 29 f.
[174] Jordan, *UVB* I, 26; v. Haller and Lenzen, *UVB* IX, 18.

[175] Falkenstein, *Topographie*, 40.
[176] Heinrich, *Tempel und Heiligtümer,* 301.

33

however, that the whole outer enclosure of the sanctuary was rebuilt during the Seleucid period, and the outer facade of the Seleucid enclosure wall shows a system of decoration with projections and recesses similar to that used in the Assyrian period. This decorative system characterizes sacred buildings, which suggests that E-anna continued to function as a sanctuary.

It seems also that the ziggurat retained its old meaning. Its form, however, was changed. In earlier periods the ziggurat in E-anna had been simply a high tower, unlike the other ziggurats in Mesopotamia, but in the Seleucid period it became stepped. The old casement wall of the enclosure in which the ziggurat stood became the outer step, a filled-in courtyard between this wall and the ziggurat the second, and the core of the old Urnammu ziggurat the third and highest step. The height of the ziggurat was increased, but probably did not exceed sixteen meters. Lenzen takes this rebuilding as a stepped ziggurat in conformity with the normal Babylonian type as an indication of the vitality of the traditional religion in Uruk and of the city's major role in a "Babylonian renaissance" during the Seleucid period.[177]

During the Seleucid period some parts of E-anna were retained or rebuilt along their old lines, whereas in other areas there were alterations. The casement wall (see F in fig. 7) that had been erected on ruins from the period of Nebuchadnezzar between the entrance court (A[1]) and the lower court (A[4]) still stood in Seleucid times, as did two temples within this casement wall that were erected under Nabonidus.[178] Within the easternmost court (A[4]) there are also some traces of Seleucid work. The Innin temple erected in this area by Karaindaš II in Kassite times was still used during the Seleucid period, as is shown by the presence of bricks with Seleucid stamps in the main base. The temple to the god Ningizzida, first erected along the line of the walls of this court by Marduk-apal-iddina and subsequently rebuilt by Sargon, Nebuchadnezzar, and finally Nabonidus, was excluded from the sacred precinct during Achaemenid times by the closing of the "narrow door" behind the temple, which led from the garden court into the lower court. The

temple was burnt some time after the accession of Darius, since a tablet dated to his reign was found in the destruction level, and was not rebuilt as a sacred structure. Instead, in the Seleucid period the ruins of this temple were built into a corner bastion of the newly rebuilt precinct of E-anna, which was made much smaller on its northeast side.[179]

Though E-anna had lost its rank as the most important temple of Uruk with the transfer of the major part of its cults to the Irigal, it is still mentioned in texts of the Seleucid period. In the offering list AO 6451, E-anna comes after the rēš and the Irigal but before the temple of the gods of TIR.AN.NA. In another text it follows the rēš, the Irigal, and the "high seat" (the high temple of the Anu ziggurat) and again precedes the temple of the gods of TIR.AN.NA. Furthermore, the Anu hymn dated to the year 61 of the Seleucid era (251 B.C.) calls Anu "lord of E-anna, lord of E'ulmaš"; according to Falkenstein, this should not be taken as an indication that Anu had become the chief god of E-anna, but rather that he had a shrine there. Falkenstein also states that it is uncertain whether the Nana shrine Eḫilianna, located in E-anna during the Assyrian and Neo-Babylonian periods, was transferred to the Irigal along with the cult of Nana; the shrine might possibly have remained in E-anna.[180]

Along with the building of the rēš and Irigal sanctuaries and the rebuilding of the Anu ziggurat, the massive rebuilding of the ziggurat in E-anna and the re-use and alteration of other parts of the complex provide evidence for the revival of Babylonian religious practices during the Seleucid period. The idea of a Babylonian renaissance at Uruk during the Seleucid period is also supported by a study of building techniques. The walls built in E-anna during the Achaemenid period use a type of "shell" construction—two faces of complete mud bricks with a fill consisting of broken bricks in between. Lenzen suggests that this technique, which differs from that used in the earlier buildings at Uruk, is derived from the stone architecture with which the Achaemenids were familiar. Under the Seleucids, there was a return to the traditional technique, whereas the Parthians used the method first seen during the period of Achaemenid rule.[181]

---

[177] Lenzen, *MDOG* 87, 39, fig. 5; idem, *UVB* XII/XIII, 19; idem, *Neue Deutsche Ausgrabungen*, 24-26.

[178] *UVB* XIV, pl. 5, caption.

[179] Lenzen, *Neue Deutsche Ausgrabungen*, 22; idem, *UVB* XII/XIII, 31; idem, *UVB* XIV, pl. 5, caption. Falkenstein had already suggested the possibility that the Innin temple was used during the

Seleucid period: Falkenstein, *Topographie*, 40; Heinrich, *Tempel und Heiligtümer*, 281.

[180] Falkenstein, *Topographie*, 40 f. Cf. Heinrich, *Tempel und Heiligtümer*, 301: "Schrifturkunden scheinen allerdings zu bezeugen, dass man dort noch weniger bedeutenden Göttern Opfer bringen konnte."

[181] Lenzen, *UVB* XII/XIII, 18 f.

After E-anna ceased to be a sanctuary during the late Seleucid or early Parthian period, poor houses and workshops were built into the ruins. The latest settlement here belongs to the Parthian period. Lenzen suggests that the inhabitants of the poor residential quarters that grew up in all three of the great sanctuaries during the Parthian period must have been foreigners; this suggestion is based on burial customs. In all of the Neo-Babylonian houses and in all Parthian houses elsewhere on the site, the dead were buried under the floors of houses; in contrast, no graves have been found within the residential quarters on the site of the three sanctuaries.[182] After the final fall of the sanctuaries, then, the local population that worshipped there must have declined or moved away.

BIT AKITU

Seleucid economic tests that mention Akitu houses, specifically an "Akitu of Ishtar" and the "High Akitu of Anu," as well as a "festival house, the temple of prayer,"[183] show that the buildings for the celebration of the New Year's festival continued in use during the Seleucid period. The evidence of the texts has now been corroborated by excavations. Nöldecke tentatively identified a ruined building about 500 meters outside the city wall to the east, near the hill Ḥamed al Waraki, as a Bit Akitu. Since the walls remain only to the height of one or two courses of brick, Nöldecke suggested that the bricks had been robbed, perhaps during the Parthian period.[184] The building has now been excavated (fig. 8), but no objects that could suggest its function have been found, and it differs in plan and room arrangement from the Akitu house in Assur, the only one known in Assyria. This building outside the city walls of Uruk, if it is indeed an Akitu house, would be the only one in Babylonia known from material remains. In spite of the absence of finds identifying the building, Lenzen states that its sacred character is made clear by the presence within the complex of three temples and by the use on the outer wall of decoration with niches, which is appropriate to a sacred structure. A sacred building in this location can only be an Akitu house.[185]

The building is square in format, abut 140 meters on a side, with rooms arranged on all four sides of a large court (ca. 86.20 x 90 meters). More than 160

rooms of various sizes have been discovered, although most of those on the northwest side have been destroyed. Thus the plan is quite complex. There were probably entrances on all four sides, but the main entrance appears to have been on the southeast; this corresponds with what can be deduced about the Akitu house from the texts. This main entrance is not flanked by towers, which is unusual for a sacred building, and it is situated close to the south corner of the entrance room rather than in the center. A long narrow room just beyond (see 3 in fig. 8) gives access to the interior court. The rooms around the courtyard include three temples, two near the southwest corner of the building (27-31, with subsidiary rooms 32-35; and rooms 36-41), and another about midway along the side that runs from northwest to northeast (115-124). Both of the temples near the south corner are accessible only from the central court, their entrances distinguished by three-stepped door frames. The temple closer to the corner has the form of a Babylonian broad room (*Breitraum*) temple (27-31), and its entrance from the court lies on the same axis as the doors between the antecella and cella; thus the cult statue, the base for which has been found, could be seen from the main court. There was no cult niche, a deviation from the usual Babylonian practice, although Lenzen suggests that one might have been painted. A staircase in one of the subsidiary rooms (33) led to the roof. The entrance to the second temple lies on a different axis from the door to the cella, and there is no antecella, so the long inner court (36) occupies the entire space taken up in the first temple by court and antecella. Again, the cella lacks a cult niche, but its walls are lined with benches on either side. On one of these were five offering hearths with ashes and remains of bones. One of the subsidiary rooms (38) contains a well. Though each temple has its own entrance, they are connected by a passage; thus they form a unit. The corner posts of the doors in these two temples were uninscribed, and contrary to Assyrian-Babylonian practice, neither temple has foundation deposits at the doors. The third temple (115-124), whose main entrance is from outside the building on the northeast, consists of an inner court, at the back of which lie an antecella and cella of the same width (117, 122-123) and a number of subsidiary rooms. In this case the cult chamber was

[182] Ibid., 31; Lenzen, *UVB* XV, 24.

[183] Falkenstein, *Topographie*, 43; Heinrich, *Tempel und Heiligtümer*, 333.

[184] Heinrich, *UVB* V, 39 f.

[185] Lenzen, *MDOG* 87, 65 f.; idem, *UVB* XII/XIII, 40 f. The description that follows in the text is based on Lenzen, *UVB* XII/XIII, 35-40, pls. 7, 19-21; and idem, *MDOG* 87, 55-67, figs. 14-16.

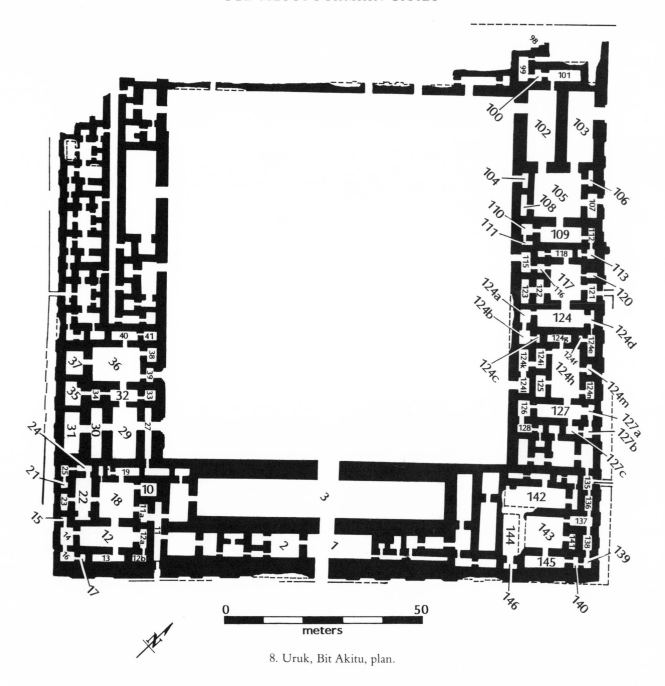

8. Uruk, Bit Akitu, plan.

not visible from the entrance, for although the door from the outside lies on approximately the same axis as the doors between the antecella and cella, the door from the entrance room into the inner court is displaced a bit to the right—a simple form of the bent-axis approach. The entrance door is not marked by stepped jambs, as were the doors to the two temples on the southwest side of the court-yard. There is indirect access to the third temple from the main courtyard of the building through rooms 115 and 116; the entrance door from this court is not distinguished in any way. The group of rooms on the southeast side of the temple (124 and the small rooms around it), though clearly forming part of the temple complex, resembles the dwelling houses that occupy much of the building.

Most of the rest of the building, in fact, consists of houses, the two largest occupying the south and east corners on the principal facade. The house in the south corner (10-26) is accessible from the outside by a small door to the west of the main entrance to the building; it is also indirectly accessible from the large entrance room (3). The equally large house in the east corner (135-46) is accessible only from the outside on the northeast side, which leads Lenzen to argue that it was less important than the house at south corner. The southwest corner of the complex included a number of small houses. The northwest corner is occupied by a group of rooms (98-103) that resembles a house in some ways, but that includes two large rooms (102, 103), one accessible from the outside, the other from the court. Another large house, located directly southeast of the temple on the northeast side of the building, consists of a number of rooms grouped around court 124h. This house is unusual in being accessible only from the central court of the building. Heinrich argues that in spite of their house-like character, these groups of rooms served not as dwelling houses but as rooms for temple service.[186] A tablet found in the archive in E-anna shows that gardens must have belonged to the Bit Akitu, and this textual evidence has received slight confirmation in the patterns of vegetation around the complex.[187]

Excavations have not provided solid evidence for the date of the building. Lenzen states that both of the temples near the southeast corner show three building periods but that it is impossible to date these phases. The format of the bricks does not permit a precise dating, and the brick stamps differ slightly from those usual at Uruk. The temples within the complex resemble the Neo-Babylonian temples in E-anna and those in the Seleucid Irigal and Bit reš sanctuaries. Lenzen originally suggested a Seleucid date for this large extramural complex on the basis of rather fragile evidence: the size, the fact that all of the elements are united within one rectilinear structure, and the close relationship of the temples near the southwest corner to the Anu-Antum temple in the Bit reš.[188] In a later publication he repeated the statement that three building periods could be distinguished and added that the ceramic evidence indicated that the complex could

have been begun in the Neo-Babylonian period and rebuilt during the Seleucid period.[189] There is no indication in the publications of a change in plans between the Neo-Babylonian and the Seleucid buildings. If, then, the Bit Akitu was originally built in the Neo-Babylonian period, the later builders merely followed the old scheme.

The building just discussed is the only possible Akitu house known archaeologically at Uruk.[190] Neo-Babylonian texts name at least two and possibly three Akitu houses; and Seleucid economic texts mention an Akitu of Ishtar and one of Anu. Falkenstein noted, however, that the Neo-Babylonian texts that speak of work done in or near the Akitu house speak only of an Akitu house without specifying a deity. When Falkenstein wrote, the ruins of the building just discussed were unexcavated, but he noted that the structure, already tentatively identified as the Akitu house, could have housed several cellae. He suggested, then, that either Anu and Ishtar had separate Akitu houses close together, or that they could both have been accommodated within one large complex. The ritual texts dealing with the New Year's festivals of Anu and Ishtar make it clear that a large part of the ceremonies took place in the courtyard. Anu had a "high seat" in the courtyard of his Akitu house, on which he sat facing the rising sun. After the ceremonies in the courtyard, he was conducted to his cella, accompanied by various deities, including Enlil and Ea. Seats are also named for Ishtar and Antum, as well as for subsidiary deities, including Nana. According to another ritual text, Ishtar, like Anu, had a "high seat" in the court of her Akitu house. This same text also records cellae for Ishtar, for Anu's chair, and for Nana.[191] Since the Akitu house here described contains three temples, as well as numerous other rooms, it would easily be possible for both Ishtar and Anu to be accommodated within it. The presence of so many dwellings within a sacred complex is somewhat puzzling, however. Lenzen suggests that they might have housed the priests and their attendants during the New Year's festival, which lasted several days.[192] In any case, what is important for my purposes is that this Akitu house was apparently either built for the

---

[186] Heinrich, *Tempel und Heiligtümer*, 334.

[187] Lenzen, *UVB* XII/XIII, 41; Falkenstein, *Topographie*, 43.

[188] Lenzen, *MDOG* 87, 66; idem, *UVB* XII/XIII, 37, 41 f. Heinrich, *Tempel und Heiligtümer*, 333, accepts a Seleucid date.

[189] Lenzen, *Neue Deutsche Ausgrabungen*, 26, fig. 5.

[190] Lenzen suggested in 1955 that a group of ruins south of the city, observed by Loftus but not yet excavated, might be another

Bit Akitu (*MDOG* 87, 65). Heinrich, *Tempel und Heiligtümer*, 333, also mentions this, as well as a third group of ruins of a large building outside the city walls.

[191] Falkenstein, *Topographie*, 42-44. Cf. Heinrich, *Tempel und Heiligtümer*, 333.

[192] Lenzen, *MDOG* 87, 65. Cf. Heinrich's suggestion that the "houses" served instead for temple business.

first time or rebuilt in its original form during the period of Seleucid rule, thus testifying once again to the revival of Babylonian religion during this period.

Though it is not explicitly stated in the excavation reports, it appears that the building lost its sacred function during the Parthian period. Lenzen reports that a massive terrace was laid at the east end of the building to support a large house. The house cannot be dated, but the discovery of a number of graves shows that it lasted for a long time. The burial practices suggest that the inhabitants were local people,[193] in contrast to the population of the poor settlements that grew up in the ruins of the three great sanctuaries within the city walls.

COMPARISON OF THE SELEUCID SANCTUARIES AT URUK TO EARLIER BABYLONIAN TEMPLES

The Bit rēš sanctuary and, as far as its plan can be determined, also the Irigal follow the traditional forms of Babylonian religious architecture. Not enough is yet known about E-anna in the Seleucid period to allow a discussion of its plan, but it appears that the general scheme of multiple courts surrounded by casement walls, often including temples, remained through the Seleucid period. Thus the builders of the Bit rēš and Irigal sanctuaries had a local model available. In addition, there was at least some Seleucid work at Esagila, the temple of Marduk in Babylon, which therefore must have remained visible.

The Bit rēš—the only sanctuary of Hellenistic Uruk whose plan is sufficiently well preserved to allow detailed discussion—does not simply copy any one earlier Babylonian temple, but is rather a new creation using the old concepts. In spite of the general similarities, it differs in details from many earlier sanctuaries, just as these earlier sanctuaries in turn differ in certain respects among themselves, presumably in response to cult requirements. The Bit rēš is bigger than most of the earlier sanctuaries—201 x 162 meters, as opposed to 77.30 and 79 meters (north and south, respectively) by 85.90 and 86.10 meters (east and west) for the main building at Esagila, excluding the east court. The Irigal is even bigger, measuring 198 x 205 meters. The size alone allows greater complexity, the creation of a large number of courts. Perhaps the best way to approach the question of the relationship of the Bit rēš

to earlier Babylonian temple complexes is to make a detailed comparison with a group of the earlier temples. I shall use Esagila, as it apparently survived into the Seleucid period, and three Neo-Babylonian temples from Babylon—the Temple of Ninmach, Temple Z, and Epatutila—as being relatively close in date to the Seleucid sanctuaries of Uruk.

Like the earlier sanctuaries on which it is modelled, the Bit rēš complex is surrounded by a high wall. The main gates are marked by projecting towers, whereas lesser projections decorate the rest of the outer walls. The numerous courts are surrounded by rooms, some of which were temples, presumably to subsidiary deities, others of which served other unknown purposes. The inner walls of these courts were also decorated with projections and recesses. Furthermore, remains of baked bricks bearing glazed reliefs of lions, stars, and rosettes show that the Seleucid builders continued to use a traditional type of Babylonian decoration, though the exact position of these glazed bricks on the walls is uncertain.

The Bit rēš is closely related to Esagila (fig. 9),[194] from which it differs mainly in having a greater number of courts and attendant chapels. Esagila is comparable in size and general organization to the Anu-Antum temple proper in the Bit rēš sanctuary and court VI in front of it (see fig. 4). At Esagila, the main court of the temple with its surrounding rooms is preceded to the east by a forecourt. The main door into the forecourt is set just off the axis of the door from the forecourt into the main court, which in turn lies on the axis of the doors into the antecella and probably also the cella. An unusual feature at Esagila is the presence of a door in the middle of each outer wall of the temple complex, arranged on two cross axes. The entrance doors along the principal east-west axis are flanked by strongly projecting towers, unlike the rather vestigial ones in the Anu-Antum temple. But like Esagila, the Bit rēš also has an off-axis approach to the temple proper: the door into court VI, which by its position serves as the northeastern forecourt to the temple, lies slightly off the axis of the doors leading into court I and the antecella and cella of Anu. It is probable that there was a gate in the outside wall of the complex behind the cella of Anu, as in the wall behind the main cella at Esagila, but damage makes it impossible to be sure. The one side gate into the

---

[193] Lenzen, *UVB* XII/XIII, 35.

[194] Weissbach, in Wetzel, *Haupttheiligtum*, 4-13, pls. 3-5; Heinrich, *Tempel und Heiligtümer*, 310-12, figs. 387-88, 391.

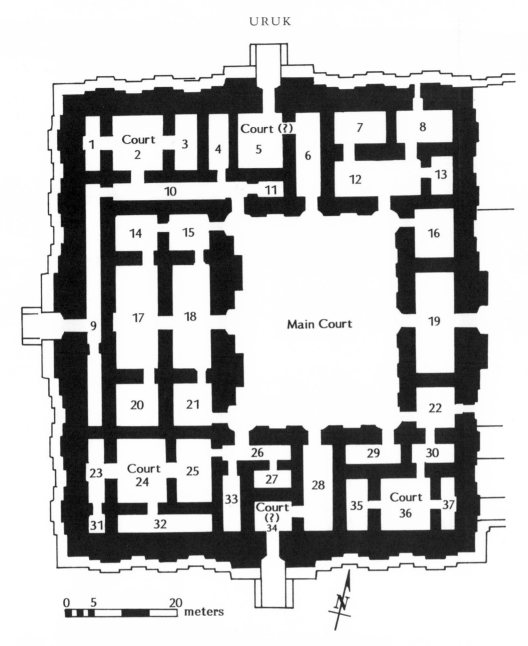

9. Esagila, the temple of Marduk in Babylon.

Anu-Antum temple, on the southeast, instead of giving access to the main court, as at Esagila, leads into a small self-contained group of rooms that form an independent temple (19-21). Though the main cella of Esagila has not been excavated, it almost certainly lay behind the antecella, at the rear of the court, as in the Anu-Antum temple. In each case, the rooms around the court include at least one subsidiary temple (rooms 19-21 in the Anu-Antum temple; the rooms around court 36 and also

cella 12 at Esagila). The disposition of the rooms is generally more symmetrical at Esagila than in the Anu-Antum temple, as far as the incomplete state of the excavations at Esagila allows the plan to be determined, but Esagila clearly provides a precedent for the general organization of the Bit rēš.

E-mach, the temple of Ninmach in Babylon, was apparently built by Nebuchadnezzar (fig. 10).[195] In its general layout, it is strikingly similar to the Anu-Antum temple within the Bit rēš sanctu-

[195] Koldewey, *Die Tempel von Babylon und Borsippa*, 4–17, pl. III; Heinrich, *Tempel und Heiligtümer*, 313 f., figs. 400, 402.

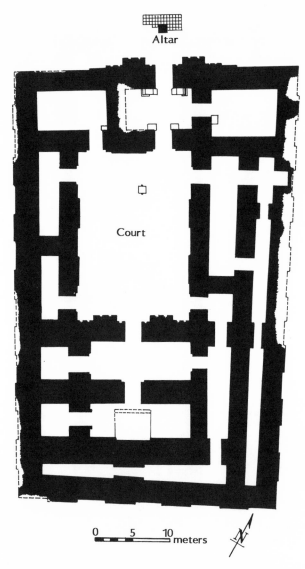

Altar

Court

0 5 10 meters

N

10. E-mach, the temple of Ninmach in Babylon.

ary. Like the Anu-Antum shrine, it consists essentially of a main court, at the rear of which lies an antecella-cella complex and around which are situated a number of narrow rooms. In both cases, entrance to the court is gained through a room flanked by two other rooms, one of which is open to it, while the other is self-contained. In the Anu-Antum temple, however, the room has its own entrance from court VI in front of the temple, whereas the room in E-mach opens into the inner court. The main entrance to E-mach is flanked by towers, unlike the entrance to the Anu-Antum temple, probably because in E-mach this was also the entrance to the

complex from the outside. A further difference is that at E-mach the altar lies outside the entrance gate on its axis, whereas in the Anu-Antum temple a base is placed in the courtyard directly in front of the entrance to the antecella-cella complex. In both temples the walls of the court are decorated with shallow projections and recesses. In E-mach, however, the entrance to the antecella is marked by particularly prominent projections; this is not true in the Anu-Antum temple. The antecella-cella complex in both cases consists of two rooms of the same width and depth with their doors on the same axis. In both cases the shallow cult niche that characterizes Babylonian temples is placed in the back wall with a base on the floor in front of it; and in both cases the antecella-cella complex is flanked by narrow rooms: two rooms on one side corresponding to the antecella and cella, respectively, accessible from those rooms but not to each other; and one long corridor-like room on the other side. These arrangements differ in detail, for the Anu-Antum temple has two cellae rather than one. Behind the cella in E-mach is a narrow corridor, which, if it was used as a corridor, and not as the space for a staircase to the roof, as Heinrich suggests, might correspond in the Anu-Antum temple to the space between the cella wall and the rear wall of the complex as a whole.

There is an important difference in principle between the two temples, however. The doors into the antecella and cella of Anu lie on the same axis as the entrance into court I, so that the cult image would have been visible from the entrance door. In E-mach, on the other hand, the entrance doors lie on a different axis from the doors of the antecella and cella, creating a modified bent-axis approach. Heinrich suggests that there was originally a subsidiary entrance into a corridor on the east side at E-mach. Furthermore, the cult niche and the base in front of it are placed approximately in the center of the rear wall of the cella of Anu, as if symmetry were important, whereas in E-mach the niche and the base are strongly off-center, showing that having the niche on the axis of the door was more important than symmetry in the room.

Temple Z at Babylon, which probably dates to the middle years of Nebuchadnezzar and was perhaps dedicated to the goddess Gula,[196] shows a different version of the modified bent-axis approach (fig. 11). Koldeway describes the temple as being divided into two parts: an eastern section, with a

[196] Koldewey, *Die Tempel von Babylon und Borsippa*, 18-24, pl. V; Heinrich, *Tempel und Heiligtümer*, 316 f., fig. 401.

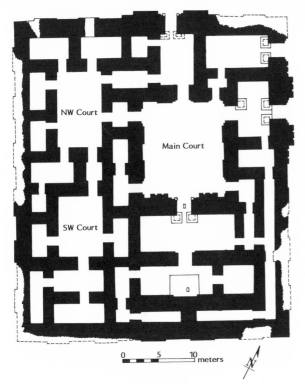

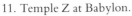

11. Temple Z at Babylon.

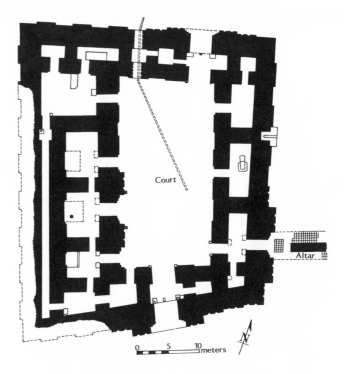

12. Epatutila, the temple of Ninurta in Babylon.

principal court, around which are grouped the cult rooms; and a western section, with two smaller courts, around which are grouped rooms used for non-cult purposes. Two gates lead into the main court, one on the north opposite the antecella-cella unit but on a slightly different axis, and another on the east; the latter was perhaps the principal entrance.[197] This entrance from one side recalls one of the paths of approach to the Anu-Antum temple in the Bit rēš, through the door on the northwest from court V (see fig. 5). In Temple Z, as in E-mach, the cult niche and the base are off-center, though on the line of the doors. The door to the antecella is distinguished here by quite strong projections. As in E-mach and the Anu-Antum temple, the antecella-cella complex at Temple Z is surrounded by a group of subsidiary rooms, though the arrangement here is more complex than in either of the other two. Temple Z resembles the Bit rēš complex in having a line of courts with surrounding rooms laid out parallel to the main court

and its antecella-cella complex. The arrangement of the courts and rooms even recalls that of court VII and west court VIII in the Bit rēš. Heinrich disputes Koldewey's interpretation of the rooms around the western courts of Temple Z as secular, however, and suggests very tentatively that they might have served as living quarters for a college of priests.[198] A further similarity between Temple Z and the Anu-Antum temple is that in both cases a room to the east of the principal entrance room has an independent entrance. Next to this room in both cases stands another room, also with an eastern entrance, but in Temple Z this room opens onto the main court of the temple, whereas in the Anu-Antum temple it leads to a small independent complex.

Epatutila, the temple of Ninurta in Babylon (fig. 12), was built by Nabupolassar.[199] Epatutila differs quite strongly from E-mach and Temple Z, though the basic scheme of a court surrounded by rooms is the same. The main entrance, marked by towers, lies on the east side near the corner. Two other en-

[197] This arrangement is also seen in the Temple of Ishtar of Agade in Babylon (Heinrich, *Tempel und Heiligtümer*, 314, fig. 403).

[198] Ibid., 295, 317; Koldewey, *Die Tempel von Babylon und Borsippa*, 18.

[199] Koldewey, *Die Tempel von Babylon und Borsippa*, 25, calls it

the temple of Ninib, but Wetzel, *Hauptheiligtum*, 11, and Heinrich, *Tempel und Heiligtümer*, 317, identify it as a temple of Ninurta. For Koldewey's description of the temple, see *Die Tempel von Babylon und Borsippa*, 25-33, pls. VI, VII.

trances on the north and south sides are placed on different axes; Koldewey suggests that these doors distinguish Epatutila as a processional temple. The temple has three cellae on the long west side; the entrances from the cellae to the court are marked by projections, and there are no antecellae. As in E-mach and Temple Z, the cult niches and bases are lined up with doors but are not in the center of the back wall. The main entrance is not quite on the axis of the southernmost cella.

Thus, with the exception of Epatutila, these late Babylonian temples share a similar scheme: a main court, at the rear of which lies the antecella-cella group, with its subordinate rooms; an outer door into the main court that lies on a different axis from the entrance into the antecella-cella complex, and in several cases, either the principal entrance or a secondary one on one of the long sides of the temple, perpendicular to the doors into the antecella-cella; and subsidiary rooms, including cult rooms for other deities, arranged around the sides of the court in a generally symmetrical fashion. The Anu-Antum temple with court VI follows the same general principles. It differs from most of the temples of Babylon in that the cult image would have been visible from the outer entrance into the main court. On the other hand, the approach to the temple from the outside is more complex.

SOCIETY AT URUK IN THE HELLENISTIC PERIOD

Numerous clay tablets found in the archives of the Bit rēš and elsewhere at Uruk attest to the continuation into the Seleucid period of the Akkadian language, the traditional religion, and the old laws. The Bit rēš housed a sizeable archive. Almost all of the Seleucid tablets found in Babylonia up to 1938 came from Uruk;[200] moreover, recent excavations have revealed a new cache of Seleucid texts from a room in the southeast outer wall of the rēš sanctuary. Van Dijk suggests that the Louvre texts probably came from this same area.[201] The Irigal may also have housed a small archive, for sixteen fragments of texts, mostly from the reign of Demetrios I (162-150 B.C.), were found there.[202] In spite of the

importance of these Hellenistic cuneiform archives, however, the striking decline in the number of cuneiform texts dealing with juridical and administrative matters between the sixth and fifth centuries and the third and second centuries, respectively, suggests that clay tablets were beginning to be replaced by parchments and papyri, and Akkadian by Aramaic or Greek. Goossens argues that Akkadian was essentially a dead language by the Hellenistic period.[203]

The relative size and strength of the native population and the vitality of the old language and customs in comparison to the population of Hellenized Babylonians and Greek settlers at Uruk are hard to determine for a number of reasons. It is clear that the city was Hellenized to some extent, but the degree of Hellenization is disputed. Among the factors that make the question difficult to answer are the following. First, the cuneiform texts almost all come from temple archives and are therefore likely to represent the more conservative elements of the population; it seems that relatively few families are represented in the Bit rēš archives.[204] Second, it is often hard to tell whether a person with a Greek name was a true Greek or a Hellenized Babylonian; the number of persons with Greek names but Babylonian ancestors suggests that the latter were in the majority.[205] Finally, much of the evidence for Hellenization is indirect; Greek documents do not survive, so their existence is attested only by the bullae that were used to seal parchments and papyri.

The great importance of the major temples in the life of Uruk in the Hellenistic period is made clear not only by their enormous size but also by the textual evidence. Especially the Bit rēš played an important role in both the religious and the administrative life of the city. The majority of the cuneiform texts found in the archives there are scientific or religious texts. Civil archives—transactions involving temple property or the sale of prebends, records of sales of slaves and urban real estate—were also kept there.[206] Other records, presumably in Greek but perhaps in some cases in Aramaic, were also housed in the sanctuary, as is revealed by the discovery of numerous clay bullae

[200] Aymard, "Une ville," 5 f.

[201] Van Dijk, *UVB* XVIII, 43.

[202] v. Haller, *UVB* VIII, 56 f.; Doty, *Cuneiform Archives*, 47.

[203] Aymard, "Une ville," 5 f.; Rostovtzeff, "Seleucid Babylonia," 22. Rostovtzeff probably overstates the size and importance of the Greek population of Uruk; this question is discussed more fully below. Goossens, "Au déclin," 222-44; cf. Sarkisian, "Self-

governing Cities," 70; and Heinrich, *Tempel und Heiligtümer*, 302.

[204] Goossens, "Au déclin," 228-34; Aymard, "Une ville," 16 f. The implications will be discussed more fully below.

[205] Aymard, "Une ville," 31 f; Oelsner, "Kontinuität und Wandel," 112 f.

[206] Aymard, "Une ville," 16; Rutten, *Contrats*, 133-99; Doty, *Cuneiform Archives*, 51.

used to seal documents on parchment or papyrus. These bullae normally bear the stamp of a royal official, the *chreophylax* ("registrar") of Orchoi (Χρεοφυλακικός Ὄρχων), with the name of the city given in its Greek transcription, and a record of tax payment. The Bit rēš may have housed the civic record office.[207]

Analysis of the documents has suggested to some scholars that the persons appearing in the cuneiform archival texts belonged to a relatively restricted group of families, closely connected with the temples. The majority of the people mentioned in the contracts traced their descent from one of several "ancestors," suggesting a closed milieu.[208] Aymard calculates that no more than five or six scribes appeared during any twenty-year period, and he notes that the scribes were frequently related to the witnesses. The notaries came almost exclusively from two families. According to Goossens, a study of the names suggests that approximately twenty families were represented in the Achaemenid period; approximately ten, shrinking to some half dozen, under the Seleucids. He calculates that no more than one hundred men are named in the contracts and that there were no more than ten clerks in each generation.[209] Oelsner explains the presence of relatively few families by the fact that the cuneiform legal texts come mostly from family archives; since they were stored in the temple, it is not surprising that most concern temple affairs.[210]

Recently the assumption that the cuneiform archives reflect the affairs of a small group of people closely tied to the temples has been challenged. Sarkisian notes that temple servants constitute approximately ten percent of the persons named in the contracts and that most of the people involved did not derive the bulk of their living from the temple. He argues, then, that the circle of persons using contracts written in Akkadian was wider than that of temple personnel, though it was still relatively restricted. He also notes that some Greek names appear in the contracts. Although many of these persons had ancestors with Babylonian names and therefore were probably Hellenized Urukaeans, some had Greek paternal names. This suggests, according to Sarkisian, that the circle of persons using the cuneiform recording system, which he characterizes as a "city-temple society," was open to new persons (*homines novi*).[211] Doty states that Greeks did not begin to participate in transactions recorded in cuneiform until the reign of Antiochos IV Epiphanes and never participated in great numbers.[212]

The fact that none of the cuneiform documents, with one possible exception, bears the seal of the *chreophylax*[213] shows that the transactions recorded in the tablets escaped government taxation. This has been taken as an indication that the Seleucids favored the continuation of the traditional temples and granted special privileges to the old priestly circle.[214] Sarkisian has modified this theory to suggest that during the Seleucid period a new collective was formed, a "city-temple society" enjoying special privileges, including freedom from taxes. Although this society was largely made up of members of the old families of Uruk, it was also open to some Greeks. He argues that this "city" was self-governing, with a citizen-temple assembly, and that it had privileges equivalent to those of a Greek polis.[215]

Doty disagrees with both views, arguing that the factor determining whether a transaction was recorded in Akkadian or in Greek was "its susceptibility to regulation by the Greek administration."[216] The restricted nature of the contents of the cuneiform archive has long been noted.[217] With a few exceptions, only three types of transactions are recorded: sale or lease of temple prebends (called "allotments" by Doty); sales of urban real estate;

[207] Rostovtzeff published a large group of these bullae in "Seleucid Babylonia," 1-114; for the finding place, see p. 9; Goossens, "Au déclin," 227. A fragment of a bulla like the one published by Rostovtzeff and also bearing the inscription χρεοφυλακικός Ὄρχων (*chreophylax* of Orchoi) was recently found near the outer wall of the rēš sanctuary (Van Dijk, *UVB* XVI, 60, W19 233).

[208] Aymard, "Une ville," 14-20; O. Schröder, "Aus den keilinschriftlichen Sammlungen des Berliner Museums," *ZAssyr* XXXII (1918), 14-22.

[209] Goossens, "Au déclin," 228-30.

[210] Oelsner, "Kontinuität und Wandel," 108.

[211] Sarkisian, "Self-governing Cities," 75 f.; idem, "Social Role," 39. On the presence of Greeks in the cuneiform texts, see Oelsner, "Kontinuität und Wandel," 112 f.

[212] Doty, *Cuneiform Archives*, 155.

[213] Ibid., 323-28; Doty, "An Official Seal of the Seleucid Period," *JNES* XXXVIII (1979), 195-97; McEwan, "An Official Seleucid Seal Reconsidered," *JNES* XLI (1982), 51-53.

[214] Aymard, "Une ville," 18-20; Goossens, "Au déclin," 226-28; Oelsner, "Kontinuität und Wandel," 111 f., argues that the Babylonians were granted the privilege of using their own legal system for certain types of transactions.

[215] Sarkisian, "Self-governing Cities," 70, 74-81; idem, "Social Role," 35 f., 39-41 (English summary, 29 f.). Sarkisian's concept of a civic and temple community is discussed briefly in "City Land in Seleucid Babylonia," in I. M. Diakonoff, ed., *Ancient Mesopotamia* (Moscow 1969), 313 f.

[216] Doty, *Cuneiform Archives*, 333.

[217] Goossens, "Au déclin," 225 f.

and sales of slaves. Doty notes that no slave sales are recorded in cuneiform documents after the year 37 of the Seleucid era, early in the reign of Antiochos I, and concludes that Antiochos I instituted a tax on the sale of slaves. Once the tax was instituted, such sales had to be recorded with the *chreophylax* and therefore would have been written on papyrus or parchment. Doty similarly explains the disappearance of sales of arable land from the cuneiform corpus by the assumption that such land became subject to a sales tax, while sales of urban real estate remained free of tax.[218] Although Doty's arguments seem sound, the exemption of most transactions involving temple property and perquisites from government tax can still be construed as a mark of government favor toward the traditional religious system.

McEwan contends that the registration clauses that appear in sales of ration rights suggest that these transactions were subject to government tax, but he maintains that at Uruk the rations were paid to relatively low level temple personnel, whereas the holders of prebends were wealthy.[219] This argument, if correct, would suggest that the government favored the local aristocracy, which in turn held to the traditional religion. Furthermore, even if Doty is correct in his assertion that the decision about which recording system to use was based on the taxability (or lack thereof) of the transaction involved, the decision to use Akkadian is an indication of a conservative, almost archaizing milieu. Finally, even if the archives represent the activities of a rather small group of well-to-do families, it seems unlikely that only members of these families worshipped in the temples. On the contrary: the sheer size of the buildings and the amount of resources involved in their construction and upkeep suggests that large numbers of people used them. The traditional religion remained vital.[220]

Anu-uballit-Nikarchos, the builder of the first preserved Seleucid Anu-Antum temple, and Anu-uballit-Kephalon, the builder of its baked-brick replacement and of the Irigal, both belonged to one of the priestly families, the Aḫ'utu.[221] Lines 6f. of

the Anu-uballit-Kephalon building inscription are interpreted by Van Dijk to mean that Anu-uballit-Kephalon attributed the origins of the sanctuary to the work of U'anadapa in mythical times: "the rēš sanctuary, which in early times the U'an[adapa] have built."[222] Thus Anu-uballit-Nikarchos and Anu-uballit-Kephalon, who were possibly cousins,[223] must have prided themselves on belonging to the traditional milieu. At the same time, both were Hellenized to some degree, and Anu-uballit-Nikarchos in particular must have had close ties with the Seleucid king Antiochos, since he explicitly states that Antiochos gave him the name "Nikarchos."[224] Nikarchos and Kephalon were also involved in civic administration, though the exact nature of their titles and duties is disputed. Anu-uballit-Nikarchos' title was read ^{lú}*šá-nu* by Clay and translated as "second officer of Uruk" by Rutten, Aymard,[225] and others. Doty, however, prefers the reading *šaknu*, which in earlier periods meant "city governor" or "provincial governor." However the title is read and translated, it does seem to designate a civic office, probably one to which Anu-uballit-Nikarchos was appointed by the king.[226] The title held by Anu-uballit-Kephalon is usually translated "the great, the city-lord of Uruk."[227] Rostovtzeff suggests that this title is the equivalent of *stratēgos* or *epistatēs*, offices known from Dura and other Seleucid cities and often held together.[228] Doty, on the other hand, argues that the meaning of his title (^{lú}*rabû* ^{lú}*SAG ali šá Uruk* or *rab ša rēš āli ša Uruk*) is not clear but that he held an important position in the city administration.[229]

The rituals practiced in the temples of Seleucid Uruk followed earlier traditions, and the somewhat antiquarian character of the revival is clear from the number of the rituals recorded in the Seleucid texts that are copies of earlier documents. Nonetheless, these ritual texts reflected contemporary practices, as is shown by the fact that religious offices were mentioned in secular texts;[230] the traditional titles continued to be used to designate temple offices. Heinrich believes that the priests must have used collections of ancient documents to

---

[218] Doty, *Cuneiform Archives*, 323-30. Rostovtzeff, "Seleucid Babylonia," 69, had suggested that Antiochos III increased the slave tax.

[219] McEwan, *Priest and Temple*, 138 f., 149.

[220] Oelsner, "Kontinuität und Wandel," 104, 115.

[221] Bowman, "Anu-uballit-Kephalon," 232-35; Falkenstein, *Topographie*, 4 f. lines 1 f.; 31.

[222] Van Dijk, *UVB XVIII*, 47 f.

[223] Bowman, "Anu-uballit-Kephalon," 232-35; Doty doubts this: *Cuneiform Archives*, 25.

[224] Falkenstein, *Topographie*, 4 f., lines 1-3.

[225] Rutten, *Contrats*, 70; Aymard, "Une ville," 33, n.2.

[226] Doty, *Cuneiform Archives*, 21 f., 24-26.

[227] Falkenstein, *Topographie*, 6 f., lines 3 f.

[228] Rostovtzeff, "Seleucid Babylonia," 6.

[229] Doty, *Cuneiform Archives*, 22-25.

[230] McEwan, *Priest and Temple*, 65 f.; for the rites, see pp. 159-82.

create a New Year's ritual designed specifically for current practices, for this ritual was tied directly to the cult of Anu and to the Bit rēš.[231] Moreover, the priests and scribes went to considerable effort to preserve traditional documents. For instance, a tablet that lists the sacrifices to be made daily to "the deities Anu, Antum, Ishtar, Nana and the (other) deities dwelling in the Resh temple, the Irigal temple, and the Esharra temple (which is) the topmost stage of the temple-tower of Anu," is copied from tablets that "Nabua-plausur, king of the sea-land, carried off as plunder from the city of Uruk." One "Kidinanu, a citizen of Uruk, a *mašmašu* priest of Anu and Antum, a descendent of Ekurzakir, an *urigallu*-priest of the Resh temple," copied the tablet in the land of Elam and brought it back to Uruk.[232] The archive recently discovered in the Bit rēš includes texts of Sumerian literature, such as the Gilgamesh epic,[233] and catalogues of authors of Babylonian literary compositions. A list of kings recorded in the Seleucid period gives, in addition to the names of kings going back to the mythological past, the names of the Apkallu, creatures who in Sumerian mythology rose out of the sea to teach men scholarship, art, and social organization, and of the *ummānū*, or learned men, in the time of each king.[234] Many of the scribes of the Seleucid texts belonged to a great family of the Sînliqunninnī, and the colophons give their genealogy back to the distant past, thus linking them with the scholarly tradition. The texts, then, show the pride that new generations of scholars felt in their great past.[235]

The Seleucid royal cult was apparently introduced into the temples of Uruk along with the worship of traditional divinities. One text, for example, mentions offerings presented at the table of the statues of the kings. McEwan suggests that the statues were those of Seleukos and his descendants, and he argues that the royal cult was sufficiently well established at Uruk that the food offerings to the statues of the kings formed part of the prebend system. The Seleucid rulers thus used the traditional religious structure to introduce their own

cult. At the same time, the table of the statues of the kings was only one of many such tables in the temple, and there is no evidence that the royal cult played a major role in its religious life. McEwan points out that there are no remains of hymns or other compositions in honor of the rulers.[236]

The degree of royal support of the temples of Uruk is uncertain. Both the Bit rēš and the Irigal were built by city officials who were members of the old aristocracy. At the same time, Anu-uballit-Nikarchos apparently had close ties to the king, and he states that he built the temple for the lives of kings Antiochos and Seleukos.[237] This implies tacit royal support, but not the active interest that several Seleucid rulers showed in rebuilding temples in Babylon and offering sacrifices there. A text from Uruk, if correctly dated to the Seleucid period, as seems probable, may suggest that the writer gives credit to the Seleucid kings for the revival of Uruk as a seat of the old deities. The text, cast in the form of an Akkadian prophecy, records that after the coming of several kings "who will not speak right," a king will arrive who will make the cult of Anu in Uruk permanent and who will bring the gods of Uruk back from Babylon and build the temples of the gods in Uruk.[238] Heinrich suggests that the occasion for the composition of this text may have been the building of the new temples of Uruk under the reign of Seleucid kings.[239] These suggestions are rather speculative, however, and active royal support of the local temples was perhaps limited to the Babylon area, as McEwan suggests.[240]

In the temples of Uruk, there continued such traditional practices as the dedication of slaves as temple oblates, to help in the work of maintaining the temples, whereas at Babylon work was carried out by hired labor.[241] Some changes were apparently made in the administrative structure of the temples at Uruk, however. For example, the temple assembly perhaps retained power over temple decisions until the end of Seleucid rule.[242] McEwan states that at Babylon the temple administration remained es-

---

[231] Heinrich, *Tempel und Heiligtümer*, 302 f.

[232] Pritchard, *ANET*, 3rd ed., 344 f.

[233] Egbert von Weher, "Eine Fragmente der 5. Tafel des Gilgameš-Epos aus Uruk," *BaM* XI (1980), 90-105.

[234] Van Dijk, *UVB* XVIII, 44-46, 49 f.

[235] Ibid., 43 f., 49 f.; W.R. Mayer, "Seleukidische Ritual aus Warka mit Emesal-Gebeten" *Orientalia*, n.s. XLVII.3 (1978), 431-37; Falkenstein, *UVB* XV, 37, rev. lines 5-8.

[236] McEwan, *Priest and Temple*, 161 f., 194 f.; Doty, *Cuneiform Archives*, 136.

[237] Falkenstein, *Topographie*, 5, lines 14 f.

[238] Hermann Hunger, *Spätbabylonische Texte aus Uruk*, part I (*Ausgrabungen der Deutschen Forschungsgemeinschaft in Uruk-Warka 9*) (Berlin, 1976), 21-23, no. 3.

[239] Heinrich, *Tempel und Heiligtümer*, 301.

[240] McEwan, *Priest and Temple*, 193 f.; cf. Bickerman, *Institutions des Séleucides*, 123 n.4, who couples Uruk with Babylon as a city where kings built temples.

[241] McEwan, *Priest and Temple*, 192; for an example of a dedication of a slave in a temple, see Doty, *Cuneiform Archives*, 87-89.

[242] Doty, *Cuneiform Archives*, 20-22.

sentially the same as in earlier periods, but at Uruk there seems to have been a general reorganization early in the Seleucid period, with the result that essentially none of the old administrative mechanisms survived.[243]

Although the rituals and the professions associated with temple activities were retained in Uruk from earlier periods, there seems to have been an increasing separation between the prebends (rights to income from temple activities, called "allotments" by Doty) and the duties traditionally associated with those prebends. McEwan makes a distinction at Uruk between "allotments," like that of the porters, which required that duties be performed, and "prebends," which did not. The separation between the prebends and the duties originally associated with them is shown by a number of features. The persons holding the prebends did not necessarily have to practice the profession listed; and in some cases where the prebends did involve duties, it was possible to lease part of the income to someone else in exchange for his carrying out the duties. Persons could also hold multiple prebends, a situation that would only have been possible when few or no duties were required. The fractioning of the rights to temple income into days or even parts of days is a further indication that the prebends served largely as sources of income. Finally, women appear in the contracts as principals, but few women actually served in the temples, and then only in limited capacities.[244]

The temples at Uruk must have played an important role in the economic life of the city. They owned a substantial amount of land, and considerable amounts of food were offered during the four daily meals, in addition to the offerings on the occasion of festivals.[245] For the families represented in the archives, the temple offerings represented an important source of income.

The archives, unfortunately, provide our only concrete evidence about the group of people who actually used the temples. Since the persons who were able to participate in the transactions recorded

in the archives were relatively wealthy,[246] the archives provide only a limited picture, and it is necessary to make a distinction between those persons who entered into contracts recorded in cuneiform and people who used the temple. The archives do suggest a group composed largely but not exclusively of members of traditional families, but open to new people, even to Greeks. Not only did Greeks enter into contractual relationships with members of native families, they even in some cases made dedications to local deities. For example, one Nicanor, son of Democrates, dedicated a slave to "Anu, Antum, and the great gods of Uruk,"[247] thus following a traditional practice. Some of the native families were at least partially Hellenized, but there is considerable variation. For instance, Anu-uballit-Nikarchos is the only member of his family known to have taken a Greek name, but the practice continued in the family of Anu-uballit-Kephalon.[248] The size of the group of Hellenized natives at Uruk and the degree of Hellenization within this group are the subject of controversy. According to Aymard, the great majority of contracts in which Greek names appear date to the second century of the Seleucid era, that is, after 211 B.C. This would suggest that the size of the Hellenized population increased with time. There are also signs, however, that the degree of the Hellenization among the traditional milieu lessened with the passage of time. Some families reverted to using only Babylonian names after using Greek names for one or more generations.[249]

There does not appear to have been a sizeable Greek colony at Uruk. There is certainly no evidence for an organized group of Greek citizens. In contrast to Babylon, there are no Greek inscriptions at Uruk (except that found near the Temple of Gareus of A.D. 111, by a non-Greek people), and no indications of Greek civic institutions or of Greek architectural forms.

It is true that the large number of bullae found in the excavations indicates that most business transactions were registered according to Seleucid prac-

[243] McEwan, *Priest and Temple*, 140, 192 f.

[244] Ibid., 67 f., 79, 106-110, 114-20; Doty, *Cuneiform Archives*, 119-22, 284; Sarkisian, "Self-governing Cities," 72-74; idem, "Social Role," 37; for examples of the fractional division of prebends, see Rutten, *Contrats*, 199-247. Brinkman, review of McEwan, *Priest and Temple*, JCS XXV 3/4 (1983), 234 f., disputes McEwan's distinction between allotments, which required the performance of certain duties, and prebends, which did not.

[245] McEwan, *Priest and Temple*, 121 f., 134 f.

[246] Doty, *Cuneiform Archives*, 309 f.; Sarkisian, "Self-governing Cities," 75.

[247] Aymard, "Une ville," 34-36; for the dedication, see p. 35 n. 4.

[248] Bowman, "Anu-uballit-Kephalon," 232-35; Goossens, "Au déclin," 230 and 231 n. 2.

[249] Aymard, "Une ville," 36-38; Goossens, "Au déclin," 230 f. Oelsner, "Kontinuität und Wandel," 113, notes an increase in the use of double names after the end of the third century B.C. See Rutten, *Contrats*, 68-70, for a list of persons with double names. Bowman, "Anu-uballit-Kephalon," 235-42, gives a list of the Greek names at Uruk known to him.

tice, but this does not prove that the people concerned in the lost documents were Greeks.[250] To state, as Rostovtzeff does, that "Orchoi, an old site of Babylonian civilization, became a half-Greek city and a good portion of its business life was in the hands of the Greeks"[251] seems a distinct exaggeration. So little is known about the civic organization of Uruk that it is not possible to determine whether or not it was organized as a Greek polis. The assembly (puḫru) that survived from earlier times probably had power only over temple affairs, though Sarkisian suggests that the members of the assembly formed a "civic and temple community" that integrated members of the old families of Uruk with a few Greeks into a new self-governing elite.[252] The designation "Urukaean," which appears in a number of documents, might mean something like "citizen of Uruk," according to McEwan, and indicate that the persons using this expression considered themselves as part of a city, which, if not necessarily organized as polis, had a similar right. But McEwan's interpretation is dubious, and the balance of the evidence seems to suggest that Uruk did not become a polis.[253] A cuneiform text, dated to 41 of the Seleucid era (270 B.C.), was written at "Antiochia on the Ishtar canal," and seems to provide evidence for a possible Greek colony near Uruk. Since the Ishtar canal was the principal waterway of Uruk in the Seleucid period, this "Antioch" must have been near Uruk.[254] It would probably have been a Greek polis, established near an old city, just as Seleucia on the Tigris was established near Babylon. Doty suggests that some of the Greeks who appear in the cuneiform documents of Uruk were citizens of Antioch on the Ishtar canal who did not necessarily participate in the native political institutions of Uruk. The possible existence of a Greek colony in the vicinity could help to explain the apparent lack of Greek civic organization at Uruk. The colony, if it existed, cannot have been much of a success, however, since it is not mentioned in the Greek sources.

Not only did the traditional religion continue to flourish at Uruk, with at least the tacit support of the Seleucid rulers, but there is no evidence for the worship of Greek divinities. Only on the bullae and in a few terracotta figurines are Greek divinities represented, and few at that—Apollo, Athena, Nike, and Tyche on the bullae;[255] Heracles, Eros, and possibly Aphrodite and Athena among the terracottas.[256] Uruk remained a Babylonian city, at least in religion and in some legal practices for a portion of the population, apparently with at least the approval and possibly with the active support of the Seleucid rulers.

Ur

ALTHOUGH UR was apparently still inhabited during the period of Seleucid control (the latest tablet found in the ruins dates to the seventh year of Philip Arrhidaios, 316 B.C.),[257] little physical evidence survives from the last centuries of the city's existence. Woolley suggests that even under Nebuchadnezzar and Nabonidus the continued existence of Ur was bound up with the worship of its patron deity Sin (called Nannar by Woolley), and that the change in religion under the Achaemenids coupled with the decline of the canal system led to the final decline of the city. As at Babylon, Cyrus rebuilt a number of the monuments of Nabonidus, and during the Persian period the shrine of Sin was apparently maintained to some extent, since tablets of the Persian period found under the foundations of a wall in a group of rooms built on the ziggurat terrace record the bringing of offerings to the god. According to Woolley, the ziggurat was deliberately destroyed during the Persian period, probably later than the reign of Cyrus, and much of the area of the old sanctuary was clearly given over to secular uses. Pottery kilns were built on the southwest side of the ziggurat, and the area of Nebuchadnezzar's temple of Nin-Ezen apparently became a res-

---

[250] Aymard, "Une ville," 32–34.

[251] Rostovtzeff, "Seleucid Babylonia," 90.

[252] Sarkisian, "Social Role," 39–41; idem, "Self-Governing Cities," 74–82.

[253] Aymard, "Une ville," 33 f. and n. 2; McEwan, *Priest and Temple*, 157 f. McEwan's analysis of an unusual document leads him to conclude that perhaps Uruk was organized as a Greek polis ("A Babylonian *leitourgia*?" *Welt des Orients* XIII [1982], 25–30). Doty, *Cuneiform Archives*, 151–60, summarizes the evidence and the arguments based on this evidence. Brinkman, in his review of McEwan's book, also disagrees with McEwan's interpretation of the documents: *JCS* XXV 3/4 (1983), 236 f.

[254] Doty, *Cuneiform Archives*, 158, 193–96.

[255] Rostovtzeff, "Seleucid Babylonia," 31–41, nos. 19–57; 45–47, nos. 73–78.

[256] Invernizzi, "Problemi di coroplastica tardo-mesopotamica. III. La cultura di Uruk," *Mesopotamia* V–VI (1970/71), 336–38; Charlotte Ziegler, *Die Terrakotten von Warka (Ausgrabungen der Deutschen Forschungsgemeinschaft in Uruk-Warka*, VI) (Berlin, 1962), 94–96, 117, nos. 633–35, 637, 643–47; pl. 23, nos. 329–31, 333; pl. 24, nos. 338–42.

[257] Sir Leonard Woolley, *Ur Excavations IX: The Neo-Babylonian and Persian Periods* (London, 1962), introduction and p. 46, n. 1; H. H. Figulla, *Ur Texts* IV (London, 1949), no. 43.

idential quarter.[258] Apparently no remains of Seleucid buildings were found.[259]

There is, however, slight evidence for Seleucid concern with Ur. A fragmentary chronicle frequently mentions Antiochos, the crown prince, probably Antiochos the son of Seleukos I, who was made co-regent in charge of the eastern satrapies in 294/93 B.C. Parts of the text of the chronicle record the removal of dust from Esagila, but another section is concerned with Egišnugal, the temple of the god Sin at Ur. Grayson suggests that Antiochos reestablished the regular income of the temple.[260]

Girsu

THERE IS little evidence of activity on the site of Girsu from about the beginning of the second millennium to about the middle of the second century B.C., though the site apparently remained inhabited. During the Seleucid period, however, one Adad-nadin-akhé installed himself at Girsu (Telloh), apparently as the ruler of a small domain. Parrot suggests that after the Seleucid abandonment of the area, the Parthians bothered little with the marshy area in southern Mesopotamia. Adad-nadin-akhé built a palace in the ruins of the *eninnu*, Gudea's sanctuary of Ningursu. He built the palace partly of reused bricks of the period of Gudea, but he also added some bricks stamped with his own name, given first in Aramaean, then in Greek characters. The bricks imitate those of Gudea in clay, size, and shape. The palace is divided into an official, public area, centered around a great court, and a private, residential section. Adad-nadin-akhé also gathered statues of Gudea from various sanctuaries and placed them in the great court, which thus became a sort of museum.[261] Though no evidence for a religious structure of the Seleucid or Parthian period has been found at Telloh, Adad-nadin-akhé's display of the statues of Gudea in the court of his palace demonstrates respect for the past greatness of the city and for old traditions.

Nimrud

EZIDA, the temple of Nabu at Nimrud, was built in a monumental form probably by Adad-nirari III and dedicated in 798 B.C. by Bel-tarsi-iluma, the governor of Calah. It was modified in the time of Sargon and apparently remained in use until the fall of the city; the last written document dates to about 616 B.C. Probably soon after the fall of the city in 614, the area of the temple was occupied by squatters. At some uncertain point, later than the squatter occupation but considerably earlier than the series of Seleucid settlements, which began about the middle of the third century B.C., a poor attempt was made to repair some parts of the temple. The presence of an altar in one of the courts of Ezida suggests an attempt to revive the cult.[262] A coin with an obverse type of Alexander the Great as Heracles, dating to cạ. 300 B.C., was found by the Fish Gate.[263]

Hellenistic villages grew up especially on the ruins of the old palace on the acropolis south of Ezida, but some remains of houses and more of graves were also found above Ezida. Coin evidence suggests that these small villages, six levels of which have been identified in the area south of Ezida, began about the middle of the third century B.C. and continued until the time of the Parthian conquest, about 140 B.C. Some of the graves associated with these villages contain antique seals, an indication of the archaizing interests of the settlers of the Hellenistic period. Coins and amphora handles provide evidence for trade with the Syrian coast and Greece. Like Dura-Europos, Nimrud in this period formed part of a currency unit with Antioch and the Syrian coast rather than with Seleucia on the Tigris.[264]

This rather slim archaeological evidence corresponds reasonably well with the statement by Xenophon that the city was deserted when he passed through (401 B.C.) but had been a large city called Larissa and inhabited by the Medes in ancient times (*Anabasis* III.4.7). He describes the walls and the

[258] Woolley, *Ur Excavations* IX, introduction, 49, 51; idem, *Ur Excavations* V: *The Ziggurat and its Surroundings* (Oxford, 1939), 144 f.

[259] Woolley, *Ur Excavations* IX, introduction.

[260] Grayson, *Chronicles*, 26, 120, chron. 11, obv. lines 6-9:

6 [. . .] *regular offerings* for Sin of Egishnugalu, Sin, lord of [. . .]

7 [Antiochus,] the prince, in the temple of Sin, Egishnugalu . . . [. . .]

8 [. . .] they bowed down. The prince [*presented*] one sheep as an offe[ring]

9 [. . .] Egishnugalu, the temple of Sin, lord of [. . .]

[261] André Parrot, *Tello* (Paris, 1948), 150-55, 309-313, fig. 33.

[262] David Oates, "Ezida: the Temple of Nabu," *Iraq* XIX (1957), 35-38; M.E.L. Mallowan, *Nimrud and Its Remains* (London, 1966), I, 282-87, 298.

[263] M.E.L. Mallowan, "The Excavations at Nimrud (Kalḫu), 1956," *Iraq* XIX (1957), 10.

[264] Mallowan, *Nimrud and its Remains*, I, 285, 296, 299-314; Oates, *Studies*, 63-66.

ziggurat and reports that the few inhabitants climbed the ziggurat to watch the troops pass.[265] The mound was apparently deserted after the destruction associated with the Parthian conquest, probably because the greater security of a stable regime made it unnecessary to live on an inconveniently high tell.[266] Thus at Nimrud the temples ceased to function as such during the Hellenistic period, and the ruins of Ezida served only as bases for houses and graves. Unlike Assur, this city was deserted during the Parthian period.

Nineveh

THERE IS some evidence for the establishment of Greek forms of civic organization at Nineveh. There seems to have been a gap in occupation from the time of the city's destruction in 612 B.C. until the Seleucid period, though some repair work was done on the Temple of Nabu before the Greek occupation. Ceramics and coins found in the excavations may suggest continued occupation in the Parthian period and perhaps also trade with the Roman world or the passage of Roman armies.[267] The evidence of Greek civic organization is provided by an inscription found during the 1904 excavations of the Nabu temple. It records a dedication by one Apollophanes, the son of Asklepiades, in honor of the θεῶν ἐπηκό[ων] (the gods who listen [to prayers]) on behalf of Apollonios, *stratēgos* and *epistatēs* of the city (στρατηγοῦ καὶ ἐπιστάτου τῆς πόλεως) presumably Nineveh. The line giving the date is unfortunately damaged, but Thompson and Hutchinson suggest a date in the third century of the Seleucid era (i.e., the first century B.C.). This inscription replaces an earlier one, almost totally illegible. If the date is correct, the inscription would fall within the period of Parthian control. The titles *stratēgos* and *epistatēs* go back to the Seleucid period, however, and probably indicate that the civic organization was established during the period of Greek political control.[268] The only other Greek inscription from Nineveh known to Thompson and Hutchinson, a list of the Macedonian months, dates to the third century A.D.

Oates suggests that the main Hellenistic town might have lain in the plain below the mound of Nineveh. He supports this in part by the presence in this area of a small shrine of Hermes. The statue, a relatively simple work, cannot be dated on stylistic grounds, but it seems to me more likely to fall within the Parthian than the Hellenistic period. It apparently stood on a raised platform at the back of a long narrow cella; there is also a side room that would have been entered from the cella. Oates relates the type of the shrine to Assyrian prototypes.[269]

Arslan Tash

ARSLAN TASH, near the Euphrates in northern Mesopotamia, was an important provincial Assyrian city, especially during the reign of Tiglathpilesar III (eighth century B.C.), when one of a number of his royal residences was constructed in the city. After the fall of the Assyrian empire, Arslan Tash lost its importance. Nonetheless, a small temple of the Hellenistic period, as well as some pottery, lamps, and terracottas, provide evidence of continued occupation or reoccupation after the Greek conquest.

The small structure at Arslan Tash is built on the ruins of the Assyrian palace at a level 1.65 meters above the floor of the palace. Basalt statues from the Assyrian period were reused in the foundations. The Hellenistic building consists of two rooms, a pronaos that is slightly wider than it is long, and a smaller naos. The building is oriented almost exactly due east. The walls are built of unbaked bricks, the dimensions of which correspond to Babylonian measurements, and the pavement within the building consists of a packing of small pieces of limestone. The door between the two rooms is preceded by two steps. The opening is flanked by engaged columns in soft limestone; these are roughly picked and perhaps were never finished. At a later period the size of the door between the rooms was reduced by placing stone blocks against the piers. Two column drums, also in soft limestone, were found in the northeast corner of the first room.[270]

Thureau-Dangin's dating of the building is based

---

[265] Oates, *Iraq* XIX (1957), 36-38; David and Joan Oates, "Nimrud 1957: The Hellenistic Settlement," *Iraq* XX (1958), 136; Mallowan, *Nimrud and its Remains*, I, 299.

[266] David and Joan Oates, *Iraq* XX (1958), 136 f.; Mallowan, *Nimrud and its Remains*, I, 310.

[267] R. Campbell Thompson and R. W. Hutchinson, "The Excavations of the Temple of Nabu at Ninevah," *Archaeologia* LXXIX

(1929), 106 f., esp. 107 n. 1.

[268] Ibid., 140-42; Oates, *Studies*, 61.

[269] Oates, *Studies*, 61; Mohammed Ali Mustapha, *Sumer* X (1954), 280-83, pls. 1-3 (in Arabic); Colledge, *Parthian Art*, 84, pl. 5.

[270] F. Thureau-Dangin et al., *Arslan Tash* (Haut-Commissariat de la République française en Syrie et au Liban, *Bibliothèque Archéo-*

largely on its architectural forms, particularly the remains of columns, and on its high level in relation to the destroyed Assyrian palace. The form of the building suggests that it was a religious structure, but unfortunately no objects that would suggest its purpose have been found. Pottery, lamps, and a terracotta figurine found in the upper levels of the tell suggest a date for the Hellenistic occupation ranging from the third and second centuries B.C. to the early years of the first century A.D. Thureau-Dangin suggests that in spite of the columns, the plan is of Babylonian origin. The reason for this suggestion is that the long sides of the rooms are

parallel rather than perpendicular to the facade. The plan closely resembles that of the heroon of Kinéas at Aï Khanoum in its first state, however, though the heroon of Kinéas has a pronaos with two columns *in antis*. Bernard suggests that the form of the heroon of Kinéas is derived from Macedonian tomb architecture and that its use in the colony at Aï Khanoum shows the importance of the Macedonian element in the Greek colonies of the Orient. He states that the temple or heroon at Arslan Tash demonstrates that this form existed also in Hellenized Syria.[271]

logique et Historique, XVI) (Paris, 1931), 5-16, figs. 2, 3, pl. XVI.1-2.

[271] Bernard, *Fouilles d'Aï Khanoum* I, 96-100.

2

GREEK COLONIES

Seleucia on the Tigris

AT SELEUCIA on the Tigris, founded by Seleukos Nicator (Pausanias I.16.3; Pliny, *NH* VI.30.121f.), there are remains of several structures that possibly date to the Seleucid period and that might have had a religious function (fig. 13). The most conspicuous of these is the artificial mound called Tell ʿUmar (fig. 14), which still rose sixteen meters above the plain at the beginning of the excavations in 1927. Both the function and the date of the structure are uncertain.

Tell ʿUmar went through a number of building periods. In its latest phase, which has now been dated to the Sasanian epoch on the basis of a hoard of coins of Chosroes II found in a ditch that was probably used for mixing earth for the bricks,[1] the structure consisted essentially of a central tower of unbaked bricks surrounded by a mound contained by an elliptical enclosure wall. This central tower, 18 meters high in its present state of preservation, was constructed at the same time as the elliptical enclosure wall, as the American excavators had conjectured. The space between the central tower and the outer wall contains two kinds of fill: a lower layer of red clay and rubbish from the debris of earlier buildings , and an upper fill consisting of layers of greenish sand alternating with layers of reeds. This latest phase represents a reconstruction, how-ever, probably after a period of abandonment. In this reconstruction, the form of the mound was changed and perhaps also its purpose was altered. Although the older structure was probably religious (see below), there is no evidence to suggest that this was true of the Sasanian construction; Invernizzi repeats Waterman's suggestion that it might have been a watchtower.[2]

At the present stage of the excavations, it is not possible to define clearly the earliest building phases at Tell ʿUmar.[3] Sparse coin finds would appear to date the original construction in the first century A.D., though Invernizzi, on the basis of the Seleucid date of an archive building that is probably associated with the complex, suggests that the structure might have been built in the Seleucid period.[4] The latest Parthian phase, the most clearly defined and best known at present, can probably be dated to the late second or early third century A.D. on the basis of coins of Vologases III found in layers belonging to this phase; it also overlies a structure in which a hoard of coins was found that had been issued in A.D. 121-125 under Vologases II.[5]

Destruction and the fact that excavations are still in progress make it difficult to determine the exact form of the building in its various phases, but in its pre-Sasanian phases the outer wall was polygonal rather than circular,[6] and apparently also the upper floors of the pre-Sasanian monument were not

---

[1] Invernizzi, *Mesopotamia* III-IV (1968/69), 11-16. Invernizzi's reports on the excavations at Tell ʿUmar have been published in *Mesopotamia*.

[2] Leroy Waterman, *Second Preliminary Report Upon the Excavations at Tel Umar, Iraq* (Ann Arbor, 1933), 75-78; repeated in Hopkins, *Topography*, 8-12; Invernizzi, *Mesopotamia* III-IV (1968/69), 14-17.

[3] Professor Invernizzi told me in April 1979 that he felt the division of the remains of the Parthian period into three phases proposed in *Mesopotamia* II (1967), 13-25, was premature.

[4] Invernizzi, *Mesopotamia* III-IV (1968/69), 17, 29 f., 75 f.; see below.

[5] Invernizzi, *Mesopotamia* II (1967), 18, 24 f.

[6] Ibid., 11 f.

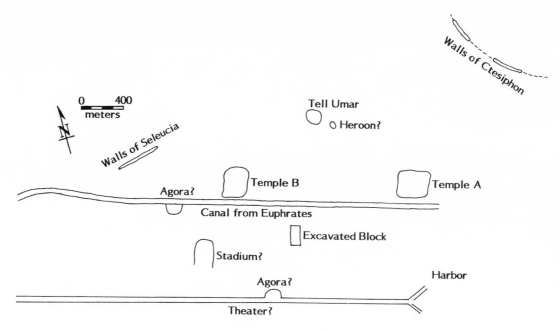

13. Seleucia on the Tigris, sketch plan of city.

solid, but contained rooms.[7] In addition, a number of rooms and courts lay on the northwest side of the monument.

The reconstructed plan of the building in its latest Parthian phase is based on the remains of the earlier structures and is to some extent conditioned by them. The enclosure wall in this period was polygonal, and part of its outer facade was perhaps found on the northwest side. This facade has the appearance of a series of steps, perhaps due to its ruined condition. In this phase there was a solid projection in the center of the northwest side, recalling the central staircase of Babylonian ziggurats. It is not certain that this solid projection actually supported a staircase; it might instead have been a terrace on which sacred rites could take place. In the latter case, it would have been accessible from the bank of the main mound, which in turn would have been reached by a staircase to the north of the projection. One side of the projection forms the south wall of a room, called the "pink room" from the color of its wall plaster; it was probably roofed. To the north of this room in turn was the so-called blue courtyard. Both might have served cult purposes.[8] There were also rooms on the upper levels.

The earlier levels have not yet been fully ex-

plored, and it is therefore difficult to discuss their form in a coherent fashion. It appears, however, that the area under the solid projection of the latest Parthian phase contained rooms, since an earlier phase of the pink room included a door leading into the area later covered by the projection. The original layout of the pink room probably belongs to the earliest phase. In its earliest stages, then, the whole of the projecting body was probably composed of rooms. That these rooms were devoted at least in part to cult purposes is suggested by the presence in two of them of rectangular bases in baked brick, probably altars. On the other hand, in the lowest level of some of the rooms and courtyards, the discovery of pithoi let into the floors or of ovens suggest domestic use.[9] At the south end of the present limit of excavations a group of rooms was found around a courtyard, all belonging to the earliest phase. These might have been domestic. Thus the plan in the earliest phases was quite different from the later plan, and Invernizzi suggests that it might have had a more Mesopotamian character. The corners of the building appear to be oriented approximately to the cardinal points, as in earlier Mesopotamian temples.[10]

The building at Tell ʿUmar is unusual and with-

[7] Invernizzi, *Mesopotamia* III-IV (1968/69), 25.

[8] Invernizzi, *Mesopotamia* II (1967), 13-24, pl. I, figs. 2-5.

[9] Invernizzi, *Mesopotamia* III-IV (1968/69), 19-22, pl. I, rooms

22c, 130p, figs. 8, 9; idem, *Mesopotamia* II (1967), 20 f.

[10] Invernizzi, *Mesopotamia* V-VI (1970/71), 18 f., figs. 6-8; idem, *Mesopotamia* II (1967), 24.

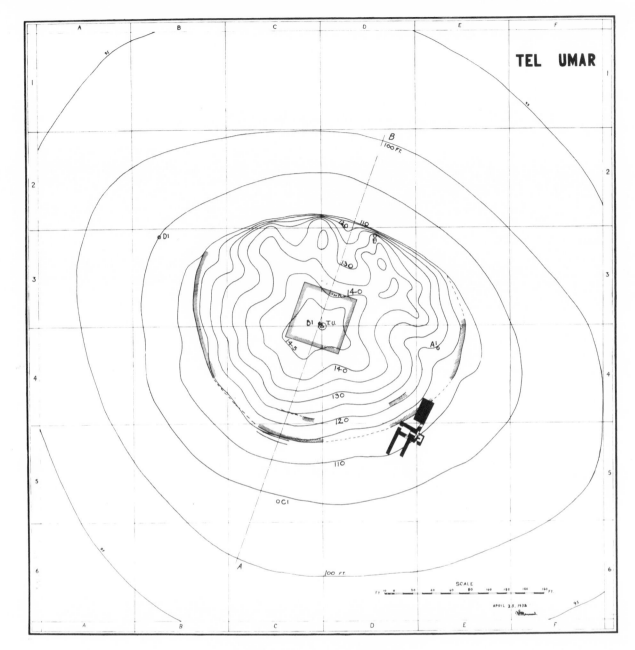

14. Seleucia, contour map of Tell ʿUmar.

out exact parallels. It has at least a superficial resemblance to a ziggurat,[11] a resemblance that becomes especially striking in the latest Parthian phase, with the presence of a central projection, particularly if this projection supported a staircase. In addition, the grouping of rooms and courtyards against the mound recalls the occasional placement of temples against a ziggurat in earlier Mesopotamia, as in the thirteenth-century Assur temple at Kar-Tukulti-Ninurta.[12] Tell ʿUmar differed from a ziggurat in that the upper floors of the structure contained a number of rooms. Nonetheless, the generally Mesopotamian character of the building is clear. Greek elements are limited to a few pieces of architectural

[11] Cf. Hopkins, *Topography*, 10 f.

[12] Andrae, *Wiedererstandene Assur*, 92, fig. 42 (2d ed., pp. 134-36, figs. 116-17); Tilman Eickhoff, *Kār Tukulti Ninurta. Eine mittelas-*

syrische Kult- und Residenzstadt (*Abhandlungen der Deutschen Orient-Gesellschaft* XXI) (Berlin, 1985), 27-35.

decoration, none of which can be associated with a specific room, and all of which probably date to the Parthian period.[13]

It seems unlikely that the mound of Tell ʿUmar goes back to the pre-Seleucid period, although a baked brick inscribed with the name of Marduk-balatsuiqbi, king (or prince) of Karduniash, who ruled in Babylon in the ninth century B.C., was found approximately one meter below the loose debris on the top of the mound. Waterman has argued that this position could not be accidental.[14] This might suggest that the original construction is Neo-Babylonian, an idea tentatively accepted by Colledge.[15] There appears to be no other evidence for a pre-Seleucid occupation of the site, however. A number of cuneiform inscriptions of Neo-Babylonian date have been found, but Pettinato suggests that the bricks on which they were inscribed were brought in from elsewhere as building materials, noting that Nebuchadnezzar's defensive wall must have passed nearby.[16] Since the ancient sources state clearly that Seleucia was founded by Seleukos Nicator, it seems likely that the inscribed brick found in Tell ʿUmar was brought from elsewhere, probably Babylon, and that the whole structure is Seleucid at the earliest. The hypothesis of a post-Babylonian origin is also confirmed by the peculiar form of the structure, since it does not conform closely to Babylonian models, unlike the sanctuaries at Uruk.

As stated above, Invernizzi suggests a possible Seleucid date for the construction of Tell ʿUmar, on the basis of the dates of tablets found in an archive housed in a nearby building. The dated tablets range from 82 to 133 of the Seleucid era (230/29 to 179/78 B.C.), apart from an isolated tablet of 158 of the Seleucid era (154/53 B.C.). There are some gaps in the years represented.[17] Though the archives building is separated from Tell ʿUmar by a street, Invernizzi argues that the two formed part of the same complex. As he points out, the practice of keeping archives, both religious and economic, in temples is an old one in Mesopotamia, and it probably continued here. In addition, the situation of the smaller tells around Tell ʿUmar suggest the possibility that it was enclosed in a large courtyard

that included other buildings associated with the administration of the sanctuary. The archives building would have been one of these. It is possible, as Invernizzi notes, that not all of the rooms of the so-called archives building necessarily housed archives; some could have been used for administrative purposes or as staff living quarters, or could even have played some role in the rituals of the sanctuary. Some confirmation for this idea is found in the fact that the southernmost room excavated in 1969 and 1970 contained no bullae. Invernizzi further suggests that a large open area to the east of the eastern block of rooms of the archives building might have been part of the large courtyard of the sanctuary complex.[18]

If Invernizzi's hypothesis that the archive building was attached to the complex of Tell ʿUmar and if the Seleucid date and religious purpose of Tell ʿUmar are accepted, then the situation at Seleucia would be closely parallel to that at Uruk. At Seleucia also the archive, which was mostly concerned with the salt tax, would show the economic importance of a sanctuary in the life of a city. In the case of the Seleucia archive, moreover, the fact that the bullae were government documents would provide evidence of the use of a sanctuary to house civil archives and, indirectly, of the interest of Seleucid rulers in large-scale sanctuaries in their cities.[19]

A cuneiform tablet of Seleucid date found on the surface in the area of the archives building cannot necessarily be associated with that building, according to Doty. It records the dedication of one or more slaves as oblates to the god Nergal by a man with a Greek name, Cebros, for the life of Seleukos the king. Doty suggests that since the major temple of Nergal was in Cutha, the tablet either might have been brought to Seleucia from Cutha or might record the dedication of a slave in Cutha by a resident of Seleucia.[20] If the tablet can be associated with the archives building, it would provide evidence that the building could house religious as well as civil archives. Seleucid tablets were apparently found in Tell ʿUmar, but their content is unknown.

The so-called Parthian villa excavated by the American expedition[21] also falls within the hypo-

---

[13] Invernizzi, *Mesopotamia* II (1967), 31 f.; idem, *Mesopotamia* III-IV (1968/69), 26 f., figs. 25-28.

[14] Waterman, *Second Preliminary Report upon the Excavations at Tel Umar, Iraq*, 75-78; repeated in Hopkins, *Topography*, 8-10.

[15] Colledge, *Parthian Art*, 41.

[16] Invernizzi, *Mesopotamia* V-VI, (1970/71), 49 f.

[17] Invernizzi, *Mesopotamia* III-IV (1968/69), 119 f.

[18] Ibid., 29 f., 33-36, 75 f.; Invernizzi, *Mesopotamia* V-VI (1970/71), 21 f.

[19] Invernizzi, *Mesopotamia* III-IV (1968/69), 73-76.

[20] Lawrence Timothy Doty, "A Cuneiform Tablet from Tell ʿUmar," *Mesopotamia* XIII-XIV (1978/79), 91-98.

[21] Manasseh, in Leroy Waterman, *Preliminary Report upon the Excavations at Tel Umar, Iraq* (Ann Arbor, 1931), 9-17.

thetical enclosure at Tell ʿUmar. Invernizzi stated in 1968-69 that since the masonry of the building had completely disappeared, its function could not be determined, but that it could have functioned as part of a sanctuary complex.[22] Hopkins has reinterpreted the building as a Seleucid heroon. His interpretation is based primarily on the discovery of a fragmentary inscription under the floor of one of the rooms of the building, which names priests of dead Seleucid kings and of the living ruler, and secondarily on the resemblance of the plan of the building to the plans of the temples of the Parthian period at Dura-Europos.[23]

McDowell, the first to publish the inscription, states that it was "built into a sub-surface wall of a Parthian structure in trial trench 4." He read the surviving portions as follows, with some restorations:

Ἀντιό]χου δὲ σω[τῆρος
βα]σιλέως δὲ
]ξενον ἱερ[ο]μνή[μονος .
]ς ἀγωνοθετοῦ μ
ταμί[α]ς Ὠτας
]κεστράτου[24]

The date of the inscription, the names of the kings referred to, and the circumstances of the dedication are uncertain. McDowell, Mouterde, Rostovtzeff, and Hopkins have offered different opinions about the name of the living king and therefore about the date of the inscription; these opinions are based in part on estimates of the number of letters to be restored in the missing portions of the stone and in part on differing reconstructions of the historical circumstances. McDowell suggested that the second king was Seleukos II, but Rostovtzeff preferred Seleukos III.[25] Mouterde suggested Antiochos II Theos,[26] and Hopkins has suggested Demetrios II on the basis of a complex historical ar-

gument about the internal power struggles of the Seleucid dynasty. Hopkins translates the restored inscription as follows: "The priest of Seleucus Nicator and of Antiochus Soter, such and such (the name of the priest), son of so and so, and the *hieromnemon* (he who piously calls to mind the name), of Demetrius Soter and of King Demetrius Nikator, such and such (the name of the *hieromnemon*) son of Philoxenos(?), and such and such son of so and so who presided at the games, and Otas the supervisor and such and such an official son of so and so (Nikestratus ?) [dedicated this building or this gift]."[27] The restorations are so extensive that the translation is speculative in the extreme.

In any case, the identity of the reigning king is relatively unimportant for my purposes. The inscription clearly refers to priests of the cult of the Seleucid rulers. Unfortunately, the object of the dedication is not preserved. Rostovtzeff assumed that the inscription was on an architrave and therefore was a building inscription, but Mouterde points out that the dimensions suggest instead a plaque, which was perhaps set into the wall of a temple to commemorate some work there. Hopkins argues that the location of the stone beneath the floor of the entrance room of the later building (fig. 15, room 11) suggests that the fragmentary inscription was placed near the entrance to the earlier building also.[28]

Hopkins states that there were four levels of occupation in the area of the building he identifies as a Seleucid heroon. The earliest, level IV, is poorly known, consisting essentially of some long walls that ran across the area later occupied by the central courtyard. The first monumental structure, level III, is dated by Hopkins to the reign of Demetrios II (145-140 B.C.), on the basis of the inscribed fragment discussed above, which he associates with this building level. The structure of this period,

---

[22] Invernizzi, *Mesopotamia* III-IV (1968/69), 29 f.

[23] Hopkins, *Topography*, 13-25.

[24] Robert Harbold McDowell, *Stamped and Inscribed Objects from Seleucia on the Tigris* (Ann Arbor, 1935), 258 f. The inscription is too fragmentary to allow a translation. Hopkins's translation, based on his suggested restorations, is given below.

[25] Rostovtzeff "Πρόγονοι," *JHS* LV (1935), 66.

[26] Mouterde, review of McDowell, *Stamped and Inscribed Objects, MélUSJ* XIX (1935), 119 f. Mouterde suggested the following restoration of the inscription:

1. [Ἱερεῖς θεοῦ Σελεύκου (cf. *OGIS*, 246,1)—or [Ἱερεῖς Σελεύ-
   κου Νικάτορος Ἀντιό]χου δὲ Σω|τῆ
2.]ρος ὁ δεῖνα τοῦ δεῖνος βα]σιλέως δὲ [Ἀν-
3.]τιόχου θεοῦ (??) ὁ δεῖνα v.g. Φιλο]ξένου, ἱερομνή-
4. [μονες (?) ὁ δεῖνα———]ς ἀγονωθέτου, [sic] M.

5. |———τοῦ δεῖνος|, ταμία⟨ι⟩ Σωτᾶς
6. |τοῦ δεῖνος, ὁ δεῖνα . . . . . κεστρατου[ς] (?).

[27] Hopkins, "A Stele from Seleucia on the Tigris," *MélUSJ* XXXVII, fasc. 12 (1960/61), 237-46; the conclusions are repeated, with some modifications, in Hopkins, *Topography*, 24. Hopkins restores the inscription as follows:

Ἱερεὺς Σελεύκου Νικάτορος Ἀντιό]χου δὲ Σω[τῆρος
ὁ δεῖνα τοῦ δεῖνος καὶ Δημητρίου Σωτῆρος βασ]ιλέως δέ
Δημητρίου Νικάτορος ὁ δεῖνα τοῦ φιλο]ξένου ἱερ[ο]μνή-
μων καὶ ὁ δεῖνα τοῦ δεῖνος ἀγωνοθετοῦν
καὶ———]ταμί[α]ς Ὠτᾶς
καὶ———ὁ δεῖνα τοῦ- -]κεστράτου

Obviously, both Hopkins's restoration and that of Mouterde are very speculative.

[28] Hopkins, *Topography*, 24.

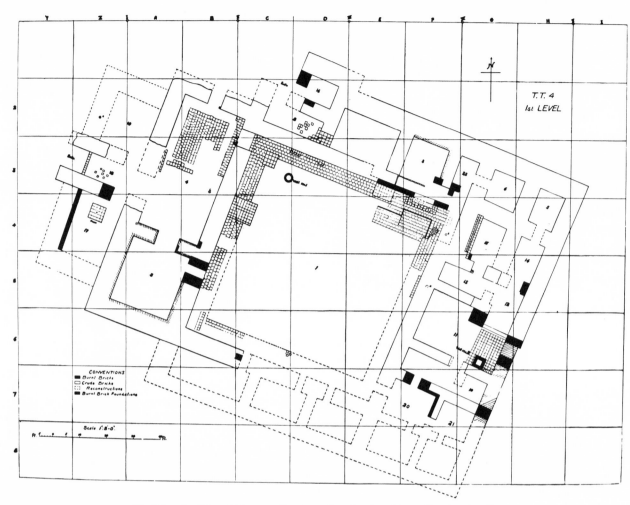

15. Seleucia, Seleucid heroon(?), plan of level II (Parthian villa, first level).

which survives only partially, was probably similar in plan to the well-preserved level II, according to Hopkins. He dates level II to the period following the revolt of Greek citizens against the Parthians in A.D. 39-43.[29] Minor modifications were made, apparently after the passage of Trajan, and the building was abandoned, probably after the expedition of Verus. The dating of the phases, then, is essentially based on the assumption that changes in the building are connected with known historical events. Hopkins finds a measure of corroboration for his dating of level III in the presence in the area of architectural terracottas of late Hellenistic type. The coin evidence is inconclusive.[30]

I shall begin the description of the supposed heroon with level II, the only well-documented building phase (figs. 15, 16).[31] The building, oriented roughly east-west, is organized around an open court approximately 21.80 meters on a side (1). On the west side were a number of small rooms grouped around a larger room (11), which lies approximately on the central axis of the court and which probably served as an entrance to the complex. The entrance into the court, however, probably lay in one of the rooms to the south (20), thus preventing a view into the court from the outside. Between two of these western rooms (13 and 15) is a door socket made of part of a column base of Per-

[29] Ibid., 16 f.; McDowell, in ibid., 159 f., suggests that it was instead the native inhabitants who revolted.

[30] Ibid., 13 f., 16 f.

[31] This description is based on Hopkins, *Topography*, 13-23, and Manasseh, in Waterman, *Preliminary Report upon the Excavations at*

Tel Umar, Iraq, 9-17. The dimensions of the building were apparently not recorded, but the plan reproduced here as fig. 15 was drawn to a scale of 1 inch to 8 feet. The size of the court is given as 72 feet square.

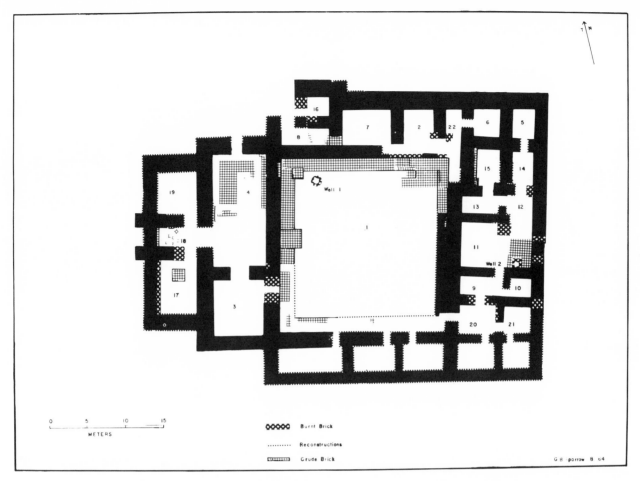

16. Seleucia, Seleucid heroon(?), restored plan of level II, as published in Hopkins, *Topography*, 18, fig. 20.

sian type. Hopkins suggests that this base might have come from the earlier building,[32] but it seems more likely to have been brought from Babylon, where similar column bases were found.[33] A single row of rooms lined the north side of the court, and a similar row is restored on the south.

On the west side of court I is a complex that Hopkins interprets as a pronaos-naos unit. The room directly west of the court is divided into two rooms of unequal size. The entrance from the court lies in the southern, smaller room (3). The north wall of the northern room (4) projects slightly beyond the north wall of the court, and this room can be entered directly from the outside. The northern portion of this room is paved with baked brick. Hopkins states that this paved area served a function similar to that of the *salles aux gradins* in some of the temples of Dura as a place for spectators to

stand to watch a cult performance that took place in the southern part of the room.

The westernmost section of the building was badly destroyed, and therefore its original form is uncertain. As restored, the western portion consists of two rooms of unequal size (17, 19), divided by an alcove (18). A line of baked bricks running south from about the mid-point of the south wall of alcove 18 is shown on the plan drawn at the time of the excavation (fig. 15). This row of bricks can perhaps be interpreted as the inner face of the west wall of room 17, and its terminus at the south may mark the south edge of the room. The presence of an elaborate drain in the floor suggests that the area housed some activity that necessitated the use of water. The west and north walls of room 19 are wholly restored (compare figs. 15 and 16). The entrance from room 4 into the rear area is not pre-

[32] Hopkins, *Topography*, 18-22, figs. 6, 11, 15.

[33] E. Schmidt, "Die Griechen in Babylon," 802-806, figs. 10, 11.

served, but it is restored as aligned with the alcove (18). The fact that the walls of the alcove ended in baked-brick piers perhaps suggests that the opening was arched, but Hopkins states that the roof was probably flat. A line of baked bricks across the floor of the alcove is interpreted by Hopkins as either steps to a podium or the line of a foundation before the platform for the cult image. There is no evidence for a west wall to this alcove. Hopkins' interpretation of the western end of the building as a naos divided into three parts, an arrangement that is frequent in the temples of Dura-Europos,[34] is dependent on the acceptance of the hypothetical restoration, and the elaborate drain in the floor of room 17 of the Seleucia building is without parallel in the naoi of the temples at Dura-Europos. Manasseh's analysis of the western end of the building at Seleucia differs radically from that of Hopkins; he suggests that alcove 18 served as the entrance from the outside into room 4, which he considered an unroofed court.[35] In view of the absence of a rear wall to alcove 18, Manasseh's interpretation is possible.

The idea that the level II building had a sacred function is perhaps supported by the discovery of a construction in the northeast corner of the courtyard that is interpreted by both Manasseh and Hopkins as a small shrine. It consists of a rectangular "altar-like" structure against the wall, in front of which is laid a rectangular platform made of baked brick and surrounded by a raised border of bricks. To the right is a small oval block of baked bricks, and a conduit runs between the two. Manasseh suggested that victims were sacrificed here in front of an image placed higher on the wall.[36]

This shrine overlies a very different construction in the building of the lower level. In the court at this earlier level was a large baked-brick vat connected by a conduit with a reservoir that was also constructed of baked bricks and lined with bitumen. Manasseh interpreted this complex as a factory for the production of date wine and molasses.[37] Hopkins, on the other hand, suggests that the vat and

reservoir provided water for ablutions.[38] The importance of water in the building is shown also by the presence of wells in the court in both phases, and the elaborate drain in room 17 (mentioned above).[39]

The earlier phase (level III) is otherwise very poorly preserved. Remains of walls found beneath the "pronaos" of level II (rooms 3 and 4) suggest four rooms in a line. The north wall of these rooms lies close to the north wall of the "naos" of level II; the south wall is lost. The east-west walls of the earlier phase have the same orientation as walls along the south side of the court and of the later room 11. Cisterns and wells below the level of the later court suggest that there was an open court in this phase also. Fragments of simas found in the reservoir and the cistern are attributed by Hopkins to the building at level III. He dates them to the last half of the second century B.C. on the basis of the style and degree of care in manufacture, stating that they "form a sharp contrast with the better baked, more carefully designed, fragments from the lowest level." If the attribution of these simas to the level III building is correct, the building would have had a gabled roof.[40] There is no evidence for columns in the court of the earlier building. As Hopkins points out, this would have been unusual in the Hellenistic period, though the court of the building identified as the heroon at Pergamon had no columns in its earliest phase.[41] The evidence for the early form of the building at Seleucia is, however, so fragmentary that no definitive statements about its form are possible.

The identification of the two successive structures at Seleucia as two phases of a heroon to the Seleucid kings is based on rather slight evidence. The inscription shows that a cult of the deified rulers existed at Seleucia, and its finding place in the foundations of the later building perhaps suggests that the original heroon is represented by the earliest phase of this structure. Apparently no objects that suggested the function of the first building have been found; and the vat and reservoir could have

[34] Hopkins, *Topography*, 17-23.

[35] Manasseh, in Waterman, *Preliminary Report upon the Excavations at Tel Umar, Iraq*, 11.

[36] Ibid., 12 f., fig. 5; Hopkins, *Topography*, 20, fig. 13.

[37] Manasseh, in Waterman, *Preliminary Report upon the Excavations at Tel Umar*, Iraq, 14-17, fig. 6.

[38] Hopkins, *Topography*, 23. He rightly rejects his alternate suggestion that it was an apparatus for changing water into wine.

[39] Ibid., 16-23; Manasseh, in Waterman, *Preliminary Report upon the Excavations at Tel Umar, Iraq*, 9-12, figs. 3, 4.

[40] Hopkins, *Topography*, 16, 23. Goldman's discussion of the fragments of architectural decoration is organized largely on the basis of pattern type rather than of finding place, and thus is not very useful in establishing the decorative program of any one building. (Goldman, in ibid., 127-48; simas from TT4, the area identified by Hopkins as the Seleucid heroon, are discussed on 133, fig. 7).

[41] Ernst Boehringer and Friedrich Krauss, *Altertümer von Pergamon IX: Das Temenos für den Herrscherkult* (Berlin and Leipzig, 1937), 5, 34 f.

had an industrial rather than a religious purpose, as Manasseh suggests.

Not enough remains of the first phase of the building to allow comparisons with Greek heroa, though if Hopkins is right in suggesting that its plan resembled that of the later structure, a tentative discussion is possible. The heroa of Calydon and Aï Khanoum consist of a chapel above a crypt; there is no crypt at Seleucia. The heroon at Calydon consists of a colonnaded court at the rear of which is a long cult room with a deep niche; a corridor runs along the entrance wall, and rooms line one side of the court. The form of the heroon of Kinéas at Aï Khanoum is very different from that of the later phase of the building at Seleucia. It consists of a pronaos-naos complex. The pronaos, which has columns *in antis*, is slightly wider than the naos. Bernard suggests that this plan was derived from Macedonian tomb architecture, and he notes that the existence in the Hellenistic levels of Arslan Tash of a building of similar plan shows that the type had spread to the Near East.[42] The building on the acropolis of Pergamon is identified as a temenos for the ruler cult on the basis of its similarity to other such buildings, especially at Calydon and Priene. It underwent a number of rebuildings, but in its main period it consisted of a peristyle court, at the rear of which was a wide foreroom preceding a narrow, deep cult room. A double row of rooms lined the side of the court opposite the cult room.[43] This building somewhat resembles the Seleucia structure.

Hopkins suggests that the late structure at Seleucia represents a rebuilding of the earlier heroon as a reaffirmation of the Greek descent of many of the citizens of Seleucia. The location of the shrine of the later structure above the vat and reservoir of the earlier structure suggests to him that the rites and ceremonies connected with the earlier building were carried out also in the later one.[44] The complete change in apparatus, however—from arrangements for the provision of water to a possible sacrificial altar—would seem to argue instead for a change in function.[45] Hopkins also supports the idea of a rededication of the building to the founder of the city by the Greek citizens of Seleucia after the revolt of A.D. 39-43, suggesting a possible historical parallel with Dura-Europos, where a building

that may have been an early form of the Temple of the Gaddé was erected between ca. 50 B.C. and A.D. 50. In one of the cult reliefs of a later building on the site, dated to A.D. 159, the Gad of Dura is crowned by Seleukos Nicator, thus stressing the Greek foundation of the city. The sacred character of the building of 50 B.C.-50 A.D. and its dedication to the Gaddé are not absolutely clear, however, for they depend on an assumption of continuity in the purpose of the block in which the building is located.[46] The suggestion of a sacred function for the later building in Seleucia also depends in part on the analogy of its plan with that of many Dura temples, but that analogy is based in turn on a proposed restoration of the western portion of the building.[47] Thus, the Dura parallels do not provide conclusive evidence for a sacred function for the building at Seleucia. If the level II building did have a religious function, the rituals are likely to have been different from those of the earlier structure. The re-use of the inscription in the foundations might even support the idea that the new building was not a heroon. Even if the construction in the court of the later building was a shrine, its presence does not necessarily imply that the entire building was a temple; a courtyard shrine could have served for household worship.

Of the two buildings included within a hypothetical courtyard surrounding the mound of Tell ʿUmar, one certainly and the other probably dates to the Seleucid period. Both the Seleucid date and the primary function of the archives building are clear, and the inscription found in the foundations of the second building raises the possibility that in its early phase it was a heroon to the Seleucid kings. The dates of these two structures offer some support for the Seleucid dating of Tell ʿUmar suggested by Invernizzi, and the proximity of the probable heroon to Tell ʿUmar makes the idea that the latter had a religious function plausible. Hopkins' interpretation of Tell ʿUmar differs from Invernizzi's. Hopkins dates the later tower and the associated circuit wall to the later half of the city's existence, possibly to the second half of the first century A.D., but this is probably incorrect. He argues that the dimensions of the unbaked bricks of an earlier interior structure followed a Greek system, but that the structure could have been built

[42] Bernard, *Fouilles d'Aï Khanoum* I, 85-102, pls. 12, 13.

[43] Boehringer and Krauss, *Altertümer von Pergamon* IX, 5, 34 f., 81-85.

[44] Hopkins, *Topography*, 12 f., 23.

[45] As Hopkins seems to recognize: *Topography*, 13.

[46] Brown, *Dura Report* VII/VIII, 222-29, figs. 53, 54. See the discussion in the chapter on Dura.

[47] Compare Hopkins, *Topography*, 14, fig. 6, the plan of the building drawn at the time of the excavation (my fig. 15), with the restored plan in *Topography*, 18, fig. 11 (my fig. 16).

during either the Hellenistic period or the period of Parthian control. He suggests that the early platform of mud brick might represent the foundations for a monumental altar and tentatively dates the construction of the artificial mound to the period shortly after the Parthians had taken control of Seleucia. By analogy with both Nippur and Assur, he suggests that Tell ʿUmar might have served as the Parthian citadel, but that the mound might also have been connected with an as yet undiscovered temple and thus might have served a religious as well as a secular purpose. Unlike Invernizzi, Hopkins feels that there is no cogent reason for connecting Tell ʿUmar with the heroon, which lay a block to the east. To Hopkins, the location of the heroon suggests that the Seleucid palace might have been nearby, perhaps in a sunken area to the east of Tell ʿUmar, and thus the Parthian citadel could be construed as replacing it.[48] If the ziggurat at Assur retained a religious function, as seems likely, that site would no longer provide an example of a former ziggurat serving as a citadel.

In addition to Tell ʿUmar and the possible heroon, two structures in Seleucia probably belonging to the Parthian period have been identified as temples by the American excavators (Temples A and B on fig. 13). Both appear to consist of an open courtyard, identifiable before excavation as a large depression, which is associated with a theater or a theater-like structure. The idea that the poorly preserved structure B is a temple is based on its superficial similarity to A, though in fact the idea that A is a temple is itself based on rather vague analogies to structures that are certainly temples. Structure A is located near the east corner of the mound and just north of the east-west canal. The location of structure B, on the west side of the city and in the same position in relation to the east-west canal, is for Hopkins an indication that it also is a temple enclosure.

Temple A consists of a large open courtyard surrounded on all four sides by a roofed corridor (fig. 17).[49] Traces of floors were found outside the surrounding corridor on the southeast and southwest, and on the southwest side there was also a small theater-like structure in mud brick. The central courtyard, 28 x 26 meters in size, has two successive plaster pavings, and the foundations of a small rectangular structure, perhaps an altar, were found in the middle of the court. The absence of a sub-

stantial layer of ash above the floor and of any indication of supports suggests that the central court was unroofed. It was apparently delimited by a wall, observable in the excavation only as an empty space, 2.25-2.50 meters wide, in which no traces of bricks or floor were found. On the other side of this space was the surrounding corridor, 5.10-5.60 meters wide. The area of the corridor was filled with a heavy layer of ash and charcoal that contained occasional bits of palm fiber; this suggests that it was roofed in wood. On the east side there are projections at the corners, perhaps forming antae, and another projection in the center of the east side perhaps marks the entrance. Within the courtyard were found fragments of architectural members—sections of columns, torus and scotia bases, pseudo-Ionic capitals, all in brick; and other sections of brick that perhaps came from blind arches. The fact that all of these fragments were found within the court suggests that the perimeter wall was decorated with engaged columns and pilasters supporting arches, though there might also have been an open arcade. The height of the columns can be calculated at 9-10 meters on the basis of the distance of the fallen segments from the walls. Other bricks were decorated with leaf and tendril or leaf and grape designs, and still others with griffins.[50] Remains of statues in marble and bronze found in the court and adjacent areas include a foot of a marble statue that was over life-size and the arm of a bronze statue. These could have belonged to acrolithic and acrometallic cult statues, as Hopkins suggests.

To the south of the building lie a few strips of pavement, and beyond a break in the pavement stands a mud-brick theater measuring 14 x 21.50 meters, with remains of about ten rows of steps. There is a semicircular orchestra, but no trace of a back wall or a stage.

No solid evidence for the date of Temple A exists, for coins dating from both before and after the Parthian conquest were found in the excavations. Hopkins suggests a date in the early Parthian period (second century B.C.) for the original building, on the basis of the coin evidence and of the architectural form of the building, which, according to him, belongs to Parthian rather than Hellenistic traditions. The building was certainly burned, and Hopkins suggests that this burning took place under Trajan. He states that although it is not clear

---

[48] Hopkins, *Topography*, 8-12, 24 f.
[49] Ibid., 119-23, pl. X.

[50] The architectural decoration from Temple A is discussed by Goldman in ibid., 131 f.

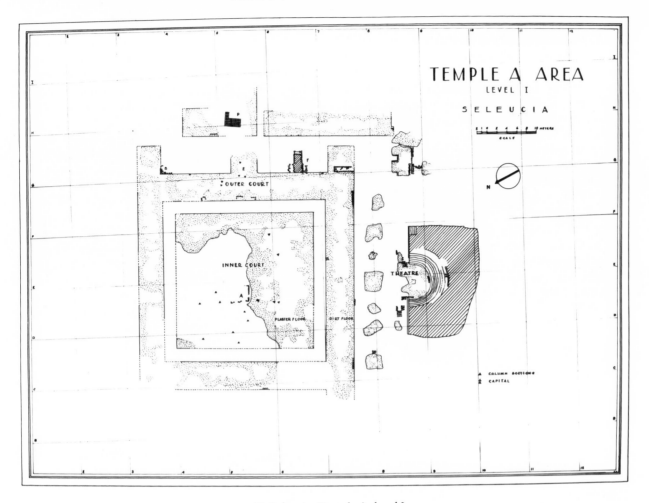

17. Seleucia, Temple A, level I.

whether the area was abandoned after the invasion of Lucius Verus in 165 or during the reign of Septimius Severus (A.D. 193-211), it is probable that the temple continued in use until the second century A.D. and therefore that the arms and armor found in the temple belonged to the soldiers of Septimius Severus. The late occupation of the area included both dwellings and simple graves.

The second depression, labelled Temple B, is also located along the canal from the Euphrates. The incomplete state of the excavations makes it impossible to determine the form of the complex with any certainty. Remains of six steps and the orchestra of a mud-brick theater, facing toward the east, have been excavated. A few traces of a plaster floor, close to a wall and probably belonging to the "temple," were found at a depth of one meter. Hopkins states that here, as in Temple A, the thea-

ter apparently lay to the south of the temple. Remains of architectural decoration in baked brick similar to that in the area of Temple A have also been found.

As with Temple A, dating evidence is slim. A number of Seleucid coins from the middle of the second century B.C. were found in the excavations of the theater and adjacent areas, and Parthian coins, the earliest dating from 121 to 83 B.C., were found in and around the graves in the area. On the basis of the "Parthian" form of the structure, Hopkins suggests that Temple B was built toward the beginning of the Parthian period, about 140 B.C., and that occupation continued until the end of the second century B.C. The excavations were quite superficial, however, so that it is possible that there is a Seleucid occupation layer that has not been reached. The graves would belong either to the period after the invasion of Verus or after the reign of Septimius Severus.[51] Hopkins further argues that the positions of Temples A and B on the east and west sides of the city suggest that the royal center of the city and therefore the palace lay between the two precincts, at least in the Parthian period, but probably already under the Seleucids.

Temple B, like Temple A, was a very simple structure. It probably had a courtyard and certainly a small theater. The idea that Temple A (and by extension Temple B) were sacred structures is based largely on analogy and on an assumption about the development of the "Parthian" temple. Hopkins considers the most significant feature of Temple A to be the presence of a covered ambularium around a hypaethral shrine. He compares the Seleucia temple to the Sasanian fire temple at Bishapur and to the shrine at Shami, which had the form of an open court, perhaps with a portico on the inside; the Shami temple does not have a surrounding corridor.[52] The square temple behind the Temple of Shamash at Hatra is surrounded by a corridor, but the central space was certainly roofed. Hopkins notes that the buildings at Seleucia differ from the temples of the Parthian period at Uruk (the Gareus Temple, and the small temple built into the Anu-Antum precinct) and at Dura. He argues that the temples at Seleucia mark a stage in the development that culminated in the domed fire temples of Sasanian Iran, with the vaulted sanctuary at Hatra forming an intermediate step. There is no reason to expect a fire temple of Iranian type at Seleucia, however, and the Hatra temple was not a fire sanctuary (see below, Hatra section).

As Hopkins notes, the association of a theater with a temple was a Syrian phenomenon, attested at Dura, at Sî' in the Hauran, and in the sanctuary of the Syrian gods at Delos. At Dura the theatrical areas were incorporated into the pronaos of the temples, whereas in the sanctuary of the Syrian gods at Delos, the theater took the form of a simple Hellenistic theater,[53] like the theaters of Temples A and B at Seleucia. In all the cases cited by Hopkins, the theaters are attached to or form part of sanctuaries of a more elaborate architectural character than the Seleucia buildings. Hopkins' suggestion that at Seleucia the theatrical areas were largely reserved for the Parthian nobility, thus explaining the introduction of a Syrian theater into an Arsacid temple, does not seem reasonable, as there is no

reason to assume a large Iranian population at Seleucia.

In some ways the closest analogy to Temple A at Seleucia is provided by the conjectured earliest stage of the sanctuary of Artemis at Dura, reconstructed by Brown as a long rectangular open court with an altar in the center and fronted by a vestibule (fig. 30). Doric columns from this structure that were reused in the building that succeeded it prove that the first building must have been at least in part columnar. Brown compares this open-air precinct to the Delphinium at Miletus and hence considers it Greek in type. He dates it to the third or second century B.C. on various grounds: pottery finds, coins, the style of the columns.[54] The structure at Dura differs from the one at Seleucia in being rectangular rather than roughly square and in (apparently) not having the isolating corridor. There is no theater associated with the Dura temple.

The evidence from Seleucia is inconclusive. No incontrovertibly religious structure has been found. Rather surprisingly for a Greek colony, no temple of Greek form has been found, and, with the possible exception of the "Seleucid heroon," none of the structures that may be religious has a Greek plan. This may be due to the accidents of discovery. Only a small fraction of the area of the city has been excavated, and in few of the excavated portions has the Hellenistic level been reached. This is true specifically in the areas of the so-called Temples A and B. Temples A and B, if they are sacred structures, resemble in form a number of Syrian temples. The re-use of the inscription mentioning priests of the Seleucid ruler cult might mean that the earliest building on the site of the so-called Parthian villa was a heroon of Hellenistic date. If Hopkins' further suggestion that its plan was similar to that of the later building is correct, then it would resemble in some respects the heroon at Calydon and the building at Pergamon identified as the temenos for the ruler cult, but would differ from the heroon of Kinéas at Aï Khanoum. Tell 'Umar obviously recalls a ziggurat; if a Seleucid dating is accepted, then a variation on an indigenous religious form would have been used at the beginning of the city. Thus the one thing that can be clearly stated is negative: no solid evidence for the existence of a religious structure of Greek type has been found at Seleucia.

The incomplete state of the excavations and the

[51] Ibid., 123 f., fig. 32.

[52] For Shami, see Schippmann, *Feuerheiligtümer*, 227-33.

[53] Philippe Bruneau and Jean Ducat, École française d'Athènes, *Guide de Délos* (Paris, 1965), 142-44, fig. 31.; E. Will, "Le sanctuaire

syrien de Délos," *Annales archéologiques de Syrie* I (1951), 77-79.

[54] *Dura Report* VI, 408-411, fig. 28, and pl. XIII. This sanctuary is discussed in the chapter on Seleucid Dura.

poor preservation of the remains make the assessment of the general architecture of Hellenistic Seleucia difficult. The "Hippodamian" grid plan of the city is clearly established,[55] and the bullae found in the archives and in the private houses provide clear evidence of the use of the Greek language and of the establishment of Seleucid administrative practices. On the other hand, there is no unequivocal evidence of the existence of civic architecture of Greek form. A semicircular depression on the south side of the city near the ancient caravan road is identified by Hopkins as the cavea of a theater. Massive piers of mud brick, labelled "Gate" or "South Gate of Seleucia" in the excavation catalogue and in later plans and drawings, are considered by Hopkins as evidence for the presence of a theater. He states that "the stage [of the theater] was connected with the terrace north of the wall with engaged columns," and suggests that the "terrace" might have been the skēnē. His observation that the plans of the site do not include diagrams of the seats and that neither the height nor the breadth of the steps was established raises doubts about the identification of this depression and the associated terrace as a theater. As Hopkins points out, a theater was considered an indispensable part of a Greek city, and at Babylon one was established early in the life of the Greek colony. Hopkins suggests that an open space south of the depression and terrace at Seleucia might have been a porticoed square similar to the so-called palaestra at Babylon. He also notes, however, that the architectural ornaments found in the theater at Babylon are lacking at Seleucia.[56] The architectural remains at Seleucia, then, do not provide firm evidence for the presence of a theater. The shape of the depression does suggest the cavea of a theater, and theaters were built both at Babylon and at Aï Khanoum. On the other hand, the nearby Seleucid colony of Dura-Europos apparently lacked a theater.[57] Perhaps the theater at Babylon served as the regional theater, though of course this idea does not correspond well with Pliny's statement that Seleukos founded Seleucia to reduce the population of Babylon.

The evidence for the existence at Seleucia of an agora or agorai is equally dubious. Two depressions, one near the supposed theater and another beside the Euphrates canal, might be agorai (see fig.

13), according to Hopkins,[58] but no finds, either of achitectural remains or of objects, confirm this suggestion. Indeed, recent excavations in the "agora" perhaps suggest that a building was erected relatively late in the city's history in an area that had previously not been used for monumental purposes.[59]

The architecture of the early days of the colony of Seleucia on the Tigris is very poorly known. Many of the early buildings probably either have disappeared or have been buried so deeply that they still await discovery. With the evidence now available, it is not possible to draw conclusions about the religious or civil architecture of the colony, though the lack of evidence for Greek forms remains striking.

Aï Khanoum

THE SITE of Aï Khanoum in northern Afghanistan, located on the river Kokcha, a tributary of the Amu Darya (Oxus), has revealed for the first time a Greek colony in Bactria. Although the excavations have not been completed, and therefore any conclusions are necessarily preliminary, the general chronological limits of the city's occupation are fairly clear. Furthermore, the excavations of the two temples so far discovered are sufficiently far advanced—in one case, completed—to permit discussion. Neither the date of the founding of the city nor its ancient name is certain. Bernard hesitates between the period of Alexander's sojourn in Central Asia (329-327 B.C.) and the time between this sojourn and the reconquest of the oriental portion of the Seleucid empire by Seleukos I between about 311 and 303 B.C. The fact that none of the buildings so far excavated can be dated before the early third century B.C. supports the idea of a foundation during the reign of Seleukos I. Bernard nonetheless still leans toward the idea that the city was founded by Alexander. He states that the strategic value of the site would not have escaped Alexander's notice and that the extent of the cultivable lands around the site would have made it an attractive place for Alexander to settle his soldiers.[60]

The date of the final destruction and the sequence of destruction in the various parts of the city also

---

[55] Hopkins, *Topography*, 1-4.

[56] Ibid., 26 f. Unfortunately, Hopkins has published no plan of the remains in this area.

[57] Perkins, *Art*, 15.

[58] Hopkins, *Topography*, 2 f., 26 f.

[59] M. Negro Ponzi, "Excavations in Squares X6/XXX96

('Agora')," *Mesopotamia* III-IV (1968/69), 53-55.

[60] Paul Bernard and H.-P. Francfort, *Études de géographie historique sur la plaine d'Aï Khanoum (Afghanistan)* (Paris, 1978), 12-15; Bernard, *Fouilles d'Aï Khanoum I*, 105-107; Bernard, "Problèmes d'histoire coloniale grecque," 110.

present uncertainties. It has been suggested that the administrative quarter (now called the palace) was burned ca. 100 B.C. and that this burning, which was followed by a squatter occupation, marked the end of the Greek city as such, particularly the end of its civic and religious institutions. In the *temple à redans*, however, the fire followed rather than preceded the squatter occupation, which would appear to suggest that the abandonment of Greek institutions preceded the fire. One possibility, raised in 1971, is that the two fires were separate, the one in the administrative quarter being the work of squatters, whose settlement might have in turn been destroyed in the catastrophe that resulted in the burning of the *temple à redans*.[61] A hoard of coins discovered in 1972-73 in a house outside the walls might suggest, however, that the city was destroyed by the end of the reign of Eucratides, since the hoard contains no coins of Heliocles, the son of Eucratides, and the last king of Bactria. By this hypothesis, the northeastern part of Bactria, including Aï Khanoum, would have been lost to Greek rule earlier than the western part.[62] Finds in the treasury of the palace support the theory that the city was destroyed during or immediately following the reign of Eucratides. The construction of the treasury was part of the last and most grandiose building campaign in the palace, which is probably to be attributed to Eucratides. The treasury was used for only a short time and was never entirely completed. A Greek inscription on a jar used to store money and found in the treasury is dated to the year 24 of an unknown era. Bernard and Rapin suggest tentatively that the era was an otherwise unattested one of Eucratides, whose reign, according to their hypothesis, would have ended in approximately 145 B.C. rather than in 155, as previously thought. The destruction of Aï Khanoum would then have fallen between about 147 and 145 B.C. A number of Indian coins of a type that did not normally circulate in Bactria were found in the treasury. As the number is too great to be explained by trade, Ber-

nard and Rapin suggest that they might represent either tribute from India to Bactrian kings or war booty, perhaps connected with Eucratides' conquest of northwest India.[63]

The architecture and planning of Aï Khanoum reveal a mixture of Greek and oriental elements, often within the same complex. This mixture is complicated and must be deliberate. The plan of the city, with a wide northeast-southeast street traversing it, an acropolis, and a lower city in which the public buildings are concentrated, is derived from the Milesian school of urban planning.[64] The propylaia on the main road also follow a Greek scheme.[65]

The palace at Aï Khanoum (initially called the "administrative quarter") mixes Greek and oriental forms. It is organized around a series of monumental courtyards. A Rhodian peristyle courtyard in the northeastern part of the building gives access through a hypostyle hall to a series of rooms whose arrangement recalls the plan of the harem in the palace of Xerxes at Persepolis.[66] According to Bernard, the Corinthian capitals of the peristyle court appear to be descendants of an old oriental type of capital in Greek guise, rather than being derived from the Greek world. Similar types of Corinthian capitals are found at Palmyra in the first century B.C.[67] The column bases belong to the Attic-Ionic type, although one campaniform base was found in the foundations of the south portico, and other bases of the Achaemenid plinth and torus type were used in the propylon and in a nearby room.[68] The excavators have hesitated about the date of these bases of Achaemenid form. Two possibilities have been suggested: 1) that they were reused from monuments of the Achaemenid period; and 2) that they were made shortly after the arrival of the Greek settlers by craftsmen trained in the Achaemenid tradition or in a local tradition, so far unattested. In *Fouilles d'Aï Khanoum* I (1973), Bernard argued in favor of the first hypothesis,[69] but in 1976 he dated these column bases to the early days of

[61] Bernard, *Fouilles d'Aï Khanoum* I, 110 and n. 14.

[62] Bernard, *CRAI* (1974), 305-308; Francfort, *Fouilles d'Aï Khanoum* III, 2. Bernard has published a series of preliminary reports on the excavations of Aï Khanoum in *CRAI*.

[63] Bernard and Rapin, "Le Palais. La Trésorerie," *BEFEO* LXVIII (1980), 23-27, 36-38; Bernard, "Problèmes d'histoire coloniale grecque," 115.

[64] Bernard, *Fouilles d'Aï Khanoum* I, 113 f. A plan of the city is found in Bernard and Rapin, "Campagne de fouille 1978 à Aï Khanoum (Afghanistan)," *BEFEO* LXVIII (1980), pl. I.

[65] Olivier Guillaume, *Fouilles d'Aï Khanoum* II: *Les Propylées de la rue principale* (Mémoires de la délégation archéologique française en Af-

ghanistan XXVI) (Paris, 1983); Bernard, *CRAI* (1978), 441-44; Olivier Guillaume, Jean-Claude Liger, and Régis de Valence, "Les propylées sur la rue principale," *BEFEO* LXVIII (1980), 7-9, pls. IV, V.

[66] Bernard, "Traditions orientales," 249-57; idem, *Fouilles d'Aï Khanoum* I, 114-20.

[67] Bernard, *Fouilles d'Aï Khanoum* I, 32, 119 f.; Bernard, "Chapiteaux corinthiens hellénistiques d'Asie centrale découverts à Aï Khanoum," *Syria* XLV (1968), 111-51.

[68] Bernard, *Fouilles d'Aï Khanoum* I, 19-21, 28-31, figs. 1, 4, 5.

[69] Ibid., 119 f.

Greek colonization, suggesting that they derived from Iranian prototypes. He concludes that though the plan of the palace is related to those of the palaces at Susa and Babylon, the architectural decoration is almost exclusively Greek.[70]

In the northern part of the palace, a large Doric court gives access to a treasury, which consists of a series of narrow rooms arranged perpendicularly around a courtyard. The treasury is related in form to the Achaemenid treasuries at Persepolis and at Altyn in Bactria, as well as to the treasury at Nysa, the first Parthian capital. The finds in the treasury demonstrate the ties of Aï Khanoum to both Greece and India. One of the rooms apparently housed a Greek library, and the accounts and records of contents of the jars containing coins, incense, and olive oil were written in Greek. Unworked semiprecious stones must have come largely from the Hindu Kush, and a shell plate with inlays in semiprecious stones must have come from India.[71]

Thus the plan, the architectural details, and the finds from the palace at Aï Khanoum show a mixture of Greek and non-Greek, or oriental, elements. The grandiosity of the building also sets it apart from Greek palaces, and Bernard suggests that the palace at Aï Khanoum is a creation of the Greek architects of the Orient, probably modelled on the royal residences of the Seleucids and the Lagids.[72]

The excavators suggest that the placement of the propylaia at the point where a street runs perpendicularly from the main street to the lower part of the city—which included the palace, the gymnasium, the heroon of Kinéas, and the mausoleum—may have been dictated in part by a desire to restrict access to these buildings, particularly the palace. They further suggest that a policy of restricted access might have operated in favor of the Greeks and of the local aristocracy on whom the Greeks would have depended for support.[73]

Other buildings at Aï Khanoum appear more purely Greek in type. In its earliest phase, the heroon of Kinéas had a plan based on the plans of simple Macedonian tombs. It later took the form of a simple Greek temple, with a naos fronted by a pronaos with columns *in antis*.[74] The theater appears to belong to the normal Hellenistic theater type, though the raised loges are somewhat unusual;[75] and a fountain of Greek type built on the banks of the Oxus in about the middle of the third century B.C. has also been discovered.[76] Finally, the gymnasium seems to resemble the gymnasia of the Greek world, though a large rotunda of unknown purpose belonging to the second phase is unusual. The excavators suggest that buildings like this might have served as a model for the "round temple" at Nysa.[77] Both the gymnasium and the theater are larger than would have been necessary to accommodate the inhabitants of Aï Khanoum, and Bernard suggests that both were designed to serve in addition the population of the entire territory. He further notes that the buildings of Greek form are associated with specifically Greek institutions.[78]

Thus the civic architecture of Aï Khanoum shows a mixture of Greek and oriental forms, with Greek forms predominating. The two temples so far discovered, on the other hand, utilize forms derived from Mesopotamia, and the third religious structure, a simple podium, is probably derived from Achaemenid traditions.

Temple à Redans

The *temple à redans*[79] was set within a sanctuary along the main north-south road of Aï Khanoum. The *temple à redans* proper was preceded by a slightly larger temple (phase V) of a similar but less elaborate plan (figs. 18, 19). The east side of the temple of phase V, which was the first on the site, was set directly on a natural bed of river pebbles, but an artificial terrace of pebbles 1.20 meters high was laid to support the west side. The building is

[70] Bernard, "Traditions orientales," 249-57.

[71] Bernard, *CRAI* (1978), 444-60, figs. 14-20; Bernard and Rapin, *BEFEO* LXVIII (1980), 15-38. The Greek inscriptions are discussed by Rapin, "Les inscriptions économiques de la trésorerie hellénistique d'Aï Khanoum (Afghanistan)," *BCH* CVII (1983), 315-72.

[72] Bernard, *Fouilles d'Aï Khanoum* I, 114; idem, *CRAI* (1978), 444-46.

[73] Guillaume, Liger, and de Valence, *BEFEO* LXVIII (1980), 7. Cf. the vaguer statement in Guillaume, *Fouilles d'Aï Khanoum* II: *Les propylées de la rue principale* (Paris, 1983), 1.

[74] Bernard, *Fouilles d'Aï Khanoum* I, 85-102, 115.

[75] Bernard, *CRAI* (1976), 314-22, figs. 19-21; idem, *CRAI*

(1978), 429-41, figs. 5-10.

[76] Bernard, *CRAI* (1976), 307-313, figs. 14-18; idem, *CRAI* (1978), 429; P. Leriche and J. Thoraval, "La fontaine du rempart de l'Oxus à Aï Khanoum," *Syria* LVI (1979), 171-205.

[77] Bernard, *CRAI* (1978), 421-29, figs. 2-4; the round building is discussed on pp. 427 f., fig. 4. Serge Veuve and Jean-Claude Liger, "Le Gymnase," *BEFEO* LXVIII (1980), 5 f.

[78] Bernard, "Problèmes d'histoire coloniale grecque," 113 f., 117.; idem, "Traditions Orientales," 245.

[79] In Francfort, *Fouilles d'Aï Khanoum* III, the temple is called the *temple à niches indentées*. I shall retain the original term, *temple à redans*, which has passed into the literature.

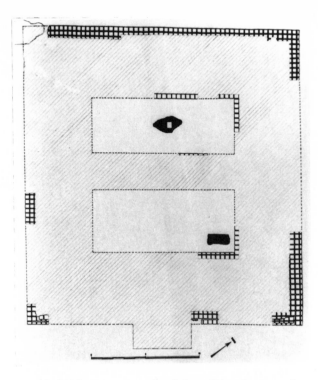

18. Aï Khanoum, temple of phase V (predecessor of
temple à redans), plan.

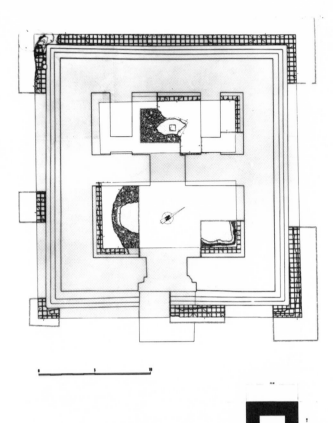

19. Aï Khanoum, *temple à redans*, phase IV and earlier temple
(phase V) superimposed.

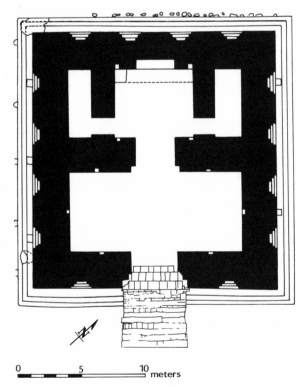

20. Aï Khanoum, *temple à redans*, phase IV, plan.

almost square; the north side is 24.50 meters long, the south 24.40 meters, the east 23.80 meters, the west 23.50 meters. The unusual thickness of the walls (5.57 meters on the north and west, 6 meters on the east) suggested to the excavators that here, as in the later temple, the wall was surrounded by a stepped crepis. Soundings have shown that the interior consisted simply of an antecella and a cella, each of which occupied the entire interior width of the building (12.10 meters); the cella was 4.60 meters deep. Thus the plan is like that of the later building, except that in the later phases the cella was flanked by two sacristies. The remains of the floors of beaten earth found in both the cella and the antecella are at a level more than one meter higher than the ground level outside, confirming that this temple, like the later one, must have been approached by steps. In the center of the cella stood an

21. Aï Khanoum, *temple à redans*, east facade, phase with platform covering stepped podium.

altar of unbaked bricks, 0.60 meters on a side and 0.60 meters high, with traces of ashes on top. This altar in turn enclosed an earlier, smaller one, 0.40 meters on a side.[80]

The simple plan of this temple and its almost square form recall the form of Temple A at Assur, the original building of which is dated by the excavators to the Neo-Babylonian period (fig. 66). That temple, 18 meters wide and 19 meters deep, was also divided into a cella and an antecella of the same width; but it differed from the temple of phase V at Aï Khanoum in that the outside walls were decorated on the outside with projections and recesses, in the Babylonian tradition.[81] The outer walls of the temple of Phase V at Aï Khanoum were apparently smooth. The other main difference between true Babylonian temples and the earliest

phase of the temple at Aï Khanoum is that Babylonian temples have a cult niche in the center of the rear wall of the cella, whereas the sounding suggests that at Aï Khanoum the rear wall was straight.

The date of this first temple at Aï Khanoum can be determined mainly by working backward from the dates of the various phases of the temple that replaced it, although the pottery from the fill does show that the building was constructed during the Greek period. Bernard has tentatively dated the temple of phase V to the beginning of the third or perhaps even to the last quarter of the fourth century B.C.[82]

The temple of phase V was replaced by another, the *temple à redans*, which retained the same form, with slight modifications and repairs, through three successive states (IV, III, II) (figs. 19-25). The

[80] Bernard, *CRAI* (1971), 414-25, figs. 18-21.
[81] Haller, *Heiligtümer*, 81.

[82] Bernard, *CRAI* (1971), 429 f.

22. Aï Khanoum, *temple à redans*, view from southeast, phase with platform covering stepped podium.

temple à redans, like the earlier building, was oriented to the southeast, in accord with the street plan. Its plan was essentially square, though the north and south sides (22.40 and 22.60 meters, respectively) were slightly longer than the east and west sides (21.70 and 21.75 meters, respectively). The temple rested on a crepis of three steps, which were whitewashed. The thick walls (2.80 meters) of the temple proper were decorated with an evenly spaced series of recesses with triple indentations, two on the front of the building and four on each of the other three sides. The walls consisted of mud brick, strengthened with a wooden framework of vertical and horizontal beams, and were probably topped with a double cornice of baked bricks, the remains of which were found in the fill on the north, east, and south sides. The building was approached on the east side by a stair five meters wide, resting on foundations of unbaked bricks, and its interior was 1.70 meters above the level of the ground. On the lower six of the ten steps are the remains of joints in lime mortar, in which was set a revetment of baked bricks. The entrance, 3.60 meters wide, was set in the center of the east side and shows traces of arrangements for closing the door.[83]

The interior, like that of the temple of phase V, was divided into an antecella that occupied the whole interior width and a cella. In this and the succeeding phases, however, the cella was flanked by two narrower rooms (sacristies?), each accessible from the cella. The door of the cella, on axis, was a bit narrower than the entrance door (3.05 meters wide) and had no arrangements for closing. In the

[83] Bernard, *CRAI* (1969), 327-34; idem, *CRAI* (1971), 425-27, figs. 17, 18, 22-24.

center of the rear wall was a relatively shallow (0.75 meters) rectangular niche, as in Babylonian temples, and a bench 1.07 meters wide and made of unbaked bricks ran along the rear wall.[84] The temple apparently stood without a cult statue for some years.

At some stage in the life of the *temple à redans*, three bases of unbaked brick were set against the wall of the front room beside the door to the cella. It is not clear from the preliminary reports whether these belong to the first state of the building;[85] since they do not appear in the plan in *CRAI* 1971 (417, fig. 17), it is probable that they do not. These bases supported two statues of clay and one of stucco. Francfort suggests on the basis of remains of bronze, wood, and nails found around the south base that that statue was set in a frame or *naiskos*.[86]

On and within the crepis of baked brick that surrounds the building were placed objects used in the cult rites. Six bases of unbaked brick stood on the upper step of the crepis: one in the center of the rear (west) side; three on the south side, one in front of each of the corner recesses and one between the two central recesses; and two on the north side, one in front of the recess at the west end of the wall and another against the wall between the two easternmost recesses. These bases have the form of a truncated pyramid, 0.40-0.60 meters on a side at the base, and ca. 0.30 meters high. The fact that a depression for ashes survives on the best preserved one—that in the middle of the south side—shows that they were altars. Two phases of construction of the bases are visible.[87] Already during phase IV, libation vessels of a local, non-Greek form were buried in the crepis at the rear of the temple; there were thirty-two of these vessels in all (figs. 23, 24). This rite continued throughout the life of the temple, as is shown by the fact that vases were also buried in the platform that was built around the crepis during phase II.[88] The possible significance of the rites represented by the deposit of these vases will be discussed below.

The temple was set in a precinct ca. 60 meters on a side. Bases in unbaked brick were found in the courtyard, on various floors belonging to phase IV. One of these, set against the northeast corner of the temple, was quite large—ca. 4 meters long and 1.10 meters wide on the north side, 1.60 meters long and

0.50 meters wide on the east side. The excavators suggest that it probably had two steps but that the top was subsequently removed. In front of the east facade, about 4 meters from the southeast corner, stood a row of three bases. They are preserved up to 0.40 meters in height; their dimensions are 1 x 1 meters; 1 x 0.95 meters; and 0.90 x 1.15 meters. A fourth and smaller one (0.70 x 0.50 meters) is located 2.50 meters to the north of this row and seven meters from the facade. These bases might have been either altars or offering tables.

In the next stage, phase III, the level of the courtyard was raised by a fill that sloped from ca. 0.50 meters high at the foot of the east facade of the temple to a shallow covering 0.05 meters deep on the west side of the temple; this declivity was created to allow rainwater to run off. Raising the level of the courtyard in turn brought about modifications in the facade: the first step of the crepis was covered for a large part of the facade, and the bases constructed during the previous phase in front of the southeast corner of the temple were cut down to the level of the new fill, which in any case almost covered them. A new access stair of ten steps was built above the old one. Some sort of repair was made to the upper part of the south side of the temple; the supports for the necessary scaffolding were set into the top step of the crepis.[89] The interior arrangements were not greatly changed, though apparently during this phase benches in unbaked bricks were added along the side walls of the cella.[90] The exterior changes had little effect on the appearance of the temple.

In the following phase, phase II (fig. 25), which was probably the last in the life of the temple as a religious edifice, considerable changes were made. A massive platform in unbaked brick was built around the temple, covering the crepis of the two preceding phases; and a new means of access, either a stair or a ramp, was constructed. The stone steps of the preceding phase were reused in this construction. This platform suffered heavy wear in spite of repeated rebuildings, thus indicating the relatively long duration of this phase. A dentil cornice in baked bricks apparently adorned the top of this platform and a similar cornice crowned the building.[91] The level was hardly raised in comparison to the floors of the previous stage, perhaps indicating

---

[84] Bernard, *CRAI* (1969), 335 f., fig. 14; idem, *CRAI* (1970), 322; idem, *CRAI* (1971), 426, plan on p. 417, fig. 17.

[85] Bernard, *CRAI* (1969), 329-33, 344.

[86] Ibid., 344 f., figs. 19, 20; Francfort, *Fouilles d'Aï Khanoum* III, 110.

[87] Bernard, *CRAI* (1971), 426, fig. 23.

[88] Bernard, *CRAI* (1970), 327-30; idem, *CRAI* (1971), 427.

[89] Bernard, *CRAI* (1971), 427-29, fig. 23.

[90] Bernard, *CRAI* (1970), 322.

[91] Bernard, *CRAI* (1969), 346-49, figs. 9-11, 23.

23. Aï Khanoum, *temple à redans*, west (rear) face, with vases buried at foot of stepped podium.

24. Aï Khanoum, *temple à redans*, west, detail.

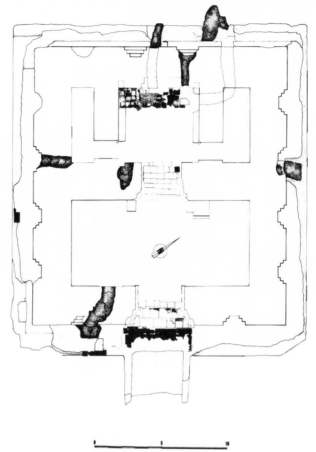

25. Aï Khanoum, *temple à redans*, phase II.

that an attempt was made to maintain the floor level of the courtyard.

Modifications were made also to the cella. In this phase, for the first time, arrangements were apparently made for the installation of a cult statue. The rear bench of phase IV of the temple was covered with another bench, this one in baked bricks, 0.80 meters high and 1.40 meters deep. A large rectangular cavity near the center reinforced with masonry of pebbles and lime mortar must have supported something heavy, probably a cult statue. Near the southwest corner of this base was a smaller cavity for a statue of clay or stucco, which had disappeared before the final fire.[92] Columns may also have been added to the cella during this period. One stone base of Attic-Ionic type, perhaps reused, was found near the west bench; it was probably not *in situ*. A wooden Ionic capital reused as a step in the final phase of the building was found in front of the south sacristy. The capital is elongated and shows traits characteristic of the Ionic capitals of the Orient, as at Ikaros, Nysa, and the early phases of Palmyra.[93] If this column base and capital came originally from the temple, it would mean that Greek architectural elements had been added to a building of Mesopotamian form. Since no traces of interior supports remain from the earlier phases, columns cannot have been necessary for support. Perhaps, as Francfort suggests, the columns supported a canopy over the cult statue.[94]

The fragments of a cult statue, in marble, represent exclusively hands and feet. The statue must have been colossal, two to three times life size. A fragment of the left hand shows that the fingers were bent around an added object (a scepter?); only small fragments of the right hand remain. The surviving part of the left foot, 0.27 meters long, is cut smoothly at the back, which suggests that the statue was acrolithic, with the other parts made in another material, probably clay. The foot is shod in a sandal of Greek type, decorated with a winged thunderbolt. Given the dimensions of the cella, the statue was probably seated. Since the thunderbolt on the sandals is an attribute of Zeus, Bernard has suggested that the statue might have represented Zeus enthroned, as seen in Greco-Bactrian and

---

[92] Ibid., 329, fig. 14; Bernard, *CRAI* (1970), 322; idem, *CRAI* (1971), 429.

[93] Bernard, *CRAI* (1969), 349-52, figs. 24, 25.

[94] Francfort, *Fouilles d'Aï Khanoum* III, 107, states only that the capital came from someplace in the sanctuary. For the possible original use of the capital, see p. 109.

Greco-Indian coins, with a scepter in his left hand and a winged Nike on his right.[95] The excellent modeling and finish suggest Greek workmanship. The niche behind the statue was perhaps decorated with a painting on cloth glued to gilded wood, but the surviving portions of the painting are too fragmentary to allow a reconstruction. Parts of a frieze of walking lions remain, and as Francfort points out, this is an old oriental motif. Considerable remains of the temple furnishings were found, although it is not always possible to determine the contents of individual rooms, due to the chaotic state of the debris left by the pillagers, nor to be absolutely certain that objects found in the disturbed layers came originally from the temple rather than from another part of the sanctuary. The temple apparently contained several large pieces of furniture in wood with fittings of ivory and bronze. Bronze plaques were also found, and the presence of small objects in ivory, gold rosettes, and bits of gold leaf shows the richness of the temple's contents.[96]

The dating of phases III and II is based on coin evidence. A coin of Seleukos I found in the fill under the floor of phase III indicates that the floor is contemporary with or later than his reign, and a coin of Diodotos II found in the masonry of the platform of phase II dates this phase to his reign (248-235 B.C.) or later. Therefore, the *temple à redans* (phase IV) must have been constructed in the first half of the third century, and the modifications of phase II should be dated in the second half of that century.[97] This chronology, proposed in 1971, may perhaps need to be modified in the light of Gardin's revised ceramic chronology of 1974.[98]

The exact sequence of events leading to the final destruction of the *temple à redans* and its sanctuary is uncertain. It has been assumed on the basis of the discovery in the temple of such mundane objects as storage jars and mortars that phase II marks the end of the life of the sanctuary as such, and that during the following period of squatter occupation the temple was deconsecrated and turned into a storeroom before being destroyed by fire, probably during the first century B.C.[99] This analysis is based on the assumption that the temple was sacked twice: first by the post-Greek occupants of the site, and later by the people who put an end to the life of the

city. Francfort has noted that the destruction of the cult statue can be attributed with certainty to the post-Greek inhabitants, and he therefore raises the possibility of the continuation of a local cult after the disappearance of the Greek statue, until the final fire.[100]

The *temple à redans* was set in a sanctuary in which seven levels have been identified, the seventh being virgin soil and the first being the surface of the archaeological level. The five phases of the temple have so far not been coordinated with the seven phases of the sanctuary, at least in published works.[101]

I shall not discuss the sanctuary in detail, since its form is not relevant to my purposes, but shall concentrate on those elements that are indicative of cultural origins and can shed light on cult practices. The sanctuary was roughly 60 meters on a side. Coin evidence indicates that it was not founded before the reign of Antiochos I. From its earliest phase it included a small side chapel, which was originally built on the south side of the precinct but was later transferred to the north side. The original south chapel was small and rectangular in plan (7.60 x 5 meters); it had a small cella and a vestibule with two wooden columns that rested on stone bases of the Achaemenid plinth and torus type. The chapel on the north side, which was probably built considerably later, had a plan like that of the earliest form of the heroon of Kinéas—a reversed T with a vestibule wider than the cella. Two column bases of the Attic-Ionic type stood in its cella. This plan, which according to Bernard is based on a Macedonian tomb type, thus lasted throughout the whole history of the city; it was apparently used first for funerary and later for religious architecture.[102] The interior portico of the sanctuary courtyard appears to show a mixture of Greek and oriental column bases, with oriental predominating in the present state of the excavations. A four-columned portico on the south side has two anta bases of Greek type and one column base of Achaemenid type, probably reused; and a portico along the southern enclosure wall, probably of late date, also uses column bases of oriental type, a torus on a square plinth.[103] Thus the architectural character of the sanctuary was mixed, as in the administrative

---

[95] Bernard, *CRAI* (1969), 338-41, figs. 15, 16.
[96] Francfort, *Fouilles d'Aï Khanoum* III, 32-34, 107-111.
[97] Bernard, *CRAI* (1971), 429 f.
[98] J.-Cl. Gardin, *CRAI* (1975), 193-95.
[99] Bernard, *CRAI* (1969), 352-55; idem, *CRAI* (1970), 327; idem, *CRAI* (1971), 429.

[100] Francfort, *Fouilles d'Aï Khanoum* III, 125.
[101] See Gardin, *CRAI* (1975), 193-95, for the ceramic chronology and its coordination with the levels of the sanctuary.
[102] Bernard, *CRAI* (1974), 295-298, figs. 8-11.
[103] Bernard, *CRAI* (1970), 333, figs. 24-26, 28.

quarter. An open water channel ran along the south side of the sanctuary from east to west. This channel was fed by another, which ran along the main road.[104]

Since no inscriptions have been found, the identity of the deity worshipped in the sanctuary remains conjectural. It is possible to make some suggestions based on the fragments of the cult statue and on the traces of cult installations in the temple and the sanctuary, but the evidence is incomplete and to some extent contradictory. The fact that the surviving foot of the cult statue is clad in a sandal decorated with a winged thunderbolt would suggest that the god is Zeus, but the oriental architecture of the temple seems inappropriate for a purely Greek deity. Therefore, Bernard has tentatively suggested that the deity might have been Zeus-Ahuramazda, as in Commagene. He has also suggested that the practice of making libations in the earth around the base of the temple and then burying the vases used for these libations in the crepis (later in the platform) around the temple seems suitable for a chthonic deity rather than for Zeus or Zeus-Ahuramazda.[105] Francfort points out that since this rite is unknown both in Greece and in the Orient, it is probably local. He tentatively suggests that the temple may have been dedicated to one or more local divinities whose relationship to the deity represented by the cult statue (of Zeus?) remains to be elucidated.[106] Again, the presence of an open water channel running along the south side of the sanctuary seems to show that water was more important here than in the usual Greek cult. The presence of a secondary chapel makes it possible to suggest tentatively the presence of a cult of Anahita, the goddess of living water, according to Bernard.[107] There is, however, no solid evidence that a goddess was worshipped in the sanctuary. The original provenance of the gilt silver plaque of Cybele found under the late floor of the south sacristy of the temple is uncertain, and therefore the plaque cannot be used in the interpretation of the cult.[108]

Other cult installations are even less enlightening. The presence of altars built against the walls of the temples and of altars or offering tables in the courtyard allows one to say that sacrifices were offered, not to specify the nature of those sacrifices.

Also in the area of the sanctuary approximately forty small limestone pedestals were found; twelve came from the temple, the others from the court or from the rooms around it. These bases belong to five types, including one in the form of an oriental column base—a torus on a stepped plinth—and another in the form of a miniature Attic-Ionic base. Here again both Greek and oriental forms are represented. The use of these pedestals, which have also been found elsewhere in Afghanistan, is unknown, but the fact that they were found in a sanctuary suggests that they had some cult function, perhaps as supports for thymiateria.[109]

Thus, the evidence for the form of worship and the identity of the deity housed in the temple is inconclusive and in part contradictory. It is in any case clear that the rites, and therefore probably also the deity, were not purely Greek.

EXTRAMURAL TEMPLE

The second temple so far discovered at Aï Khanoum, the *temple hors les murs* or "extramural temple," has been identified as a religious building largely on the basis of its striking similarity to the *temple à redans*, since no cult objects or inscriptions have been found. This building is located on the prolongation of the principal north-south street of the city, about 100 meters north of the main part of the city. As in the *temple à redans*, a later building encased an earlier one of similar form, though in this case the earlier building was smaller than the later one. So far only two phases have been identified, and no suggestions about possible dates have been made.

The later building, a rectangle 35.50 x 20.50 meters, rested on a three-stepped base 38.50 long by 26.50 meters wide and 1.80 meters high (fig. 26). The building faces approximately north and was approached by a flight of steps on that side. On the south, east, and west sides, the walls of the building proper were set at the edge of the podium, but they were slightly set back on the north side. The outer walls were decorated with a series of recesses and projections, as in the *temple à redans*, except that the recesses were simply rectangular, not stepped back. Around the roof was a cornice of baked bricks, ele-

---

[104] Bernard, *CRAI* (1974), 298, fig. 11; idem, *CRAI* (1970), 337.

[105] Bernard, *CRAI* (1974), 298; idem, *CRAI* (1970), 327-30.

[106] Francfort, *Fouilles d'Aï Khanoum* III, 125.

[107] Bernard, *CRAI* (1974), 298.

[108] Bernard, *CRAI* (1970), 339-47, fig. 31; Francfort, *Fouilles d'Aï Khanoum* III, 93-104, 124 f., pl. XLI. Bernard and Francfort have

discussed the north Syrian character of the plaque and the impossibility of identifying the goddess with any of those known from Central Asia.

[109] Bernard, *CRAI* (1970), 337-39, figs. 29, 30; Francfort, *Fouilles de Aï Khanoum* III, 81-84, pls. 28, 29, XXXVI, XXXVII.

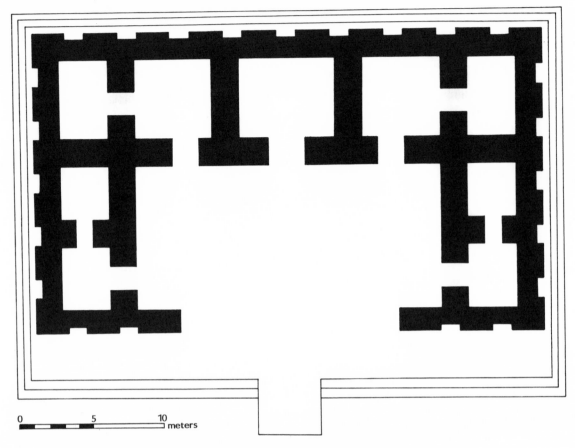

26. Aï Khanoum, extramural temple, later phase, plan.

ments of which were found especially on the south side of the building. The wide entrance on the north side led into a sort of rectangular *parvis* open to the sky, which was lined by rooms on the other three sides. The three main rooms on the south side were raised 0.50 meters above the courtyard and were approached by a flight of steps. Of these, the central room was the largest and was also the only one that did not communicate with another room; each of the rooms that flanked it opened both onto the courtyard and onto another narrower room in the corner of the building. On both the east and west sides were sets of two narrower rooms, the northernmost opening onto the courtyard, the more southern accessible only from the room in front of it. As in the *temple à redans*, the three-stepped podium was later encased in a platform of masonry. The earlier building (fig. 27) was slightly smaller, 20.15 x 15.80 meters. Like the later structure, it rested on a three-stepped podium of slightly

greater dimensions—23.80 x 20.80 meters—but still 1.80 meters high; the south (rear) side was reused in the later building. In this earlier structure a series of three rooms occupied the south side; as in the later structure, they were raised about 0.50 meters above the open courtyard onto which they faced. The central room was again the largest. In this phase there were no rooms on the east and west sides.[110]

As Bernard notes, a number of features point to the sacred character of these structures: their monumental character, the use of projections and recesses as exterior decoration, the limited number of rooms all facing onto a courtyard. Behind the building was a monumental wall, the interior face of which was also decorated with projections. The similarities to the *temple à redans* are also evident: the stepped podium, the decoration of the outer wall with projections and recesses, the use of a dentil cornice of baked bricks. Even though the plan dif-

---

[110] Bernard, *CRAI* (1974), 287-89, figs. 4, 5; idem, *CRAI* (1976), 303-306, fig. 11.

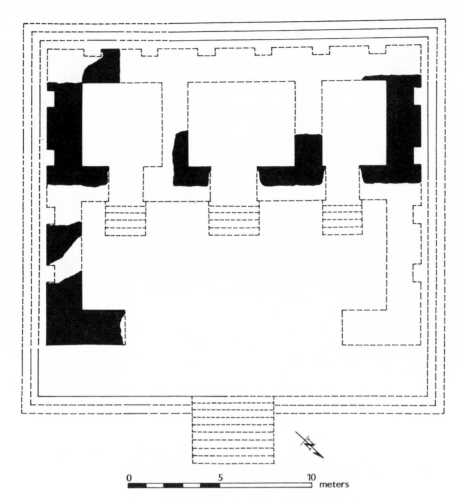

0   5   10
meters

27. Aï Khanoum, extramural temple, earlier phase, plan.

fers, the long rectangular *parvis* does recall the form of the roofed vestibule of the *temple à redans*. There is no evidence about the deity to whom the sanctuary was dedicated, but the triple cella arrangement suggests a triad. The non-Greek character of the building suggests also that the deity or deities are unlikely to have been purely Greek.

STEPPED PODIUM

A sounding at the southwest edge of the acropolis has revealed the existence of another large stepped podium set in the court of a sanctuary, but this podium does not support a building; rather it is sufficient in itself. This, as Bernard notes, recalls the statements of Herodotos (I.131f.) and Strabo

(XV.3.13f.) that the Persians worshipped their gods in the open air.[111] A podium that does not support a building also appears at Bard-è Néchandeh and may date originally to the Achaemenid period.[112] Soviet archaeologists have found a large square (ca. 21 meters on a side), three-stepped platform at a site called Pačmek Tepe in the valley of the Surkan Darya, a tributary of the Oxus. This platform apparently supported only a light enclosure in pisé. Dated on the basis of its pottery to the Achaemenid period, it can be considered a cult structure perhaps influenced by the terraces and platforms of Achaemenid Iran.[113]

Thus the religious architecture of Aï Khanoum combines various oriental traditions. The plan and the exterior decoration are derived from Mesopo-

[111] Bernard, *CRAI* (1976), 306 f.

[112] Ghirshman, *Terrasses sacrées*, 15-28, figs. 7, 12-13.

[113] Bernard, *CRAI* (1976), 307 n. 16, referring to Sh. P. Pidaev, *Drevnjaja Bactrija* (Leningrad, 1974), 33-38, fig. 2.

tamian architecture, whereas the high podia and perhaps also the dentil courses are based on Achaemenid forms. Though the similarity of the plan of the *temple à redans* to a number of the Parthian period temples at Dura is striking, the chronological gap raises difficulties in assuming a common origin. The temples at Uruk and probably also at Babylon show that traditional architecture remained alive in Seleucid Babylonia, however. Bernard, accepting Ghirshman's dating for the early phases of the temples at Masjid-i Solaiman, suggests Iran as an intermediate point between the Seleucid temples of Babylonia and Aï Khanoum. As he notes, however, Masjid-i Solaiman is located at the western edge of the Iranian plateau, so it is possible that the appearance of Mesopotamian forms there represents a local phenomenon. The reason for the choice of essentially Mesopotamian forms for the temples at Aï Khanoum remains uncertain. Bernard states that though the podium on the acropolis might have been intended for the indigenous troops of the garrison, and the extramural temple might have housed a strictly local cult, Greeks must have worshipped in the *temple à redans*. He suggests the possibility that a substantial number of the colonists came from Mesopotamia.[114]

That the temples of Aï Khanoum may represent a specifically Bactrian development is suggested by their similarity to the temple attributed to the Dioscuri at the site of Dilberdjin, located at the northern edge of the oasis of Bactria.[115] This building may date in its original form to the end of the Greco-Bactrian occupation of the site (fig. 28). Constructed in pisé, it is set at the back of a walled enclosure open to the sky. The temple proper, which measures 23 x 17.50 meters, has a deep entrance vestibule lined with benches and flanked by two rooms that open onto the court. The attribution to the Dioscuri is based on the subjects of the paintings that flank the entrance to the cella. Paintings in the vestibule, however, need not represent the principal deities of the temple. The cella, 10.50 x 5.50 meters in size, is parallel to the long axis of the building. A corridor that originally surrounded it on three sides was subsequently partially blocked to create two narrow sacristies flanking the cella and opening onto it. A low bench lines one wall of the corridor behind the cella. The temple underwent a number of rebuildings under the Kushans,

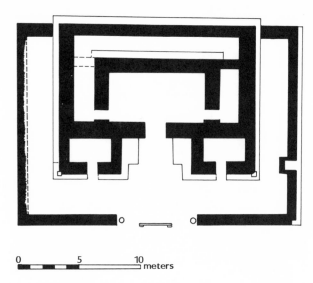

28. Dilberdjin, "Temple of the Dioscuri," phase I.

and a painting dated to the third century A.D. that represents Šiva and Parvati testifies to a radical change in cult.[116]

In its plan this unusual building recalls both of the temples of Aï Khanoum. With the creation of the sacristies, the cella area resembles that of the *temple à redans*, but the rectangular shape, the open court, and the two subsidiary rooms recall the extramural temple. The surrounding corridor of the original building is a feature seen also in the Great Temple at Masjid-i Solaiman (fig. 56),[117] and Kruglikova states that the plan also resembles that of the Temple of Heracles at the same site. The derivation of this unusual plan is unclear, but the temple may represent a Bactrian variant of the form derived ultimately from Mesopotamia.

Dura-Europos in the Seleucid Period

DURA-EUROPOS (fig. 29) was so thoroughly rebuilt during the period of Parthian control that very little evidence remains from the Seleucid period. The excavations have provided evidence for the existence of only two temples during the Seleucid period—that of Artemis and the temple that was later dedicated to Zeus Megistos. Thorough excavations in the numerous other temples of the city have revealed no trace of remains going back to the Hel-

[114] Bernard, "Problèmes d'histoire coloniale grecque," 119; idem, "Traditions orientales," 266-74.

[115] Irene Kruglikova, "Les fouilles de la mission soviéto-afghane sur la site de Dilberdjin en Bactriane (Afghanistan)," *CRAI* (1977),

[409] f., figs. 2-3.

[116] Ibid., 410-11, figs. 4-8.

[117] Ghirshman, *Terrasses sacrées*, 89, 103-108, pls. III, IV, VII, VIII. See also the section on Masjid-i Solaiman, and fig. 57.

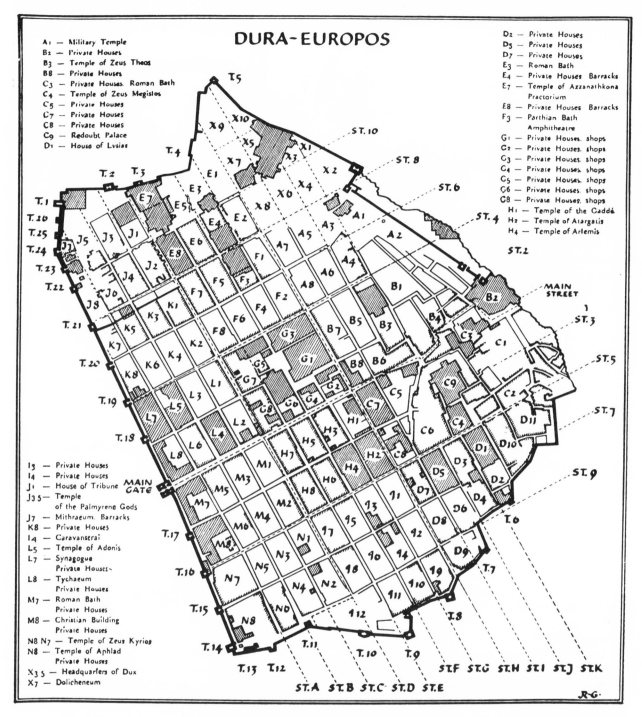

DURA-EUROPOS

A1 — Military Temple
B2 — Private Houses
B3 — Temple of Zeus Theos
B8 — Private Houses
C3 — Private Houses. Roman Bath
C4 — Temple of Zeus Megistos
C5 — Private Houses
C7 — Private Houses
C8 — Private Houses
C9 — Redoubt Palace
D1 — House of Lysias

D2 — Private Houses
D5 — Private Houses
D7 — Private Houses
E3 — Roman Bath
E4 — Private Houses Barracks
E7 — Temple of Azzanathkona
       Practorium
E8 — Private Houses Barracks
F3 — Parthian Bath
       Amphitheatre
G1 — Private Houses. shops
G2 — Private Houses. shops
G3 — Private Houses. shops
G4 — Private Houses. shops
G5 — Private Houses. shops
G6 — Private Houses. shops
G8 — Private Houses. shops
H1 — Temple of the Gaddé
H2 — Temple of Atargatis
H4 — Temple of Artemis

I3 — Private Houses
I4 — Private Houses
J1 — House of Tribune
J35 — Temple
       of the Palmyrene Gods
J7 — Mithraeum. Barracks
K8 — Private Houses
L4 — Caravanserai
L5 — Temple of Adonis
L7 — Synagogue
       Private Houses
L8 — Tychaeum
       Private Houses
M7 — Roman Bath
       Private Houses
M8 — Christian Building
       Private Houses
N8 N7 — Temple of Zeus Kyrios
N8 — Temple of Aphlad
       Private Houses
X35 — Headquarters of Dux
X7 — Dolicheneum

29. Dura-Europos, plan of city.

lenistic period. The discovery of only two religious structures that can be certainly attributed to the period of Seleucid control at Dura is perhaps surprising, though of course undue weight should not be given to negative evidence, since later rebuilding was so extensive in most areas of the city. In addition, it is possible, though perhaps not very likely, that other temples of the Hellenistic period were located in the unexcavated portions of the city. The Seleucid colony at Dura does not appear to have been particularly prosperous. F. E. Brown has pointed out, for example, that the agora buildings were completed in a truncated fashion, showing that the original scheme for the agora was over-ambitious.[118] He also states, in his unpublished manuscript on the Temple of Zeus Megistos, that most of the original building projects of the Hellenistic colony stood in an unfinished state throughout the later Hellenistic period. Thus it is possible that the two temples of which there are remains were sufficient for the population of the small colony, or that no more were built due to a lack of funds. In the present state of the excavations, Aï Khanoum provides a parallel.

Both the Temple of Artemis and that of Zeus Megistos were rebuilt so frequently that the remains of the earliest structures on the sites are exceedingly fragmentary and their reconstruction is uncertain. The earliest remains in the area of the Temple of Artemis can probably be attributed to the first Greek settlers. A date in the first years of the city's history is suggested by a number of factors: the pottery, the coin evidence, the style of the Doric columns, the divergence in the orientation from the street plan, and the difference of the plan from those of later Durene temples. The foundations of this phase suggest that there was "a long rectangular area oriented north and south, preceded by a vestibule to the south side and with other structures east and west of it" (fig. 30). The vestibule, placed at the southeast corner of the rectangular area, is preceded by two narrow L-shaped foundations, perhaps for columns and antae. Another section of foundations runs west from the vestibule, curving slightly to the south and thickening toward its west end. It is intersected just before its west end by a very small segment of another foundation running south. On the east side of the structure is a small portion of a foundation that

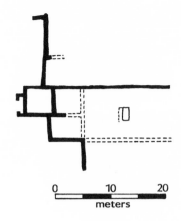

30. Dura-Europos, Temple of Artemis, plan of earliest remains.

would have intersected the east wall of the rectangular area. Brown notes that an early altar plinth corresponds in orientation with these walls and lies on the center line between the east and west walls of the rectangular area. The only remains of the superstructure are the drums and capitals of some Doric columns that were reused in the later constructions on the site. Their attribution to the earliest building is assured by the fact that some of the drums were built into two altars belonging to the construction that replaced the original precinct, and which itself was destroyed to make way for the temple of 40-32 B.C. Brown states that the foundations of the first structure are too flimsy to have supported a massive superstructure and therefore suggests an open peribolos, presumably colonnaded, with an altar in the center and a monumental propylon. He compares it to the Delphinium at Miletus.[119]

Presumably this precinct, like the later one on the site, was dedicated to Artemis, and she was probably associated with her brother Apollo, the patron of the Seleucid dynasty. An inscription found in the temple dated to A.D. 2 and recording a dedication by one Abidnerglos to Artemis and Apollo *archēgoi* ("founders"), shows that the Macedonian tradition was still vigorous after the Parthian conquest, since *archēgos* is a frequent epithet of Apollo in Seleucid inscriptions.[120] An association of Artemis with Apollo is additionally suggested by the fact that in the second period of construction there were two

---

[118] Frank E. Brown, *Dura Report* IX.1, 19-26; cf. Perkins, *Art*, 14.

[119] Brown, *Dura Report*, VI, 407-411, fig. 28, pl. XIX.1 and 2; Perkins, *Art*, 14. For the Delphinium at Miletus, see Gerhard Klei-

ner, *Die Ruinen von Milet* (Berlin, 1968), 35-38, fig. 17.

[120] H. T. Rowell and A. R. Bellinger, *Dura Report* III, 63 f., D161.

altars; probably also in the first period there was an altar to Apollo, as Brown suggests.[121]

The exceedingly fragmentary state of the remains of the earliest temple of Artemis obviously makes an analysis of its form difficult. Nonetheless, the use of Doric columns certainly suggests a Greek character, as does the probable placement of these columns in a propylon. The open courtyard, probably colonnaded, with an altar in the center, is also consistent with Greek architecture. The second phase of the temple, if Brown's restoration is correct, also has a Greek plan: that of a *naiskos* surrounded by a colonnade with two altars in front (fig. 31). This structure was torn down while still incomplete and replaced by the temple of 40-32 B.C., which has the oriental court plan typical of the temples of the Parthian period.[122] That the earliest religious structure of Dura should have had a Greek form is consistent with the Greek plan of the city as a whole.

In his unpublished manuscript on the excavations of the Temple of Zeus Megistos,[123] Brown describes the earliest form of the temple as having an almost square plan, 22.90 x 24.65 meters on the outside (fig. 32), with its entrance to the east. The rear (or western) portion was occupied by three naoi, the larger front portion by an open courtyard with a monumental altar on the axis of the entrance door and the central, and largest, naos (fig. 33). The court was entered through a Doric propylon, the proportions and form of which corresponded to those of the Hellenistic Doric order (figs. 34, 35). Brown restores the naoi with arched entrances, giving the appearance of iwans (figs. 36, 37). If this reconstruction is correct, the earliest form of the Temple of Zeus Megistos would have shown a mixture of Greek and oriental forms.

Brown's reconstruction rests entirely on the remains of the foundations of the early building that survived through successive rebuildings. One must ask, then, how much of the reconstruction is based on solid evidence. The massive ashlar foundations of the first structure appear to have survived almost intact; thus the reconstruction of an almost square structure, 22.90 x 24.65 meters on the outside, appears reasonable. In addition, a north-south cross wall (fig. 32, A) dividing the structure into two unequal portions survives; the eastern part, occupying two-thirds of the depth of the structure, is filled

31. Dura-Europos, *naiskos* of Artemis and Apollo, plan.

with a heavy paving; and remains of east-west cross walls (fig. 32, B and C) show that the western part was divided into a larger central and two smaller side rooms. In the courtyard it seems also that part of the edge of a north-south step (fig. 32, D) remains on the south side, and there are indications of a second step inside the first; this suggests that the central portion of the court was raised above the lateral portions, though all traces of pavement above foundation level have disappeared on the north side.

Although the remains of a north-south cross wall with two east-west cross walls behind it support Brown's proposed restoration of three naoi at the rear of the temple, his suggestion that they had arched entrances appears to be based on less reliable evidence. Brown notes, however, that the front (east) wall of the central naos is wider than other walls in the temple, and this wider wall extends into the side naoi by two feet of the module used in Hellenistic Dura (ca. 0.352 meters). This heavier foundation should have supported a thicker wall above, but Brown argues that the central naos

[121] Brown, *Dura Report* VI, 407 f., 410 f.

[122] Ibid., 397-408, fig. 27; Perkins, *Art*, 17 f.

[123] My description and analysis is based on Frank E. Brown's

manuscript, which he has graciously allowed me to use. A brief description and reconstruction of this earliest phase, also based on Brown's manuscript, are published in Perkins, *Art*, 15, pl. 4.

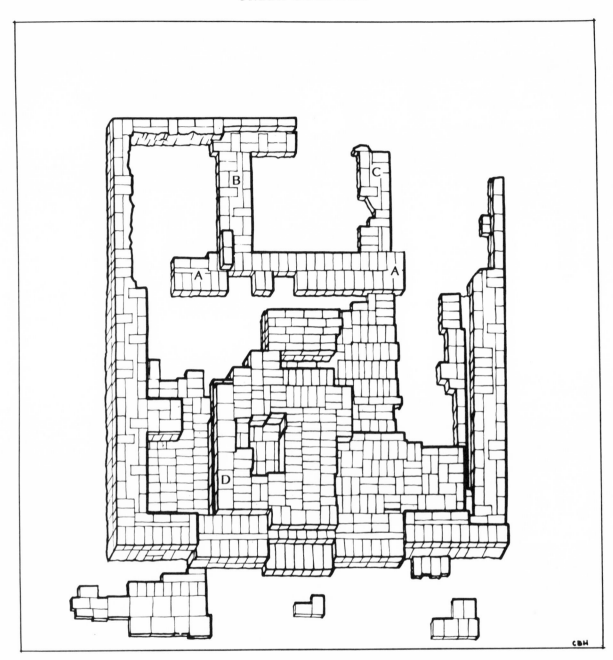

32. Dura-Europos, Temple of Zeus Megistos, plan of earliest remains.

could hardly have risen higher than the lateral ones, since only the front wall is heavier; thus he suggests that the strengthening of the wall implies that the opening to the central naos was arched. He also restores the side openings as arches, on the basis of the fact that the ends of the wider sections of the north-south cross wall coincide with the bottom step from the central to the side portions of the court and hence probably formed the edge of the openings of the naoi, openings too wide to be conveniently spanned by gypsum lintels. He arbitrarily gives the side openings a span equal to half that of the central arch. The heights of the openings and of the roof remain conjectural, as does the form of the

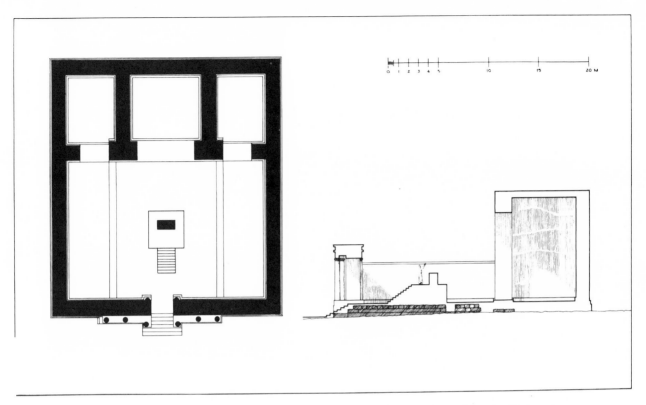

33. Dura-Europos, Temple of Zeus Megistos, period I, reconstructed plan and longitudinal section.

34. Dura-Europos, Temple of Zeus Megistos, reconstructed facade.

35. Dura-Europos, Temple of Zeus Megistos, period I,
Doric order.

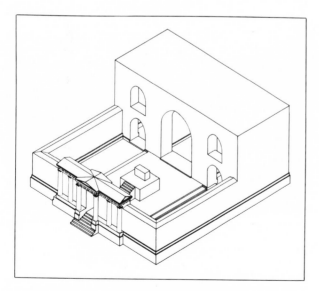

37. Dura-Europos, Temple of Zeus Megistos, period I,
isometric reconstruction.

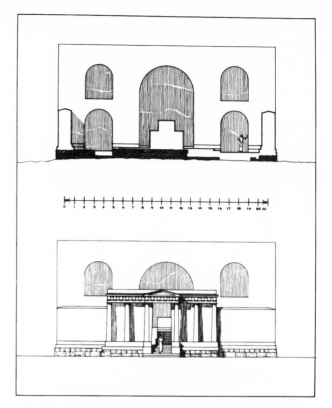

36. Dura-Europos, Temple of Zeus Megistos, period I,
transverse section.

roof, though in the absence of any evidence to the contrary, Brown assumes a timber roof.[124]

Brown argues that the massive foundation of solid masonry in the center of the courtyard must have been designed to support a considerable structure, all traces of which have vanished. His restoration of a monumental altar (figs. 33, 37) is based largely on inferences from the later history of the site. In the second period of the temple's construction, the position of the entrance was shifted slightly northward; Brown conjectures that the reason for this shift was to make the entrance coincide with a structure still standing in the courtyard on the axis of the old central naos, which no longer existed. He feels that the presence in the third and succeeding periods of a monumental altar, albeit in a different part of the building, supports the restoration of an altar in the courtyard of the first temple.

A number of elements of a small-scale Doric portico of gypsum, found reused in the building of the succeeding period, must belong to this early struc-

[124] Perkins, *Art*, 15, states that the naoi were barrel vaulted.

82

ture. These include forty-three fragments of drums of free-standing columns, four fragments of capitals, one cornice block, and one block with a section of a half-column worked on it. A number of columns were partly fluted and partly polygonal; these latter must have been set close against a wall. Therefore, Brown restores a propylon on the sections of foundation that project toward the east from the outer wall of the court (figs. 34, 37). He suggests that two columns flanked a staircase and that on either side of this central element two columns were set close against the precinct wall. The segment of an engaged column could belong to one of a pair of engaged columns framing the gate on the inside.

During the first building period, an isolated stone bicolumnar structure stood beside the southwest corner of the original temple precinct (fig. 38). Apparently the columns, unfinished, were Doric. By its position, in the center of Street K at its intersection with Street 5 (see fig. 29), it assumed the function of a gate leading not to the temple but to the Redoubt Palace; it served, that is, to mark the passage from the city proper to the isolated area on the spur of the hill that was occupied at first only by the Redoubt Palace and later also by the temple.

Apparently the temple was ruthlessly destroyed and replaced by quite a different structure (fig. 41). Brown dates this second temple to the second quarter of the first century B.C. and suggests that the destruction of the first building was connected with the capture of Dura by the Parthians in the late second century B.C. The dating of the first temple is based primarily on two types of evidence, neither conclusive. First, the sherds in the small section of undisturbed fill suggest a Hellenistic date, before the middle of the second century B.C. Second, the use of ashlar masonry, in simple fractions of a foot of ca. 0.352 meters, also suggests Hellenistic work; this masonry is most comparable to that of the second periods of the Redoubt and Citadel Palaces. The style of the Doric order is also consistent with a Hellenistic date. Further precision within this period depends on the analysis of the architectural forms and the cult of the original temple.

However the temple is reconstructed, the square shape and apparent division into a courtyard and three naoi are un-Greek, whereas the forms and proportions of the columns are those of the eastern Hellenistic Doric order. The hybrid character of the temple sets it apart from the earliest buildings of the

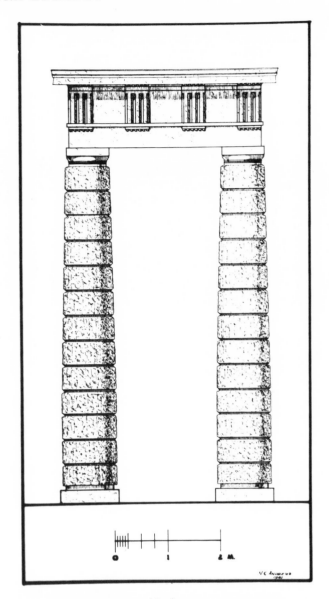

38. Dura-Europos, bicolumnar monument near the Temple of Zeus Megistos, reconstruction

colony, those of the agora,[125] which are purely Greek in type. Brown, followed by Perkins, suggests that the Temple of Zeus Megistos belongs to a second period of Seleucid construction, a period represented also by the second forms of the Redoubt and Citadel Palaces and characterized by an amalgam of Greek and eastern architectural traditions. Brown tentatively dates this second Seleucid period to the reign of Antiochos IV Epiphanes on the admittedly circumstantial grounds that the hybrid character of the buildings of this period is consistent with the Greco-Asiatic amalgam that, ac-

[125] Brown, *Dura Report* IX.1, 1-27; Perkins, *Art*, 13 f.

cording to some scholars, Antiochos IV wished to foster.[126]

Possible confirmation of a date in the reign of Antiochos IV Epiphanes is provided by inferences that can be drawn about the cult of the Period I temple. An inscription of A.D. 169/70 identifies the chief god as Zeus Megistos ("Greatest"), an epithet that corresponds to the Semitic Baalshamin.[127] The original temple might then have been dedicated to Zeus Olympios.[128] Welles has suggested that the epithet *Megistos* may be the equivalent of *Hypsistos* ("Highest"), or *Ouranios* ("Heavenly"), and that the temple might have been built as part of a religious movement sponsored by Antiochos IV Epiphanes[129] as part of an attempt to unite the diverse peoples of his empire under the worship of Zeus Olympios. Whether there was such an attempt is controversial.

It is clear that the earliest form of the Temple of Zeus Megistos utilized both Greek and non-Greek elements (the Doric order and the plan, respectively). The basic scheme, a roughly square plan with three rooms at the back of an open court, may have been derived from Babylonian architecture, but if so, it is much simplified, since Babylonian temples generally have a number of rooms around the court. An example is the Bit rēš at Uruk (fig. 4). Brown compares the heavy platform of the courtyard to the terraces of Achaemenid monumental architecture, as at Persepolis and Pasargadae,[130] and compares the complex as a whole to the platforms with triple iwans at Masjid-i Solaiman and Bard-è Néchandeh, as well as to two Parthian buildings at Assur—the so-called "Freitreppenbau" (fig. 70) and the temple built over the old Assur temple (figs. 72, 73). These comparisons need to be re-evaluated in the light of recent excavations and studies.

Ghirshman originally attributed the terraces at Masjid-i Solaiman and Bard-è Néchandeh, each supporting triple iwans, to the first Achaemenids;[131] thus they could have served as predecessors for the Seleucid Temple of Zeus Megistos at Dura. In the final report on the sites, however, he attributes the first terraces to the Achaemenid period, but suggests that each supported only a podium (with an adjacent room, in the case of Masjid-i Solaiman), not a triple-iwan structure.[132] Without the triple-iwan buildings, the similarity between the sacred structures in Elymais and the Dura Temple of Zeus Megistos vanishes. Both structures at Assur are later than the Seleucid period. The earliest form of the building over the Assur temple probably dates to the first century A.D. and had only two iwans; the third was added later, probably in the third century (figs. 72, 73).[133] The "Freitreppenbau" (fig. 70) is badly destroyed, and the reconstruction as a two-storied, triple-iwan structure (fig. 69) is based on very little evidence. (See the discussion in the section on Assur.) The Assur buildings, then, cannot serve as models for the reconstruction of the Seleucid Temple of Zeus Megistos at Dura. Brown also cites the Temple of Shamash at Hatra[134] as a more grandiose version of the triple-iwan scheme.

On the basis of these comparisons, Brown considered the Dura Temple of Zeus Megistos a Hellenistic adaptation of the old Iranian temple type, a bridge between Achaemenid and Parthian architectural forms. He argued that the Dura temple represented a more compact and organic form of the basic scheme of court and three iwans seen at Assur and Hatra, and that, as such, it was an example of the formation of a truly Seleucid architecture.

As restored by Brown, the Seleucid Temple of Zeus Megistos at Dura is indeed strikingly similar to the buildings of Assur and Hatra. But is the proposed restoration reliable? With the redating of Masjid-i Solaiman and Bard-è Néchandeh, all buildings with a row of three iwans are later than the Seleucid period. The one exception would be the fragmentary second citadel palace at Dura, if Brown's reconstruction is accepted.[135] The physical evidence for that reconstruction is slight, however,

[126] Rostovtzeff, *SEHHW* II, 703 f. Not all scholars agree with this assessment of the policies of Antiochos IV; this problem will be discussed below in the section on Antiochos IV.

[127] Welles, "Inscriptions," 139 f., no. 6. For a summary of opinions about the identification of the god, see Downey, *Stone and Plaster Sculpture*, 209.

[128] Eissfeldt, *Tempel und Kulte*, 120 f.

[129] Welles, "Gods," 54 f.

[130] Henri Frankfort, *The Art and Architecture of the Ancient Orient* (Baltimore, 1969), 218, fig. 110; David Stronach, *Pasargadae* (Oxford, 1978), 11-23, pls. 2-4.

[131] Ghirshman, "Masjid-i Solaiman. Résidence des premiers achéménides," *Syria* XXVII (1950), 205-220.

[132] Ghirshman, *Terrasses sacrées*, 14-21, 26-28, 55-70, plans I, III, pls. XLVI-XLVIII; Schippmann, *Feuerheiligtümer*, 243-48, 256-58.

[133] Andrae, *Partherstadt Assur*, 73-88; Colledge, *Parthian Art*, 47 f., fig. 18. This building will be discussed below in the section on Assur.

[134] Ghirshman, *Persian Art*, 36, fig. 50.

[135] Rostovtzeff, *Dura-Europos*, 46 f., fig. 9; Perkins, *Art*, 14 f., pl. 3. Cf. Downey, "Two Buildings at Dura-Europos and the Early History of the Iwan," *Mesopotamia* XX (1985), 111-129; idem, "The Citadel Palace at Dura-Europos," *Syria* LXIII (1986), 27-37.

so that it cannot be used to support a reconstruction of the Seleucid Temple of Zeus Megistos. Furthermore, with the exception of the restored citadel palace at Dura, all of the iwans known before the Sasanian period appear in sites further east: Seleucia on the Tigris (probably first century B.C.),[136] Assur,[137] Hatra (second century A.D.),[138] possibly Kuh-i Khwaja (second century B.C., according to Gullini; possibly Sasanian, according to Schlumberger and others),[139] and possibly Qal 'e-i Yazdigird (Parthian in date, but the presence of iwans is not certain.)[140] The origins of the iwan are obscure and controversial,[141] but it is somewhat difficult to accept the appearance of a new architectural form in a Greek colony of the Hellenistic period on the basis of such fragmentary evidence. If the naoi in the Temple of Zeus Megistos were timber roofed, as Brown assumes, then it seems possible that the openings were narrow enough to be spanned with lintels.

The Seleucid Temple of Zeus Megistos in some ways strongly resembles the two temples at Aï Khanoum, though there are numerous differences. The *temple à redans* at Aï Khanoum was roughly square in all phases of construction and was divided by a transverse wall into two approximately equal sections. The front portion was an antecella, and in the second and succeeding periods the rear section was divided into a central sanctuary and two subsidiary rooms (figs. 18-20). Thus the general scheme is similar to that of the Dura temple. At Dura, however, an open court, not an antecella, occupies roughly two-thirds of the depth of the structure. Furthermore, at Aï Khanoum, the two side rooms off the cella are relatively narrow and are accessible from the cella, an arrangement that char-

acterizes some of the temples of the Parthian period at Dura; in the early form of the Temple of Zeus Megistos, the side rooms were apparently independent naoi. The Seleucid Temple of Zeus Megistos is also closely related to the early form of the extramural temple at Aï Khanoum, which is likewise divided longitudinally into an open court and three naoi at the back; in this temple also the open court occupies roughly two-thirds of the structure. The extramural temple at Aï Khanoum, however, is rectangular rather than square (fig. 27).[142]

In its exterior appearance, the Dura temple differs drastically from those at Aï Khanoum. Both of the temples at Aï Khanoum are raised on heavy, stepped podia, perhaps derived from Achaemenid architecture.[143] This evidence for the continuation of Achaemenid traditions after the Greek conquest perhaps strengthens Brown's hypothesis that the unnecessarily heavy paving of the courtyard of the Temple of Zeus Megistos is derived from the terraces of Achaemenid architecture. Both the *temple à redans* in phases IV through II and the extramural temple in the two phases so far identified are decorated on the outside with projections and niches—complex, stepped niches in the *temple à redans*, a simple alternation of rectangular projections and recesses in the extramural temple. This type of decoration characterizes Mesopotamian sacred architecture, and the combination of the square plan with the type of exterior decoration clearly indicates the derivation of the temples at Aï Khanoum. The Temple of Zeus Megistos, on the other hand, is bounded by a wall of ashlar masonry and fronted with a Doric propylon. Thus, though the Dura structure does not resemble a Greek temple in plan, in its external appearance it would fit into a Greek

[136] Colledge, *Parthian Art*, 47 f.; Hopkins, *Topography*, 66 f., 77, 88-91, 95 f.

[137] Andrae, *Partherstadt Assur*, 2 f., 28-42, 81-86.

[138] Colledge, *Parthian Art*, 48. For the date, see Milik, *Dédicaces*, 360, 393, inscription no. 108.

[139] Gullini, *Architettura iranica*, 322-33. Gullini suggests that the form of the complex remained essentially the same from the second century B.C. to the end of the second or beginning of the third century A.D. Other scholars have doubted Gullini's dating and in particular his attribution of the iwans to the Parthian period. For example, Schlumberger suggests that the date of the complex should perhaps be lowered to the end of the Parthian or even the beginning of the Sasanian period (*L'Orient hellénisé*, 59). Klaus Schippmann also doubts Gullini's attribution of the earliest building (Stratum VI) to the Achaemenid period and suggests that it might instead represent a first phase of the Parthian building. He tentatively accepts a Parthian date, perhaps in the course of the second and first centuries B.C., for the building of Stratum V, which includes an entrance iwan (*Feuerheiligtümer*, 61-67). Ghirshman also suggests that the building attributed by Gullini to the Achaemenids should in-

stead belong to the Parthian period; this building has no iwan (*Terrasses sacrées*, 205).

[140] E. J. Keall, "Qal 'e-i Yazdigird: The Question of its Date," *Iran* XV (1977), 1-9.

[141] Schlumberger, *L'Orient hellénisé*, 186-88; Gullini, *Architettura iranica*, 326-33; Colledge, *Parthian Art*, 47 f.; E. J. Keall, "Some Thoughts on the Early Eyvan," in Dickran K. Kouymjian, ed., *Near Eastern Numismatics, Iconography, Epigraphy, and History: Studies in Honor of George C. Miles* (Beirut, 1974), 123-30.

[142] For a detailed discussion of the two buildings, see the section on Aï Khanoum. Bernard points out the similarity of the extramural temple at Aï Khanoum to the early form of the Temple of Zeus Megistos at Dura. In his estimation, they differ in that at Dura the temple proper consists only of three cellae, whereas at Aï Khanoum the *parvis* is integrated into the building ("Traditions orientales," 273; for his analysis of the religious architecture of Aï Khanoum, see pp. 266-74). It seems to me that the court at Dura and the *parvis* at Aï Khanoum fulfill similar functions, and that the buildings are equally integrated.

[143] Bernard, "Traditions orientales," 271.

city. The difference in materials—mud brick as opposed to cut stone—does not suffice to explain the differences between the Dura temple and those of Aï Khanoum. It is, after all, possible to build straight mud-brick walls and stone walls with niches; and the palace ("administrative quarter") at Aï Khanoum amply demonstrates the ability of the architects to design columns of Greek type.[144] The differences must thus represent a choice by the patrons. Paradoxically, the temples of a Greek colony in remote central Asia look Mesopotamian from the outside, while those of a Greek colony in Parapotamia look like Greek buildings. The existence, at almost the extreme ends of the Seleucid empire, of temples that combine in such diverse ways Greek, Achaemenid, and Mesopotamian elements bears witness to the complexity of cultures in this vast area.

The Cultural and Religious Policies of Antiochos IV Epiphanes

THE PAUCITY and fragmentary nature of the sources and the difficulties of their interpretation have led to the creation of conflicting pictures of the cultural and religious policies of Antiochos IV Epiphanes (175–164/63 B.C.). He is seen by some scholars as the champion of Hellenism, founding Greek colonies and establishing Greek institutions in existing oriental cities. According to one interpretation, he attempted to replace local cults with that of Zeus Olympios. Rostovtzeff and others suggest that he was trying to create a Greco-Oriental amalgam by his introduction of the cult of Zeus Olympios. Other scholars feel that Antiochos allowed considerable local autonomy in religious matters.

Part of the difficulty in establishing a clear picture of Antiochos' religious activity arises from the fact that much of our evidence is derived from Jerusalem, which was presumably a special case. The coin evidence, the other major source of informa-

tion, can be interpreted in diametrically opposed fashions.

Evidence for a policy of Hellenization on the part of Antiochos IV: Antiochos IV claimed to have founded a number of Greek cities in his empire. For scholars such as Tarn,[145] this means that he renewed the earlier policy of colonization in order to promote Hellenization. Tscherikower, however, notes that most of the names on the list are those of old cities, which therefore were simply refounded and were foundations only in the legal, formal sense.[146] As Will and others have noted, the "founding" of a Greek city on the site of an established, inhabited city, such as Babylon, could only mean the creation of a body of Greek citizens or of citizens who adopted Greek institutions within the existing oriental framework; it is impossible that all citizens would have become Greeks overnight.

The books of the Maccabees record the founding of two gymnasia in Jerusalem during the reign of Antiochos IV, one for non-Jews in Jerusalem at their request (I Macc. 1:13), the other by the high priest Jason, who also established an ephēbeion (II Macc. 4:9). This second passage also includes the ambiguous phrase τοὺς ἐν Ἱεροσολύμοις Ἀντιοχεῖς ἀναγράψαι, which Bickerman translates "to register the Antiochenes in Jerusalem" ("die Antiochener in Jerusalem aufzuzeichnen"). He suggests that these "Antiochenes in Jerusalem" would have constituted an organization of Hellenized citizens within the city.[147] Tscherikower maintained in 1927 that "those in Jerusalem" could only be understood as Hellenized Jews who called themselves Antiochenes, i.e., who wished to establish in Jerusalem a Greek polis named Antioch, an attempt that failed because of the revolt of the Maccabees.[148] Will seems to me to interpret Tscherikower's ideas too strongly as implying that Jason intended a rather radical Hellenization of the citizens of Jerusalem.[149]

In a more recent work, Tscherikower discusses the passage in II Maccabees in more detail. He

---

[144] Bernard and Le Berre, in Bernard, *Fouilles d'Aï Khanoum* I, 18-49; Bernard, "Chapiteaux corinthiens hellénistiques d'Asie centrale découverts à Aï Khanoum," *Syria* XLV (1968), 129-148; idem, "Traditions orientales," 246-57. See the discussion under Aï Khanoum.

[145] W. W. Tarn, *The Greeks in Bactria and India* (Cambridge, 1938), 183-88.

[146] Tscherikower, *Hellenistische Städtgründungen*, 176-78. For a summary of the problem, see Will, *Histoire* II, 261.

[147] Bickerman, *Der Gott der Makkabäer*, 59 n. 1. Bickerman discusses other interpretations of the phrase. His full discussion of the passage is on pp. 59-62. The English translation of *Der Gott der*

Makkabäer renders the phrase in II Maccabees 4:9 as "to enroll in Jerusalem a group known as the 'Antiochenes' " (Bickerman, *The God of the Maccabees*, trans. Horst R. Moehring [Leiden, 1979] 39).

[148] Tscherikower, *Hellenistische Städtgründungen*, 207. "Unter οἱ ἐν Ἱεροσολύμοις konnen natürlich keine anderen als hellenisierte Juden verstanden werden, die sich Antiocheer nennen, d.h. eine griechische Polis mit dem Namen Antiocheia errichten wollten."

[149] Will, *Histoire* II, 281 f.; on p. 282 he states that Tscherikower understands the passage in II Maccabees 4:9 as "faire de ce qui était à Jérusalem des Antiochéniens." His reference to Tscherikower (*Hellenistische Städtgründengen*, 161 f.) is incorrect, however.

translates the phrase in question as "register the people of Jerusalem as Antiochenes" and interprets it as meaning that "Jason received from Antiochus permission to convert Jerusalem into a Greek *polis* called Antioch." In registering the people of Jerusalem as Antiochenes, Jason would have drawn up a list of those people he deemed worthy of being citizens of the city of Antioch established at Jerusalem but would not have interfered with the right of the people to traditional forms of worship.[150]

The evidence for the events and the trends of cultural life in Mesopotamia during the reign of Antiochos IV Epiphanes is extremely sparse. We are forced to construct a picture of life in Mesopotamia during the period of Seleucid rule by using inscriptions, cuneiform tablets, and archaeological evidence of various dates, and thus it is hard to pin down the policy of any one ruler. Antiochos' interest in Babylon is suggested by the inscription naming him as the founder of the city—if the general assumption is correct that the city in question is in fact Babylon. Rostovtzeff in 1928 concluded on the basis of this and other evidence that "a new era in the history of Babylon and the other cities of Babylonia comes in with Antiochos Epiphanes," including a policy of restoration at Uruk.[151] The basis for this statement about Uruk is the number of Greek and Greek-Babylonian double names that appear in the documents. As McEwan notes, however, such names had already begun to appear during the reign of Antiochos II and increased during that of Antiochos III; there is thus no reason to attribute a policy of increased Hellenization at Uruk to Antiochos IV.[152]

Religious policies of Antiochos IV Epiphanes: There are numerous indications of the devotion of Antiochos IV Epiphanes to the cult of Zeus Olympios. He replaced the image of Apollo that had been used on the coins of Seleucid rulers during the previous century with a type of Olympian Zeus that he adopted from the coinage of Seleukos Nicator. Zeus, or the eagle, his usual attribute, also appears as a reverse type on the independent coinage of some cities of the Seleucid empire during the reign

of Antiochos IV; as the interpretation of these coins is controversial, I shall reserve discussion. In addition, Antiochos IV resumed work on the temple of the Olympian Zeus in Athens, which had been abandoned since the time of the Peisistratids.[153] Finally, he is said to have established the worship of the Olympian Zeus in the Temple of Jerusalem (II Macc. 6:2).

The devotion of Antiochos IV to Zeus Olympios seems undeniable, but interpretations of the events in Jerusalem and of the appearance of Zeus or an eagle as a type on independent coinage vary widely. Some scholars, among them Seyrig and Rostovtzeff, argue that Antiochos was trying to impose the cult of Olympian Zeus on the disparate populations of his empire in order to further Hellenization or in order to unite them in the worship of one god; others, like Bickerman, Tscherikower, and Will, suggest that the coins show the prevalence of local religion and that the events in Jerusalem were the result of an attempt to break a local revolt.[154]

Seyrig argues that Antiochos' work on the Temple of Zeus Olympios at Athens, his attempts to transform the cults at Jerusalem and Samaria into cults of Zeus, and his use of Zeus rather than Apollo as a reverse type on his coinage provide evidence that he was following a deliberate policy of replacing local cults by a cult of Zeus. He feels that the sudden appearance of Zeus as a reverse type on the coins of eight scattered cities bolsters this argument. He suggests that this "Jovian" politics makes sense, since almost all Syrians worship a celestial god; even though those gods have different names, there is a substantial unity of concept.[155] Bickerman, on the other hand, argued that the local coinage showed that cities continued their old religious traditions, and that the coins depict important local deities for the most part and images of Zeus are rare.[156]

The holy city of Hierapolis-Castabala in Cilicia is used as an argument both for and against the idea that Antiochos was attempting to replace local cults with that of Zeus Olympios. The goddess of the city, Perasia, is represented on the coins in Hellen-

[150] V. Tscherikower [Tcherikover], *Hellenistic Civilization and the Jews*, trans. S. Applebaum (Philadelphia, 1961), 161-66 and appendix III. The quotation is on p. 161.

[151] M.I. Rostovtzeff, *Cambridge Ancient History* VII (New York and Cambridge, 1928), 188 f. The inscription is discussed in the section on Babylon.

[152] McEwan, *Priest and Temple*, 195 f. Rostovtzeff, "Seleucid Babylonia," 90 f., attributes the beginnings of the policy of Hellenization at Uruk to Antiochos III. For further discussion of the subject, see under Uruk.

[153] Seyrig, "À propos du culte de Zeus à Séleucie," *Antiquités syriennes* III, 27-31 (*Syria* XX [1939], 296-300); Otto Mørkholm, *Studies in the Coinage of Antiochus IV of Syria*, Historisk-filosofiske Meddelelser udgivet af det Kongelige Videnskabernes Selbskab 40, no. 3 (Copenhagen, 1963), 16 f., 58 f.

[154] This view is also represented by Arthur Darby Nock, "The Roman Army and the Roman Religious Year," *Harvard Theological Review* XLV (1952), 208-211.

[155] Seyrig, *Antiquités syriennes* III, 27-31.

[156] Bickerman, *Institutions des Séleucides*, 232.

ized form, but the eagle is also an important coin type, either alone or under the throne of the goddess. Bickerman interprets the eagle as the bird of Hadad, though in *Der Gott der Makkabäer* he seems to suggest that the sanctuary at Castabala was secularized with the renaming of the city as Hierapolis.[157] Dupont-Sommer and Robert, on the other hand, suggest that the cult was indeed Hellenized by the Seleucids. They identify the eagle as the bird of (Olympian) Zeus and suggest the he was introduced as the paredros of the goddess, who had not previously had a consort, at the same time that the goddess was presented as a city goddess of Greek type.[158]

The interpretation of the events in Jerusalem is of course particularly difficult. Some scholars accept as accurate the statement of I Maccabees 1:41 that "the king wrote to all his kingdom that all must form one people and abandon their own traditions."[159] In this view, the establishment of a cult of Zeus Olympios in the Temple on the citadel in Jerusalem would be a manifestation of general political policy. It is also possible to interpret Antiochos' actions as a response to the Jewish revolt, however. In any case, it seems unlikely that the establishment of the cult of Zeus Olympios was the result of an attempt to force Hellenization on the population of Jerusalem. Bickerman has argued that the naming (προσονομάσαι) of the Temple in Jerusalem as that of Zeus Olympios does not mean the establishment of the cult of a new god, but rather that the hitherto anonymous god has now received the name of the god of the heavens. He further suggests that in any case the cult was not Greek, for the form of the sanctuary (which is poorly known) remained oriental and the cult was still apparently aniconic.[160] This interpretation is perhaps strengthened by the fact that the Syriac text of Maccabees gives the name of the god as "Baalshamin." Thus the temple would not have been a Hellenic sanctuary but a Syrian one, adapted to the needs of the military colonists of the Akra, most of whom would presumably have been Syro-Phoenician.[161]

Rostovtzeff suggests, largely on the basis of events in Jerusalem, that Antiochos was attempting an amalgamation of Greeks and Semites throughout his empire, to use "Greco-Semites" as a means of consolidating and unifying the empire. He argues that the introduction of the cult of Zeus Olympios was an important part of this process, since it represented "a synthesis of the leading religious ideas of his empire." He states that the god, though he bore a Greek name, was worshipped in temples of semi-oriental type and was represented in semi-oriental dress and with semi-oriental attributes.[162] His evidence for the dress and attributes, however, is not contemporary with the reign of Antiochos IV, but is drawn from the relief of the Temple of the Gaddé in Dura, carved in A.D. 159. Thus it appears that Rostovtzeff's assumption that Antiochos IV was deliberately trying to create a synthesis of Greek and Semitic elements in his empire by his introduction of the cult of Zeus Olympios in a particular form is largely based on the special case of Jerusalem, and on later and therefore suspect evidence.

The Seleucid temple of Zeus at Dura has also been interpreted as evidence for the propagation of the cult of Zeus Olympios by Antiochos IV Epiphanes by Welles.[163] Brown in his unpublished manuscript suggests dating the temple to the reign of Antiochos IV because he feels that its amalgam of Greek and Iranian forms is best understood as a reflection of an intensified policy of unification.[164] In view of the uncertainty about the date and original form of the Dura temple, however, these ideas must remain speculative.

The evidence, then, is inconclusive. That Antiochos IV had a special devotion to the cult of Zeus Olympios seems clear. It also seems that in some cases Antiochos introduced this cult alongside of or in substitution for earlier cults, but that the citizens of the Seleucid empire were for the most part free to worship their familiar deities according to their own rites. Only in Jerusalem was there an attempt to ban the traditional rituals.[165]

Dura-Europos in the Parthian and Roman Periods

THE INSCRIPTIONAL evidence suggests that there were two major bursts of temple building at Dura, the first lasting from about the middle of the first

[157] Ibid.; Bickerman, *Der Gott der Makkabäer*, 90.

[158] André Dupont-Sommer and Louis Robert, *La Déesse de Hiérapolis-Castabala (Cilicie)* (Bibliothèque archéologique et historique de l'Institut français d'archéologie d'Istanbul XVI) (Paris, 1964), 96-99.

[159] Will, *Histoire* II, 285, citing E. Mayer, W. Otto, and Abel.

[160] Bickerman, *Der Gott der Makkabäer*, 92-104; cf. the English translation, *The God of the Maccabees*, trans. Horst R. Moehring, 62-68.

[161] Will, *Histoire* II, 283-85; Tscherikower [Tcherikover], *Hellenistic Civilization and the Jews*, trans. S. Applebaum, 180-201.

[162] Rostovtzeff, *SEHHW* II, 703 f.

[163] Welles, "Gods," 54 f.; cf. Eissfeldt, *Tempel und Kulte*, 118-21.

[164] For a fuller discussion of Brown's views, see the section on Seleucid Dura.

[165] Tscherikower [Tcherikover], *Hellenistic Civilization and the Jews*, trans. S. Applebaum, 180-201.

century B.C. to about the middle of the first century A.D., and the second occurring in about the middle of the second century A.D.[166] With a few exceptions, the temples built at Dura during the periods of Parthian and Roman rule followed a court plan of Mesopotamian type, with a pronaos-naos unit normally oriented perpendicularly to the axis of the entrance and with a number of chapels around the court walls. Though the basic plan of the temples built during this time was the same, there were considerable variations in detail. It is hard to determine what factors affected the form of the buildings—date of construction, deity to whom the temple was dedicated (and therefore of course the rituals involved), clientele served by the temple. I shall first discuss the temples of Dura in roughly chronological order, beginning with the Temple of Artemis as the most thoroughly documented, and then deal with the relationships among the various buildings.

TEMPLE OF ARTEMIS

The evidence from the Temple of Artemis suggests that in this case at least there was a major change in temple type in about the middle of the first century B.C. A number of Doric capitals and column drums, some of the latter unfinished, were built into the walls of the temple constructed in approximately 40-32 B.C.; and two large altars, built in part of reused column drums of the same type, preceded the construction of this temple, although apparently by only a few years. Brown reconstructs the slightly earlier temple to which these altars belonged as a Doric *naiskos* fronted by the two altars and surrounded by a colonnade that enclosed the altars also (fig. 31). The evidence for this reconstruction is fairly slight, consisting of the bedding for the plinths of four Doric columns and a few fragments of three walls of an aedicula. Since some of the reused column drums, which presumably came from this phase of construction, were unfinished, Brown further suggests that this *naiskos* was never completed, but that its partially completed fabric was razed to allow for the construction of a new temple on an entirely different plan.[167] Even if the details of Brown's reconstruction are not accepted, the presence in the later building of reused Doric column drums and of altars that are not oriented

along the same lines as the later sanctuary suggests that the temple of 40-32 B.C. was preceded by another structure of a different type, and the number of Doric elements argues for an essentially Greek structure.

The temple that replaced the unfinished *naiskos* of Artemis and Apollo can be dated to approximately 40-32 B.C. on the basis of the date of an inscription on a column erected in 33/32 B.C. on the north side of the pronaos by Seleukos the *stratēgos*.[168] The building of this period consisted of a roughly square courtyard, within which was set a free-standing sanctuary unit (fig. 39). The court was entered through a porch on the east flanked by buttresses, and this entrance door lay on the same axis as the door to the sanctuary unit. The two monumental altars of the preceding period were respected, though they no longer lay on the axis of the sanctuary unit, but stood in front of it, to the right of the entrance. Only in the Roman period were they covered. Another altar was built in the court on the line between the entrance door and the sanctuary unit; this altar also was covered by pavement in the Roman period. The sanctuary unit, oriented at right angles to the entrance to the court, consisted of a pronaos and a naos flanked by two sacristies. Steps were placed in the pronaos some thirty to forty years after its construction, converting it into a *salle aux gradins*. The earliest dated inscription from the *salle aux gradins* falls in the year 7/6 B.C., the latest in A.D. 140/41.[169] The naos was paved with a succession of rammed earth floors, and in a final period with gypsum blocks. Underneath this last floor was a commonware jar filled with other jars containing ashes, bones of small animals and birds, and tiny ornaments, all probably the remnants of sacrifices. The jar was put into position too late in the life of the temple to qualify as a foundation deposit.

Already in its form of 40-32 B.C. the Temple of Artemis included a chapel of Aphrodite, which at that period consisted simply of a colonnade in front of the sanctuary unit.[170] At least one oikos (S[1] in fig. 40), in the northeast corner, is contemporary with the construction of the court wall and propylon.

The temple underwent a number of alterations, but none of these seem to have changed its essential character (fig. 40). The sanctuary area itself remained the same, though the seats in the *salle aux*

[166] Frank E. Brown, *Dura Report* VII/VIII, 195; Rostovtzeff, *Dura-Europos*, 20 f., 25; Rostovtzeff, "Parthian Art," 197 f. For a summary of the dates of construction of the majority of the Dura temples, see Downey, "Temples," 23-39.

[167] Brown, *Dura Report* VI, 404-408, fig. 27.

[168] Ibid., 397, 411 f.; inscription originally published by Cumont, *Fouilles*, 409 f., no. 52

[169] Cumont, *Fouilles*, 412 f., no. 57; 423 f., no. 78; Brown, *Dura Report* VI, 412.

[170] Brown, *Dura Report* VI, 397-402, fig. 25.

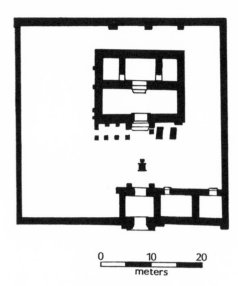

39. Dura-Europos, Temple of Artemis, building of ca. 40-32 B.C., plan.

nal south wall of the courtyard and adding enclosure walls. Several chapels were built against the south and southwest walls of this additional enclosure. The most important addition, however, was a small odeon (H) in the southeast corner. That the room served as a bouleuterion is suggested by two graffiti scratched on the seats, both commemorating one Zoilos, probably the same man, a *bouleutēs* ("senator") of Dura. Bellinger's suggestion that the room replaced the destroyed *salle aux gradins* and that it served both religious and civic purposes cannot be entirely correct, since all of the names preserved in the graffiti on the seats are male,[175] in contrast to the situation in the *salle aux gradins*. The names are also almost exclusively Semitic. In fact, the graffiti commemorating Zoilos provide an especially significant indication of the degree of Semiticization in that the city is called "Dura" rather than "Europos." Chapel I in the same section of the temple was dedicated by a group of men who called themselves Aurelioi and were *bouleutai* of Dura; the use of the name Aurelioi dates the inscription to the reign of Caracalla (A.D. 211-217) at the earliest.[176] Probably this entire section of the temple was built during the third century A.D.

Other modifications were made during the Roman period. A monumental altar located slightly to the southwest of the sanctuary unit was probably built then to replace the earlier altars, now covered by a platform.[177] A shallow pool located somewhere in the courtyard is also dated by Rowell to the Roman period.[178]

The Temple of Artemis was clearly a major civic shrine. The earliest dated inscription from the temple, of 33/32 B.C., is a dedication carved on a column by one Seleukos, son of Lysias, *stratēgos* of the city and *genearchēs*, thus a man with an official position in the city. The official character of the temple is also shown by the fact that one Gemellus, an envoy of the emperor ($\pi\rho\epsilon\sigma\beta\epsilon\upsilon\tau\grave{\eta}\varsigma$ $\Sigma\epsilon\beta\alpha\sigma\tauο\tilde{\upsilon}$), erected a cippus to Artemis. This same Gemellus also made a dedication in the Temple of Atargatis. Dedications to members of the imperial family also suggest the official character of the building. One Aurelios Heliodoros, an *epistatēs* of the city, made a

gradins were torn out and used as paving material; this alteration could argue for a change in ritual. The "chapel of Aphrodite" was enlarged and made more elaborate, and a number of subsidiary rooms—naoi and oikoi, according to inscriptions from various temples—were built. Many of these subsidiary rooms had benches around the walls and therefore were probably used for ritual dining by small groups of worshippers. Brown suggests that the oikoi in the north part of the complex may date to the first century A.D. Oikos U is dated by its inscription to A.D. 33;[171] another inscription of A.D. 118 recording the dedication of a door in oikos V is interpreted by Brown as referring only to a reconstruction of the entrance to the room.[172] A room (M) with benches in the south part of the temple contained a sieve, which perhaps suggests that food for ritual meals was prepared there.[173] Pillet states that a broad staircase in front of the north part of the facade of the sanctuary unit led to a small upper gallery for viewing ceremonies in the courtyard.[174] This staircase is not shown on the plan.

During the Roman period, the temple precinct was enlarged toward the south by razing the origi-

[171] Rowell, *Dura Report* III, 29; Rowell and Bellinger, *Dura Report* III, 55 f., D. 152.

[172] Brown, *Dura Report* VI, 399. Rowell, *Dura Report* III, 29, interprets the inscription (D. 164, p. 65) as referring to the construction of the oikos as a whole.

[173] Cumont, *Fouilles*, 443, no. 122.

[174] M. Pillet, *Dura Report* III, 5 f. Pillet also mentions a stair to the northeast of the entrance, but none is shown on the plan.

[175] Bellinger, *Dura Report* III, 22; Rowell, *Dura Report* III, 31; Welles, *Dura Report* IV, 168-71, nos. 341-44; Cumont, *Fouilles*, 444-47, nos. 123-127.

[176] Cumont, *Fouilles*, 404-409, no. 50; Rowell, *Dura Report* III, 31 f.

[177] Brown, *Dura Report* VI, 407; Rowell, *Dura Report* III, 32.

[178] Pillet, *Dura Report* III, 7 f.; Rowell, *Dura Report* III, 32.

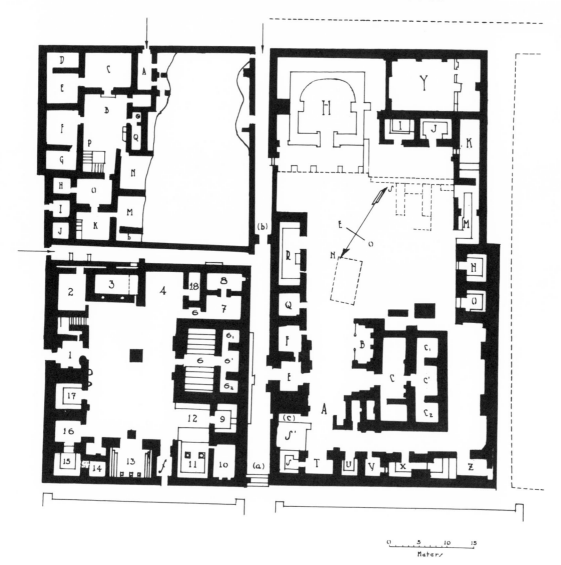

40. Dura-Europos, Temples of Artemis (right) and Atargatis (left), with priests' house.

dedication to Lucius Verus; Cumont suggests that the column on which the inscription is carved supported a statue of the emperor.[179] An inscription by the *boulē* of the city (Εὐρωπαίων ἡ βουλή) honoring Julia Domna probably came from a statue base.[180]

Dedicants named in inscriptions in the temple, except for the owners of seats in the *salle aux gradins*, were men. Both Greek (especially Macedonian) and Aramaean names appear, with perhaps a slight preponderance of Semitic names in the graf-

fiti. Thus both elements of the population appear to have mixed in the temple. The majority of the women who owned seats in the *salle aux gradins* were members of families with Greek, even Macedonian names (twenty inscriptions); the names in two additional inscriptions are Greek, and four inscriptions suggest a mixture of Greek and Semitic names within a family.[181]

Two inscriptions suggest that the goddess was served by priests rather than by priestesses. Both

[179] Cumont, *Fouilles*, 409 f., nos. 51, 52, 53.
[180] Rowell and Bellinger, *Dura Report* III, 51 f., D. 149.
[181] Cumont, *Fouilles*, 413 f., 421 f., nos. 57 and 72 (Greek); 416, 418 f., 421 f., nos. 63(?), 68, and 75 (mixed). The inscriptions are

published in Cumont, *Fouilles*, 412-26, nos. 57-84. The numbers given in the text are not entirely meaningful, as the degree of completeness of the inscriptions varies, and in some cases a crucial name must be partly restored.

inscriptions, one of A.D. 33 and one of the Roman period, record the erection of a room by members of the priesthood. The name of the priest in the earlier inscription, Ἀβεισμαχχινος, is apparently Aramaic;[182] in the later inscription, from room J in the newer part of the temple, priests of Artemis are associated with *bouleutai*.[183] This latter inscription also names a γαζζοφ[ύλαξ], presumably a temple treasurer. The room mentioned in the first inscription is called an "oikodomē" (οἰκοδομή), that in the second a "naos." Both have benches of the sort that usually suggest ritual dining.

The drastic change in plan of the Temple of Artemis in approximately 40-32 B.C. would seem to suggest a major shift in ritual and possibly also in belief, but the evidence suggests that the goddess that was worshipped in the temple retained the name Artemis, whatever changes in ritual may have occurred. Cumont had conjectured from the character of the temple plan that the goddess worshipped there must have been oriental, that "l'Artémis, adorée dans la cité macédonienne d'Europos, était une déesse beaucoup moins grecque que sémitique."[184] His argument, however, rested primarily on the finding in the temple of one graffito dedicated to Nanaia,[185] which might well represent a personal act of devotion. Artemis, on the other hand, is named in a number of important inscriptions. The most significant is a dedication to Artemis and Apollo *archēgoi* (ἀρχηγοῖς) by one Abidnerglos, dated to A.D. 2. This suggests that not only did Artemis remain Artemis, but that she even retained an epithet that particularly associated her with the Greek colony.[186] Thus it appears that a Greek goddess could be worshipped in a temple of Mesopotamian form.

TEMPLE OF ZEUS MEGISTOS, PERIODS II-V

According to Brown, "the destruction of this temple [i.e., Temple of Zeus Megistos, period I,] was singularly complete, so complete as to leave the impression of purposeful ruthlessness."[187] The destruction of the earliest building on the site should probably be associated with the Parthian conquest of Dura in the late second century B.C.

The temple of the Hellenistic period was replaced by a building (period II) of a very different type. The second structure on the site utilized the foundations of the outer walls of the first temple as far as possible, but the change in the interior arrangements was so complete that only one interior wall was reused. According to Brown's field notes and plan (fig. 41), the temple as rebuilt consisted of an independent, roughly square sanctuary unit (11, 16) set in a court that had rooms along the north and south sides. The sanctuary unit consisted of a broad pronaos and naos; the naos was slightly narrower than the pronaos because part of its width was occupied by a flight of stairs leading from the pronaos to the roof of the sanctuary. The doors to the pronaos-naos unit did not lie quite in the center of the facade of the sanctuary unit, but slightly to the south of center. A small altar stood in the courtyard, roughly on the line of these entrances. The placement of the altar might explain the off-center placement of the entrance doors, but then it is necessary to explain the placement of the altar.

In addition, the entrance into the courtyard from the street did not lie on the line of the doors into the pronaos-naos unit, but considerably to the north. Brown states that the entrance to the court in period II was shifted slightly to the north in relation to the entrance in period I, with the result that the new entrance coincided with what would have been the entrance to the period I sanctuary unit, but the latter no longer existed. He suggests as a possible reason for this shift the survival into period II of a monumental altar supported by the heavy paving of the period I court. The evidence for the presence of a monumental altar in either period I or period II is slim, however. Another possible explanation for the off-axis arrangement of the sanctuary unit could be the desire to follow one type of Neo-Babylonian temple plan, in which there is not a direct axis from the street entrance to the sanctuary unit.[188] Possible confirmation of this idea is found in the addition of a vestibule to the sanctuary unit in period V, which has the effect of screening the sanctuary more completely from the court.

In this second phase of construction, the southern side of the court was occupied primarily by two

---

[182] Rowell and Bellinger, *Dura Report* III, 55 f., D. 152.

[183] Cumont, *Fouilles*, 404-409, no. 50.

[184] Ibid., 199.

[185] Ibid., 195-204; for the inscription, see p. 411, no. 55.

[186] Bellinger, *Dura Report* III, 22; Rowell and Bellinger, *Dura Report* III, 63 f., D. 161; Downey, *Stone and Plaster Sculpture*, 170 f.; Eissfeldt, *Tempel und Kulte*, 115-18.

[187] The discussion of the Temple of Zeus Megistos is based on

Frank E. Brown's unpublished manuscript on the period I building and his notes on the field plans. The excavators of Dura used "Period I" to designate the earliest phase of a building. Eissfeldt discusses the building and gives a simplified plan in *Tempel und Kulte*, 118-21, fig. 25.

[188] E.g., the temples of Ninmach and Ninurta, and Temple Z at Babylon: Koldewey, *Die Tempel von Babylon und Borsippa*, 4-33, pls. III, V, VI, VII. See figs. 9-11 in the present volume.

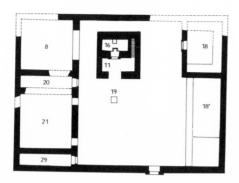

41. Dura-Europos, Temple of Zeus Megistos,
period II, plan.

large rooms (8 and 21 in fig. 41) with a narrow
room (20) between and a second narrow room (29)
between room 21 and the east wall of the court.
These narrow rooms served in effect as buttressing
corridors for the larger rooms. If Brown is correct
in restoring arched entrances, the large rooms
would have looked like iwans. Their function is
unknown. A colonnaded portico (18') occupied the
eastern portion of the northern side of the court,
and a room with benches on three sides (18), presumably a dining room, filled the western part of
this side of the court.

According to Brown, the second temple was
probably erected in the second quarter of the first
century B.C. Though no evidence is given for this
date, it is plausible, as it would place the construction toward the beginning of the first major burst
of temple building at Dura. This new phase of the
Temple of Zeus Megistos would slightly predate
the similarly radical rebuilding of the Temple of
Artemis (fig. 39), which can be dated by inscriptional evidence to roughly 40-32 B.C.[189] The two
temples are quite similar in plan.

Though the Temple of Zeus Megistos was enlarged and altered several times, most drastically
after the earthquake in A.D. 160, the basic scheme
established in the period II temple was retained
throughout its life: a roughly square sanctuary unit
consisting of a pronaos and naos of approximately
the same width, set in a courtyard with rooms, porticoes, and chapels around the outer walls. It is notable that a room for dining, a prominent feature of
many Dura temples, was already present in this
phase. A stair leading to the roof of the sanctuary
unit (11, 16) remained throughout the life of the
temple.

The Temple of Zeus Megistos underwent three
more rebuildings, but only the last of these, period
V, can be dated at all accurately on the basis of the
available evidence. An inscription of A.D. 169, discussed below, marks completion or a stage of completion of this building.[190] This phase marks a major rebuilding rather than the gradual accretions
and minor changes that characterized the third and
fourth phases; it is reasonable to assume that the rebuilding was necessitated by damage suffered in the
earthquake of A.D. 160.

It is not possible to reconstruct the sequence of
the period III and IV additions from the available
notes and plans, so the following discussion is
somewhat summary. The main outlines of the
building remained the same through phase V (fig.
42), with the period II sanctuary unit (11 and 16) remaining in use. A major addition in period III was
the erection of a monumental altar (17) that stood
in its own court; this altar lasted through the subsequent phases of rebuilding. It was enlarged in the
fourth building phase by the construction of a rubble shell around the original core. Three rooms in
the southeast corner of the block (22, 27, 28), built
in period III, do not communicate with the temple
precinct, suggesting that perhaps they formed a
small house.

Period V represents not only a major rebuilding
but to some extent a change in conception from the
earlier phases. The plan of this period almost gives
the appearance of two juxtaposed temples, each
centered around a court. The entrance to the northern court remained where it had been since period
II, on the east side. Two large rooms on the south
side of this court (20, 21) apparently collapsed in the
earthquake, however, and they remained unroofed
and no longer constituted part of the temple. Then
with the building of an additional entrance into the
sanctuary from Street 5 on the south side, the temple precinct was divided into a northern and a
southern court. The old sanctuary unit (11, 16)
continued to function, but two additional sanctuary units were built in the southern court: one in the
southwest corner (12, 14, 2), the other a single naos
(15) at the northwest end of the court, behind the
original sanctuary (16). Since the monumental altar
in room 17 remained in use, the effect of these additions was an increased number of centers of worship around the southern court.

Several changes were made around the period II
sanctuary unit in the northern court. It was isolated
from the courtyard by the building of an entrance

[189] Brown, *Dura Report* VI, 397-404.

[190] Welles, "Inscriptions," 139-42, no. 6.

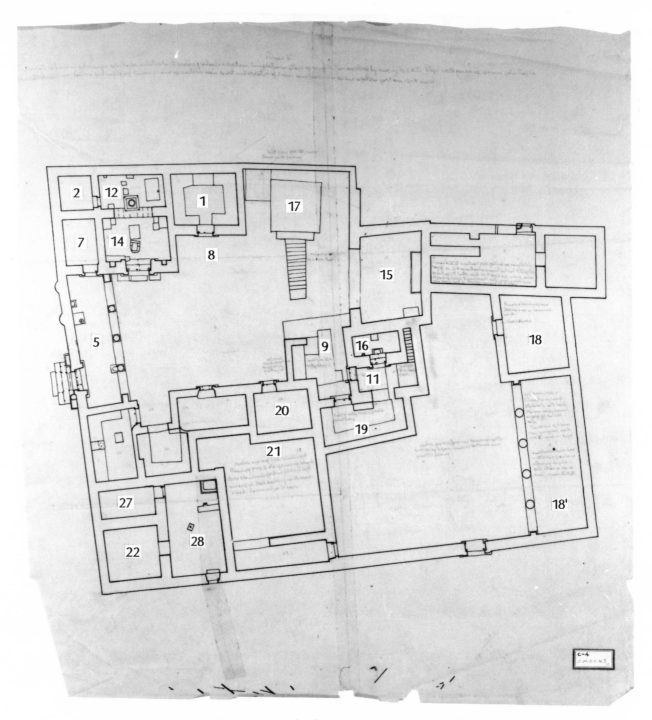

42. Dura-Europos, Temple of Zeus Megistos, periods III-V, plan.

vestibule (19) in front of it on the east. This room might also have served as a center of worship, for remains of sculpture were found there. A secondary entrance to this sanctuary unit from the southern court was provided by the construction of room 9 to the south of the pronaos-naos unit, which gave access to vestibule 19. The fragments of a life-sized statue in civilian dress found in naos 16 probably date to this period.[191] The benches in room 18 were floored over in this phase, perhaps suggesting the room no longer served for dining.

A new entrance and a portico (5) were built on the south side of the southern court. In the southwest corner of the court, the newly constructed sanctuary unit (12, 14, 2) consisted of a pronaos and naos of the same width, with the entrance on the east. Various features—bases, perhaps for altars, apparently a plinth supporting a column—are shown on the plan, but Brown's notes do not give any information that allows an interpretation. A small room (2) in the extreme southwestern corner opened from naos 12 and so probably served as a sacristy. A second small room (7) opened from portico 5 but apparently did not communicate with the sanctuary unit; perhaps it was a porter's room.

To the north of this sanctuary unit, against the west wall of the southern court, was a room (1) with benches around it, perhaps therefore a triclinium. The area in front of this (room 8) apparently had an arched entrance, the springings of which were decorated with images of Heracles in high relief.[192] To the north of room 17, which housed the monumental altar built in period III, a new naos (15) constructed in period V consisted of a single room, apparently with a wide entrance. A plinth, presumably for a statue, is shown in plan against the rear wall. A majestic, life-sized, bearded head in a polos headdress from this naos is presumably all that remains of the cult statue; it can probably be identified as Baalshamin on the basis of its similarity to the stele of Baalshamin/Zeus Kyrios from his temple at Dura.[193] A gypsum slab with a fragmentary Greek inscription apparently honoring an emperor, also found in naos 15, was probably set into the podium of a statue.[194]

The inscription of A.D. 169/70 cited above suggests that the principal deity of the temple was Zeus Megistos, which is probably the Greek name for Baalshamin.[195] Fragments of the cult statue found in the principal naos (16) were not sufficient to permit identification of the deity, but it was probably either Bel or Baalshamin.[196] Since at Palmyra, Bel always wears a cuirass,[197] whereas Baalshamin may wear either civilian or military dress, and since the statue found here was in civilian dress, perhaps Baalshamin is more likely.

The gods of the desert were prominently represented in sculpture from the temple. Naos 16 contained a stele of a nimbate and radiate god. A relief representing a god identified in the accompanying inscription as Arsu was found in vestibule 19, and a relief of a man leading a camel found under the floors of the vestibule and pronaos of this sanctuary unit might also be associated with Arsu.[198] A small relief of Heracles also came from vestibule 19,[199] and a stele of a nimbate god clad in the dress of the desert and holding a lance and a sword stood in entrance portico 5.[200] Heracles figured importantly in the temple. The figures of Heracles in high relief that adorned the springing of the arched entrance to room 8 might simply have been apotropaic, but may indicate that this area was consecrated to Heracles. The fact that three small reliefs of Heracles (including the one from vestibule 19 cited above) were found in and near the temple suggests in any case that Heracles was a *synnaos theos* of Zeus Megistos.[201]

Inscriptions and graffiti, few in number, provide some slight evidence about the worshippers in the temple. The most important inscription is that of A.D. 169/70 recording that "Seleukos, *stratēgos* and *epistatēs* of the city, built the arch, the portico, and the πλινθῖον [perhaps stone door trim] to Zeus Megistos on behalf of his safety and that of his children in accord with a vow."

[Ἔτους] απύ, Ὑπερβερεταίου γ΄.
Σ[έλε]υκος στρατηγὸς καὶ
ἐπιστάτης τῆς πόλεως τ[ὴν]
ψαλίδα καὶ τὴν στοὰν καὶ τὸ
πλινθῖον τοῦτο Διὶ Μεγίστῳ
ἀνοικοδόμησεν ὑπὲρ τῆς
ἑαυτοῦ καὶ τέκνων σω-
τηρίας κατ᾽ εὐχήν.

[191] Downey, *Stone and Plaster Sculpture*, 67-70, 209 f., no. 51.

[192] Downey, *Heracles Sculpture*, 29 f., 32, 60, nos. 31, 37.

[193] Downey, *Stone and Plaster Sculpture*, 66 f., 209, no. 50.

[194] Welles, "Inscriptions," 142 f., no. 7.

[195] Ibid., 139 f., no. 6; Eissfeldt, *Tempel und Kulte*, 120 f.; Downey, *Stone and Plaster Sculpture*, 209.

[196] Downey, *Stone and Plaster Sculpture*, 67-70, no. 51, 209 f.

[197] Seyrig, "Bêl de Palmyre," *Syria* XLVIII (1971), 87.

[198] Downey, *Stone and Plaster Sculpture*, 53-57, nos. 42, 44; 70 f., no. 52; 195-98.

[199] Downey, *Heracles Sculpture*, 21, no. 7.

[200] Downey, *Stone and Plaster Sculpture*, 71 f., no. 53.

[201] Downey, *Heracles Sculpture*, 57-61.

This Seleukos may well have been a member of an aristocratic Durene family, many of whose members held the office of *stratēgos* and *epistatēs*.[202]

The constructions mentioned in the inscription cannot be identified with certainty. It seems highly probable that the stoa was the newly constructed portico 5, since the inscription was found near the entrance to it. Perhaps then the arch refers to the entrance door, if it was arched. The interpretation of the third item, πλινθῖον, is more problematical. Brown suggests that this term, which appears also in an inscription from the Temple of Adonis and in a parchment, might refer to stone door trim.[203] Perhaps, then, Seleukos paid for the new door into the court and the portico behind it. This inscription would thus show a presumed member of an aristocratic family providing generous aid in reconstructing the temple.

The Macedonian aristocracy is perhaps also represented by the Lysanias whose name is inscribed on a fragmentary relief of Heracles from vestibule 19. He might even be the Lysanias named as priest of Zeus in a contract of sale dated to A.D. 180.[204] The prominence in the sanctuary of the gods of the desert, worshipped in Palmyra and the country surrounding it, would seem to suggest that Semitic worshippers also used the temple. Indeed the sculptor of the Arsu relief, who is apparently also the dedicant, has the Palmyrene name Ogâ.[205] Graffiti on benches, apparently from naos 12, give two Iranian names, one Semitic, and one unexplained; dipinti named Lysias and Albinus (Ἀλβεῖνος), the latter probably an army man.[206]

The increased complexity of the Temple of Zeus Megistos in its final period, particularly the building of two new naoi, perhaps reflects the introduction of new deities into the temple. It is of course impossible to determine which of the sculptures found in the temple date only from the last period and which instead survived from the earlier phases.[207] The finding of portions of life-sized statues in two naoi is particularly striking in view of the paucity of large-scale sculpture at Dura. If both statues represented Baalshamin, perhaps each naos was used by different groups of worshippers. Al-

ternatively, one of the statues might represent Bel, in which case one court might have been dedicated primarily to Bel, the other to Baalshamin. The two gods appear together in two reliefs from the region of Palmyra.[208]

The increased size and complexity might possibly reflect a renewed importance of the temple in the city's life, though there are some chronological difficulties with this suggestion. In the Seleucid period the temple, probably dedicated to Zeus Olympios, must have played an important role in the religious life of the colony, especially if it was one of only two temples in the city, as seems likely. This importance may have continued, but was more probably renewed, in the Roman period. A papyrus deed of sale of A.D. 180 is dated both in the official Roman manner and by the eponymous priests of four cults: Apollo, Zeus, Seleukos Nicator, and the ancestors (πρόγονοι). Since this dating formula is not known during the Parthian period, Welles suggests that its use represents "an innovation, an actual or supposed reintroduction of a dating method which belonged to the Seleucid period of the city's history."[209] Of the temples dedicated to some form of Zeus at Dura (Zeus Kyrios/Baalshamin; Zeus Theos), only the Temple of Zeus Megistos has remains dating from the Seleucid period; therefore, the Zeus whose priest is named in the papyrus was presumably worshipped in the Temple of Zeus Megistos.

NECROPOLIS TEMPLE

The Necropolis Temple (fig. 43) was built in 33 B.C. by two Palmyrenes, Zabdibol, son of BʿYHW of the Bnai Gaddibol, and Maliku, son of RMW of the Bnai Kumara; it was dedicated to Bel and Iarhibol. The Palmyrene inscription calls the building a *haikal*, "temple,"[210] and like the Temple of the Gaddé (fig. 50), which was also built by Palmyrenes, the Necropolis Temple is divided into two essentially separate parts. The principal court, on the north side, was entered through a gateway on the east flanked by buttresses. The gate lies on approximately the same axis as the entrance to the

[202] Welles, "Inscriptions," 139-42, no. 6.

[203] Brown, *Dura Report* VII/VIII, 168 f., no. 872; 432.

[204] Downey, *Heracles Sculpture*, 38 f.

[205] Ingholt, in Welles, "Inscriptions," 138 f., no. 5.

[206] Welles, "Inscriptions," 143 f., nos. 9-12.

[207] Downey, *Stone and Plaster Sculpture*, 233 f., 236; one relief, found under the floors of rooms 11 and 19 (fig. 42), probably dates from the first century A.D. (pp. 56 f., no. 44).

[208] A. Bounni, "Nouvelles bas-reliefs religieux de la Palmyrène," *Mélanges offerts à Kazimierz Michalowski* (Warsaw, 1966), 313 f., figs. 2, 4; Seyrig, *Syria* XLVIII (1971), 97 f., figs. 3, 4.

[209] Welles, *Final Report* V.1: *The Parchments and Papyri* (New Haven, 1959) 6 f., 130 f., no. 25; cf. also no. 37; the quotation is on p. 131.

[210] Torrey, *Dura Report* VII/VIII, 318-20, no. 916.

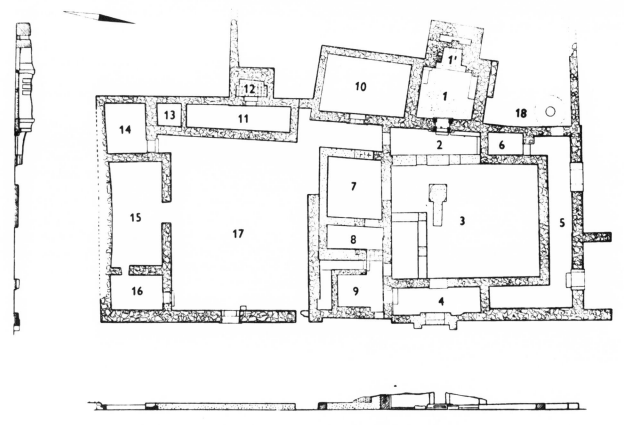

43. Dura-Europos, Necropolis Temple, plan and sections.

naos, which itself is placed askew, at an odd angle to the walls of the court. Three sides of the court are occupied by narrow rooms—an entrance vestibule (4) on the east, a portico(?)(5) on the north and a small unidentified room (6) on the west near the naos. The monumental altar lies on approximately the line between the entrance to the complex and the door to the sanctuary. Brown suggests that this stepped altar probably replaced an earlier, simpler one, arguing that stepped altars do not seem to appear at Dura until the middle of the first century A.D.[211]

The sanctuary unit (1, 1′) lies on the west side of the northern court, fronted by a portico. It consists of a roughly square pronaos with a smaller naos projecting from it; the arrangement could also be interpreted as a sanctuary with a deep cult niche. The whole unit projects from the rear wall of the court. This arrangement, which is unusual at Dura, is seen also in the Temple of the Gaddé in its fourth period (fig. 50). In the thick wall behind the naos is

a long empty space, which can be interpreted as a vestigial isolating corridor like that in the Temple of Adonis. A base for the cult statue stands at the rear of the naos, and there are remains of altars in the two front corners.

A series of three rooms lies along the south side of the court (7, 8, 9), and a stairway in the southeast room (9) gave access to the roof. Thus in this temple precinct there was access to the roof close to, though not directly above, the entrance. A small colonnaded porch in front of two of these rooms (8 and 9) should perhaps be interpreted as an aedicula for a *synnaos theos*, like a similar porch in the Temple of Bel at Dura. These rooms and porch may have been added in a second period of construction.

Though the southern court (17) is essentially separate and has its main entrance on the east, it can also be entered from the northern court, through a narrow door leading in from the portico in front of the sanctuary unit 1-1′. A small room (12), presumably a second naos, projects from the rear wall

[211] Brown, *Dura Report* VII/VIII, 322.

of the southern court; its door is approximately aligned with the main eastern entrance to this court. The walls of the naos are broken up by niches, as in the naos of the main sanctuary unit. In front of this room in the court are the foundations of a long, narrow, rectangular space (11), and to the south of this is a further small room (13). Toll interprets the foundations of room 11 as supporting a portico, by analogy with the colonnade in front of the northern sanctuary unit, in spite of the fact that no traces of plinths or bases for columns remain. It seems possible, therefore, that rooms 11 and 13 should be interpreted instead as a long pronaos with a subsidiary room, and that rooms 11, 12, and 13 could have formed a sanctuary unit similar to that in the Temple of the Gaddé. Three further rooms line the south wall of this court (14, 15, 16). The southern court and the rooms around it represent an addition to the original structure. Room 12 is perhaps the naos referred to in an inscription of A.D. 173, in which one Maribēlos, after mentioning benefactions of his parents, records his dedication of something that is now missing in the inscription and "another naos" (ἄλλον νάον). Brown leaves open the question of whether this inscription records the erection of the entire new complex or only the court and the sanctuary unit.[212] The inscription also records the gift of temple furniture of various kinds, but its poor condition makes a detailed discussion impossible.

The dedicatory inscriptions name two gods, Bel and Iarhibol. The inscription of A.D. 173, which probably records the erection of the secondary naos (12), is unfortunately fragmentary, but probably a third Palmyrene god—Arsu or Malakbel—whose painted image was found in the room, was worshipped there. Brown discusses the relationship between the location of the temple, outside the walls and in the necropolis, and its possible function. The location and the plan suggest the possibility that the building was a heroon. Brown rejects this idea, however, since the gods who were worshipped there had no connection with the cult of the dead. He suggests that the plan of the building, rather than being related to the Greek heroon, was derived from Babylonia. This unusual kind of sanctuary unit, with a broad pronaos and a deep niche

for the cult image, is known in some earlier Mesopotamian temples, as at Kar Tukulti Ninurta and the Gigparku at Ur.[213] It is also the most frequently used temple plan at Hatra. Bernard rejects the attempt to derive this plan from Babylonia. He suggests instead that the plan in the shape of a reversed T seen at Dura in the Necropolis Temple and the Temple of the Gaddé is influenced by the Greek architecture of the Orient, as exemplified by the heroon at Aï Khanoum. This structure consists simply of a naos fronted by a slightly wider pronaos, a far less complex arrangement than at Dura.[214] The similarity between the Dura temples and the heroon at Aï Khanoum is slight, and thus Bernard's argument does not seem convincing.

Another obvious explanation of the extramural location, that the temple was a Bit Akitu, built to house the Babylonian New Year's festival, is weakened both by the fact that there is no evidence that this festival was celebrated at Dura and by the fact that it was built by Palmyrenes, a foreign element at Dura.[215] Gawlikowski and Du Mesnil argue that an equivalent of the Babylonian Akitu festival was celebrated at Palmyra;[216] if this hypothesis is accepted, the Necropolis Temple could be interpreted as an Akitu house for the gods of Palmyra. Their argument rests essentially on the processional character of the colonnaded street leading past the major temples at Palmyra and on the frequency of inscriptions dated to March/April, corresponding to the Babylonian month of Nisan. I do not find the evidence persuasive. It seems more likely that the temple was designed to serve the needs of Palmyrene traders who camped outside the city. Brown notes that the Necropolis Temple is approximately contemporary with the earliest probable trace of Palmyrene elements within the city, the small chapel erected in the area that was later occupied by a temple built by Palmyrenes in honor of the Gaddé of Dura and Palmyra.[217] It is possible that at this relatively early date the Palmyrenes could not build a large temple to their deities within the city. The structure in the area later occupied by the Temple of the Gaddé was relatively small, and there is no proof that it was then used by Palmyrenes. The earliest temple within the city that was surely built by a foreign group is that dedicated to Aphlad of

[212] Toll, *Dura Report VII/VIII*, 310-16; Brown, *Dura Report VII/VIII*, 320-23, no. 918. The temple is discussed by Eissfeldt, *Tempel und Kulte*, 127-29.

[213] Brown, *Dura Report VII/VIII*, 323 f. T. Eickhoff, *Kār Tukulti Ninurta* (*Abhandlungen der Deutschen Orient-Gesellschaft* XXI) (Berlin, 1985), 27-31, fig. 8.

[214] Bernard, *Fouilles d'Aï Khanoum* I, 85-91, 98 f., Pls. 12, 13.

[215] Brown, *Dura Report VII/VIII*, 324 f.

[216] Michal Gawlikowski, *Palmyre VI: Le temple palmyrénien* (Warsaw, 1973), 81-83; R. du Mesnil du Buisson, "Les origines du panthéon palmyrénien," *MélUSJ* XXXIX (1964), 166.

[217] Brown, *Dura Report VII/VIII*, 226 f., 257 f.

Anath in A.D. 54,[218] nearly ninety years later than the Necropolis Temple.

TEMPLE OF AZZANATHKONA

The construction of the Temple of Azzanathkona (figs. 44, 45) stretched over a number of years. The date of the earliest inscribed step in the *salle aux gradins*, A.D. 12/13, gives a *terminus ante quem* for the initial construction. The latest seats are dated to A.D. 107/108, a year in which the *salle aux gradins* was probably reconstructed and enlarged.[219] An inscription dates two subsidiary rooms (12W and 14W on fig. 45) to A.D. 153; and two other rooms (8D and 9D) were built (or rebuilt?) in 161, after the earthquake of 160.[220] It is not possible to establish the exact sequence of construction for the rest of the temple.

The Temple of Azzanathkona was built against the north city wall near the Temple of Bel. Apparently the city wall, including a tower, served as the north precinct wall, though the date of the wall and its exact relationship to the various building periods of the temple are unclear.[221] There appear to have been two sanctuary units, rooms 2D-5D and rooms 9W-10, both facing east.

The entrance to the courtyard lies on the axis of the sanctuary unit 2D-5D, and a monumental altar stands in the courtyard on this same line. This sanctuary unit consists of an anteroom, a pronaos, and a naos with a small sacristy at its south side. As usual at Dura, the long axis of the sanctuary unit is perpendicular to the axis of the entrance to the court. The pronaos-naos unit is separated from the rear wall of the court and from the rooms to the south only by a relatively narrow right-angled corridor (10D). Brown interprets this as an isolating corridor like those seen in some Babylonian temples.[222] The addition of an anteroom to the pronaos-naos unit is somewhat unusual. The surviving furnishings of the anteroom are an altar, on which there were no traces of fire, and a mortar. An altar also stood in the naos just opposite the door; three holes to its front and sides could have held sacred

standards. The width of the naos is slightly less than that of the pronaos because of the chamber that flanks the naos. In most Dura temples the naos is flanked by one or more sacristies; what is unusual in the Temple of Azzanathkona is that this flanking chamber is accessible only from the pronaos.

The second sanctuary unit, 9W-10, is placed at a slightly different angle, and its front room is arranged as a *salle aux gradins*, the seats of which belonged to women whose names are inscribed on them. The great majority of the women had Greek names, as did their husbands and fathers; but a few inscriptions include only Semitic names, and there were some mixed families.[223] The cult relief is set into the rear wall just to the right of the entrance to the inner room, with two altars in front of it. An inscription of A.D. 33 found on the steps recording a dedication to Azzanathkona identifies the goddess worshipped here.[224] As in the first sanctuary unit, the inner area here is divided into a larger and a smaller room, but in this case the smaller room is accessible only from the larger. Hopkins interprets room 10 as a naos, as indeed its plan and its position behind a *salle aux gradins* would suggest.[225] The center of the room is occupied by a cupboard-like niche, however, and the discovery of thirteen large storage jars and arrangements for a shelf suggest that instead it was a storeroom.[226] Milik suggests that it was the meeting place for a thiasos.[227] The fact that the cult relief and altars were placed in the *salle aux gradins* suggests that it was the real center of worship in this unit.

The goddess Azzanathkona is not known elsewhere. An inscription from a subsidiary room dated to A.D. 161 calling her "Artemis the goddess called Azzanthkona" (᾿Αρτέμιδι θε(ᾷ) καλουμένῃ ᾿Αζζαναθκονα)[228] shows that by the second century A.D. she was identified with Artemis. The cult relief, which depicts her seated on a throne between lions, indicates that she was one of the great Syrian mother goddesses. The second element in the name seems to be related to the name of the city of Anath, down the Euphrates from Dura, and may indicate that she was originally the goddess of Anath.[229]

[218] Clark Hopkins, *Dura Report* V, 112-16.

[219] Ibid., 131; Susan Hopkins, *Dura Report* V, 180, 196, no. 545.

[220] C. Hopkins, *Dura Report* V, 131, 134-36, 142 f., 151 f., nos. 453, 468.

[221] Downey, "Temples," 24-27, summarizing earlier opinions.

[222] Brown, *Dura Report* VII/VIII, 138 f.

[223] S. Hopkins, *Dura Report* V, 180-200, nos. 510-55. The fragmentary preservation of the inscriptions makes an exact count of names impossible. In thirty-one inscriptions only Greek names are preserved, whereas four have only Semitic names and seven include

both Greek and Aramaic names in the same family.

[224] C. Hopkins, *Dura Report* V, 177 f., no. 504.

[225] Ibid., 170 f.

[226] Cf. Brown, *Dura Report* VII/VIII, 254 f., n. 21.

[227] Milik, *Dédicaces*, 203.

[228] C. Hopkins, *Dura Report* V, 142-45, no. 453.

[229] Downey, *Stone and Plaster Sculpture*, 185-87, summarizing previous scholarship. The Temple of Azzanathkona is discussed by Eissfeldt, *Tempel und Kulte,* 129-33.

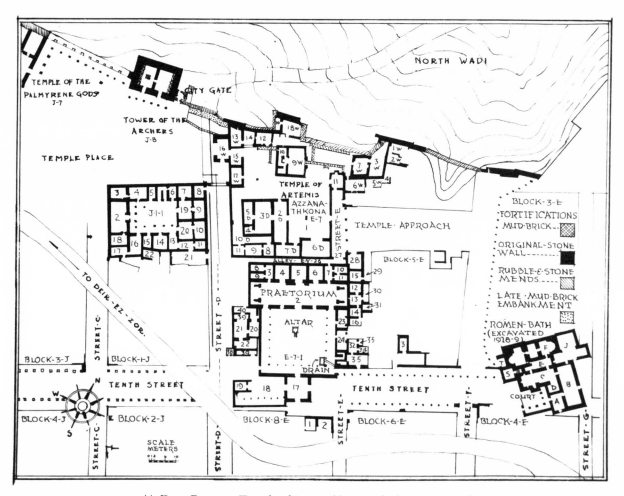

44. Dura-Europos, Temple of Azzanathkona and adjacent areas, plan.

The court of the Temple of Azzanathkona is lined by rooms built at various times. Most of these were probably chapels; many have altars, and graffiti give the names of worshippers. The evidence from the inscriptions and graffiti perhaps suggests that the various rooms and chapels were largely or partly reserved for different elements of the population. The dedicatory inscriptions of two of the rooms are preserved; both were dedicated by private citizens on behalf of themselves and their families. The inscription of A.D. 161, cited above, was found near the door between rooms 8D and 9D (fig. 45) south of the isolating corridor around sanctuary complex 2D-5D. It records the erection of an oikos to Artemis, the goddess called Azzanathkona, by one Barnabous, son of Zabidkonos, son of Rhaeibelos. The finding of mortars in both rooms suggests that they might have been used for

food preparation or storage. The excavation report does not mention benches, so probably the rooms were not used for dining. The dedicant of room 12W near the city wall gives his name as Heliodoros, son of Theodoros, called Samsbanas, son of Abidsomos. Apparently, then, he was a member of a Hellenized Semitic family. The inscription is dated to A.D. 153. At a later point, this room, along with others in the vicinity, was apparently taken over by the army, as a Latin inscription in honor of Septimius Severus Pertinax was painted on the east wall by an actuarius of the Second Ulpian cohort.[230]

In other rooms, only graffiti and the objects found there give indications of function and the identity of the worshippers. The room to the south of the entrance, 6D, was probably a subsidiary chapel, for a niche in the west wall might have held a statue of a divinity. The names in the graffiti are

[230] C. Hopkins, *Dura Report* V, 142 f., no. 453; 151 f., no. 468; 226-29, no. 561.

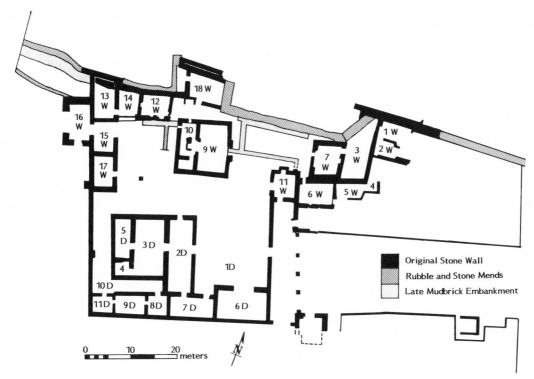

45. Dura-Europos, Temple of Azzanathkona, plan.

mostly Greek, though a few Semitic names occur. Two of the rooms in a group on the east side of the court near the city wall contain altars; in one (7W), the names are mostly Semitic, in the other (11), almost exclusively Greek.[231] The discovery of commonware vessels in another room in this corner (3W) suggests that it was a storeroom,[232] rather than living quarters for one of the priests.[233] Another group of rooms near the wall on the west side of the court was apparently taken over by the military. The discovery of papyri in room 13W suggests that it housed military records, and the graffiti in room 14W also seem to have a predominantly military character; it was probably a military clerical office.[234]

The cult relief possibly suggests that bulls were sacrificed to Azzanathkona. A small man clad in simple dress and leading a humped bull that is carved above the goddess is probably best interpreted as a temple attendant leading a sacrificial victim. Though most of the sacrifices depicted at Dura

involve incense, there is slight evidence for animal sacrifice. A ram is offered to Zeus Kyrios on the cult relief from his temple, and in the Synagogue paintings a humped bull is the regular sacrificial victim.[235] The altar in the main court of the Temple of Azzanathkona would have been large enough for animal sacrifices (1.44 x 0.90 meters).[236]

TEMPLE OF ZEUS KYRIOS

This simplest of all the Dura temples was built next to the fortification wall on the west side of the city, against tower 16 and the adjacent part of the curtain wall. In all periods the sanctuary consisted of an open court, an altar, and a cult relief set into the face of the tower (fig. 46). The original altar was built against the face of the tower in A.D. 28/29, and in A.D. 31 the cult relief of Zeus Kyrios/Baalshamin was set into the wall of the tower 5.15 meters above the floor of the court and to the left of the altar. The enclosure in this early period extended across the

[231] Ibid., 139-41; 145-50.
[232] Milik, *Dédicaces*, 203 f.
[233] C. Hopkins, *Dura Report* V, 145.
[234] Ibid., 152-66; Brown, Rostovtzeff, and Welles, *Dura Report* VI, 492-97.

[235] Downey, *Stone and Plaster Sculpture*, 186 f.; for the Synagogue paintings, see Carl Kraeling, *Final Report* VIII.1: *The Synagogue* (New Haven, 1956), 129, 138, 141, pls. LX-LXII.
[236] C. Hopkins, *Dura Report* V, 137.

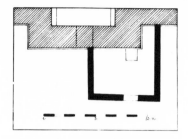

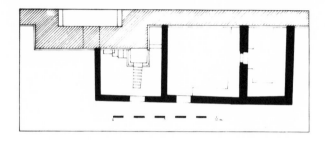

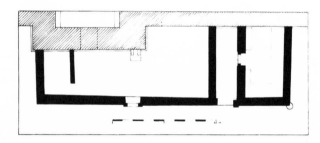

46. Dura-Europos, Temple of Zeus Kyrios,
periods I-III, plan.

northern part of the tower, not including the door. In an intermediate period the altar was enlarged and a roofed dining hall and its forecourt built north of the temenos. The forecourt could be entered only from the street, not from the temenos. In a final period, after the destruction caused by the earthquake of A.D. 160, the level had risen so that the door to the tower was blocked in any case, and in this period the enclosure was enlarged and rebuilt so as to include all of the tower. The altar of the preceding period was razed and replaced by a smaller altar, and the face of the tower around and beneath the

cult relief was whitewashed. The forecourt to the dining room was reduced to a corridor, but the separation between this complex and the temenos was maintained. The Temple of Zeus Kyrios differs from most other Dura temples in that there was no naos as such, but rather worship took place in an open court with only an altar and a cult relief. In all periods the entrance to the temenos was on the axis of the altar. Though the precinct incorporated a tower of the city wall, access to the tower was not possible from the precinct.

Brown characterizes the Temple of Zeus Kyrios/Baalshamin as a "Semitic sanctuary reduced to its barest essentials." The reasons for the placement of the temple are not clear. Brown notes that the form of the sanctuary suggests that it served a few worshippers banded together in an association. He raises but rejects the idea that the placement of the sanctuary against a tower of the city wall and the setting of the cult relief against the face of the tower suggest that the group of worshippers was military, since neither of the two inscriptions suggests that the dedicants were soldiers.[237] The altar was made by a man named Roumēs, whereas the name of the dedicant of the cult relief is given in Greek as "Seleukos the son of Leukios" ($\Sigma \acute{\epsilon} \lambda \epsilon \nu \kappa o \varsigma$ $\Lambda \epsilon \nu \kappa \acute{\iota} o \nu$) and in Palmyrene as "Bar ʿAteh, the son of Luke."[238] Furthermore, in the cult relief both the dedicant and Zeus Kyrios/Baalshamin are shown in civilian rather than military dress. The fact that the dedicant holds a ram suggests that animal sacrifices were practiced in the temple. The bones of a small fowl, the remnants of a sacrifice, were found on the altar.[239] Brown suggests the possibility that the deity "had a definite apotropaic significance, either for the fortifications in general or for Tower 16 in particular."[240]

TEMPLE OF ATARGATIS

The Temple of Atargatis[241] was erected on a site previously occupied by houses, which were razed, probably at the time of the construction of the Temple of Artemis in 40-32 B.C. It can be dated quite closely on the basis of epigraphical evidence. An inscription found in the naos records that in A.D. 31/32, Ammonios, the son of Apollophanes,

---

[237] Brown, *Dura Report* VII/VIII, 284-92. The Temple of Zeus Kyrios is discussed by Eissfeldt, *Tempel und Kulte*, 133 f.

[238] Brown and Torrey, *Dura Report* VII/VIII, 307-309, nos. 914, 915.

[239] Brown, *Dura Report* VII/VIII, 289.

[240] Ibid., 292.

[241] The following discussion is based on the published reports and an unpublished preliminary study by Henry Pearson in the Dura archives. For the general description of the building, see Pillet, *Dura Report* III, 9-11; and Bellinger, *Dura Report* III, 18-24. See also Eissfeldt, *Tempel und Kulte*, 121-23.

erected something (unspecified) on behalf of the safety of himself, Lysanias, and his brothers: Ἔτους γμτ΄. Ἀμμώνιος Ἀπολλοφάνου τοῦ Σελεύ-κου [ἀ]νήγειρεν ὑπέρ τε ἑαυτοῦ καὶ Λυσανίου καὶ ἀδελφῶν σωτηρίας.[242] On the basis of the finding place, it seems likely that the inscription refers to the naos itself. The majority of the steps in the *salle aux gradins*, which served as the pronaos, were dedicated in A.D. 61/62.[243] Two explanations for this thirty-year gap can be suggested: either the pronaos existed without steps for some thirty years, or the inscription of A.D. 31/32 refers to an early phase of the temple. Traces of rebuilding and some inscriptional evidence perhaps make the second hypothesis the more likely. The most significant evidence for the demolition of at least parts of the structure of the 30s A.D. is the discovery in a late wall between two rooms (fig. 40, rooms 9 and 10) of a reused inscription dated to A.D. 37, recording the erection of a meeting place by an association of men.[244] Chapel 2, which flanks the main entrance on the south, was erected in A.D. 92, and an inscription found in the vestibule records the erection of a chapel and its doors (τὴν οἰκοδομὴν καὶ τὰ θυρώματα) in A.D. 91. The building was damaged in the earthquake of A.D. 160; repairs were made, and an inscription shows that the temple was still in use in A.D. 225 or 235.[245]

The plan of the Temple of Atargatis closely resembles that of the Temple of Artemis (fig. 40). The main entrance to the roughly square court lies on the axis of the sanctuary unit, and a monumental altar stands in the courtyard on the same line. Both the entrance vestibule and the sanctuary unit are placed slightly to the south of the central line of the complex. The entrance was flanked by buttresses, and a staircase to the south must have given access to a roof terrace over the propylon. There is a second, subsidiary entrance in the north wall.

The sanctuary unit in the Temple of Atargatis is placed against the rear wall of the court, unlike that in the Temple of Artemis, where it is free-standing. Its axis coincides with the long axis of the court. The pronaos, whose door is flanked by small buttresses, is arranged as a *salle aux gradins*. Under its floor was found a small storage jar with bits of bone and ashes, perhaps a foundation deposit. The naos is flanked by two sacristies, as in the Temple of Ar-

temis, and small fragments of wall paintings remained in it. An altar in the court, dedicated by Gemellus, the legate of the emperor (πρ[ε]σβευ[τ]ὴς Σεβαστοῦ), was placed within a small columnar shrine to the southeast of the entrance to the *salle aux gradins*.[246] A second, uninscribed incense altar with a niche above it also occupied this shrine. Both altars were subsequently covered with plaster, obscuring the dedicatory inscription. Traces of painting too fragmentary to interpret remain on successive coats of plaster. A Doric column stood in the court, in front of the north side of the sanctuary unit. Other installations in the court included a waterproof basin and several small altars or pedestals. The paving of the court apparently dates to the second century A.D. Three superimposed stone basins found in the entrance vestibule suggest a rite of washing on entering the precinct. A second *salle aux gradins* (13) is located against the north wall of the court; its importance is emphasized by the altar placed in the court in front of its door. Three pedestals against the rear wall probably supported statues.

A number of subsidiary rooms were built against the walls of the court. Some of these surely served as chapels for the *synnaoi theoi* mentioned in the inscriptions. Four (rooms 9, 11, 15, 17) are lined with benches and thus probably served as rooms for ritual dining, and the facade of room 17 is distinguished by the presence of three rubble columns. A statue base against the rear wall of one of them (9) probably supported the image of the deity worshipped there. Rooms 10 and 11, just to the west of the north entrance, seem to form an independent unit; room 11, with a bicolumnar facade facing onto the court, serves as a vestibule to room 10, which is very narrow. There are three niches in the rear wall of room 10. A plaster mortar found in room 14 suggests that this room might have been used for food preparation. Brown suggests that a group of rooms in the southeast corner (6, 7, 8, 18) might have served as meeting place and living quarters for the priests.[247] It is not possible to trace the order of construction of the various chapels.

Abundant epigraphical evidence demonstrates that the temple was dedicated to Atargatis. The cult relief, which represents Atargatis, her consort Hadad, and the mysterious *sēmeion*, was almost

---

[242] Cumont, *Fouilles*, 427, no. 85.

[243] Ibid., 429-41, no. 90; probably no. 91; nos. 92-94, 97, 99-101, 106-108, 110-111, 113-14, 116-18.

[244] Welles, "Inscriptions," 129-31, no. 2. The inscription will be discussed in more detail below.

[245] Rowell, *Dura Report* III, 35 f.; Rowell and Bellinger, *Dura Report* III, 46-49, D. 146; 59, D. 157; 61 f., D. 159. For the finding place of the inscriptions, see Pillet, *Dura Report* III, 9.

[246] Rowell and Bellinger, *Dura Report* III, 43-46, D. 145.

[247] Brown, *Dura Report* VII/VIII, 194.

certainly modelled after the cult images in the principal sanctuary of the Syrian goddess at Hierapolis.[248] Therefore, the worship of Atargatis at Dura was related to and probably derived from that at Hierapolis. Though our lack of knowledge about the form of the temple at Hierapolis makes it impossible to compare the two, Lucian's description of the sanctuary of the Syrian goddess (*DDS* 28-41), particularly his statement that the temple is made like those in Ionia (*DDS* 30), suggests that the Dura building differed from that at Hierapolis. There appear to have been some similarities, however. They share the fact that the temple proper was set in a courtyard, and Lucian's enumeration of the deities worshipped in the sanctuary at Hierapolis shows that there, as at Dura, Atargatis shared her sanctuary with other divinities. They apparently shared some rites, as well. An inscription of A.D. 34/35 found in the Dura temple and recording the erection of phalloi ($\varphi\alpha\lambda\lambda o\acute{\iota}$) by one Ammonios, the son of Apollophanes, recalls Lucian's mention (*DDS* 28) of phalloi in the entrance to the sanctuary at Hierapolis, which a man climbed twice a year.[249] Bellinger had suggested before the discovery of the inscription that Lucian's statement might explain the purpose of the Doric column found in the courtyard of the Dura temple.[250]

The *salle aux gradins* must have been used for some sort of cult performance, but the small size of the available space shows that the number of participants must have been limited. Lucian does not mention a theatral area in the temple at Hierapolis but does describe two ceremonies that took place in the court, the descent of the images to the sacred lake ($\grave{\epsilon}\varsigma$ $\tau\grave{\eta}\nu$ $\lambda\acute{\iota}\mu\nu\eta\nu$ $\kappa\alpha\tau\alpha\beta\acute{\alpha}\sigma\iota\epsilon\varsigma$) and the pyre or torch festival (*DDS* 47-50). The first festival is unlikely to have been celebrated at Dura, since it depended on the presence of the sacred lake at Hierapolis. It is possible, however, that a modified version of the rites celebrated at Hierapolis was carried out in the Dura temple. The basin in the courtyard might even have served as a symbolic reminder of the sacred lake. It is also possible that

images were carried down to the Euphrates. Bellinger suggests on the basis of Lucian's description (*DDS* 50) and a passage in Apuleius (*Metamorphoses* VII.27-28) that the "statue of Atargatis was brought forth from the naos into the *salle aux gradins* and there worshipped with dancing and orgiastic rites by the priests to the accompaniment of music from the worshippers."[251] Cumont had suggested dances and sacred chants.[252] Will thinks it probable that the image of the goddess was displayed at the door leading from the naos to the *salle aux gradins*. The sanctuary of the Syrian gods at Delos incorporated a theater of Greek form, and inscriptional evidence supports Will's hypothesis that there also, the image of Atargatis was transported from the naos to the theater.[253] Thus the Dura temple of Atargatis probably represents the adaptation of a Babylonian type of court temple to the worship of the great goddess of Hierapolis, with the inclusion of a theatral area for ritual performances.

Inscriptions found in the temple show that Atargatis and her consort Hadad shared the temple with *synnaoi theoi*. An inscription found in a cistern that was later plastered over must have belonged to an early phase of the temple. The inscription records the offering of 100 denarii as partial payment toward some construction, perhaps a porch, dedicated to Shamash, by one "Malkiôn, son of Shomêshû, (son of) Maḥêbâ."[254] The dedicant's name is Palmyrene. The Greek version of the inscription gives the god's name as Helios. Two mysterious and otherwise unknown gods, Sasados and Saddoudan, also had altars in the temple. The dedicant of the altar to Sasados has a Latin name written in Greek letters ($\Sigma\kappa\alpha\nu\rho\iota\alpha\nu\acute{o}\varsigma$ $M\alpha\xi\iota\mu o\varsigma$); and one Masichos dedicated the altar to Saddoudan.[255] Another inscription, in Greek, records a painting for Adonis and Atargatis.[256]

The Temple of Atargatis is closely connected with the neighboring Temple of Artemis. Probably at the time of the building of the Temple of Atargatis, the section of street that separated the two was closed to wheeled traffic by a flight of two

[248] Downey, *Stone and Plaster Sculpture*, 173-80, with references to earlier literature.

[249] Welles, "Inscriptions," 128 f., no. 1.

[250] Bellinger, *Dura Report* III, 23 f.

[251] Ibid., 22 f.

[252] Cumont, *Fouilles*, 202 f.

[253] Will, "Le sanctuaire syrien de Délos," *Annales archéologiques de Syrie* I (1951), 77-79.

[254] Ingholt, in Welles, "Inscriptions," 131-37, no. 3. R. du Mesnil du Buisson, "Un bilingue araméen-grec de l'époque parthe à

Doura-Europos," *Syria* XIX (1938), 147-52, gives a slightly different translation.

[255] Rowell and Bellinger, *Dura Report* III, 59-63, D. 158, D. 160.

[256] Brown, *Dura Report* VII/VIII, 154, no. 9. Rowell and Bellinger originally restored the first divine name as Ἀδων[αίῳ, "lord," which they took to refer to Hadad because there was no evidence for the worship of Adonis at Dura, nor for his association with Atargatis (*Dura Report* III, 46-49, D. 146), objections countered by the discovery at Dura of a Temple of Adonis that apparently contained a chapel of Atargatis (Brown, *Dura Report* VII/VIII, 153-56).

steps. An arch was constructed on impost pilasters at the corner of each building.[257] Like the Temple of Artemis, that of Atargatis seems to have been a major civic shrine. Its importance is emphasized by the fact that Gemellus, an envoy of the emperor (πρ[ε]σβευ[τ]ὴς Σεβαστοῦ), dedicated an altar in this temple, as well as in the Temple of Artemis.[258] The dedication by Ammonios, son of Apollophanes, found in the naos, suggests that this Greek, who also erected phalloi in the court, played an important role in building the temple. Welles notes that the family continued its interest in the temple, as indicated by the fact that Ammonios' daughter dedicated a seat in the *salle aux gradins* in A.D. 61/62 and that his grandson presented a chapel and doors in the spring of A.D. 92.[259] The great majority of the women who owned seats in the *salle aux gradins* belonged to families with Greek, indeed Macedonian names, though a few inscriptions (probably six) include both Greek and Semitic names, and another four only Semitic ones.[260] The monumental altar in the court bears a graffito of a man with a Semitic name, Ἀββᾶς Ἀββοῦ, dated to A.D. 69/70.[261] Three of the four chapels whose inscriptions remain were dedicated by men with Greek names.[262] One of these chapels contained a money box (ταμεῖον). Another inscription, reused in the fill between oikoi 9 and 10, records the erection to the goddess of a meeting place (συνχωρεθέ<ν>τα τόπον), probably a chapel, by an association of men, in A.D. 37. There were two main dedicants, both with Semitic names, and probably fifteen others, all but two of whom had Semitic names. The association did include one man with a Macedonian name, Lysias the son of Nicophon, and one Lysimachos whose father had a Semitic name (Zebidaa). The dedication of a room by the members of an association (συνέταιροι) recalls the similar dedication of an andron in the Temple of Aphlad.[263]

A large house that occupies the remainder of the block to the south of the Temple of Atargatis is contemporary with the construction of the temple. The two originally shared a party wall and probably also communicated with one another through a door in the south wall of the temple (in room 3). In the rebuilding after the earthquake of A.D. 160, the two buildings were separated but remained closely connected; it is even possible that there was a passage between the two on the second story. The house also opens onto the narrow alley separating it from the Temple of Artemis. The close connection between the house and the Temple of Atargatis has led to the suggestion that it was the priests' house. No inscriptions and few objects were found. One room was a bakery. A painting in another room that shows a figure reclining on a bed and perhaps a priest and a thymiaterion has been interpreted as a depiction of a funeral meal.[264] In spite of the lack of finds, the close connection between the house and the temples does support the interpretation of the house as belonging to the priests.

TEMPLE OF BEL

The Temple of Bel (also called the Temple of the Palmyrene Gods) (fig. 47)[265] was built into the northwest corner of the city wall. An inscription to Zeus Soter dated to A.D. 50/51 that was found in the courtyard gives a *terminus ante quem* for the existence of some sort of cult structure here, though of course the temple could be somewhat older.[266] Pearson has identified three main phases of construction. The dates of these are uncertain, but the third phase may plausibly be connected with alterations necessitated by the earthquake of A.D. 160.

The northernmost tower of the western part of the city wall was included within the boundaries of the temple, and this tower apparently functioned as

---

[257] Brown, *Dura Report* VI, 401.

[258] Rowell and Bellinger, *Dura Report* III, 43-46, D. 145.

[259] Cumont, *Fouilles*, 427, no. 85; Welles, "Inscriptions," 128 f., no. 1; Rowell and Bellinger, *Dura Report* III, 59, D. 157. See above for further discussion of these inscriptions.

[260] The fragmentary state of the inscriptions makes certainty about family names impossible. In twenty-two inscriptions only Greek names remain (Cumont, *Fouilles*, 427-38, nos. 85-109, 112A, 113), but in many cases only the men's names are preserved. In addition, most of these inscriptions date to A.D. 61/62 and thus record the dedications of one year. Four other inscriptions that are probably connected with the *salle aux gradins* include only Greek names (Cumont, *Fouilles*, 440-42, nos. 116-119; Rowell and Bellinger, *Dura Report* III, 42 f., D. 144).

[261] Welles, "Inscriptions," 137, no. 4.

[262] Rowell and Bellinger, *Dura Report* III, 50, D. 148; 59, D. 157; 61 f., D. 159.

[263] Welles, "Inscriptions," 129-31, no. 2. For the inscription in the Temple of Aphlad, see Hopkins, *Dura Report* V, 114-16, no 418.

[264] A. Naudy, *Dura Report* III, 25-27; Rowell, *Dura Report* III, 33-35.

[265] The description of the temple is based on the published report and an unpublished manuscript by Henry Pearson in the Dura archives. For the architecture, see Cumont, *Fouilles*, 29-41; Hopkins, *Dura Report* II, 67 f.; idem, *Dura Report* V, 290 f.; Eissfeldt, *Tempel und Kulte*, 134 f.

[266] Hopkins, *Dura Report* II, 91-93, H. 4; Eissfeldt, *Tempel und Kulte*, 134 f.

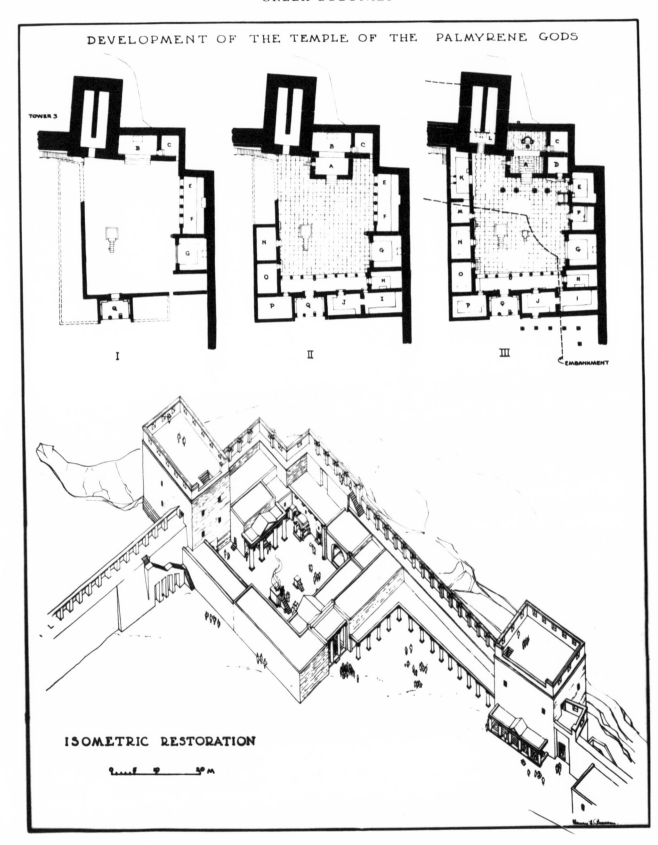

DEVELOPMENT OF THE TEMPLE OF THE PALMYRENE GODS

ISOMETRIC RESTORATION

47. Dura-Europos, Temple of Bel, periods I-III, plan.

part of the temple. The sanctity of the tower is suggested by the fact that altars were placed in it, the most important being an altar dedicated to Zeus Megistos on the occasion of the earthquake and another dedicated to Iarhibol by a Roman chiliarch.[267] Von Gerkan argued that the presence of the temple was taken into account in the rebuilding of the tower and the parts of the city wall next to it, stating that "in the construction the proprietorship of the ground floor of the tower by the Temple of the Palmyrene Gods was foreseen." He concluded from the fact that the part of the city wall that constitutes the west wall of the naos of the temple was completed later than the tower "that the temple plan was foreseen in the building of the wall."[268] The original line of the wall bounding the temple court on the south is uncertain, but Pearson in his unpublished manuscript suggests that in the first two periods of the building's life the southern wall did not run all the way to the tower, leaving access between the temple and the stairs to the sentry-go. The entrance to the precinct, a colonnaded porch (Q) in the eastern wall, lay on the axis of neither the naos nor the tower but rather in between. The monumental altar that stood in the court on the axis of the entrance dates to the first period of construction. The reason for its placement is unknown. Only the base remains, suggesting that it fell into disrepair or was levelled at some time. In the third phase an altar was built on the axis of the pronaos-naos complex. It is not clear whether the original altar survived into this period.

In the original temple structure, as shown on the plan (fig. 47.I), the naos consisted of a single room (B) facing east, with its long axis perpendicular to the long axis of the court. A subsidiary room (C) accessible from the naos occupied the space between the naos and the corner of the city wall. In the second phase of construction, a pronaos (A) of the same width as the naos and approached by steps was added. The pronaos could also be entered through a small subsidiary door in its southeast corner. In the third phase, a portico of four columns was added in front of the pronaos. It is not clear what provisions were made for a cult image in the first two periods, but a line of plaster extending a short distance from the rear wall of the naos

(shown as a dotted line in plans I and II) is interpreted by Pearson as the remains of a central altar or table. Since there are no foundations, these traces cannot be remains of a pedestal for a cult statue. The huge, presumably divine figure in the badly damaged painting on the rear wall of the naos may well have been the original cult image.[269] In the third phase, the cult image was presumably housed in a free-standing aedicula in the center of the naos, and statuettes of Iarhibol and ʿAglibol may have been placed in small niches in the front pillars.[270]

As usual at Dura, the court of the temple was lined with a number of rooms built at various periods. The plan suggests that in the first phase the structure was fairly simple, including, in addition to the naos and sacristy, only a large room (G) lined with benches on three sides, and a portico (E-F), both along the north side of the court. A gap between two buttresses of the city wall forms a niche in the center of the rear wall of the portico. In the second phase additional rooms were added; some are equipped with benches and were therefore presumably used for ritual dining (G and H on the north side of the court, I, J, and P on the east, and N and O on the south). Small tables or altars also stood in some of these rooms. In the top of an altar in room E are three indentations filled with soot. In this second phase the courtyard was paved with brick, and another portico was built along the inside of the entrance facade. In the third phase the portico E-F on the north side of the court was apparently converted into two rooms, so that there were now five rooms on the north side of the court. An additional room (D) filled the space between the pronaos and the north wall of the court. In front of the westernmost of the rooms along the north wall (E) a small aedicula was built, presumably to house the image of a *synnaos theos*.[271] Rectangular bases attached to the front of the columns of this aedicula may have supported statuettes.

The construction of the large room K, which closed the south side of the court, is contemporary with alterations made to the tower, probably in connection with earthquake damage, and the small room M that opens onto room K was probably built at the same time. Room K was certainly a center of worship, for it is adorned with paintings de-

[267] Hopkins, *Dura Report* II, 86-91, H. 2, H. 3; Eissfeldt, *Tempel und Kulte*, 135.

[268] A. Von Gerkan, *Dura Report* VII/VIII, 31 f. The chronological relationship between the city wall and the Temple of Bel remains unclear; on the subject, see Pierre Leriche, "Chronologie du rem-

part du brique crue de Doura-Europos," *Syria* LXIII (1986), 78-82, fig. 14 and n. 32.

[269] Cumont, *Fouilles*, 74-76, tableau III, pls. XLII.2, XLIII; Perkins, *Art*, 37.

[270] Cumont, *Fouilles*, 31 f.

[271] Ibid., 35.

picting the eunuch Otes performing a sacrifice to five Palmyrene deities; the accompanying inscription calls him the builder of an exedra, a term that is probably to be understood as referring to the room, but which may refer instead to a columnar aedicula that was later installed in the center of the back wall on a low bench that ran around three walls.[272] The aedicula perhaps held a cult statue, and lamps may have been placed in niches in the walls on either side of it. The date of the paintings is uncertain. Brown suggests a date around the 150s or 160s on the basis of stylistic similarities between the Otes paintings and the dated paintings of the Temple of Adonis.[273] Perkins, on the other hand, suggests a third-century date on the basis of the epithet *bouleutēs* ("senator") used to identify one of the participants, and she feels that the style of the paintings is consistent with such a date.[274] The temple was still undergoing rebuilding in the third century A.D., as is indicated by the re-use in the pavement of a stone bearing a defaced inscription to Severus Alexander and Julia Mamaea dated to A.D. 230.[275]

Cult furniture and small altars survive in various parts of the temple. For instance, several incense altars and small bases stood in the entrance portico, and an additional broken columnar altar was built against one of the columns of the interior colonnade. These installations suggest the offering of sacrifices on entering the precinct. A small incense altar was also attached to the stair of the monumental altar in the courtyard, and a shallow plaster basin stood in front of room F. Other minor installations—a niche, a reed shelf, and irregularly placed peg holes in the walls of the pronaos; and a small shelf in the wall in front of room E—might have supported ex-votos.[276]

The temple appears to have been dedicated to the triad of Bel, Iarhibol, and ʿAglibol—with Bel as the paramount god. Other deities are also named in graffiti. Identification of Bel with Zeus probably explains the presence in the temple and tower of altars and dedications to Zeus.[277] The painting of the eunuch Otes in room K shows him sacrificing to the Palmyrene triad of Bel, Iarhibol, and ʿAglibol, together with a fourth god, probably Arsu, and an almost obliterated fifth deity, perhaps a goddess.[278] The three gods represented in the painting that shows the sacrifice of the tribune Julius Terentius and the members of the twentieth Palmyrene cohort are harder to identify, but they are probably Iarhibol, ʿAglibol, and Arsu.[279]

Evidence from inscriptions and graffiti shows that all segments of the population worshiped in the Temple of Bel. Its importance in the civic life of Dura is suggested by the fact that the city (ἡ πόλις) erected an altar to Zeus Megistos on the occasion of the earthquake of A.D. 160 inside the tower that is included in the temple precinct.[280] The presence of Macedonian families is amply demonstrated by the lavish paintings offered by one Conon, depicting himself and the members of his family. The men of the family have Greek names, but Conon's daughter is called Bithnanaia. Lysias, the son of Conon, son of Patroclos, probably the son of the Conon in the painting,[281] dedicated a chapel with an upper story to Zeus Megistos on behalf of himself and his grandchildren in A.D. 115. Another member of the Greek aristocracy, Zenocrates, son of Seleukos, son of Ammonios, dedicated an altar to Zeus Soter in A.D. 50/51 on behalf of Seleukos, son of Lysias, a *stratēgos* and *epistatēs* of the city.[282] Another inscription, unfortunately not found *in situ*, records the erection of a ψαλίς by one Athenodoros, son of Aristodemos, who is called Rageibēlos, son of Machchisaios (Ῥαγειβηλος Μαχχισαίου), thus a Hellenized Semite. Cumont suggests that the ψαλίς might have been a niche to hold a divine image, or, less probably, a vaulted entrance.[283]

Persons with Semitic names also played a prom-

[272] Ibid., 38, 364 f., no. 9. Cumont argues on the basis of Greek usage that the term "exedra" refers to the whole room. Cf. also Brown, *Dura Report* VII/VIII, 156, n. 20. Perkins (*Art*, 47) identifies the exedra of the inscription with the later aedicula; this is also Pearson's interpretation. For the paintings, see Cumont, *Fouilles*, 122-36, tableaux XVII, XVIII, pls. LV-LX.

[273] Brown, *Dura Report* VII/VIII, 163.

[274] Perkins, *Art*, 47.

[275] Cumont, *Fouilles*, 357 f., no. 3.

[276] Information from Pearson's manuscript.

[277] Cumont, *Fouilles*, 379 f., no. 17; 387 f., no. 25; Hopkins, *Dura Report* II, 86-92, H. 2, H. 4; Seyrig, *Dura Report* IV, 68-71, no. 168.

[278] Cumont, *Fouilles*, 122-34, pls. LV-LVIII; H. Seyrig, "Hiérarchie des divinités de Palmyre," *Antiquités syriennes* I, 28 (*Syria*

XIII [1932], 191); R. du Mesnil du Buisson, *Les Tessères et les monnaies de Palmyre* (Paris, 1962), 173 f.

[279] Downey, *Stone and Plaster Sculpture*, 213 f., with references to earlier literature. For the painting, see Cumont, *Fouilles*, 89-100, tableau VI, pls. XLIX-LI.

[280] Hopkins, *Dura Report* II, 86-90, H. 2.

[281] Cumont, *Fouilles*, 355 f., no. 1; 359-61, no. 5; *contra*, see Perkins, *Art*, 40 f., who dates the Conon painting in the second century A.D. and suggests that Lysias could be an ancestor rather than a descendant of Conon.

[282] Hopkins, *Dura Report* II, 91-93, H. 4.

[283] Cumont, *Fouilles*, 356 f., no. 2. Part of the date is missing. Cumont restores it to read 470 of the Seleucid era, or A.D. 159.

inent role in the sanctuary. The eunuch Otes probably dedicated the large room K; at the least he decorated it with paintings. It is notable that the second
sacrificant depicted in the painting, Iabsumsos, son
of Abdaathes (Ἰάβσυμσος Ἀβδαάθητος) is a *bouleutēs* (βουλευτής).[284] Eunuch priests are also apparently named in a graffito scratched on an altar from
the pronaos.[285] A particularly important graffito
probably lists the rotation of priests in the temple
service; all of the names are Semitic.[286] The graffiti
in the building contain primarily Semitic names,
but Greek and Latin names also appear, and a number of graffiti show a mixture of Greek and Semitic
names within a family.[287]

Two graffiti specify occupations of people. One
Bargatēs, a barber (Βαργάτης κουρεὺς), is mentioned twice; Cumont suggests that he was perhaps
the official barber of the temple. Another graffito
mentions a baker (ἀρτοκοπῶ), probably the temple
baker, and a number, either the number of years he
had worked for the temple[288] or a sum of money
given to him.[289] The army is also strongly represented in the temple. The most significant indication of the army's presence is the painting depicting
a sacrifice by the tribune Julius Terentius and members of the twentieth Palmyrene cohort to a group
of Palmyrene gods; the priest, Themēs, the son of
Mokimos (Θέμης Μοκίμ[ου]), had a Semitic name.[290]
A legionary priest (ἱερεῖ λεγι[ω]ναρίῳ) with an unusual Semitic name (Ἀββᾶυι, in the dative) is included in a list of names in a graffito in the naos.[291]
Individual soldiers also made dedications in the
temple. Thus, one Scribonios Mucianos, a chiliarch, dedicated an altar in the tower to Iarhibol,[292]
and Aurelios Diphilianos, a soldier of the fourth
Scythian legion, dedicated an altar placed in front
of room E "to [his] national god, Zeus Betylos,
[god] of the dwellers along the Orontes": Θεῷ
πατρῴῳ Διὶ Βετύλῳ τῶν πρὸς τῷ Ὀρόντῃ. The use of
the *gentilicium* Aurelius probably dates the inscription after the *Constitutio Antoniana*.[293] A dedication
to Alexander Severus and Julia Mamaea was reused
in the pavement of the court, doubtless after the

damnatio memoriae of A.D. 235;[294] it is not certain,
however, that the inscription originally came from
the temple.

Graffiti provide an unusually full picture of cult
furnishings and gifts offered in the Temple of Bel.
An inventory dated to A.D. 165/66 scratched on the
north wall of the pronaos lists thirty-seven golden
images and two smaller ones, presumably statues
of divinities, as well as an image of Patroclos and
one of Conon, son of Abissaios. Cumont suggests
that the latter were probably portrait statues but
might simply have been statuettes dedicated by the
two men. A list of offerings made on the twentieth
day of the intercalary month of Dystros and during
the month of Dios includes three images, two of
which are described as small; these were probably
statues and statuettes. This list also includes a number of drinking cups and four perfume flasks.[295]
Gifts of jewelry for the gods are frequently recorded. One group of graffiti on the south wall of
the naos specified that some of the jewelry—rings,
bracelets, necklaces, and a fibula—was for the neck
and arms of the gods; this implies that the
jewelry adorned statues.[296] A fibula (φίβλα)
is also part of a long inventory. The interpretation
of this and other graffiti is made difficult by the fact
that many of the words are unfamiliar and incomplete; in some cases the graffiti contain Latin words
written in the Greek alphabet. Possessions listed in
the inventory in question include three candelabra—one of gold, one of silver, one carved—and
other objects whose identity is uncertain: perhaps
boxes (καμ[ψ]άκια), plates for sacrifice ([γ]αβαθὰ),
objects that might have been either shields or shallow bowls (εἰσκοτ[λ]α δύω). The word τοράλλια is
interpreted by Cumont as a Greek form of the Latin
toralia, "bed cover"; if this interpretation is correct,
the presence of a bed cover might imply the rite of
a lectisternium, well known at Palmyra.[297] Another
graffito perhaps suggests an offering of clothing, if
Cumont's interpretation of λακέρνια as a diminu-
tive of the Latin *lacerna*, a military cloak, is correct.
This same list includes cups, a plate, a box for salt

[284] Ibid., 364–66, no. 9.

[285] Hopkins, *Dura Report* II, 94 f., H. 5.

[286] Cumont, *Fouilles*, 381–83, no. 20.

[287] Ibid., 366 f., nos. 10, 11; 375–77, no. 14; 379, no. 16; 390, no.
28; 392 f., nos. 33, 34; 394, no. 37; R. du Mesnil du Buisson, *Inventaire des inscriptions palmyréniennes de Doura-Europos*, new ed. (Paris,
1939), 9 f., nos. 16, 17; Welles, *Dura Report* IV, 172–75, nos. 351,
357, 358 (Semitic); Cumont, *Fouilles*, 380 f., no. 18; 383–87, nos.
21, 22, 24; 398–400, no. 44; Welles, *Dura Report* IV, 172–75, nos.
352–358 (Greek, Latin, and mixed).

[288] Cumont, *Fouilles*, 383–85, nos. 21, 22.

[289] R. du Mesnil du Buisson, *Inventaire des inscriptions palmyréniennes de Doura-Europos*, 24.

[290] Cumont, *Fouilles*, 89–114, tableau VI; 363 f., nos. 8 a and b.

[291] Ibid., 375–77, no. 14.

[292] Hopkins, *Dura Report* II, 90 f., H. 3.

[293] Seyrig, *Dura Report* IV, 68–71, no. 168.

[294] Cumont, *Fouilles*, 357 f., no. 3.

[295] Ibid., 385–87, no. 23.

[296] Ibid., 369–72, no. 12; Downey, *Stone and Plaster Sculpture*,
151.

[297] Cumont, *Fouilles*, 372–75, no. 13.

(ἁλιά), and perhaps baskets (κάφ[φ](ινοι)?).[298] A lamp is mentioned elsewhere.[299] Cups appear to have been the most common offering.[300]

An inscription in Aramaic but written in Greek letters that records an offering in the temple presents great difficulties. Levi della Vida translated it, with many reservations, "Deux lingots d'or sur la main de la statue, le 2 Nisan, Barzakikè."[301] Du Mesnil combined two alternatives rejected by Levi della Vida to read "deux globes d'or pour la main du dieu."[302] Milik removes the statue (or the god) from the inscription, translating the first line "deux fromages d'or, ʿAbdšalmâ," which he explains as models of goat cheese left by a shepherd.[303] Teixidor objects to this idea as odd, preferring to translate instead "two molds," while recognizing that his is merely a fourth hypothesis.[304]

Cumont restores a line in another inscription, εμτα φραγ[ελλίον?] φρα[γ(έλλιον?)] to give φραγελλίον, "flagellum." He suggests that the whips might have been used for ritual flagellation, as in the rites of the galli in the cult of Cybele, or they might have been a divine attribute, as in the cult of Jupiter Heliopolitanus.[305] In view of the fragmentary state of preservation, it is probably best not to build any hypotheses about cult practice on this inscription.

In spite of the difficulties of interpretation, the cult installations, paintings, inscriptions, and graffiti in the Temple of Bel provide unusually full information about temple rituals and personnel. The inscriptions and graffiti show that all segments of the population, including both civilians and the military, worshipped in the temple, and the dedication of an altar by the city suggests that the temple played a role in the official life of the city as well.

TEMPLE OF APHLAD

The Temple of Aphlad, god of the city of Anath, occupied the southwest corner of the city wall (fig. 48). An inscription recording the erection of an andron to Aphlad by the members of an association shows that the temple was in existence by A.D. 54.[306] The temple came to consist of a number of rooms loosely arranged around a courtyard in which stood a number of monumental altars. The city wall formed the western and southern boundaries of the precinct; but the temple lacked a temenos wall. The sacred area was presumably entered through the open space on the east side, between two chapels, or rooms for ritual dining (rooms 5 and 6). There are two sanctuary units, both facing east. One, the andron of the inscription (1), which also contained the cult relief, is located along the northern side of the area. It is a single room with benches lining three sides. An aedicula attached to the rear wall held the image of Aphlad; there is a shelf in front of the aedicula and an incense altar in front of that. A shallow niche is set into the entrance wall, on the inside and to the south of the door. Outside and to the north of the door stands a high rubble shaft with an indentation on the top. Since there are no traces of fire, Hopkins suggests that this shaft was used for libations rather than for incense offerings. The other sanctuary unit (2A-2B), a more conventional pronaos-naos group, is free-standing. Hopkins sugests that these rooms were erected when the first pavement of the area was already in use, since the west end of the naos rests on fairly deep fill. The plan shows a shallow projection, too shallow to serve as a statue base, in the center of the rear wall of the naos, but no altar was found. The only trace of cult furniture was a bowl set into the floor just within the doorway, perhaps to hold water for ritual ablutions. Fragments of wall paintings were found; their condition precludes reconstruction, but they included a female head in a high headdress and other fragments of large-scale figures.

It appears from the plan that a wall extending to the east from the northern wall of the andron (1) formed the northern side of the temenos. Apparently, however, this side of the sanctuary grew up piecemeal. Hopkins states that the first room to be built was the easternmost and largest (6); its rear wall projected a bit beyond the line of the north wall of the andron, and it was lined with benches on three sides. According to Hopkins, at the time of the building of the second chamber (8), a curtain

---

[298] Ibid., 378 f., no. 15.

[299] Ibid., 383 f., no. 20 bis.

[300] Ibid., 369-72, no. 12, line 7; 375-77, no. 14, line 2; 378 f., no. 15, line 1; 383-85, no. 21.

[301] Ibid., 367 f., no. 11.

[302] R. du Mesnil du Buisson, *Inventaire des inscriptions palmyréniennes de Doura-Europos*, 33 f., no. 51; accepted by Mouterde in a review of Du Mesnil's monograph, *MélUSJ* XXII (1939), 152.

[303] J. T. Milik, "Inscription araméenne en caractères grecs de Doura-Europos et une dédicace grecque de Cordoue," *Syria* XLIV (1967), 289-91.

[304] J. Teixidor, "Bulletin d'épigraphie sémitique," *Syria* XLVII (1970), 375 f., no. 85; cf. Downey, *Stone and Plaster Sculpture*, 151.

[305] Cumont, *Fouilles*, 375 f., no. 14, line 3, and commentary.

[306] Hopkins, *Dura Report* V, 113-16, no. 418. The architecture is discussed by Hopkins on pp. 98-104. See also Eissfeldt, *Tempel und Kulte*, 139 f.

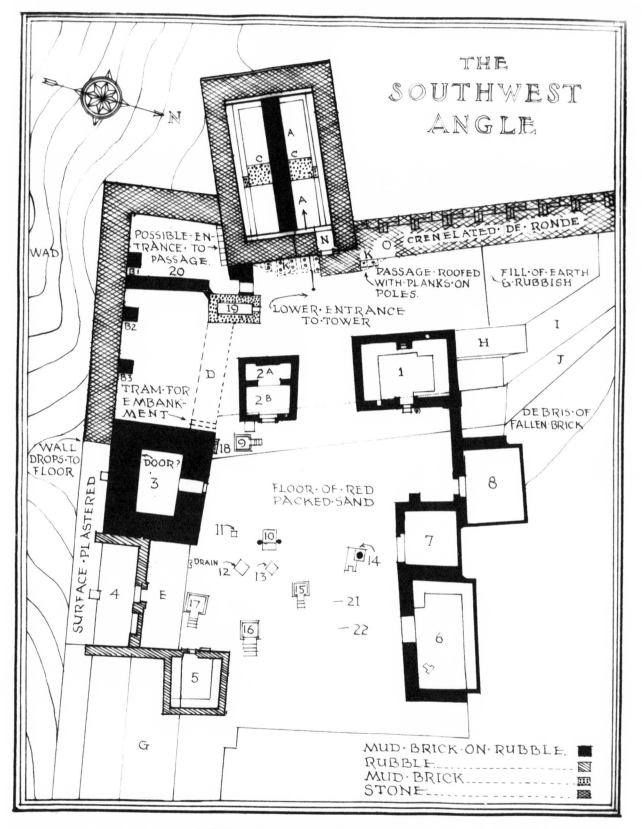

48. Dura-Europos, Temple of Aphlad, plan.

wall was extended to connect the andron with room 6; room 8 lay to the outside (north) of this wall, but was entered through the temple precinct. The only find in this room, a large basalt mill, suggests that it might have been used for the preparation of grain for ritual meals eaten in other rooms (e.g., 6 and 5, both of which have benches). Finally, room 7 was built in the space between rooms 8 and 6.

On the east side of the sanctuary, opposite room 6, a smaller chamber (5) opened to the interior of the precinct, and benches lined two walls. Two additional rooms were built against the southern city wall. The easternmost of these (4) was relatively shallow and apparently was open toward the wadi on the south side. Next to this a tower with heavy walls was built (3), perhaps in the Roman period, and curiously, on the inside of the wall; its door opened into the temple court. In the court were a number of free-standing altars, mostly grouped in its western section. One (9) was located close to the sanctuary unit 2A-2B and partially blocked its entrance; because of this and because its base was covered by the second pavement of the court, Hopkins argues that it must have been one of the earliest altars built. It is hard to relate the altars to specific rooms, which suggests that they might have been independent centers of worship. Hopkins relates altar 10 to the sanctuary unit 2A-2B on the basis of the fact that it is almost aligned with this sanctuary, but since it lies some distance in front of the sanctuary unit and is slightly smaller than some of the other altars in this part of the court, this assumption is somewhat questionable. Two small pedestals in the court (12, 13) may have been statue bases.

The Temple of Aphlad is more loosely organized than the majority of Dura temples, and it is anomalous in its lack of an enclosure wall. In some respects, it resembles the rustic sanctuaries in the steppe area to the northwest of Palmyra, particularly the sanctuary of ʿAbgal at Khirbet Semrine.[307] On the other hand, it does resemble especially the Temple of Bel at Dura in its incorporation of a tower of the city wall, and indeed von Gerkan suggests that the Temples of Bel and Aphlad were located so as to put the two most vulnerable corners of the city under divine protection.[308] The incorporation of a tower of the city wall into a temple

precinct is a feature of the Temple of Azzanathkona as well, which also resembles the Temple of Aphlad in having two sanctuary units and a large number of subsidiary rooms.[309]

Aphlad, called in the inscription on the cult relief the "god of the village of Anath on the Euphrates," is otherwise unknown. The cult relief probably copies the image of the god in his temple at Anath.[310] Aphlad may well have been related to the goddess Azzanathkona, whose name suggests a connection with Anath. Unfortuntely, nothing is known of the shrine of Aphlad at Anath (assuming there was one), and therefore the peculiarities of the Temple of Aphlad at Dura cannot be explained on the basis of its relationship to its parent shrine.

The inscriptional evidence suggests that the sanctuary of Aphlad was erected by a small group of people. The inscription on the cult relief records that Adadiabos, the son of Zabdibolos, son of Silloi, erected the foundation of the temple ($\tau\dot{\eta}\nu$ $\dot{\alpha}\varphi\epsilon\dot{\iota}\delta\rho\nu\sigma\iota\nu$ $\tau\alpha\dot{\nu}\tau\eta[\nu]$ $\iota\epsilon\rho\sigma\tilde{\nu}$) on behalf of the safety of himself, his children, and all his house. The andron was erected by the members of an association consisting of eleven men, members of six families, on behalf of the safety of the *stratēgos* Seleukos, themselves, and their children. All of the names and patronymics of the members of the association are Semitic with the exception of Theogenēs, perhaps a Greek version of a Semitic name.[311] The graffiti from the andron, however, include both Greek and Semitic names in roughly equal numbers.[312]

TEMPLE OF ZEUS THEOS

The Temple of Zeus Theos (fig. 49) was erected over the remains of modest private houses, beginning probably in the early second century A.D. The inscription on the lintel of the gate leading in from the street is dated in August/September, A.D. 114, and probably marks the completion of the "public" portions of the complex. An altar reused in a late counterwall is also dated to A.D. 113/14, but another inscription shows that the chapel unit on the north (24–30) was only dedicated in A.D. 120/21.[313] Brown suggests that the temple complex was essentially complete by that time.

The temple follows the court plan usual for

[307] D. Schlumberger, *La Palmyrène du Nord-Ouest* (Paris, 1951), 14–22, fig. 5.

[308] Von Gerkan, *Dura Report* VII/VIII, 35.

[309] On the inclusion of towers in sacred precincts at Dura, see Downey, "Temples," 21–29.

[310] Hopkins, *Dura Report* V, 112 f., 118 f. Eissfeldt, *Tempel und*

Kulte, 139 f.; Downey, *Stone and Plaster Sculpture*, 193 f., with references to earlier literature.

[311] Hopkins, *Dura Report* V, 113-16, nos. 416-418.

[312] Ibid., 120-27, nos. 419-447.

[313] Brown, *Dura Report* VII/VIII, 194 f., 212-15, nos. 886-888.

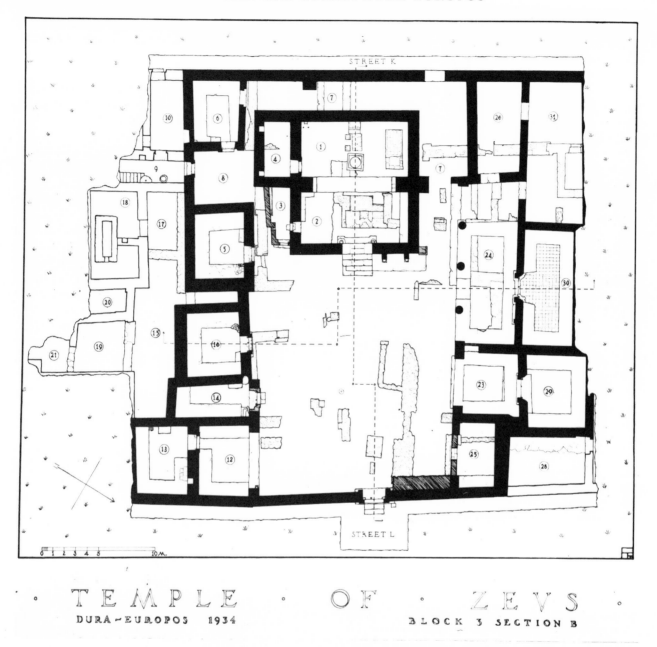

TEMPLE OF ZEVS

DURA-EUROPOS 1934   BLOCK 3 SECTION B

49. Dura-Europos, Temple of Zeus Theos, plan.

Dura, with a modest entrance lying in the east wall, just off the axis of the sanctuary unit. The slight shift of axis between the entrance and the sanctuary unit might be due in part to the fact that the temple was constructed over earlier houses. There was no monumental altar in the courtyard, though several incense altars stood there. The sanctuary unit (1, 2) consisted of a pronaos and naos of the same width, with their long axis oriented perpendicularly to the long axis of the courtyard; a sacristy (4) opened off the naos on the south side. A projecting sacristy is

seen also in the Temple of Bel (fig. 47). The sanctuary unit at the Temple of Zeus Theos was free-standing, though separated by only a narrow space from the rear wall of the precinct and the flanking rooms; Brown describes it as isolated by a circumambient corridor and compares it in this respect to the Temple of Azzanathkona (figs. 44, 45). The pronaos was approached by a staircase, and an aedicula projected into the courtyard from its front wall to the right of the door. Similar aediculae are found in other Dura temples (Atargatis, Bel, the

113

Gaddé, and Adonis), and they appear to be dedicated to *synnaoi theoi*.

The cult furniture of the naos is unusually well preserved. A round altar that stands in the center might, according to Brown, have taken the place of the altar that at Dura usually stood in the courtyard. The base of what was probably a second altar, provided with sockets to carry off the liquid from libations, stood in the southwestern corner of the naos. A plinth erected against the rear wall was probably designed not to support a cult statue but simply to offer symbolic support to the painted image of a god that dominated the rear wall of the naos. In front of this plinth stood a rectangular altar or table. Square bases beside this might have served as altars, as supports for candelabra or other paraphernalia, or as supports for a seat or shelf. A broad bench that stood in the north corner of the room might have served for a lectisternium, like those known at Palmyra; in that case, the altar might have been used in this rite. Room 4, opening from the naos on the west and equal to it in width, probably served as a sacristy or treasury, on the evidence of provisions for locking the door between the two rooms, the presence of niches in the walls, and the discovery of jewelry in the room.

Around the walls of the court stood a series of chapels, presumably erected at various times. Some utilized the walls of preexisting houses as foundations. Three were preceded by a foreroom (24, 30; 23, 29; and 12, 13); and in the largest complex (24, 30) the foreroom was a porch with three columns *in antis*. Most of the chapels were lined with benches, probably for ritual dining. The fact that four of the chapels on the south side of the court include stoves and that the walls are blackened with smoke leads Brown to suggest that food was actually prepared in them.[314] A graffito in chapel 13 preserves the beginning of an account (λόγος), with the name of one man, Adeos ('Αδέος).[315] Brown suggests that room 6 at the rear of the temple served as a meeting place for the priests, and that some of the rooms in the house to the south of the temple precinct perhaps were converted to serve as living quarters for the priests.[316]

In general terms, the Temple of Zeus Theos conforms to the plan that was normal for temples at Dura during the Parthian period. It differs from most of them in two respects: 1) there was no mon-

umental altar in the courtyard; 2) the main entrance was not flanked by towers or buttresses, nor is there evidence for provision for access to the roof anywhere in the temple.

Unfortunately, the name of the god is of little help in explaining these peculiarities. He is named twice, once as Zeus and once as Zeus Theos. All that this really tells us is that he was an important god, probably one of the many Syrian Baals.[317] Eissfeldt discusses the possibility that the name Zeus Theos is a Greek version of a Semitic title. He prefers the explanation that Zeus Theos is an Iranian-Parthian god, on the basis of an inscription from the temple, to be discussed shortly, in which the dedicant is called *Europaios* and τῶν πρώτων ("of the first"), interpreted by Eissfeldt as a Parthian court title.[318] The painting on the rear wall of the naos has been reconstructed as showing a god clad in Parthian dress, standing in front of a horse-drawn chariot and crowned by victories. As Brown points out, the paintings from the temple, which also include images of donors and sacrificants, closely resemble those from the Temple of Bel. The rites depicted include incense and wine sacrifices, as well as offerings of fruit.[319]

The inscriptions from the Temple of Zeus Theos give a relatively restricted range of names, perhaps suggesting that the temple served relatively few, primarily aristocratic families. The dedicatory inscription on the lintel of the gate from Street K into the court gives the name of an individual, Seleukos son of Theomnēstos, son of Antiochos, a member of the old Dura aristocracy. Though this inscription is quite fragmentary, the names can be reliably restored on the basis of the dedicatory inscription of the large two-room chapel 24–30, erected in A.D. 120/21.

Ἔτους βλυ΄.
Σέλευκος
Θεομνήστου
τοῦ Ἀντιόχου
Εὐρωπαῖος καὶ
τῶν πρώτων
ἀνήγειρεν Διὶ Θεῶι
τὸν ναὸν καὶ τὰ
θυρώματα καὶ
τὴν τῶν εἰκόνων
γ[ρ]αφὴν πᾶσαν.

[314] Ibid., 183-94.
[315] Ibid., 217, no. 900.
[316] Ibid., 194.
[317] Ibid., 195 f., 213 f., nos. 887, 888.

[318] Eissfeldt, *Tempel und Kulte*, 142-44.
[319] Brown, *Dura Report* VII/VIII, 196-210, fig. 50, pls. XXI-XXV.

Translated, this inscription reads: "Year 432. Seleukos, the son of Theomnēstos, son of Antiochos, [a] *Europaios* and [one] of the first, erected to Zeus Theos the naos and the doors and all the painting[s] of images." The epithet *Europaios* denotes full civic rights and was, according to Brown, probably restricted to the aristocracy consisting of the descendants of the original Greek settlers. The sense of τῶν πρώτων, "of the first," is less certain. Brown raises the possibility that it is an abbreviated form of a Parthian court title, τῶν πρώτων φίλων, "of the first friends," but argues that it is better to understand the words with *Europaios*, perhaps to indicate that Seleukos served as a member of a municipal council.[320] Welles, on the other hand, accepts the title as referring to Parthian court rank.[321] Thus Seleukos was in any case a member of the old Dura aristocracy and perhaps held a Parthian court title as well.

The sacrificants whose images adorned the side walls of the naos apparently were members of two families: the "Lysias" family, represented by Olympos, son of Lysias and perhaps his sister Mekannaia; and the "Bargates" family, more numerous here but otherwise unknown at Dura. The Biddaios whose name appears in the naos may be a member of the Lysias family, if the Biddaios, son of Lysias who dedicated an altar in A.D. 160/61 is the same man or one of his descendants.[322] The naos paintings thus included both Greek and Semitic names, mixed in the same family.

The fact that altars were immured in a late wall built beside the entrance perhaps suggests a change of ownership of chapels. One of the altars found in this wall is inscribed with the name Demetrios, son of Diodoros, and the date A.D. 113/14.[323]

The prominent placement of the inscription of Seleukos, son of Theomnēstos, on the lintel of the gate into the temple would seem to suggest that he was responsible for the building's construction, though of course the inscription might refer only to the erection of the gateway.[324] Two inscriptions found reused in and near the Mithraeum that refer to an unknown, presumably destroyed, temple provide an instance of an individual building a temple. The first inscription, which should belong to the late first century A.D., records that "Epinicus, the herald and priest of the god, erected this naos [to the god] for the safety of himself and his children, decorating it also with paintings" (the phrase "to the god" is omitted from Welles' translation): Ἀνήγε[ι]ρε[ν] Ἐπίνικος κήρυξ καὶ ἱερεὺς τοῦ θεοῦ τὸν ναὸν θεῶι ὑπὲρ τῆς ἑαυτοῦ καὶ τέκνων σωτηρίας καὶ ζωγραφήσας εἰκόνας.

The second inscription, dated to A.D. 116/17, records the renovation and enlargement of the naos by Epinicus' son Alexander after the departure of the Romans from the city: Ἔτους ηκυ´. [Ἀν]ακαινίσας Ἀλέξανδρος Ἐπινίκου τὸν ναὸν τοῦ[τ]ο?. . . . A third inscription, of A.D. 118/19, records the erection of an oikos, presumably a secondary chapel in the temple, by Alexander. As Welles notes, the fact that the dedicants were priests of the god suggests that the naos erected by Epinicus and renovated by Alexander was not simply a chapel in another temple, but rather "the central chapel of the god's worship."[325] The Temple of Aphlad also provides a parallel. The inscription on the cult relief records that an individual erected "this foundation of a sanctuary" (τὴν ἀφείδρυσιν ταύτη[ν] ἱεροῦ), and the andron was built by members of an association.[326]

Perhaps, then, the Temple of Zeus Theos was erected largely at the expense of a private citizen to serve a relatively restricted group of Dura citizens, members of the aristocracy devoted to a particular form of Zeus. The rituals in the temple presumably did not require either a monumental altar or stairs.

TEMPLE OF THE GADDÉ

The Temple of the Gaddé, dedicated apparently to Malakbel and the Gaddé of Dura and Palmyra, served the religious needs of a group of Palmyrenes resident in Dura.[327] It was built over the remains of earlier private houses, and even in its final period, when it became a full-fledged temple, the northern half of the complex retained in many respects the character of a house, both in plan and in function. The temple in its definitive form is dated to approximately A.D. 159 by the inscriptions on the cult reliefs.[328] Since the evidence for the sacred character of the two phases that preceded this structure rests essentially on the differences of their plans from the usual Dura house plan and on their similarity to the last structure, I shall begin the discussion with this final building, Brown's Period IV.

[320] Ibid., 212-15, nos. 886-888.

[321] Welles, "Gods," 60 f.

[322] Brown, *Dura Report* VII/VIII, 215-17, nos. 890-899.

[323] Ibid., 182 f., 213, no. 887.

[324] Ibid., 195.

[325] Welles, *Dura Report* VII/VIII, 128-34, nos. 867-869.

[326] Hopkins, *Dura Report* V, 112-16, nos. 416, 418.

[327] Brown, *Dura Report* VII/VIII, 257 f.; Eissfeldt, *Tempel und Kulte*, 123-27.

[328] Brown, *Dura Report* VII/VIII, 256.

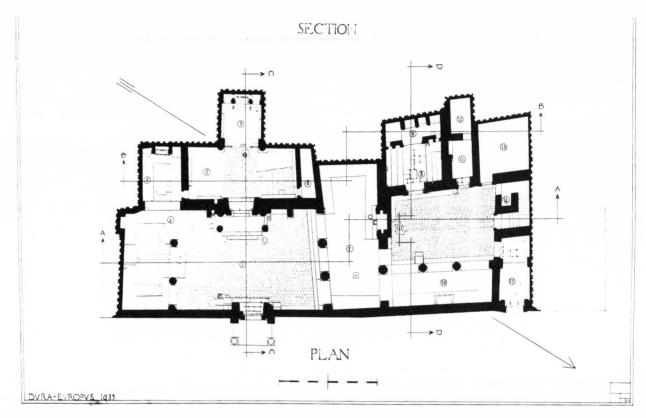

50. Dura-Europos, Temple of the Gaddé, period IV, plan

The complex of the Gaddé (fig. 50) is divided into two interconnected sections.[329] The southern part was the temple proper; the northern part of the block, previously occupied by houses, became a sort of chapter house, combining religious and secular functions. The temple court was entered through a propylon flanked by buttresses and fronted by columns, with the propylon lying slightly off the axis of the entrance to the naos. The sanctuary unit, placed at the back of the open court, consisted of a broad pronaos and a narrow naos that projected beyond the courtyard wall (2, 3). There was no monumental altar in the court, but rubble altars were built against the entrance wall. The sanctuary unit was entered through a colonnaded porch, to the south of which an aedicula, dedicated by one "Malku, son of Iarhai, son of Nasor," projected from the facade of the pronaos. A foundation deposit consisting of a commonware pot containing amulets and a bronze bowl was found under the floor of the pronaos. A narrow bench ran around its walls. The rear wall of the naos was occupied by three arched niches, which contained the cult reliefs. The pronaos was flanked by two narrow rooms accessible from it. The southern room (5) was apparently a secondary naos, since its end wall was occupied by three arched niches, presumably to hold images of a triad of divinities. The large room (4) that occupied the southern side of the court served in some respects as a pronaos to this secondary naos, but at the same time, the low benches mark it as a room for ritual dining. A podium with an altar beside it must have been topped by a painted or sculptured image of a *synnaos theos*.

The southern and northern sections of the complex were connected by a long narrow room (7), which was open to the southern court (1) through a colonnade. The northern half of room 7 served as a chapel, with an aedicula in front of which stood an altar. A low bench ran around its three walls. The northern part of the temple complex retained much of the character of a house. It was organized around a court with a portico on its east side; the presence of two altars in the court emphasized its sacred

[329] Ibid., 234-55, figs. 67-71; for the inscription of Malku, see p. 281 f., no. 911.

116

character. At the back of the court was a complex consisting of two rooms (8 and 9); an altar or altars in the outer room show that it was used at least partly for religious purposes. Graffiti on the bases of the niches against the wall of the inner room (9) list groups of men and their contributions of cakes or barley, doubtless for sacred meals. All of the men have Semitic names, though one man's father is named Lysanias; another is called a veteran (οὐε-τρανὸς). The recording of contributions of food suggests that the room was a storeroom and that the niches held cupboards. Brown points out that this unit resembles the *salle aux gradins* and the adjacent room of the Temple of Azzanathkona (9W, 10) (figs. 44, 45); he suggests that the inner room in the Temple of Azzanathkona might also have been a storeroom.[330]

A base large enough to have supported at least two statues and bearing a fragmentary Latin inscription of the twentieth Palmyrene cohort stands in colonnade 10, on the eastern side of the northern court. The remains of the inscription give no indication of the identity of the subjects of the dedication. The use of Latin perhaps suggests a dedication to the imperial family rather than to deities, and Brown suggests that the statues might have been those of Septimius and his sons or of Caracalla and Geta.[331] Other rooms in the northern part of the complex do not seem to have served specifically religious purposes and probably served as meeting rooms.

Before this final phase, the area was occupied partly by houses but also, in two preceding periods, partly by a complex that may have had a sacred character. Some of the houses that occupied the block in the earliest period were later replaced by a complex that lacked the characteristics of domestic structures (period II, fig. 51). At the rear of a court was a room (2a) with benches around it, like the chapels of Dura temples, and this room gave access to another one (2b) that was distinguished by a hearth and with an isolating corridor (6a) behind. The isolating corridor, which is a feature of the sanctuary unit in some Dura temples (e.g., the Temple of Adonis), suggests that this room served as a naos and that the hearth was used for sacrifices. The idea that this complex was sacred in function is also supported by the later history of the block.[332]

The following period brought changes to this

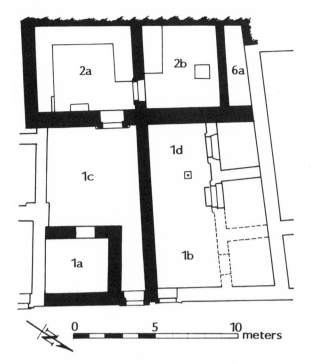

51. Dura-Europos, Temple of the Gaddé, period II, central complex, plan.

central complex (period III, fig. 52). It was divided into two sections, each with its own court, and the presumed naos of the preceding period (room 2b in fig. 51) was turned so that the isolating corridor of the preceding period became a sacristy; a new isolating corridor was built behind the room. The entrance to the court was placed just off the axis of the entrance to the sanctuary. The second room, now entered through its own courtyard, lost its character of a pronaos and became simply a meeting room. In a subsequent period the two rooms were thrown together.[333] These two periods can be dated only by working back from the date of the final building and, to some extent, by ceramic evidence. Brown suggests that period III apparently began about the middle of the first century A.D.; period II must have covered most of the preceding century.[334]

The three cult reliefs of the principal naos of the temple in its final period were dedicated in A.D. 159 by Hairan, the son of Malku, the son of Nasor. The central relief apparently represented Malakbel in a chariot pulled by griffins, i.e., in his solar aspect;

[330] Ibid., 276 f., nos. 904, 906; 254 n. 21.
[331] Ibid., 277, no. 906.
[332] Ibid., 220-28, figs. 53-54.
[333] Ibid., 229-32, fig. 55.
[334] Ibid., 256 f.

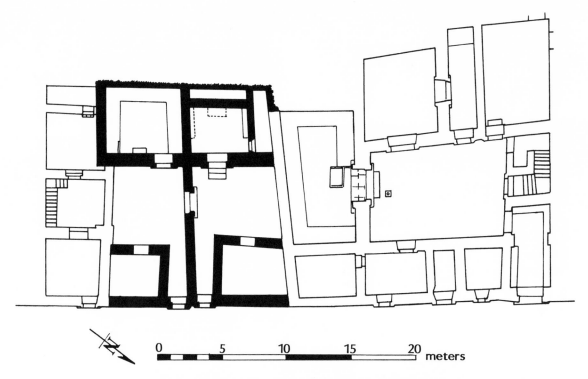

52. Dura-Europos, Temple of the Gaddé, period III, plan.

the flanking reliefs depicted the Gaddé of Dura and Palmyra.[335] A small sculpture found in the naos bears a dedication to the Palmyrene sun god, Iarhibol, though the iconography is that of the moon god, ʿAglibol.[336] The dedicants of the cult images of naos 3 and of the aedicula on the entrance facade were members of a wealthy Palmyrene family, and the gods whose painted and sculptured images were placed in the temple were Palmyrene. As Brown states, the division of the complex into two units, one wholly sacred and the other partly secular, suggests that the worshippers were members of an association that required meeting and social rooms.

The plan of the sanctuary proper, with a broad pronaos and a niche-like naos, is unusual at Dura; the closest parallel is the Necropolis Temple (fig. 43). Since the worshippers in both temples were Palmyrenes, perhaps the plan was associated with the Palmyrene community at Dura, though it does not resemble the temples of Palmyra itself.

TEMPLE OF ADONIS

The Temple of Adonis (fig. 53) was constructed during the second half of the second century A.D. over the remains of private houses, which were demolished to make way for it.[337] There were two main building periods. The first, from ca. 150 to 160, saw the temple as a whole completed; during the second, ca. 175 to 182, various rooms were added and a number of minor improvements made. The Temple of Adonis occupies the entire eastern half of a block. Probably because it was built over the remains of private houses and used existing foundations to some extent, and also because the area available for building was restricted, the temple differs in significant respects from the plan that is usual at Dura. The court is extremely long and narrow, with the entrance on the eastern long side. The entrance is flanked by buttresses, and a staircase next to it presumably led to an elevated terrace over the propylon. The main sanctu-

[335] Torrey, *Dura Report* VII/VIII, 277-79, nos. 907-908; Brown, *Dura Report* VII/VIII, 258-64, pls. XXIII-XXXV.1; Downey, *Stone and Plaster Sculpture*, 14-22, 208 f., 216, nos. 4-6.

[336] Brown, *Dura Report* VII/VIII, 264 f., pl. XXXV.2; Torrey,

Dura Report VII/VIII, 279-81, no. 909; Downey, *Stone and Plaster Sculpture*, 62-64, no. 47; 214 f.

[337] Brown, *Dura Report* VII/VIII, 135-58, pls. IV-V, figs. 42-43; Eissfeldt, *Tempel und Kulte*, 144-47.

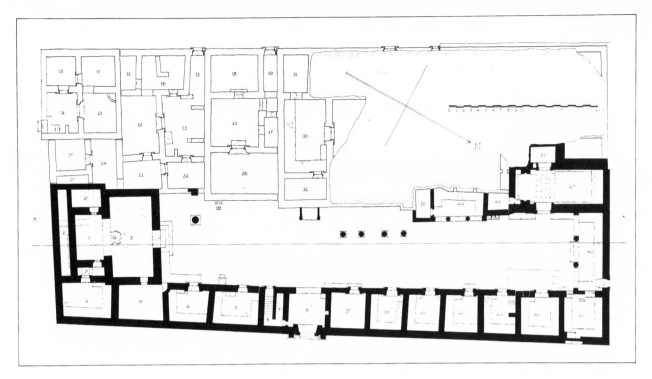

53. Dura-Europos, Temple of Adonis, plan.

ary unit is placed not opposite the entrance, as is usual at Dura, but at right angles to it, occupying most of the south side of the complex—a bent-axis approach. The sanctuary unit consists of five rooms—a broad pronaos, a slightly narrower naos flanked by two sacristies, and an inaccessible isolating corridor behind the naos and sacristies (rooms 1, 2, 2^1, 2^2, 3). A naos flanked by two sacristies is found also in the Temples of Artemis and Atargatis (fig. 40). Brown compares the isolating corridor behind the sanctuary to corridors that isolate the sanctuary units from the courtyard walls in the Temples of Azzanathkona (figs. 44, 45) and Zeus Theos (fig. 49). In the latter two temples, however, the corridors were open at both ends and gave access to a subsidiary room or rooms. Brown suggests that in the Temple of Adonis the isolating corridor seen in the temples of Babylon and Borsippa has been "reduced to its ultimate attenuation. The corridor here has become a mere symbol, functionally meaningless, architecturally useless and wasteful."

The foundation deposit in the pronaos, an empty jar, is, according to Brown, a type characteristic of coastal Palestine.[338] The naos includes neither an altar nor a statue plinth, and the image of the god in the presence of worshippers was painted on the rear wall.[339] Two rooms flanked the sanctuary unit on the east side: the corner room (9), with low benches that skirt the walls, was accessible only from one of the sacristies, and so was probably reserved for the use of the priests; the second room (9^1) was originally accessible only from the pronaos, but later a small door was cut from the courtyard. A secondary sanctuary unit (rooms 47, 48, 51), located in the northeast corner of the complex, consisted of a broad pronaos (47), oriented with its long axis parallel to that of the court, and a small eastward facing naos (51) behind. The lintel over the door from the court into pronaos 47 bears an inscription to Atargatis, apparently dated to A.D. 152. The dedicant's name is missing, but the surviving portion records the dedication to Atargatis on behalf of the safety (σωτηρίας) of his wife and children.[340] According to Brown, the arrangement of the pronaos suggests that it served the same function as the *salles aux gradins* of other temples. The south portion of the room was raised and treated as a stage, the north

338 Brown, *Dura Report* VII/VIII, 137-39.
339 Ibid., 158-63, fig. 44.

340 Ibid., 167 f., no. 870.

end as an orchestra surrounded by seats. Piers set against the east and west walls, probably to support an arch, framed the southern section, and seats stood beside the piers. Benches ran around the three walls of the northern end of the room. Two cuttings in the west bench presumably held something light: standards, candelabra, or votive offerings. A seat at the end of the west bench bears a dedication by one "Barlaas, also called [Ly?]sias, son of Bargates, treasurer" (Βαρλάας, ὁ ἐπικαλούμενος [Λυ]σίας Βαργάτους, γαζοφ[ύλαξ]), dated to A.D. 178.[341] He was presumably a temple official. The fact that the one inscribed seat bears only a man's name differentiates this room from the *salles aux gradins* in the temples of Artemis, Atargatis, and Azzanathkona, where all of the seats belonged to women. Brown suggests that this room corresponded to the *deiktērion* (δεικτήριον) of the Adonis festival at Alexandria and that it was used for pantomimic dances.[342]

A niche was built into the entrance wall of the naos (50), but no trace of cult image was found, nor are there any remains of provisions for a cult image on the rear wall. Room 48, a later addition to the group, probably served as a sacristy. In A.D. 181/82 the area to the south of this room was filled with a portico and a small room (49, 50), called in the dedicatory inscription a peristyle (περίστυλον) and wine cellar (οἰνοτυχεῖον). At about the same time, a portico was built in the courtyard next to the peristyle.[343]

The court did not contain a monumental altar, though numerous small altars and thymiateria were placed around its edges. Rubble altars stood against the facades of a number of chapels (5, 45, 46, 48), and a single rubble column of uncertain function stood on a plinth 0.52 meters above the earlier court level and somewhat to the west of the entrance to the main sanctuary unit. It corresponds to a rubble anta in the west wall of the court. Brown notes that its resemblance to Hellenistic funerary and honorary bicolumnar monuments that carried statuary suggests the possibility of a similar function for the Dura column and pier. He also points out a parallel to the pairs of columns that stood before several West Semitic sanctuaries. As a third possibility, he suggests that "the pier and column with their en-

tablature served primarily as an effective frame for ritual expositions before the gates of the sanctuary." A base with a hole for some cult object, probably a standard, stood against the west wall of the court just north of this isolated columnar monument. Two horned altars stood in front of the base, and their fire-blackened bowls were periodically refurbished with whitewash, suggesting a long period of use.[344] A base supporting a standard topped with a crescent is shown on a relief from the Temple of Atargatis.[345] The placement of the altars in front of the base suggests that whatever it supported was an object of worship. An arched aedicula stood against the wall of the court facing the entrance to the temple precinct. The floor was paved, and apparently no traces of a statue base were found.[346]

The north end of the temple court, opposite the main sanctuary unit, was closed by a portico (42). In a second building period, a small entrance was cut into the north wall. Along the east side of the court were nine chapels, all very uniform; with one exception, their walls were lined with benches on two or three sides. In one case (chapel 44), a stair led to an upper story. Finds of amphorae in two chapels and of a jar stand in another suggest that these three rooms were used for sacred banquets. Chapel 38 was dedicated by a group of eight men belonging to seven different families, all with Semitic names.[347] The inscription on the door lintel to chapel 5 states that Aneinis, son of Mēmaraios, the high priest, erected the *plintheion* (πλινθεῖον) in A.D. 157/58. The meaning of the word *plintheion* is obscure, but Brown suggests that it might refer to stone door trim.[348] Presumably, Aneinis was a high priest of Adonis. A man with a Semitic name, Thaesamsus, son of Iabsymsus, also called A———, son of Zabidadus, erected an altar to the god Adonis against the court facade of this chapel for the safety (σωτη[ρ]ίας) of himself and his wife Eklapat in performance of a vow (κατ᾽ εὐχήν). If the end of the inscription is translated correctly, the donor had "the right to make a burnt offering privately(?) to the god each year," thus a special privilege.[349]

The fragmentary inscription on the lintel over the entrance to chapel 46 preserves only one name,

---

[341] Ibid., 145 f., 170 f., no. 184.

[342] Ibid., 156.

[343] Ibid., 146 f., 171 f., no. 875.

[344] Ibid., 148-51, fig. 41.

[345] Baur, *Dura Report* III, 117 f., pl. XIX.1; Downey, *Stone and Plaster Sculpture*, 145 f., 178 f., no. 178.

[346] Brown, *Dura Report* VII/VIII, 148 f., fig. 40.

[347] Ibid., 140-42, 168, no. 871.

[348] Ibid., 168 f., no. 872. θξυʹ. Ἄνεινις Μημαραίου ἀρχιειραίως ἀνήγειρεν τὸ πλινθεῖον.

[349] Ibid., 169 f., no. 873. The end of the inscription reads: ἐφ᾽ ᾧ[. . .].ι καρπῶσαι κατ᾽ αὐτὸ[ν] τῷ αὐτῷ θεῷ κατ᾽ ἐνιαυτόν.

Demetrios (Δημήτρι[ος or [ου); since the ending of the name is missing, Demetrios might have been the dedicant, his father, or his grandfather.[350] In any case, Demetrios is one of the few non-Semitic names in the temple.

The "peristyle and wine cellar" were built by two men with Semitic names, Solaeas, son of Boubaeus, and Gornaeus, the jailor, son of Mēmaraeus, "at their own expense in performance of a vow for the use of themselves and their descendants in perpetuity": Ἔτους γφυ΄, Σολαίας Βουρβαίου καὶ Γορναῖος Μημαραίου δεσμοφύλαξ, οἰκοδόμησαν περίστυλον καὶ οἰνοτυχεῖον εἰς τὰ Ἀδώνιδος κατ᾽ εὐχήν, εἰς διακονίαν αὐτοῖς καὶ ἐπίγονοι εἰς ἐῶνα ἐκ τῶν ἰδίω[ν] ἀνηλωμάτων.

Brown states that the title "jailor" (δεσμοφύλαξ) perhaps refers to a municipal office. Since the office of jailor is a relatively modest one, however, he suggests the possibility that the title might instead have a religious, even a mystical significance, possibly connected with the rites of Adonis. That the title might identify Gornaeus as a temple official is supported by the use of titles in other inscriptions from the temple: high priest (ἀρχιειραίως) or treasurer (γαζοφ[ύλαξ]).[351]

Graffiti and one dipinto from the temple give other names, almost all Semitic. The most important of these is an elaborate dipinto in Greek from peristyle 49, in which four men, all called Aurelios and all with Semitic names, honor Septimius Aurelios Heliodoros, son of Lysanias, a priest of Apollo. The use of the *nomen* Aurelios dates the inscription after the *Constitutio Antoniniana* in A.D. 212. That the man who is honored belonged to the aristocracy is suggested both by his father's name and by the fact that he holds the priesthood of Apollo, one of the Seleucid cults.[352] It is notable that few women appear in the inscriptions and graffiti. In addition to the inscriptions by men on behalf of their wives already cited, an inscription on a crude gypsum base found in the court names Mēcamea, daughter of Bēteos.[353]

Adonis, the chief deity of the temple, is named in the dedication of the peristyle and of an altar in front of chapel 5.[354] Presumably, it was Adonis

whose painted image adorned the rear wall of the principal naos (1). The second sanctuary unit (47-51) was dedicated to Atargatis, who at Dura was apparently the mother-consort of Adonis. The association of Adonis with Atargatis at Dura is shown also by the dedication in the Temple of Atargatis of a painting to Adonis and Atargatis.[355] A fragmentary relief of Atargatis and one of a camel-riding god, probably Arsu, were found in portico 42 of the Temple of Adonis.[356]

The Temple of Adonis follows in general terms the normal plan at Dura—a court with a sanctuary at one end and with chapels along the walls. It differs, however, in several respects from the usual arrangement. In other Dura temples, the sanctuary unit faces east and is placed opposite the entrance to the court, though sometimes on a slightly divergent axis. Here the sanctuary unit faces north and closes one end of a long narrow court, whose entrance is on the east side, at right angles to the sanctuary facade. There was no monumental altar in the courtyard, as there was in most Dura temples. On the other hand, the Temple of Adonis does exhibit many of the features that characterize the sanctuaries of Dura. The type of sanctuary unit—a broad pronaos and a naos flanked by two sacristies—is seen at Dura in the Temples of Artemis and Atargatis; and the isolating corridor behind the naos also finds parallels in other Dura temples. The arrangement of the secondary sanctuary unit dedicated to Atargatis as a *salle aux gradins* with a naos behind is characteristic of the temples dedicated to goddesses at Dura. The monumental entrance flanked by buttresses and with access to a roof terrace relates the building to most of the temples erected at Dura in the Parthian period.[357]

The Temple of Adonis at Dura is the only one so far discovered that was dedicated to Adonis as the principal god.[358] In fact, the lack of sanctuaries dedicated to Adonis had led to doubts about whether he was, properly speaking, a god rather than some sort of *daimon*.[359] As Eissfeldt points out, the discovery of the Dura temple effectively resolved such doubts.[360] The festival of Adonis at Byblos was celebrated in the temple of Astarte-Aphrodite, ac-

[350] Ibid., 173, no. 877.

[351] Ibid., 169-72, nos. 872, 874, 875.

[352] Ibid., 172-75, nos. 876, 879-884; 179, additional note.

[353] Ibid., 173 f., no. 878.

[354] Ibid., 153, 169-72, nos. 873, 875.

[355] Rowell and Bellinger, *Dura Report* III, 46-49, D. 146 (wrongly restored); Brown, *Dura Report* VII/VIII, 154 and n. 9.

[356] Brown, *Dura Report* VII/VIII, 163-67, pl. XXXI.1, 2; Dow-

ney, *Stone and Plaster Sculpture*, 47 f., no. 33; 55 f., no. 43; 172, 196 f.

[357] Downey, "Temples," 21-39.

[358] Eissfeldt, *Tempel und Kulte*, 144-47.

[359] Wolf Wilhelm Grafen Baudissin, *Adonis und Esmun* (Leipzig, 1911), 177 f.

[360] Otto Eissfeldt, *Adonis und Adonaj, Sitzungsberichte der Sächsischen Akademie der Wissenschaften zu Leipzig*, Philologisch-historische Klasse 115.4 (Berlin, 1970), 16, 22 f.

cording to Lucian (*DDS* 6): Εἶδον δὲ καὶ ἐν Βύβλῳ μέγα ἱρὸν Ἀφροδίτης Βυβλίης, ἐν τῷ καὶ τὰ ὄργια ἐς Ἄδωνιν ἐπιτελέουσιν. Strabo (XVI.2.8) does say, however, that the city was consecrated to Adonis: ἡ μὲν οὖν Βύβλος ἱερά ἐστι τοῦ Ἀδώνιδος.

It is difficult to determine if the anomalies in the Dura Temple of Adonis are due to its being dedicated to Adonis or to the exigencies of the long narrow site that was previously built upon. Brown suggests that the bent-axis entrance to the sanctuary and the lack of a monumental altar in the court reflect a foreign architectural tradition. He suggests that "the builder attempted to compromise with the ruling convention [at Dura] by reproducing the normal sanctuary plan and other features of Mesopotamian derivation and by placing his monumental entrance in the east side with an *aedicula* on the axis opposite."[361] If Birgitte Soyez is correct in suggesting that the large Roman temple of the acropolis of Byblos served for the celebration of the festivals of Adonis,[362] it cannot have provided a model for the temple of Adonis at Dura. In any case, the bent-axis approach was common in earlier Mesopotamian temple architecture.

DOLICHENEUM

The Dolicheneum (fig. 54) was located in the northern part of the city, in the area taken over for the Roman military camp. The building must have been completed by A.D. 211, the date of a Latin dedicatory inscription found just in front of the entrance. Jupiter Dolichenus shared the temple with the god Turmasgade, whose name appears on the door jamb of the westernmost of the two naoi, and a mysterious goddess called in an inscribed relief only Kyria, "the lady."[363] Most of the dedicants named in the inscriptions found in and around the building were soldiers, so that it is probable that the temple was built by members of the garrison and that the worshippers were largely if not entirely military. The names were almost exclusively Latin and Greek.[364] No Semitic names appear in the inscriptions, but one possibly Semitic name,]Βαρναῖος[, occurs in a dipinto and another on a jar stamp.[365]

The temple was centered around a colonnaded court, with the entrance to the court on the south side flanked by buttresses, and a long corridor leading into the court. The axis of the entrance lay between the entrances to the two cellae that were placed against the rear wall of the court. The eastern cella (19) is marked as the more important one by its slightly larger size and the aedicula against the rear wall. This cella presumably belonged to Jupiter Dolichenus. The western cella (20), which according to the inscription on the door jamb belonged to Turmasgade, has no cult furniture, but since the cella is almost equal in size to the eastern one, the two gods were probably of nearly equal importance. Beside the main cella was a large room, probably a sacristy, though it was not accessible from the cella; a small room beyond could be entered only from this sacristy. A large chapel on the east wall of the court (13) probably belonged to Kyria, since the relief depicting her was found in its court. A second chapel, to the right of the entrance (3), was lined with benches and therefore was probably used to serve the ritual meal that was part of the cult of Jupiter Dolichenus.

The temple underwent major modifications, probably in connection with an increase in the size of the garrison around 251, the date of the dedication of two altars (fig. 55).[366] The most important change was that the "sacristy" of the first period was taken over as part of the barracks. Two monumental altars, apparently lacking in the first temple, were built in the court more or less on the axes of the entrances to the two cellae. Slightly in front of the eastern altar was a low round object of uncertain purpose. In this period an additional room (24) was built in the northwest corner of the court; as it has a low bench along the back wall and was decorated with paintings of priests and worshippers, it was probably a chapel. A Bacchic graffito found on one of the walls might indicate that Dionysos was worshipped there.[367] Room 13, the chapel of Kyria, had rather elaborate furnishings at this stage: heavy, broad benches lined the north and south walls; an aedicula formed by two piers and a stone shelf stood against the east wall, with holes in the top of the shelf presumably to hold a cult image. A stone hearth just north of the doorway

[361] Brown, *Dura Report* VII/VIII, 155; the plan and function of the various rooms of the temple are discussed on pp. 153-57.

[362] Birgitte Soyez, *Byblos et la fête des Adonies* (Leiden, 1977), 23-28, fig. 7.

[363] J. Frank Gilliam, *Dura Report* IX.3, 107-110, no. 970; 115-19, nos. 974, 976; the possible significance of this group of divinities is

discussed by Gilliam on pp. 130-34.

[364] Ibid., 107-124, nos. 970-78, 983, 987; 130.

[365] Ibid., 122, 124, nos. 982, 986.

[366] Ibid., 110-14, nos. 971-972. For the architecture, see Perkins, *Dura Report* IX.3, 97-106, figs. 9-11.

[367] Gilliam, *Dura Report* IX.3, 122, 134, no. 979.

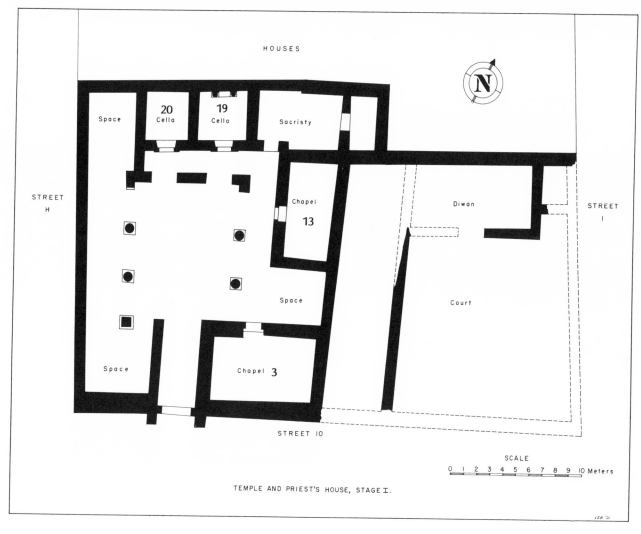

54. Dura-Europos, Dolicheneum, period I, plan.

might have been used for sacrifices. The presence of a pottery jar with a rubble-work structure built around it suggests that room 9 on the east side of the court, which was created by building a wall between the chapel next to the entrance (3) and the chapel of Kyria (13) was probably used for the preparation of sacred meals to be eaten in the chapel of Kyria. The area to the west of the entrance corridor (2) was also lined with benches but was open to the court through the colonnade; perhaps some sort of screen wall in a perishable material shut it off from the court.

In spite of being built to "foreign" gods, the Dolicheneum follows the court plan normal for Dura temples of the Parthian period. As Perkins points

out, it is the only one of the temples built at Dura during the Roman period to utilize this plan. It differs from the other Dura court temples in some respects, however. Whereas the sanctuaries of the other Dura temples face east, the two naoi in the Dolicheneum face south. Since most temples to Jupiter Dolichenus are oriented east,[368] the southward orientation of the Dura building may be due to the exigencies of the site. The long entrance corridor of the Dolicheneum is without parallel in Dura temples; and the colonnaded court is unusual, though the courts of both the Temple of Bel and the Necropolis Temple have partial porticoes. Though other temples have subsidiary chapels for *synnaoi theoi*, the twin naoi are also without parallel; pre-

[368] P. Merlat, *Iupiter Dolichenus* (Paris, 1960), 166 f.

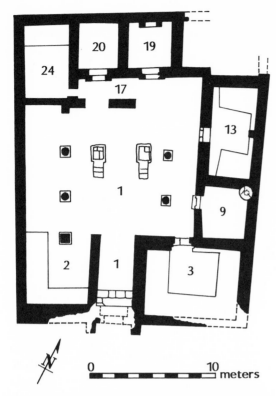

55. Dura-Europos, Dolicheneum, period III, plan.

ably, the rituals performed in the Dura Dolicheneum were sufficiently similar to those in the majority of Dura temples that the same type of plan was suitable. Certainly the monumental altars of the final phase of the building and the chapels for ritual dining suggest similar cult practices.

Summary

ALL but a very few of the temples built at Dura during the periods of Parthian and Roman control follow the Babylonian court plan. Only the Mithraeum, the temple built by the Roman archers, and the building identified by Rostovtzeff as a Tychaeum but by Pillet as a customs house, do not. The Mithraeum, in spite of being built above ground, conforms fairly closely to the normal Mithraic sanctuary type,[371] which was presumably dictated by the requirements of the cult. The little temple built by the archers of the *Cohors II Ulpia Equitata* consists of a single room fronted by a distyle *in antis* porch. Except for the fact that the roof of the cella was supported by four pillars,[372] the building had the form of a simple Roman temple and was probably influenced by Roman traditions. Not only were the builders soldiers in the Roman army, the inscription expressly states that they were Roman citizens: ". . . coh(ortem) II Ulpiam eq(uitatam) civium romanorum sagittariorum. . . ."[373] A building to the northeast of the Palmyrene Gate in Dura is identified by Pillet as a customs house on the basis of its location, but as a Tychaeum by Rostovtzeff.[374] It is a small square structure, the roof of which was supported by four pillars. Two periods of construction have been identified. The entrance of the earlier period, a single door on the east side, was altered in the Roman period to form three monumental doors, the central one flanked by columns. A pillar built against the rear wall in the earlier period was retained in the Roman period, and pedestals were added against two of the pillars that supported the roof. Rostovtzeff suggested that the pillar and the pedestals originally bore painted dedications, of which no trace remains. He notes the presence of a number of inscriptions and graffiti to Tyche in the Palmyrene Gate and argues on that basis that she must have had a shrine nearby, which he identifies with this

sumably, they result from cult necessity. Finally, the naoi are unusual in being single rooms, lacking a pronaos, though they are screened from the court by a passage behind the north side of the colonnade. Porticoes in front of the sanctuary are also seen in the Necropolis Temple and in the third stage of the Temple of Bel.

Temples to Jupiter Dolichenus did not follow a uniform plan, unlike Mithraea, though there are some common elements. These temples were generally located near military camps. Many appear to have been designed for large congregations. They were often located near a spring or include a cistern. Most of the temples in Germany also had a cellar of uncertain use, and rooms for gatherings, especially for ritual meals, were often associated with the temple proper.[369]

Apparently, the rites of Jupiter Dolichenus did not require a particular building form, and Schwertheim notes that the surviving buildings provide little evidence about cult rites.[370] Presum-

[369] A. H. Kan, *Juppiter Dolichenus* (Leiden, 1943), 34-36.
[370] Elmar Schwertheim, *Die Denkmäler orientalischer Gottheiten im römischen Deutschland* (*EPRO* 40) (Leiden, 1974), 311 f.
[371] Pearson, *Dura Report* VII/VIII, 64-82.

[372] Pillet, *Dura Report* II, 16 f., pls. V, XXXV.2.
[373] Hopkins, *Dura Report*, 83-86, H. 1.
[374] Rostovtzeff, *Dura Report* III, 37-39, pl. VII; Pillet, *Dura Report* III, 13.

building. Obviously, the idea that this building was sacred rests on very slender evidence. Thus, of the three buildings that do not follow the court plan, both the Mithraeum and the Temple of the Roman Archers are associated with the Roman army,[375] and the Mithraeum had to conform to specific cult requirements. The sacred character of the third structure is open to question.

Although the majority of Dura temples adhere to the same basic scheme, there is considerable variation in such matters as the relation between the entrance and the sanctuary unit; the exact form of the sanctuary unit, including the number and position of sacristies; the presence or absence in the court of monumental altars and their placement; and other elements of the temple. The factors that underlie this variety are hard to determine. Cult requirements presumably explain many of the features of each temple, but our lack of information about the rituals makes this factor difficult or impossible to assess. It is possible also that temples built for particular groups of worshippers (e.g., the Temple of the Gaddé, the Necropolis Temple; the Temples of Aphlad and Zeus Kyrios) had certain specific requirements. This notion is supported by the fact that the Necropolis Temple (fig. 43) and the Temple of the Gaddé (fig. 50), which apparently were built for Palmyrenes and served a largely Palmyrene clientele, share a number of characteristics that other Dura temples lack. It is also possible that both Aphlad and Azzanathkona were connected with the city of Anath, and again their temples (figs. 44, 45, 48) share certain characteristics. Some of the temples went through a number of rebuildings, and the desire to preserve some of the features of the earlier phases probably explains the position of such things as altars. Another factor that might possibly have affected the form of some temples is the presence of preexisting houses in the area; both the desire to reuse earlier walls as foundations and constraints on available space may explain some of the peculiarities of the Temples of Adonis and the Gaddé.

I have shown elsewhere that with the exception of the Temple of Zeus Theos, all of the temples built on the court plan during the Parthian and Roman periods at Dura incorporated towers into their structure.[376] Four temples—Bel, Zeus Kyrios, Aphlad, and Azzanathkona—included an actual tower of the city wall within their precinct. In a sec-

ond type, access is provided to an elevated terrace over the entrance—Atargatis and Adonis—or to the roof of the naos—Zeus Megistos, periods II-V. In a third type, the entrance is flanked by buttresses but no access to the roof is provided—Necropolis Temple, Artemis, Gaddé, and Dolicheneum. The Temple of Adonis (fig. 53) belongs to a mixed type, since its entrance is flanked by buttresses, and this characterization might also apply to the Necropolis Temple (fig. 43), in which access is provided to the roof of a room near the propylon.

The pronaos-naos unit is normally placed with its long axis at right angles to the long axis of the court—Bel, Aphlad, Artemis, Azzanathkona, Atargatis, Zeus Theos, and Zeus Megistos—though in some cases the court is nearly square. The principal sanctuary units of all of the temples except those of Adonis and Jupiter Dolichenus are oriented to the east; that of Adonis faces north, and the naoi in the temple of Jupiter Dolichenus face south. In both cases, the unusual orientation is probably the result of the exigencies of the site rather than of cult practices, though the lack of comparative material for the Temple of Adonis makes it difficult to say in that case. The main sanctuary unit is usually placed on the axis of the entrance—Artemis, Atargatis, Azzanathkona—or just off that axis, with a deviation so slight that it may not be deliberate—Necropolis Temple, Gaddé, Zeus Theos.

The principal sanctuary unit of the Temple of Zeus Megistos in the second and succeeding periods (figs. 41, 42) lies considerably off the axis of the entrance to the temple, and neither of the two sanctuary units built around the south court in the last period of construction lies on the line of the door into the court. The reasons for the off-axis placement of the principal sanctuary unit are not clear, but the arrangement may result, as Brown thinks, from the history of the site, or it may be based on the Babylonian bent-axis approach. Constraints of space and previous construction on the site probably explain the positions of the naoi around the south court. The naos of the Temple of Adonis (fig. 53) lies on the south side of the court, oriented perpendicularly to the entrance. This bent-axis approach could easily be due to the constricted building site but might reflect some cult requirement. The entrance to the Dolicheneum (fig. 54) lies between the doors of the two naoi; this po-

[375] For the Mithraeum, see Rostovtzeff and Torrey, *Dura Report* VII/VIII, 83-88.

[376] Downey, "Temples," 21-39.

sition may reflect the roughly equal importance of the two divinities worshipped there.

The placement of the sanctuary unit in relation to the walls of the court also varies. In the temples of Atargatis and Bel, the sanctuary is built against the rear wall of the court; and the two naoi in the Dolicheneum also stand against the rear wall. In the Necropolis Temple, the Temple of the Gaddé, and the secondary sanctuary unit of the Temple of Adonis, the pronaos is built against the court wall and a niche-like naos projects from it. The sanctuary units of the temples of Aphlad and Artemis are free-standing, as is the principal such unit in the Temple of Zeus Megistos. In the temples of Azzanathkona and Zeus Theos the sanctuary unit also stands free in the court but is separated from the rear wall and the subsidiary rooms to the side only by a relatively narrow space; Brown interprets this arrangement as a version of the isolating corridor seen in some earlier Babylonian temples. If this interpretation is correct, it would seem to apply also to the Temple of Artemis. The main sanctuary unit in the Temple of Adonis is separated from the outer wall of the court by a space interpreted by Brown as a vestigial isolating corridor. The similar blind space behind the cult niche in the Necropolis Temple might be another example of the same phenomenon.[377]

The standard sanctuary unit at Dura consists of a pronaos and a naos of roughly the same width, but the arrangements of the naos vary, and its width may be reduced by the presence of one or more sacristies. There are no sacristies in the Temple of Aphlad, and the principal naos in the Temple of Zeus Megistos also lacks sacristies, though its width is reduced by a staircase leading to the roof. A vestibule is added to the pronaos-naos unit in the Temple of Azzanathkona, and the width of the naos is reduced by the presence of a room accessible only from the pronaos. In the temples of Artemis, Atargatis, and Adonis, the naos is flanked by two sacristies accessible only from the naos. The pronaos-naos units of the Necropolis Temple and the Temple of the Gaddé differ from the usual Dura type. In both cases, there is a long pronaos and a niche-like naos that projects from the rear wall of the court. The plan may have had some significance for the Palmyrene community at Dura, though it is not used at Palmyra itself.[378] The second sanctuary

unit in the Temple of Adonis, which was dedicated to Atargatis, also follows this scheme, and the plan occurs frequently in the smaller temples at Hatra. Each of the naoi of the Dolicheneum consists of a single room, without a pronaos; a room next to the eastern naos in the building of the first period might have served as a sacristy, though it is not accessible from the naos. The temples of Aphlad and Zeus Megistos also include a naos without a pronaos, as well as sanctuary units of the more usual type.

A *salle aux gradins*, normally associated with a naos behind it, is a feature of the temples dedicated to goddesses at Dura. The pronaos of the Temple of Artemis was set up as a *salle aux gradins* in the later first century B.C. The steps were removed, probably in the Roman period; and in the Roman period also, an odeon was built in the newly added south portion of the court. It is not clear whether the odeon took over the functions of the *salle aux gradins* to some extent, though, as I have argued above, the inscriptional evidence makes that seem unlikely. The pronaos of the Temple of Atargatis (fig. 40) was a *salle aux gradins*, and a second such chamber was built against the north wall of the temple. The *salle aux gradins* in the Temple of Azzanathkona (figs. 44 and 45, room 9W) seems to have served as the main center of worship in that unit, since it also contained altars and the cult relief; the inner room was probably a storeroom. Finally, the outer room of the sanctuary unit dedicated to Atargatis in the Temple of Adonis (fig. 53, room 47) was apparently arranged as a *salle aux gradins*, and a room (8 in fig. 50) in the Temple of the Gaddé had benches arranged in a fashion similar to the steps in the *salles aux gradins* of other temples. In the Temples of Artemis, Atargatis, and Azzanathkona, all of the seats belonged to women, so whatever ritual was performed there was probably reserved for women. The one name preserved on a seat block from the sanctuary of Atargatis in the Temple of Adonis is male, however, and room 8 in the Temple of the Gaddé (fig. 50) is also an exception. The benches in that room do not bear inscriptions, and the names painted on the cupboards of the inner room are those of men who provided food. Whatever ritual was performed in this room in the Temple of the Gaddé thus probably differed from those in the *salles aux gradins* of the temples of goddesses. It is interesting that according to the inscriptional

[377] Brown, *Dura Report* VII/VIII, 138 f., 183, 311.

[378] For temple types at Palmyra, see Malcolm A. R. Colledge, *The Art of Palmyra* (Boulder, Colo., 1976), 26-29, figs. 6, 7; Paul Collart and Jacques Vicari, *Le Sanctuaire de Baalshamin à Palmyre*

(Neuchâtel, 1969); A. Bounni and N. Saliby, "Six nouveaux emplacements fouillés à Palmyre," *Annales archéologiques de Syrie* XV (1965), 126-35.

evidence, the Temple of Artemis had the earliest *salle aux gradins*, suggesting that perhaps this feature was introduced first in the temple of a Greek goddess.

It has often been noted that theatral areas appear to be characteristic of some Syrian temples, or of temples dedicated to Syrian deities. A theater built above a long terrace forms part of the sanctuary of the Syrian gods at Delos.[379] In the sanctuary of Baalshamin at Sî´ in the Hauran, a Nabataean inscription on the entrance to a porticoed courtyard, recording the dedication of an inner and outer temple and a portico with its covering, uses the Greek word *theatron* transcribed into Semitic characters.[380] The two buildings of the Parthian period at Seleucia on the Tigris that have been identified as temples also include a theatral area (see the discussion in the section on Seleucia). As Will notes, a theater was a possible but not a necessary part of Syrian sanctuaries.

Another frequent feature in the temples of Dura is the presence in the courtyard of a monumental altar or altars. In a number of temples a large altar was placed on the axis of the naos—the Temple of Artemis as rebuilt in 40-32 B.C. (but not in its later phases), Atargatis, the Temple of Bel in its third phase, and the Dolicheneum as rebuilt in approximately A.D. 251. In the Temples of Bel and Artemis there were also altars that were not aligned with the sanctuary unit. The entrance to the Temple of Bel (fig. 47) was aligned with a monumental altar rather than with the entrance either to the naos or to the tower included in the precinct. The position of this altar recalls the sanctuary of Zeus Kyrios (fig. 46), in which worship must have centered around an altar placed opposite the entrance, and there was no sanctuary unit properly speaking. The two altars that belonged to the phase of the Temple of Artemis just preceding the rebuilding of 40-32 B.C. (fig. 31) were preserved in that rebuilding, though they no longer stood on the axis of the sanctuary unit. In the Roman period, both these early altars and the altar erected on the axis of the sanctuary unit were paved over, and other altars were

erected in the court to the southeast of the sanctuary. The monumental altar in the court of the Necropolis Temple (fig. 43) was positioned slightly off the axis of the sanctuary unit, which was itself askew (thus the off-axis position might not be significant). The Temple of Zeus Megistos (fig. 42) in the third and succeeding phases included a monumental altar set in its own courtyard. A number of altars stood in the precinct of Aphlad (fig. 48); since few if any of them seem to stand in a clear relationship to a naos or chapel, they were probably the focus of independent worship. There was no monumental altar in the courts of the temples of Adonis, Zeus Theos, or the Gaddé, though in all these cases a number of relatively small rubble altars were placed against the walls of the court in various places. According to the plan, there was no monumental altar in the first period of the Dolicheneum.

The courts of the Dura temples were lined with a number of rooms, conventionally called "chapels." In the inscriptions, rooms of this type were called *naos* (ναός), *oikos* (οἶκος), and *oikodomē* (οἰκοδομή), apparently interchangeably.[381] Brown also notes that the term *exedra* (ἐξέδρα) is used of one such room in the Temple of Bel, and *andrōn* (ἀνδρών) designates a single room in the Temple of Aphlad. Some of these rooms were dedicated to *synnaoi theoi* of the chief deity. A sanctuary unit in the Temple of Adonis, for example, was dedicated to Atargatis. Some of these subsidiary rooms had arrangements for the placement of cult images—(Temple of Atargatis, room 9; Temple of the Gaddé, rooms 4 and 5—or were painted with images of worshippers and divinities—Necropolis Temple, room 12; Temple of Bel, room K; Dolicheneum, room 24 in fig. 55). The majority of these rooms were dedicated by private individuals on behalf of their families, by members of the clergy and their families,[382] or by colleges of men.[383]

A number of features suggest that most of these subsidiary rooms were used for ritual dining. Many were lined with benches on two or three walls. In others amphorae were set into the floor, or a plaster jar stand or cooler was found. The pres-

[379] Ernest Will, "Le sanctuaire syrien de Délos," *Annales archéologiques de Syrie* I (1951), 59-79.

[380] Enno Littman, *Publications of an American Archaeological Expedition to Syria* IV, 85-90; Littman, *Publications of the Princeton University Archaeological Expeditions to Syria in 1905-1906 and 1909*, division IV, section A: *Nabataean Inscriptions from the Southern Haurân* (Leiden, 1914), 76-78, no. 100. For the architecture, see Howard Crosby Butler, *Princeton Expedition*, division II, *Ancient Architecture in Syria*, section A, part 6: *Sî (Seeia)* (Leiden, 1916), 374-85. Cf. Will, *Annales archéologiques de Syrie* I (1951), 75 f.

[381] Brown, *Dura Report* VII/VIII, 156 f. n. 20. For a discussion of the meaning of the term *exedra* used in the inscription from the Temple of Bel, see above, p. 108.

[382] Rowell and Bellinger, *Dura Report* III, 55 f., 59, 61, D. 152, D. 157, D. 159 (Temple of Atargatis); Hopkins, *Dura Report* V, 142 f., no. 453 (Temple of Azzanathkona); Cumont, *Fouilles*, 404-409, no. 50 (Temple of Artemis); Brown, *Dura Report* VII/VIII, 168 f., no. 872 (Temple of Adonis).

[383] Hopkins, *Dura Report* V, 113-16, no. 418 (Temple of Aphlad); Brown, *Dura Report* VII/VIII, 168, no. 871 (Temple of Adonis).

ence of stoves in four of the chapels in the Temple of Zeus Theos makes it likely that food was actually prepared in them.[384] The dedication of a wine cellar in the Temple of Adonis also suggests that ritual banquets were held there.[385] The idea that the Dura chapels were rooms for dining is also supported by the presence in the temples of the rural area to the northwest of Palmyra of similar chapels that were clearly used for ritual dining. Ovens were found near the temples, and a number of chapels contained kraters, some of which were dedicated to the god of the sanctuary.[386]

The derivation of the plans of the Dura temples from Babylonia has long been noted.[387] The Dura temples, however, do not simply reproduce the plans of earlier Babylonian temples but are new creations based on old principles. Part of the variety in the Dura temples, in fact, comes precisely from the selective adoption of Babylonian features. Thus, although nearly all of the temples under discussion are organized around a court surrounded by a multitude of chapels, and most have a broad pronaos-naos complex, the exact form of the sanctuary unit and its placement within the court varies. Only some of the Dura temples have the isolating corridor that is a standard feature of Babylonian temples, for example. The Dura temples also incorporate a number of features that Babylonian temples lack and, conversely, lack certain features characteristic of Babylonia. A monumental altar in the court, more or less on the axis of the naos, is a frequent feature of the Dura temples. Although monumental altars are frequent in earlier Babylonian temples, they are generally located outside the temple, on the line of the main entrance, rather than within the court.[388] An altar does stand in the court of the Seleucid Anu-Antum temple at Uruk (fig. 5), so perhaps this placement is a late development. The naoi of the Dura temples also lack the cult niche that is a constant feature of Babylonian temples, and which occurs also in the late temples of Uruk, even in the rather Romanized Temple of Gareus (fig. 59). It is possible that the aediculae that housed the cult statue in some Dura temples—Gaddé and Bel—represent a Westernized version of the same feature. In no case are the exterior walls of the Dura temples decorated with projections and recesses in the Babylonian fashion. The theatral areas that characterize the temples of goddesses at Dura are a feature of Syrian rather than of Babylonian cults.

The evidence from the Temple of Artemis and possibly also from the Temple of Zeus Megistos suggests that the Babylonian court plan was introduced to Dura in about the middle of the first century B.C. At least in the case of the Temple of Artemis, the mid-first-century temple represented a radical change in plan, since it apparently replaced an unfinished structure of Greek type that was demolished to make way for it. This radical shift in plan, especially in the temple of a goddess worshipped by the Greek settlers, would seem to argue for a deliberate shift in policy. The court plan appears to have been suitable for the worship of a variety of divinities—gods and goddesses, Greek and Semitic, including Palmyrene gods.

Unfortunately, not enough is known of the history of Dura to suggest plausible reasons for the shift to a court plan of Babylonian type. It cannot be connected with the Parthian conquest, which occurred in 114-113 B.C.,[389] some seventy-five years before the rebuilding of the Temple of Artemis. The spate of temple building that began at this time and continued until about the middle of the first century A.D. suggests a period of increased prosperity, but that fact would not account for the adoption of a radically different type of temple plan. There does not seem to be evidence of any infusion of Babylonian elements into the population at this time. On the contrary, evidence suggests that the Greco-Macedonian aristocracy maintained itself, though by this time there was a strong admixture of Aramaean elements. The inscribed seats in the *salles aux gradins* in the Temples of Artemis, Atargatis, and Azzanathkona show that the women of the most prominent families in Dura worshipped in these temples, and the majority of these women, for the most part wives of men with Macedonian names, themselves had Greek names; a few Semitic names appear, but they are less than ten percent of the total. A few native families also are recorded as having worshipped with them.[390] Thus

[384] Brown, *Dura Report* VII/VIII, 140-42, 157 (Temple of Adonis); Perkins, *Dura Report* IX.3, 104 (Dolicheneum); Brown, *Dura Report* VII/VIII, 194 (Temple of Zeus Theos).

[385] Brown, *Dura Report* VII/VIII, 146 f., 171 f., no. 875.

[386] Schlumberger, *La Palmyrène du Nord-Ouest* (Paris 1951), 101-105; J. Starcky, "Autour d'une dédicace palmyrénienne à Šadrafa et à du ʿanat," *Syria* XXVI (1949), 55-67.

[387] Cumont, *Fouilles*, 169-71; Bellinger, *Dura Report* III, 18-24.

[388] E.g., the temple of Ninmach and Epatutila at Babylon: Koldewey, *Die Tempel von Babylon und Borsippa*, pls. III, VII (figs. 10, 12).

[389] Bellinger, *Final Report* VI: *The Coins* (New Haven, 1949), 199-201.

[390] Welles, "The Population of Roman Dura," *Studies in Roman*

it does not seem that the appearance of temples of Babylonian type should necessarily be connected with an increase in the Semitic elements of the population.

One possibility is that the increased prosperity evidenced by the surge of building activity is in part the result of increased trade and therefore of growing awareness of Babylonian traditions on the part of the people of Dura. An increased openness to foreign communities at about this time is suggested by the fact that the first traces of religious activity by the Palmyrene community occur in this period, with the building of the Necropolis Temple in about 33 B.C. The evidence from the agora suggests that the transition from Greek agora to oriental bazaar began in the last quarter of the second century B.C., at the time of the transition from Greek to Parthian political control. Brown suggests that the end of Greek political control led to the "abandonment of the Greek conception of the agora as the characteristic expression of the economic life of the city."[391] The orientalization of the temples is a later manifestation of the same phenomenon.

PAINTING AND SCULPTURE AS EVIDENCE FOR RITUALS AT DURA-EUROPOS

Paintings and cult reliefs from temples at Dura provide additional evidence about rites performed there. The burning of incense on an altar or thymiaterion seems to have been the most common rite. Frequently offerings of wine were associated with incense sacrifices, and often priests or sacrificants are depicted washing leaves or branches in tall vessels. Probably these actions represent different stages in the same ritual. As the paintings from the Temple of Bel provide the most complete evidence, I shall begin the discussion with them.

One of the paintings in the naos of the Temple of Bel depicts a sacrifice celebrated by two priests at the expense of Conon, son of Nikostratos, and his family. The first priest washes a reed-like plant in an elaborate vessel, while holding in his left hand a pitcher, a patera, and two knives. The second priest offers incense over a columnar altar. In his right hand he holds a bowl, the red interior of which identifies the contents as wine, and two knives;

thus he is performing an incense and wine sacrifice. Cumont interprets these rites as preliminaries to an animal sacrifice, which is not depicted but which is implied by several features of the painting: a band held by Conon, which Cumont interprets as a fillet to adorn the victim's horns; and a mysterious dumbbell-like object, also held by Conon, which Cumont interprets as a mace to stun the victim, who would then be killed by the priests' knives.[392] As the evidence for animal offerings at Dura, especially sacrifices of large animals, is otherwise rather slight, Cumont's interpretation may not be correct. The band could be a wreath, and the object held in Conon's left hand is too mysterious to support any interpretation. It is hard to explain the knives held by the priests in rites involving only plants, wine, and incense, however.

The ritual of washing a plant is also shown in two other paintings from the pronaos of the Temple of Bel, one depicting a lone priest, the other four men in civilian dress.[393] Another painting from the pronaos depicts Julius Terentius, tribune of the twentieth Palmyrene cohort, offering incense on a thymiaterion to a triad of Palmyrene gods in the presence of members of his cohort.[394] Paintings in room K depict Otes performing an incense sacrifice over a flaming thymiaterion, while a small acolyte behind him holds a cup and ladle, probably for wine. A second sacrificant holds his right hand over the thymiaterion, probably offering incense, while holding twigs in his left hand. His acolyte holds a ciborium and a patera. This sacrifice is offered to five Palmyrene gods.[395] The well-preserved paintings from the Temple of Bel thus suggest a relatively restricted range of rites.

More fragmentary paintings from other temples apparently depict similar, though not necessarily identical, rites. For example, the side walls of the naos in the Temple of Zeus Theos were covered with paintings showing worshippers, probably arranged in three registers. The surviving fragments suggest that here wine and incense sacrifices were combined with offerings of fruit.[396] The even more fragmentary remains of the sacrificants from the paintings on the rear wall of the naos of the Temple of Adonis provide evidence only for incense sacrifices.[397] A graffito from the Temple of Azzanath-

Social and Economic History in Honor of Allan Chester Johnson, ed. P. R. Coleman-Norton (Princeton, 1951), 262-64; Downey, *Heracles Sculpture*, 80.

[391] Brown, *Dura Report* IX.1, 43. For the evidence for the date of the changes, see pp. 30-42.

[392] Cumont, *Fouilles*, 45-48, 66-70, pls. XXXII-XXXV.

[393] Ibid., 72 f., pls. XXXI, XLI, XLII; 76-83, pls. XLIV-XLVII.

[394] Ibid., 89-100, pls. XLIX-LI.

[395] Ibid., 122-34, pls. LV-LVIII.

[396] Brown, *Dura Report* VII/VIII, 196-210, fig. 50, pls. XXI-XXV.

[397] Ibid., 158-63, fig. 44.

kona apparently depicts an incense sacrifice to Iar-hibol.[398] Cult reliefs to several deities—Aphlad, the Gaddé, Nemesis—also depict incense sacrifices. Adadiabos, the dedicant of the Aphlad relief, and Hairan on the relief of the Gad of Dura hold an incense bowl and an alabastron, implying that liquid was offered as well.[399] One relief showing a camel-riding god, probably Arsu, apparently illustrates an offering of fruit and flowers on an altar.[400]

A few sculptures imply animal offerings. The dedicant of the Zeus Kyrios relief holds a ram, presumably an offering to the god,[401] and the bull in the background of the Azzanathkona relief is probably being led to sacrifice.[402] More dubious evidence is provided by a group showing a female figure beside a youth holding an animal; the larger scale of the woman suggests that she is a goddess, and the animal could be an offering. Another very fragmentary sculpture might represent a priest and an animal victim beside an altar.[403]

[398] Hopkins, *Dura Report* V, 152-56, pl. XXXVI.1-3.
[399] Downey, *Stone and Plaster Sculpture*, 7-9, no. 1; 14-19, nos. 4-5; 29-31, no. 9.
[400] Ibid., 55 f., no. 43; Brown, *Dura Report* VII/VIII, 165-67, pl. XXXI.2.

[401] Downey, *Stone and Plaster Sculpture*, 31-34, no. 10.
[402] Ibid., 11-14, no. 3.
[403] Ibid., 99, no. 87; 144 f., no. 176.

3

IRAN

Masjid-i Solaiman

THE SITE of Majid-i Solaiman in Elymais was probably sacred already in Achaemenid times. According to Ghirshman, a podium and an *atašgah* stood on the terrace, and offerings made near the podium show that it remained a sacred spot at least through the beginning of the Sasanian period.

Ghirshman suggests that after the Greek conquest, the Macedonians enlarged the terrace and erected their own temples on it.[1] Two temples stood on this expanded terrace. Ghirshman attributes the larger one (the "Great Temple") to Athena Hippia; the reasons for this attribution will be discussed below. A statue of Heracles belonging to the Parthian period was found in the smaller temple, and Ghirshman suggests that the temple was dedicated to him already in the Seleucid period.[2] A low, almost symbolic wall separated the part of the terrace occupied by the sanctuaries of the Macedonians from the section with the podium used by the Iranians. The dating of the expanded terrace and the early form of the two temples to the Seleucid period is based largely on small objects found in the excavations: on votive offerings such as terracottas, small bronzes, and jewelry, and on the pottery.[3] The material is not extensive, however, and the Seleucid date may not be correct. David Stronach has said that on several visits to Masjid-i Solaiman while the excavations were in progress he saw no pottery that he would classify as Seleucid.[4]

The plan of the early form of the Great Temple

could not be determined but Ghirshman suggests that it was not very different from that of the Parthian period. The temple of the Parthian period has an unusual plan (fig. 56).[5] Its perimeter is roughly square (31 x 33.08 meters), and a corridor running along all four sides separates the central block of the sanctuary from the outer wall. Four entrances led into this outer corridor: one at either end of the north side, which was the principal facade, and one in the east and one in the west wall; these last two entrances were placed not quite opposite one another. The principal facade was elaborately articulated. Ghirshman restores a portico three columns deep, arranged in rows of eight, seven, and six columns, moving out from the facade. The principal entrance, located near the northeast corner, was distinguished by a projecting threshold, and a row of three stairs ran along the front wall on either side of the entrance. In the northwest corner of this facade stood a low podium to which access was given by three steps on the east side. A second door on the north facade led from the podium into the isolating corridor. Behind the corridor on the north side (5-13), a long narrow vestibule (12) gave access to a large court surrounded on all four sides by narrow benches. The pronaos-naos unit lay on the west side of this court and occupied the width of the court and vestibule 12. They were entered by two sets of doors leading, on the same axis, first into the pronaos and then into the naos. The temple thus used a bent-axis approach. A water jar was placed under the pavement of the pronaos near the north-

---

[1] Ghirshman, *Terrasses sacrées*, 55-77.
[2] Ibid., 90-96.
[3] Ibid., 76-91.
[4] Personal communication.

[5] Ghirshman, *Terrasses sacrées*, 89. The description given here is of phase IIIa, which, according to Ghirshman, presents the most complete plan (p. 105 f., fig. 36, plans III, V, VII). For other phases, see pp. 103-108, figs. 36, 37, 41, plans III, IV, VII, VIII.

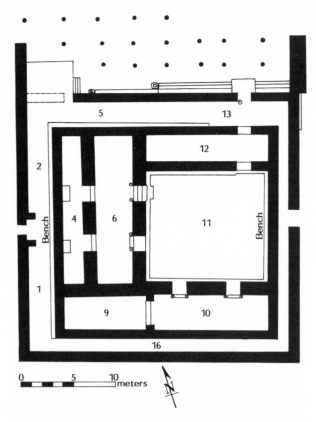

56. Masjid-i Solaiman, Great Temple, phase IIIa, plan.

door, on the line of the north, and principal, door into the antecella, led into the cella; this door was flanked by two bases, perhaps for statues. The small room (13) to the north of the antecella might have served as a sacristy, but since it opened only to the outside, this is uncertain. Low stairs stood against the front wall of the temple flanking the main entrance to the antecella. Ghirshman compares them to the steps of the *salles aux gradins* at Dura, and indeed they could have served as benches for spectators of sacred rites that took place on the terrace in front of the temple. The *salles aux gradins* of the Dura temples are rooms incorporated into the building, however, not simply stairs in front of it. Ghirshman also compares the steps in front of the Temple of Heracles to the steps that surround the *temple à redans* at Aï Khanoum, but those steps form the base of the temple and are unlikely to have been used for spectators. Ghirshman suggests that the steps in front of the Temple of Heracles were not original, but seem to have been added later, "à l'époque où ce sanctuaire devint celui d'Héraclès iranien, le dieu Verethragna."[6] The temple underwent a number of modifications and additions; in particular, several subsidiary chapels were built (12, 14-15, 18). Except for the steps, these did not change its essential character.

The plan of the Great Temple is unusual, but does seem to be related to Babylonian religious architecture. The basic scheme—a court, behind which are situated an antecella and cella of the same width—is seen, for example, in the Irigal (fig. 6) and Anu-Antum (fig. 5) temples at Uruk. At Masjid-i Solaiman, however, there were two doors into the antecella and cella, whereas in Mesopotamian temples there was only one. There were no cult niches in the cella at Masjid-i Solaiman, but two altars stood against the rear wall on the line of the doors. The separation of the core of the building from the perimeter wall by an isolating corridor is also seen in both the Irigal and the Anu-Antum temples, but the form is somewhat different. At Masjid-i Solaiman, the isolating corridor runs uninterruptedly around all sides of the central block, whereas in the temples at Uruk there was a corridor, properly speaking, around only two sides of the sanctuary unit, with courts on the other two sides. As Ghirshman points out, the corridor of the Great Temple at Masjid-i Solaiman could have been used for circumambulation, unlike the isolating corridors in the Uruk temples.[7]

east wall, and a drain from outside the building channelled water into it. Two altars stood against the rear wall of the naos on the axis of the doors. Between the court and the isolating corridor (16) on the south side of the building, a long room (10) was entered from the court through two doors on the south. A second room (9) behind it, which occupied the space to the south of the pronaos-naos complex, was accessible only from room 10. Ghirshman suggests that the two rooms might have been sacristies. In a later phase a door was apparently opened from the pronaos into room 9.

On the upper part of the terrace stood a smaller temple, apparently dedicated to Heracles (fig. 57). The temple, which faced approximately east, was rectangular, consisting of a long antecella (5), a cella (6) and an additional room opening to the outside (13). Room 13 was placed between the antecella and the north wall of the temple, thus reducing the length of the antecella. As in the Great Temple, two doors gave access to the antecella. Low benches ran along its northeast and northwest walls. A single

[6] Ibid., 90 f., fig. 33; 118 f., plans III, IV, VII, VIII; pls. XLIII, XLV, XLVIII, XLIX, LX.1. The quotation is on p. 191.

[7] Ibid., 189 f.

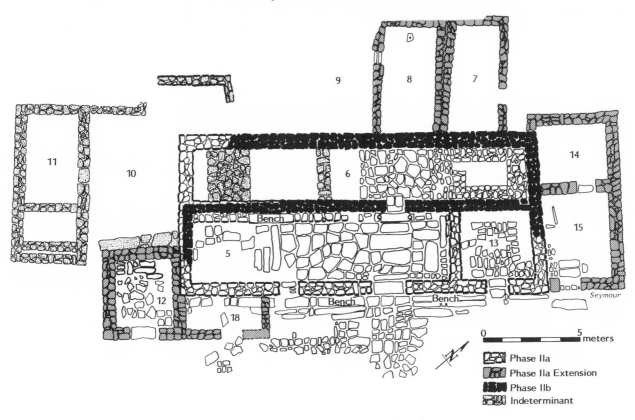

57. Masjid-i Solaiman, Temple of Heracles, plan.

The Irigal and Bit rēš sanctuaries were far more complex than the temple at Masjid-i Solaiman. Not only were there more subsidiary rooms around the main court, there were also numerous courts, each with their own subsidiary rooms. The main entrance to the Irigal was apparently perpendicular to the entrances to the cellae, as at Masjid-i Solaiman, and one of the entrances to the Bit rēš was also placed at right angles to the entrances to the cellae. In both the Irigal and the Bit rēš, however, the entrance to the main court lay on the axis of the door to the chief cella. The small Temple of Heracles on the upper terrace at Masjid-i Solaiman can be seen as a simplified version of the Great Temple. The antecella-cella unit is very similar, but there is no court. Ghirshman notes the derivation of the plans of the two temples at Masjid-i Solaiman from Babylonian architecture, and he especially stresses the similarity of the Great Temple to the Irigal. He notes that the scheme of a sanctuary unit consisting of a long antecella and a cella of the same width appears also at Aï Khanoum and Dura-Europos, and

he suggests that the temples of Masjid-i Solaiman bridge the gap between Mesopotamia and Central Asia. The temples of Masjid-i Solaiman show, in his opinion, that there is no gap in continuity (geographical) in the erection of religious buildings on a Babylonian plan by Seleucid rulers. This suggestion depends on the acceptance of Ghirshman's dating of the two temples at Masjid-i Solaiman to the Seleucid period, however, and of his assumption that the early form of the Great Temple was like that of the later building, which is well preserved.[8]

In any case, the temples of Masjid-i Solaiman do not simply repeat the Babylonian plan, but modify and vary it. For example, the complete circumambulatory corridor around the central block of the Great Temple is not found in Babylonian temples, but anticipates, as Ghirshman says, the circumambulatory corridors of such buildings as the Square Temple at Hatra and Sasanian fire temples. Isolating corridors are seen in the houses of Aï Khanoum and other Central Asian sites, so the origins of this feature may lie in the eastern part of the Iranian

[8] Ibid., 187-91. Cf. Bernard, "Traditions orientales," 269 f.; Bernard, in J. Deshayes, ed., *Le Plateau iranien et l'Asie Centrale des ori-*

gines à la conquête islamique (Colloques internationaux du Centre National de la Recherche Scientifique, no. 567) (Paris, 1977), 265.

world.[9] The arrangement of the antecella-cella unit in the Great Temple, with two doors into each and two altars against the rear wall of the cella, is also different from the arrangements in Babylonian temples, presumably in response to the needs of the cult. The lack of entrance towers and the fact that the exterior walls are not decorated with projections and recesses further differentiate the Great Temple from Babylonian temples, including those of Seleucid Uruk. Finally, the portico in front of the main entrance, the only sign of Western influence, is not seen in the temples of Uruk, Dura, or Aï Khanoum.

Ghirshman attributes various column capitals, none found *in situ*, to the portico of the Great Temple. One of these, found near the entrance to the temple, seems to echo the Achaemenid tradition. This capital, cut in one piece with the top of the column, consists of two addorsed protomes of animals with prominent female breasts and legs ending in hooves. The heads are missing, but Ghirshman suggests that the animals were sphinxes. He attributes another capital, this one with three female heads, found in the Temple of Heracles, to the Great Temple, because the latter was the only building on the terraces that had columns. The third capital, found even further away, bears an acanthus leaf decoration.[10] If Ghirshman's attribution of all three of these capitals to the portico in front of the Great Temple is correct, then the building was indeed remarkably eclectic.

Although the statue of Heracles from the small temple demonstrates that at least in the Parthian period it was dedicated to Heracles, it is not so clear to whom the Great Temple was dedicated. Ghirshman attributes the temple, which he dates to the Seleucid period, to Athena Hippia on the basis of the discovery in and near the temple of two small bronze images of Athena and a number of votive terracottas of Macedonian riders.[11] The use of a few small votives as a means of determining the deity to whom a temple was dedicated seems dubious, however, and it is probably better to leave the question open. Ghirshman argues from the presence of two altars in the cella of the Great Temple in the Parthian period that it was dedicated to a pair of di-

vinities, whom he identifies as Anahita and Mithras on the basis of the images on a bronze plaque found in the antecella.[12]

Bard-è Néchandeh

BARD-è NÉCHANDEH in Elymais, like Masjid-i Solaiman, is a sacred complex consisting of a series of terraces built against a hillside. Though the two complexes are only eighteen kilometers apart, the major temple at Bard-è Néchandeh differs significantly from the Great Temple at Masjid-i Solaiman. The upper terrace at Bard-è Néchandeh, which is also the oldest, probably goes back to the Achaemenid period; its existence at least as early as the first part of the second century B.C. is demonstrated by the discovery of a number of coins of Seleucid rulers. A simple podium stood on this terrace, and in its third phase, a small building, perhaps a sacristy, was attached to it.[13] A large platform, on which stood a podium with a room next to it, is also seen at Masjid-i Solaiman.

A second phase at Bard-è Néchandeh, in which a terrace was added in front of the upper one, can perhaps be dated to the reign of Kamniskires I (189-140 B.C.?) on the basis of numismatic and epigraphical evidence.[14] In a third phase, an additional terrace was built in front of the first two, and a temple of unusual plan was erected on this lower terrace (fig. 58). The cella, a rectangular room whose roof was supported by four columns arranged in a square, was flanked on three sides by long, shallow, rectangular rooms, which were accessible only from the cella and did not communicate with one another. In front of the temple was a double portico of eight columns. Under the threshold of room 1, behind the cella, a foundation deposit consisting of nearly five thousand coins was found. The coins included one minted under Kanishka and four Parthian obols, which permit the dating of the temple, or at least of its last restoration, to the second century A.D. Numerous fragments of columns were found, including one decorated with four figures in relief. Ghirshman also discovered a capital with four figures in relief: two men in long tunics, an

[9] D. Stronach, "On the Evolution of the Early Iranian Fire Temple," *Hommages et Opera Minora* XI: *Papers in Honor of Professor Mary Boyce*, 610-12, 617-19, 624-27. For the central Asian houses, cf. Henri-Paul Francfort, "Le plan des maisons gréco-bactriennes et le problème des structures de type 'megaron' en Asie Centrale et en Iran," in J. Deshayes, ed., *Le Plateau iranien et l'Asie Centrale*, 267-80.

[10] Ibid., 110-14, pls. XC.2, XCIII.1-3; 32, 41.

[11] Ibid., 78-81, 89, pls. XCVII.3; C.1, 2; CXII.2, 3; CXIII.1, 5; CXIV.4, 5; 35, 43-44, 66.

[12] Ibid., 191-93.

[13] Ghirshman, *Terrasses sacrées*, 5, 15-28.

[14] Ibid., 39; J. Harmatta, in ibid., 289-303.

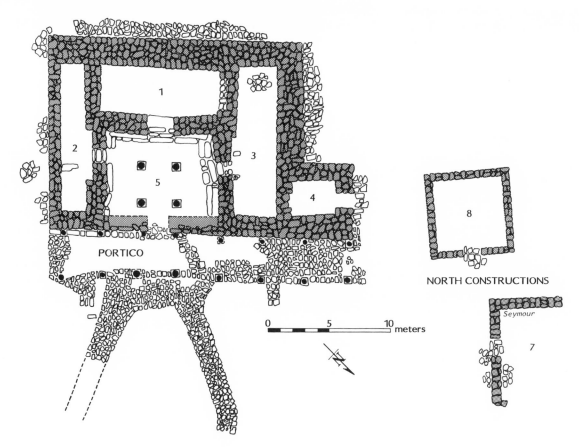

58. Bard-è Néchandeh, temple, plan.

armed man, and an armed woman. He interprets the two figures clad in military dress as Anahita and Mithras.[15]

In addition, parts of thirteen statues in the round, five high reliefs, and fragments belonging to perhaps an additional half-dozen statues were discovered on the upper terrace.[16] All apparently represented men in Parthian dress. Obviously, statues were a frequent votive offering at Bard-è Néchandeh. The profusion of statues recalls Hatra, but at Hatra statues of women as well as of men were dedicated.

The plan of this temple, unlike that of the Great Temple at Masjid-i Solaiman, is not based on a Mesopotamian scheme. A number of religious buildings that included a room whose roof was supported by four columns have been found in the area ranging from Iran and Central Asia through the Hauran, though there is a geographical gap be-

tween Iran and Syria. Schippmann has argued that the plan originated in Iran.[17] The buildings discussed by Schippmann served a variety of religions, including Buddhism in Central Asia, and they differ among themselves in a variety of ways. The common element is a square or slightly rectangular room, the roof of which was usually supported by four columns. This room formed part of different sorts of complexes, and may have served either as a principal room (e.g., a cella, or a room housing the sacred fire in fire temples) or as a subsidiary one. In one of the earliest, the "āyadana" at Susa, a tetra-style room was fronted by a portico and vestibule and was surrounded on three sides by a corridor. This complex was set at the back of a court. The corridor at Susa allowed for circumambulation, unlike the rooms at Bard-è Néchandeh. Ghirshman dates the "āyadana" to the second century B.C. at the earliest,[18] but Dieulafoy and others date it to the

[15] Ibid., 39-46, figs. 16-19, plan II; pls. XXIV.1-5, 18 A-D.
[16] Ibid., 30 f., 48-50, pls. XXV-XXXVI.

[17] Schippmann, *Feuerheiligtümer*, 480-99.
[18] Ghirshman, *Terrasses sacrées*, 197-200.

reign of Artaxerxes II (404-358 B.C.).[19] The fire temple at Kuh-i Khwaja, in the Seistan, underwent a number of rebuildings. In its earliest phase, however, its plan was remarkably similar to that of the "āyadana" at Susa. Gullini dates this phase to the Achaemenid period.[20] His dating is doubted by other scholars, however, who attribute this phase of the building to the Parthian period at the earliest.[21]

The area of the so-called Fratadara temple, below the terrace at Persepolis, is a large complex including a number of rooms and streets. The room identified by Herzfield as a temple cella is roughly square, the roof was supported by four pillars, and a three-stepped base stood a little in front of the rear wall. The room was flanked on all four sides by narrow corridors, with those on the east (front), north, and south opening into the cult chamber, although the rear (west) corridor apparently did not. According to Herzfeld's plan,[22] the corridors did not communicate with one another, and in that respect, the plan is similar to that of the temple at Bard-è Néchandeh; but at Bard-è Néchandeh, there was no corridor in front of the cella, and all of the side rooms opened from the cella. The cult room in the temple at Persepolis was fronted by a double portico, apparently consisting of two rows of four columns each, again recalling Bard-è Néchandeh. Suggested dates for the square temple at Persepolis range from the Achaemenid period to the third century B.C. The function is uncertain, but most scholars identify it as a fire temple.[23]

Somewhat similar plans are also widespread in Central Asia—at Surkh Kotal, Mansur-Depe, Merv, and Pendjikent—but they are all later than the temple at Bard-è Néchandeh and differ from it in significant respects. The "Square Hall" at Old Nysa dates from an earlier period, but shares with Bard-è Néchandeh only the fact that the roof was supported by four columns.[24]

A number of temples in the Hauran also had a roughly square cella with a roof supported by four columns. The Temple of Baalshamin at Sî', which was built in 33/32 B.C., was situated at the back of a porticoed court. The roughly square cella, with four columns supporting the roof, was fronted by a two-columned porch and surrounded on all four sides by a corridor. The small Temple of Dusares next to it was similar, as were the temples at Sūr and Sahr.[25] The sanctuary of Baalshamin at Palmyra followed the same organizational principles as these Nabataean temples, and Collart suggests that the scheme was derived from the Nabataean area.[26] The square room in the Palmyrene sanctuary apparently lacked the four columns that characterized most of the other buildings discussed. The relation between the Syrian sanctuaries and those of Iran and Central Asia is unclear.

Thus the temple at Bard-è Néchandeh is not related to Mesopotamian prototypes. Rather, it shows a version of a temple plan that was probably developed in Iran. Ghirshman suggests that the temple was dedicated to Anahita and Mithras, and that Ahuramazda was worshipped on the podium on the upper terrace.[27] Although this attribution is based on very slender evidence, a temple of Iranian plan would seem appropriate for Iranian divinities.

---

[19] For a summary of the dating question, see Schippmann, *Feuerheiligtümer*, 272-74, and Stronach, "On the origins of the Iranian Fire Temple," *Hommages et Opera Minora* XI (1985), 619-22.

[20] Gullini, *Architettura iranica*, 263-72.

[21] Schippmann, *Feuerheiligtümer*, 61-70; Ghirshman, *Terrasses sacrées*, 205; Stronach, "On the Origins of the Iranian Fire Temple," *Hommages et Opera Minora* XI (1985), 618 f.

[22] E. Schmidt, *Persepolis* I (Chicago, 1953), 55 f., fig. 16.

[23] Schippmann, *Feuerheiligtümer*, 180-85; Stronach, *Hommages et Opera Minora* XI (1985), 612-14.

[24] Ghirshman, *Terrasses sacrées*, 205-213, figs. 46-51.

[25] Howard Crosby Butler, *Publications of the Princeton University Archaeological Expedition to Syria in 1904-1905 and 1909*, division II, *Ancient Architecture in Syria*, Section A, *Southern Syria*, Part 6, *Sî'* (Leiden, 1916), 372-90; idem, *Princeton Expedition* II.A.7, *The Ledja* (Leiden, 1919), 428 f., 423; Schippmann, *Feuerheiligtümer*, 481-84; Ghirshman, *Terrasses sacrées*, 219-22, figs. 55, 56.

[26] Collart and Vicari, *Le Sanctuaire de Baalshamin à Palmyre* (Neuchâtel, 1969), 190-98.

[27] Ghirshman, *Terrasses sacrées*, 50, 196.

4

PARTHIAN MESOPOTAMIA

Parthian Uruk

THE RELIGIOUS architecture of Uruk during the period of Parthian control differs both in scale and in character from that of the Seleucid period. Whereas the monumental Seleucid sanctuaries were built in traditional Babylonian forms for the worship of old deities, the one temple that can be certainly dated to the Parthian period is built in a style that shows clear signs of Roman influence and is dedicated to a new god, Gareus. The other probable Parthian temple in Uruk, a small structure built against the southeast wall of the Anu-Antum temple, is dated by the excavators to the Parthian period on the basis of its obvious secondary character and its un-Babylonian plan. This dating is plausible, for such an addition would have been unlikely while the Anu-Antum temple was still functioning. Although the remains of Parthian Uruk have been little explored,[1] and it is therefore possible that other sanctuaries await discovery, the contrast is striking between the monumental Seleucid constructions and the small Parthian temples that are known.

The Temple of Gareus is located on a mound to the southeast of the Bit rēš and Irigal sanctuaries. This mound is separated from the nearby hills by a deep hollow,[2] a separation that was further emphasized at one time by a heavy fortification wall. Schmidt suggests that this fortress served as a kind of "Fluchtberg" at a time when the great city walls of Uruk had fallen or at any rate were no longer functional. This fortification, the earliest Parthian

construction on the site, cannot be precisely dated, but the temple of Gareus, erected after the fortification wall had lost its protective function, provides a *terminus ante quem* of A.D. 111. Schmidt argues that the wall was built to protect a foreign population in Uruk, perhaps the Dollamēnoi named in the inscription found near the temple.[3] The architectural forms suggest that this whole area represents a zone at least of foreign influence, and possibly of foreign population, with ties to the West. The influence of Roman architecture, for example, is clearly seen in a set of domestic baths that were built later than the fortification wall and either slightly before or roughly contemporary with the construction of the Temple of Gareus. The plan of these baths is closely similar to that of baths in private houses in Pompeii, and alien to the traditions of Mesopotamian architecture. Schmidt suggests that they may well have been built for a group of people who wished to retain part of their traditional way of life in a foreign land.[4] The Temple of Gareus shows mixed Babylonian and Roman or Romanized forms.

The Temple of Gareus is identified and a *terminus ante quem* for its building given by a Greek inscription found nearby:

Ἔτους ΒΚΎ μηνὸς Δείου
Ἀρτεμίδωρος Διογένους ὁ
ἐπικαλούμενος Μινναναιος
Τουφαιου στοιχῶν τῆι τῶν προ-
γόνων αὐτοῦ ἀγαθῆι προαιρέσει
ἀνέθηκεν Γαρει θεῶι χωρίον Δα-

---

[1] J. Schmidt, *BaM* V (1970), 76.
[2] Heinrich, *UVB* VI, 33.
[3] J. Schmidt, *BaM* V (1970), 89-91; idem, *UVB* XXVI/XXVII,

57-59, 61. On the identity of the Dollamēnoi, see below.
[4] J. Schmidt, *BaM* V (1970), 91-93, fig. 12; idem; *UVB* XXVI/XXVII, 59-61, pls. 14a, 70.

ιαμεινα· τὸ δὲ κοινὸν τῶν
Δολλαμηνων ὃν εὐχά-
ριστον ἔκρ[ι]εινεν ἀμεί-
ψεσθαι ἀντὶ ἀναθέματος · ἀν-
δριάντα αὐτῶι στῆσαι ἐν ναῶι Γαρειος
στεφανοῦν τε αὐτὸν ἐν ἑκάστηι γε-
νεθλιακῆι αὐτοῦ τὸν σύνπαντα χρόνον
οὔσηι ἕκτηι Ἀπελλαίου, παρειστᾶν αὐτῶι
ἱερόθυτον καὶ ἀπὸ τοῦ αὐτοῦ ἱερο-
θύτου πέμπειν αὐτῶι Ἀρτεμι-
δώρωι ὀσφὺν εὐσεβείας
καὶ εὐνοίας ἕνεκεν.

The following is a partial translation: "In the year 442, in the month of Deios, Artemidoros, son of Diogenes, who is also called Minnanaios, son of Touphaios, following the good resolution of his ancestors, dedicated the χωρίον Δαιαμεινα to Gareus the god. The association [κοινὸν] of the Dollamēnoi decided, in thanks, to repay the dedication by erecting a statue to him in the Temple of Gareus. . . ."

Assuming that the era used is the Seleucid one according to the Babylonian calculation, the date is October/November, A.D. 111. The Dollamēnoi are an unknown people, but Meier suggests that they might have been the inhabitants of the land Δολομηνή, which Strabo (XVI.1.1) mentions as near Nineveh. Though they cannot be Greek, it is clear that they knew the language. It is striking to find not only a Greek inscription but also Greek religious customs (offering a statue of a person in a temple and crowning it on his birthday) at Uruk in so late a period. The god Gareus is otherwise unknown.[5]

The Temple of Gareus (fig. 59), constructed in baked brick and covered in stucco, may be considered as having an interior plan of Babylonian type encased in an exterior of Romanized form.[6] The relatively small interior (10.50 x 13.70 meters) is divided into two rooms of equal breadth, like the cella and forecella arrangement of Babylonian temples. The inner room also has a cult niche in the rear wall with a statue base in front of it, again in Babylonian fashion. A fragment of a life-size bronze foot shod in a soft shoe of Parthian type, which was found in a later house in front of the west corner of the temple, might have belonged to the cult statue.[7]

Above the cult niche is a light shaft, and to either side of the niche, 1.20 meters above the floor, angled passages one meter high are built into the wall; their purpose is enigmatic.

The outer walls of the temple are decorated with engaged columns, between which are arcades consisting of engaged pilasters that support arches; at the top of each arcade is a narrow, blind window (see figs. 60, 61). To either side of the door are round niches set within blind arcades, and above the niches are blind windows like those on the other three walls. Heavy rectangular pilasters mark the rear corners. The architectural details are clearly the result of strong Mediterranean influence, but they have been combined in ways that would have seemed strange to a Roman eye. The columns have Ionic bases in molded brick, but flutes (in stucco) like those of Doric columns. Small fragments of volutes suggest that the capitals were flat and Ionicizing. The bricks that top the pilasters have profiles like a Lesbian cyma and the relief ornament appropriate to that molding. The bricks just below this molding are decorated with strange dragon-like winged creatures, rather like griffins with serpents' tails. A brick of the same format, but decorated with a dog, which was found in the debris, presumably also came from a pilaster. The Lesbian leaf ornament and the animals were cut out of the bricks rather than molded into them, and the details were finished in stucco.[8]

The reconstruction of the elevation of the Gareus temple is uncertain, though some elements—the thickness of the columns, the form of the bases, and the general form of the capitals—are known. Heinrich concluded from the relative scarcity of brick in the debris that the temple was never much higher than it is at present. The reconstruction by von Haller shows rather stubby proportions; the calculation of the height is apparently based both on the relative absence of bricks in the debris and on a rather vague notion that in the Parthian period there was little feeling for proportions. Heinrich states that von Haller's reconstruction of the crowning of the temple as a horizontal zone with two levels of moldings, which form projecting consoles over each column, is perhaps based too closely on [classical] rules (fig. 60).[9] J. Schmidt agrees that von Haller's reconstruction is too clas-

[5] Christian Meier, "Ein griechisches Ehrendekret vom Gareustempel in Uruk," *BaM* I (1960), 104-114. The significance of the inscription will be discussed in more detail below.

[6] Heinrich, *UVB* VI, 33 f.; J. Schmidt, *UVB* XXVI/XXVII, 61 f.

[7] Heinrich, *UVB* VI, 35, pl. 30a.

[8] Ibid., 33-36, pls. 12-13, 23-26. See the drawings in J. Schmidt, *UVB* XXVIII, pl. 43b and c.

[9] Heinrich, *UVB* VI, 34, pl. 13.

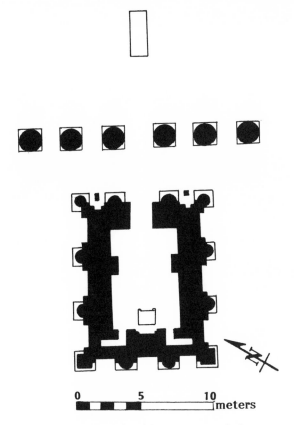

59. Uruk, Temple of Gareus, restored plan.

might have stood in the niches of his hypothetical second story;[10] Heinrich had suggested that statues might have stood in the niches of the entrance facade. Meier thought that the baked-brick base in front of the north aedicula on the entrance facade might have supported the statue of Artemidoros mentioned in the inscription.[11]

One of the strangest features of the Temple of Gareus is the presence about five meters in front of and parallel to the entrance facade of a row of six columns with very heavy foundations, twenty-five bricks deep; the temple itself, in contrast, is simply set on a layer of tamped mud. Heinrich suggests that these deep foundations were laid in an attempt to keep the columns from being set unevenly in the thick debris that forms the building field. The columns are 1.30 meters in diameter, thus noticeably thicker than the half-columns of the main building; and they are not aligned with the engaged half-columns; thus they could not have constituted a true peristyle. Furthermore, the plan of the bases suggests that the columns were joined by arches, giving the effect of a wall with openings rather than of a colonnade. Since no traces of foundations for columns have been found on the other three sides of the temple, there cannot have been a surrounding colonnade. Heinrich suggests that the columns formed part of a court, the other walls of which were made of mud brick.[12] Schmidt disagrees with this idea but concedes that the relation of the columns to the facade of the temple remains unclear. He notes, as does Heinrich, that although the spacing of the columns, especially the outer two, gives the impression of a peripteros, both the absence of any traces of columns on the other three sides of the building and the lack of an axial relationship between the columns in front of the temple and the half-columns on the facade of the building make the idea of a peripteros unlikely. Schmidt's drawing of two possible axial spacings of columns on the long side of the building shows the lack of structural relationship between the conjectural peristyle and the body of the temple proper.[13]

The exterior form of the Temple of Gareus, with its engaged columns, blind arcades, and niches flanking the entrance, is based on the architectural principles of the Roman world. Details of the architectural ornament, such as the Ionic bases of the engaged columns and the Lesbian cymas that crown the pilasters, represent transformations of an

sical in appearance. He also states that the fact that the temple is now known to have been placed within a temenos (see below) raises the question of its proportions, since the temenos wall must have stood at least as high as the ruins of the temple to make it a meaningful construction. The temple, he feels, should have stood higher than the temenos wall, and thus he suggests a two-storied restoration (fig. 61). This gives the columns slimmer proportions and also necessitates a second level of blind arcades on the walls. According to Schmidt, the zone above the architrave was covered with a design in relief of back-to-back triangles separated by a continuous horizontal line. Pieces of these bricks, some of which have holes for attachment, were found in the excavations. Emphasizing the tentative nature of his suggested restoration, Schmidt also restores a crowning of stepped battlements decorated with arrows on the basis of the frequent occurrence of such decorations at Uruk. He further suggests that statues, fragments of which were found in the area,

[10] J. Schmidt, *UVB* XXVIII, 35, 38, fig. 12.
[11] Meier, *BaM* I (1960), 105.

[12] Heinrich, *UVB* VI, 34 f.
[13] J. Schmidt, *BaM* V (1970), 94; idem, *UVB* XXVIII, 34 f., fig. 11.

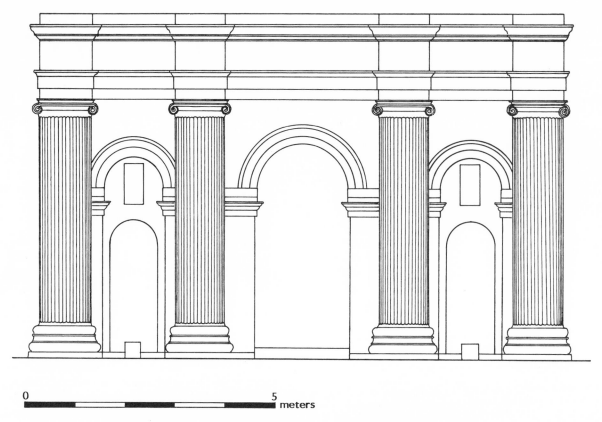

0   5 meters

60. Uruk, Temple of Gareus, northeast facade, reconstruction by von Haller.

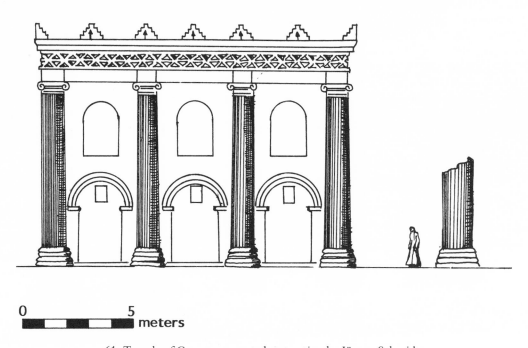

0   5 meters

61. Temple of Gareus, suggested restoration by Jürgen Schmidt.

original Greek form analogous to ornamentation seen at Seleucia and Babylon during the Parthian period. The strange snaky-tailed griffin and dog plaques that decorated the tops of the pilasters of the Temple of Gareus find their closest parallels at Seleucia and Hatra. Fragments of a baked-brick frieze found at Seleucia in the excavations of the porticoed street show the same combination of fantastic animals and architectural moldings of a debased Greek type. The Seleucia frieze is described by Negro Ponzi as showing "a lion attacking a humpbacked bull in front of a winged griffin,"[14] but it looks more like two griffins attacking a bull; floral motifs that suggest the traditional tree of life separate the animal combats. As at Uruk, the designs in the Seleucia frieze are cut out of the brick and covered in stucco. Both the animal combat motif and the form of the griffins in the Seleucia plaques are closer to Greek models than are the monsters on the Uruk bricks. The frieze of the so-called "Hellenistic temple" (the Temple of Bar Maren) at Hatra is decorated with confronted griffins, elongated and strangely flat;[15] and again, the Hatra griffins are closer to Greco-Roman prototypes than are the Uruk dragon-griffins. The tritons of the same frieze also come out of the Greco-Roman repertoire, and the moldings of the Hatra temple are based on Greco-Roman prototypes combined in odd ways. The fantastic animals that decorated the Temple of Gareus at Uruk might well represent a continuation of the Babylonian tradition of decorating buildings with real and fantastic animals in molded brick, especially as this tradition is attested in the Seleucid Bit rēš and Irigal sanctuaries.

The odd placement of a row of columns in front of the Gareus temple without a discernible connection to the temple or to a surrounding courtyard is unparalleled. The peripteros at Assur, however (fig. 68), with its odd combination of an interior plan of vaguely Babylonian form with a colonnade on three sides, shows a similar juxtaposition of seemingly unrelated forms. (This building is discussed in the section on Assur.) Likewise, the "Hellenistic temple" (or Temple of Bar Maren, fig. 75, E) at Hatra, a peripteral temple on a podium surrounded by an outer colonnade on a lower level and with columns on a slightly different axis,[16] pro-

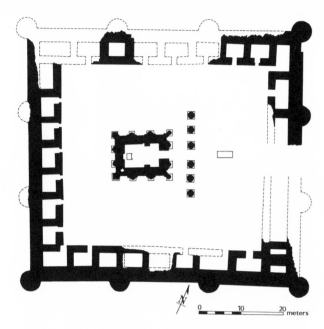

62. Uruk, Temple of Gareus in temenos, schematic plan.

vides an example of an encasing exterior without a clear relationship to the inner building.

Recent excavations have revealed that the Temple of Gareus stood within a temenos 60 x 63 meters in size (fig. 62). This temenos was laid out on a different orientation from that of the fortification wall that was the earliest Parthian construction on the site. Though the temporal relationship between the wall and the temple cannot be determined exactly, the wall had apparently lost its defensive function by the time the temple was built.[17] The temenos wall, constructed in a mixture of baked and unbaked brick, had round towers at the corners and probably also two round towers on each side, though the poor state of preservation makes the exact form difficult to determine. The northwest corner, much of the northwest wall, and a long stretch on the northeast side of the enclosure have been destroyed by channels dug by torrential rains. The entrance to the court was probably in the destroyed section of the northeast wall, opposite the door of the temple. On the inside of the temenos wall, rooms opened to the court, but did not intercommunicate, and in the courtyard in front of the temple, on the axis of the door, is a mass of bricks that

[14] Invernizzi, "The Excavation of Tell ʿUmar," *Mesopotamia* II (1967), 31 f., fig. 17; idem, "Problemi di coroplastica tardo-mesopotamica," *Mesopotamia* V-VI (1970/71), 333 f.; M. Negro Ponzi, "Excavations in Squares CLXXI, 54/55/63/64/74 (Porticoed Street)," *Mesopotamia* V-VI (1970/71), 35 f., figs. 38, 39; the quotation is on p. 36.

[15] Safar and Mustapha, *Hatra*, 347.

[16] Ibid., 345, 381 f., 388, 391 f.

[17] J. Schmidt, *UVB* XXVI/XXVII, 59.

might be the remains of an altar. The temenos wall just described is the second to have been built. It was preceded by another, to which rooms were added in a second phase, and remains of occupational debris suggest that this earlier phase had a long life. This wall was levelled, and a fill as much as 0.50 meters thick was laid as a foundation for the second wall, which is contemporary with the Gareus temple. Schmidt suggests that there may have been an earlier temple contemporary with the first precinct wall, all traces of which would have been removed in levelling operations for the Gareus temple.[18]

Apparently while the Gareus temple and precinct were still in use, additional walls were built in parts of the court. Two walls running west from the corner pilasters at the rear of the temple to the temenos wall formed a room whose function is unclear. Schmidt describes the room as a dead space. To the north of the temple, other walls formed two courts or rooms paved with baked bricks, and other remains of a paved court are visible. The purpose of these additions is unclear.[19]

Schmidt in his most recent discussion of the stratigraphy of the site states that within the area of the Gareus temple precinct, nine building periods are visible. There are some traces of construction that predate the earlier temenos wall. After the temple went out of use, it was at first separated from the surrounding area by low walls. Later, the area was filled with houses, in which at least four phases of use are discernible.[20]

The complex stratigraphy of the constructions within the temenos makes it difficult to determine the various phases of construction, but it appears that initially the Gareus temple stood axially and in isolation within the temenos wall. This differentiates it from the Seleucid sanctuaries of Uruk and from earlier Babylonian temples, which were also surrounded by high walls but which included a multiplicity of courts and rooms. Schmidt notes the similarity between the temenos of the Gareus temple and Sasanian and Ummayed palatial architecture. He reports that excavations in the Merkes section of Babylon, north of the Ishtar temple, have revealed a temenos like that at Uruk; according to

the excavator, the ruins are to be dated in the Parthian period. Also at Hatra the temenos preceding the present one, and therefore dated to ca. 50 B.C., had round towers and rooms on the inside, according to Schmidt and Mustapha.[21] The placement of a temple within a fortress-like temenos may represent a Near Eastern tradition going back to the Seleucid period. The temple at Ikaros-Falaika in the Persian Gulf, which probably dates to the third century B.C., also stood in a temenos, this one with square towers.[22]

It is ironic that in spite of the unusually full information supplied by the inscription found near the Temple of Gareus, we actually know little about the temple's place in the culture of Uruk. The Dollamēnoi were presumably not natives of Uruk, and the temple's placement within an area that was clearly separated from the rest of the city and that was originally fortified perhaps suggests that the Dollamēnoi were an alien people worshipping their own god. As Meier points out, lack of evidence makes it difficult to assess the significance of a Greek inscription at Uruk in the second century A.D. The Dollamēnoi cannot have been Greeks, nor was Gareus a Greek god, yet the fact that the inscription is largely grammatically correct suggests that the dedicators had strong relations with the Greek-speaking world. The double names Artemidoros-Minnanaios and Diogenes-Touphaios suggest that the person being honored and his father were either Hellenized Dollamēnoi or Hellenized citizens of Uruk, though occasionally Greek residents in the Near East took local names. Most of the honors decreed in the inscription—dedication of a statue of a benefactor in a temple, crowning it on his birthday; offering an animal in his name—are known in Greek, not Babylonian, practice. Only the giving of a portion of the sacrificial animal to the person honored does not correspond to Greek custom, but neither is it Babylonian.[23] The epithet θεὸς ("god") applied to Gareus finds parallels at Dura-Europos, where an otherwise unknown but Semitic god, Aphlad, worshipped by a small group of men from Anath, was called "Aphlad the god,"[24] and another deity was named simply Zeus Theos.[25] The parallel especially with

---

[18] J. Schmidt, *UVB* XXVIII, 30-35, figs. 8-10, pls. 13-15, 39-41.

[19] Ibid., 36, pls. 14a, 15b, 50.

[20] Ibid., 36-38. Heinrich suggested that one phase of houses preceded the building of the temple and that six followed after it went out of use (*UVB* VI, 35).

[21] J. Schmidt, *UVB* XXVIII, 33 f.

[22] K. Jeppesen, *Le rayonnement des civilisations grecque et romaine sur*

les cultures périphériques (8ᵉ Congrès international d'Archéologie classique, Paris, 1963) (Paris, 1965), 541-44, fig. 1.

[23] Meier, *BaM* I (1960), 110-14.

[24] Ἀφαλαδῳ θεῷ; Ἀφλαδ λεγουμένου θεοῦ τῆς Ἀναθ κώμης (Hopkins, *Dura Report* V, 112-15, nos. 416, 418).

[25] Brown, *Dura Report* VII/VIII, 214, no. 888.

the Aphlad inscription might reinforce the idea that the epithet was applied to make clear the divinity of an otherwise unknown local god.

The Dura evidence further supports the idea that the god Gareus might have been worshipped by a small population of foreigners resident in Uruk. One of the inscriptions found in the precinct of Aphlad at Dura states that the andrōn was erected by members of an association (ἑταιρεία).[26] A similar term was used in the inscription found near the Gareus temple. The Temple of the Gaddé at Dura was apparently established and maintained by a group of Palmyrene merchants resident at Dura, for the purpose of maintaining the worship of their native gods along with the Gad (Fortune) of Dura.[27] Thus Meier's suggestion that the worshippers of Gareus were a small group of merchants seems plausible.[28]

The interior arrangements of the Temple of Gareus suggest that worship might have followed Babylonian practices, at least in part. The cult statue presumably stood on the base in front of the cult niche. It would have been dramatically illuminated at times by light from the shaft directly above the niche. The passages in the rear wall to either side of the cult niche probably played some unknown role in the cult. The fragmentary bronze foot found in a later house in front of the temple, which might possibly have come from the cult statue, is shod in a soft shoe, somewhat similar to those worn at Dura-Europos and at Hatra.[29] Even if the foot did come from the cult statue, all that we can say is that the footgear suggests that the figure might have worn Parthian dress.

The only other temple that can be attributed to the period of Parthian control at Uruk is the small, one-roomed structure built against the southeast wall of the core building of the Anu-Antum temple (fig. 4). The remains of the southeast wall of Anu-uballit-Kephalon's building formed one of the long sides of this small temple, and the structure's secondary character is obvious from the fact that it does not bond with the wall of the Anu-Antum temple, as well as from differences in the architectural decoration. In fact, its obviously secondary character and non-Babylonian decoration lead to its dating in the Parthian period. It appears from Jor-

dan's report that there can have been no significant difference in floor level between this addition and the Seleucid Anu-Antum temple.[30]

The three newly constructed walls of this temple were made of baked brick set in gypsum mortar and defined an interior space that measured 4.60 by 4.35 meters. The entrance door, in the northeast wall, was flanked by narrow rectangular pilasters, and the southeastern wall was decorated with engaged three-quarter columns at its corners and an engaged half-column in the middle. The segment of the rear wall abutting the wall of the old Anu-Antum temple was marked by a shallow pilaster; a similar shallow projection in the middle of the rear wall is restored by Jordan as a half-column. The heavy foundations were carried for a few courses above the level of the floor to support the engaged columns and pilasters, between which were thin (0.45 meter) screen walls; these screen walls created niches in the interior corresponding to the intercolumniations. The interior effect, then, was of pilasters resting on a bench. In the pilaster in the middle of the rear wall, thus on the axis of the door, was a small niche, 1.07 meters high, 0.57 meters wide at the bottom, 0.38 meters wide at the top. The niche was closed at the top by two diagonally placed bricks, and was 0.40 meters deep. The interior walls show traces of lime mortar with a thin coating of gypsum plaster.

A baked-brick projection 0.92 meters wide and 1 meter long rises from the floor in front of the niche in the center of the rear wall of the building; it is so badly preserved that the excavators were unable to determine whether it was a staircase or a base. Under the floor were found more than one hundred baked clay cones, whose bases were covered with blackish brown glaze.[31] These objects obviously recall the cones used to form the mosaic decoration of E-anna in the fourth millennium B.C.[32]

The small temple against the Anu-Antum temple, then, appears to combine Babylonian forms with architectural details derived at some remove from the Roman world. The interior arrangement, with a base (if it is that) in front of a niche, both of which lie on the axis of the door, recalls that of a Babylonian temple. The niches in earlier Babylonian temples were deeper, however, and therefore could

[26] Hopkins, *Dura Report* V, 113-15, no. 418.

[27] Brown, *Dura Report* VII/VIII, 257 f.

[28] Meier, *BaM* I (1960), 114.

[29] Heinrich, *UVB* VI, 35, pl. 30a. For Dura, see Cumont, *Fouilles*, 45, pl. XXXI, XXXII. For Hatra, see Ghirshman, *Persian Art*, 86, fig. 98; 94, fig. 105; 99, fig. 110.

[30] Jordan, *Uruk-Warka*, 36-38, pls. 14, 18, 43b, 73a and b.

[31] Ibid., 37, pl. 85b.

[32] Henri Frankfort, *Art and Architecture of the Ancient Orient* (Baltimore, 1969), 9, pl. 2; Anton Moortgat, *The Art of Ancient Mesopotamia* (London and New York, 1969), 3, pl. 2.

have held a cult statue. The niche in the late temple at Uruk is too shallow to have held a statue, and Jordan suggests that it could have sheltered, at the most, a cult symbol. The exterior treatment of the building, with engaged columns or pilasters corresponding to pilasters in the interior, is based on Hellenistic or Roman models, rather than on the traditional Babylonian decorative scheme, with its projections and recesses. The terracotta cones, if they belonged to this temple, suggest the continuation of some traditional Babylonian forms of decoration. Jordan states, however, that it is not known where they were originally used. He restores the facade with tall narrow arcades and pseudo-Ionic capitals on the basis of architectural fragments found by Loftus.[33] Although these fragments may have had nothing to do with the small temple built into the ruins of the Anu-Antum temple, the general resemblance of this building to the temple of Gareus makes Jordan's restoration plausible.

Jordan suggests that this temple—a small chapel, as he calls it—might have been built by the Parthians for their own use, while the Anu-Antum temple still served the needs of the defeated Babylonians. It seems more likely, however, that the small temple was built after the Bit rēš had ceased to function as a sanctuary, and that the new temple was intended to serve the needs of the inhabitants of the rather poor residential quarter that grew up in the ruins. The village was surrounded by a fortification wall. The sanctuary had taken on the appearance of a fortification already during the Seleucid period, but Lenzen dates the baked brick *kisu* at the northeast end of the precinct to the Parthian period, partly on technical grounds. Thus the village was clearly separated from the surrounding area. Lenzen has suggested that the villages that grew up in the ruins of the three great sanctuaries during the period of Parthian control at Uruk were inhabited by a different and non-local population from that of the city that occupied the entire eastern part of the mound.[34] He raises the possibility that the inhabitants of the villages within the old sanctuaries were Parthians, an idea that he feels is strengthened by the location of the building he calls a Mithraeum between the Bit rēš and the Irigal. His identification

of the building as a Mithraeum rests solely on the presence of benches and on its apsidal form, which recalls that of the Wallbrook Mithraeum in London. A fragmentary terracotta mold of a man kneeling on the back of a bull, which was found on the surface near the Anu ziggurat, has been considered Mithraic. Only the legs of the man are preserved.[35] Neither the form of the building nor the iconography of the mold support the identification, however; as Lenzen concedes, Mithraea are not usually apsidal; and the terracotta lacks the snake, dog, and scorpion that are usually present on Mithraic reliefs and is too small to be a cult relief.[36]

It seems prudent not to speculate on the ethnic identity of the inhabitants of the village within the Bit rēš, but the fortification of the village and the difference in burial customs do suggest that the inhabitants were of different stock from the people who inhabited the east part of the mound. The present evidence suggests, then, that the two temples so far known at Uruk in the Parthian period may have been built by foreigners who inhabited separate, fortified areas.

Nippur

At Nippur, where the assembly of the gods under the leadership of Anu and Enlil met,[37] Ekur, the temple enclosure of Enlil, apparently ceased to function as such after the Neo-Babylonian period. The Enlil temple in its monumental form was founded by Urnammu of the third dynasty of Ur. The last major work was undertaken by Assurbanipal, who rebuilt the ziggurat and the Enlil temple. Repair work by Nebuchadnezzar II shows that the temple was still in use during the Neo-Babylonian period, but there are no traces of Seleucid or early Parthian work in the area.[38] Coins found in unstratified contexts all over the site suggest occupation in the third and second centuries B.C. and again in the first and second centuries A.D.[39] Although few unequivocal traces of Seleucid activity have been found in the city, Oelsner argues that the discovery of an administrative document dated to the seventh year of Philip Arrhidaios' reign (317/316 B.C.) provides concrete evidence that the life of the city con-

[33] Jordan, *Uruk-Warka*, 37 f., pl. 30a.

[34] Lenzen, *UVB* XII/XIII, 31; idem, *UVB* XV, 24 f.

[35] Lenzen, *MDOG* 87, 46-55; idem, *UVB* XII/XIII, 32-34, pls. 6, 16-18; idem, *UVB* XIV, 18-20, pls. 6d, 7, 8, 45a, idem, *Neue Deutsche Ausgrabungen*, 26 f., fig. 6.

[36] H.J.W. Drijvers, "Mithra at Hatra," *Acta Iranica* IV: *Études*

Mithriaques (1978), 183 f., argues against the existence of a Mithraeum in Uruk.

[37] Thorkild Jacobsen, *The Treasures of Darkness* (New Haven, 1976), 20 f., 188.

[38] Donald E. McCown and Richard C. Haines, assisted by Donald P. Hansen, *Nippur* I (Chicago, 1967), 4-6, 25-27.

[39] Keall, *Late Parthian Nippur*, 43-45.

tinued later than had previously been thought.[40] He also argues for the identification of the *oppida Hipparenum* named by Pliny (*NH* VI. [30]. 123) as a site of "Chaldaean learning" (*Chaldaeorum doctrina*) with Nippur rather than Sippar, and on this basis suggests that the city was the seat of a late Babylonian astronomical school.[41] The status of the city in the Seleucid period remains highly uncertain.

Ekur (fig. 63), which enclosed the Temple of Enlil as well as the ziggurat, must have survived as an impressive ruin when it was turned into a fortress beginning around A.D. 65. Three distinct phases of growth, each apparently lasting only a short time, can be traced; the last phase probably dates to about A.D. 150.[42]

Coin evidence suggests that the nearby Temple of Inanna, queen of Heaven, was rebuilt as a temple during the same period as the phase III occupation of the fortress on the site of the temple of Enlil, i.e., during the second century A.D. (fig. 62).[43] Oelsner, citing a conversation with Falkenstein in which he expressed the original opinions of the excavators, suggests that the rebuilt temple should be dated to the Seleucid period on the basis of its similarity to the Seleucid temples of Uruk.[44] Heinrich also accepts a Seleucid date on the same basis. He notes that the building is not dated by archives and states that a few finds could be intrusive.[45] The coin evidence, though slight, seems sound, however. Crawford suggests that the late temple was still dedicated to Inanna,[46] but there is no textual or other evidence on this point. Heinrich doubts that the temple of this phase was still dedicated to Inanna, noting that the arrangements of the cella suggest the worship of two equal deities. Since Inanna had no consort, he raises the possibility of a later rebirth of the cults of Enlil and Ninlil.[47]

The age of the earliest temple has apparently not yet been determined, but the earliest well-preserved temple dates to Early Dynastic II (ca. 2750-2600 B.C.). The huge size that characterizes the Inanna temple in its various phases is evident already in this Early Dynastic II structure, which is approximately 96 meters long and 28 meters wide at its southeastern end, the widest point. An interesting feature of this temple is the existence within the complex of an independent shrine, which Crawford suggests may reproduce an early small shrine of Inanna.[48] The temple was rebuilt frequently, but a particularly important rebuilding is dated to the Ur III period (ca. 2100-2000 B.C., fig. 63). The last identifiable rebuilding before the late period was apparently Assyrian, and the plan of this building seems to have differed from that of the Ur III temple.

The builders of the late temple (fig. 64) apparently cleared the site down to the level of the Ur III temple and erected an enormous platform as a substructure for their new construction. In the process they destroyed the southeastern part of the Ur III temple and brought in some fill from another location, perhaps the Temple of Ninurta. Quantities of earlier material from various periods were found in this fill. The late temple retained the orientation of the Early Dynastic II and Ur III temples, and it also followed a traditional Babylonian court plan. It was a sizeable construction, some 96 meters in length and 62.50 meters in width. Two sanctuary units, side by side, each consisted of an antecella and a cella of the same width; another smaller group of rooms in the south corner of the complex may also have been a sanctuary unit. The entrances to the antecellae appear to have been distinguished by projections and recesses, and the cellae had a cult niche in the center of the back wall on the axis of the doors. An isolating corridor ran around two sides of the joined sanctuary units, and the approach to these units must have been quite indirect. There are a number of small rooms in the outer wall of the complex.[49] The plan is thus quite similar to those of the Bit rēš and Irigal sanctuaries in Uruk. The temple was replaced by another poorly preserved Parthian structure of unknown purpose.[50]

Thus the evidence from Nippur is contradictory.

[40] Oelsner, "Nochmals 'Hipparenum (Plinius nat. hist. VI 123) = Nippur?'" *Altorientalische Forschungen* IX (1982), 269 f.

[41] Ibid., 259-62; Oelsner, "War Nippur Sitz einer spätbabylonischen Astronomenschule?" *Wissenschaftliche Zeitschrift der Friedrich-Schiller Universität Jena* 20, no. 5 (1971), 141-49. Keall uses this same passage to argue that Nippur had lost its importance as a religious center by the first century A.D. (*Late Parthian Nippur,* 17).

[42] The preliminary report by James Knudstad and Edward John Keall, *Sumer* XXIV (1968), 95-106, has been summarized and amplified by Keall, in *Late Parthian Nippur,* 21-43. The fortress is also mentioned briefly in McCown, Haines, and Hansen, *Nippur I,* 19. Cf. also Clarence S. Fisher, *Babylonian Expedition of the University of Pennsylvania, Excavations at Nippur,* Part I (Philadelphia, 1903), 17

f.; H. V. Hilprecht, *Die Ausgrabungen der Universität von Pennsylvania im Bel-Tempel zu Nippur* (Leipzig, 1903), 31-33, fig. 18.

[43] Keall, *Late Parthian Nippur,* 55 f.; 56 n. 2, 61, fig. 18; idem, *JAOS* XCV (1975), 625 and n. 14.

[44] Oelsner, "Kontinuität und Wandel," 104.

[45] Heinrich, *Tempel und Heiligtümer,* 303, 334 f., fig. 424.

[46] Vaughn E. Crawford, "Nippur, The Holy City," *Archaeology* XII (1959), 77.

[47] Heinrich, *Tempel und Heiligtümer,* 303, 335.

[48] Crawford, *Archaeology* XII (1959), 79-81; illustration on p. 75.

[49] Ibid., 77-82; plan on p. 74; Keall, *Late Parthian Nippur,* 55 f.

[50] Crawford, *Archaeology* XII (1959), 77 f.

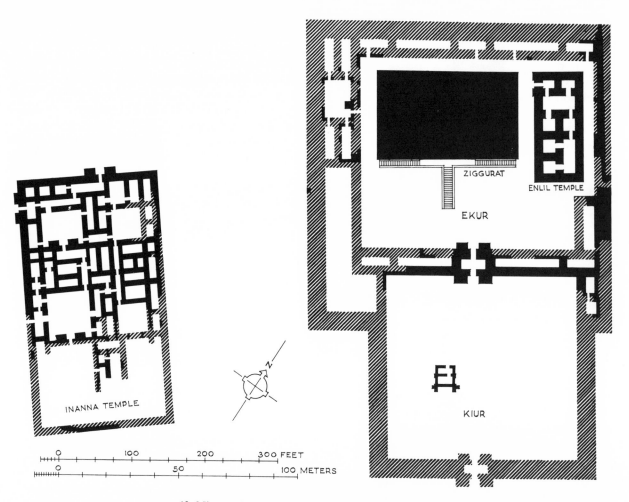

63. Nippur, Inanna Temple (Ur III period) and the Ekur.

64. Nippur, Inanna Temple, Seleucid or Parthian period.

Although the ziggurat and the Temple of Enlil were transformed into a fortress during the Parthian period, if the coin evidence is accepted, the temple of Inanna was rebuilt along traditional lines. Keall suggests that it "survived as a relic of religious conservatism."[51] Nippur, then, differs from Uruk in that there is a lack of unequivocal evidence for Seleucid work; but whereas at Uruk the major temples went out of use during the period of Parthian control, at Nippur the temple of Inanna seems to have been rebuilt.[52]

Assur

WITH THE FALL of the Assyrian kingdom in the late seventh century B.C., the city of Assur lost its importance. Assur was taken, and the Babylonian conquerors rebuilt the city on a much smaller scale. The inhabitants were apparently poor people. The temples were destroyed, and the great temple of the god Assur was not rebuilt after the conquest. Rather, two small structures of Babylonian plan were constructed in what had been the south forecourt of the temple, probably by the conquerors. It is not known to whom these temples were dedicated, but it seems unlikely that the Babylonians would have erected temples to the conquered god Assur.[53]

With the Achaemenid period and the arrival of the Greeks, Assur appears to have become an even less important city. An occasional Achaemenid coin and a few scattered finds of Greek terracottas remain as testimony of those periods, but there are no traces of building activity. Oates observes that no pottery of Hellenistic type like that found at Kalhu (Nimrud) is known from Assur, and he suggests that the decline of the city after the fall of the Assyrian empire was natural, since the local agricultural economy depended on irrigation canals built and maintained by the Assyrian kings.[54] Andrae has suggested that the city, essentially forgotten during the Achaemenid period, reappears in

Xenophon's *Anabasis* (II.4.28) as Kainai, the inhabitants of which crossed the Tigris on inflated animal skins and supplied the retreating Greeks with cheese and milk.[55] Barnett, however, identifies Xenophon's Kainai with Tikrit, south of Assur.[56]

Only after the Parthian conquest of Mesopotamia did Assur come to life again. The date of its revival is uncertain, but the revitalization of the city can plausibly be connected with the emergence of the Tigris as an important strategic boundary, which in turn is probably linked with the arrival of the Romans in the Near East during the first century B.C. Because of the long hiatus in major occupation and the possible change of name during this hiatus, Andrae doubts that the town of the Parthian period was still called Assur, in spite of the evidence for the worship of the god Assur in this town. Little is known of the history of the Parthian city, but Andrae suggests, plausibly, that its history is likely to have been closely linked with that of Hatra. Thus he distinguishes three phases of building activity during the Parthian period at Assur. He argues that the first, most prosperous phase might have been ended by an attack by Trajan in A.D. 116, and the second, poorer phase by a more thorough destruction by Septimius Severus in A.D. 198.[57] Schlumberger, more skeptical, states that all the excavations allow us to determine is that nothing is preserved as early as the Seleucid period or as late as the Sasanians.[58]

Apparently the most important religious buildings of Parthian Assur are grouped between the ruins of the old Enlil-Assur ziggurat and the Tigris (fig. 65). The area to the east of the ziggurat was apparently cleared during this time, since the Parthian buildings there rest on the living rock. Haller infers from the fact that at least some of the Parthian buildings had a cult character that the area was probably also sacred in the Assyrian period.[59] An irregularly shaped area bounded by the ziggurat on the west, by walls and colonnades on the south and east, and by the cliffs at the edge of the city on the north, encloses the peripteros and the "Freitrep-

---

[51] Keall, *Late Parthian Nippur*, 17.

[52] Hilprecht mentions another temple of the Parthian period located halfway between the Shatt en-Nil and the ziggurat. He describes it as small and originally domed, with a stepped altar (Hilprecht, *Die Ausgrabungen der Universität von Pennsylvania im Bel-Tempel zu Nippur*, 35). Since he gives no plan of the building and it is not discussed by more recent authors, it is impossible to assess its form or date.

[53] Andrae, *Wiedererstandene Assur*, 164 f. (2d ed., 237-39, figs. 216, 217); Haller, *Heiligtümer*, 81; Andrae, *Partherstadt Assur*, 71. Heinrich states that it is possible that one of the leaders installed by Nebuchadnezzar built both temples. He also feels that it is probable

that the inhabitants of Assur dedicated temples to the old city god and perhaps also to his consort Scherua, whose cults survived into the Parthian period (*Tempel und Heiligtümer*, 296, 317 f.).

[54] Oates, *Studies*, 61 f.

[55] Andrae, *Partherstadt Assur*, 1-3; idem, *Wiedererstandene Assur*, 169-71 (2d ed., 248).

[56] R. D. Barnett, "Xenophon and the Wall of Media," *JHS* LXXXIII (1963), 25.

[57] Andrae, *Partherstadt Assur*, 1-3.

[58] Schlumberger, *L'Orient hellénisé*, 113.

[59] Haller, *Heiligtümer*, 6; Andrae, in Haller, *Heiligtümer*, 4.

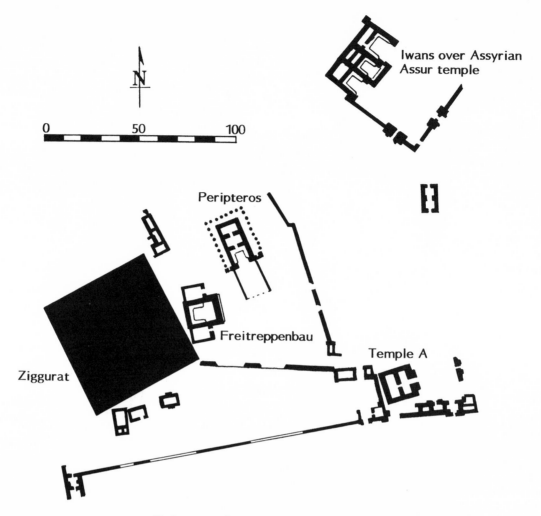

Iwans over Assyrian Assur temple

Periptéros

Ziggurat

Freitreppenbau

Temple A

65. Assur, northeastern section of Parthian city.

penbau''; Andrae considers this the agora.[60] To the south of this enclosed area is another long, narrow courtyard, and Temple A lies in its own small court to the east of this. Some little distance away, at the northeast corner of the city, lies the temple built over the old Assur temple; it has its own forecourt.[61] Andrae interprets this entire walled sector of the city as an acropolis.[62]

The religious buildings of Parthian Assur give evidence of both change and continuity. New sanctuaries dedicated to the old gods stand on the sites of at least three of the old sanctuaries, according to Andrae.[63] The temple that was built over the ruins

of the old Assur temple was dedicated to Assur and Scherua, as inscriptions testify, but its triple-iwan form is totally unrelated to the earlier Assur temple. Temple A, originally built on a Babylonian plan, probably shortly after the fall of the city, and dedicated to an unknown divinity, was rebuilt on the same plan and dedicated apparently to Heracles.[64] The festival house of Assyrian times was rebuilt during the Parthian period on its old plan.[65]

On the other hand, certain temples were not rebuilt. Parthian houses and kilns were built into a layer of debris that formed in post-Assyrian times over the ruins of the Sin-Shamash temple.[66] No re-

[60] Andrae, *Partherstadt Assur*, 6 f.

[61] Ibid., 58 f.

[62] Andrae, *Wiedererstandene Assur*, 176 f. (2d ed., 255, fig. 33).

[63] Andrae, *Partherstadt Assur*, 6.

[64] Ibid., 71-88; Andrae, *Wiedererstandene Assur*, 173-75, fig. 73 (2d ed., 249-52, fig. 288).

[65] Andrae, *Wiedererstandene Assur*, 176 (2d ed., 249); idem, *Partherstadt Assur*, 89 f.; Haller, *Heiligtümer*, 74-80.

[66] Haller, *Heiligtümer*, 90.

mains of the Parthian period were found on top of the Anu-Hadad temple,[67] and in any case, already in the late Assyrian period a secular building and private houses occupied much of the area.[68] Residential quarters also grew up over the ruins of the temples of Ishtar and Nabu.[69] The discovery of one inscription mentioning the god Nabu was interpreted by Jensen as a possible indication that this god had a cult place there,[70] and Andrae suggested on the same basis that a temple of Nabu that has not been found was built in the Parthian period, perhaps over the ruins of the late Assyrian temple.[71] It seems more likely, however, that the inscription reflects a private act of devotion.

Although the ziggurats of Anu and Hadad appear to have been almost totally destroyed by the Parthian period, the principal ziggurat, that of Assur, remained a prominent landmark. Andrae suggests that it functioned as a citadel, perhaps with the residence of the satrap (totally vanished) on its summit.[72] It seems possible, however, that the ziggurat might have retained its religious function, as did the Anu and E-anna ziggurats in Uruk. This problem will be discussed below.

TEMPLE A

As stated above, the temple of the chief god Assur was destroyed at the fall of the city in 614 B.C., and not rebuilt by the Babylonian conquerors. Instead, two small and simple temples were built in what had been the forecourt. One of these, Temple N, belongs to the simplest possible Babylonian temple type (fig. 66). It consists simply of one broad room with a cult niche in the rear wall and a base in front of the niche; there are no towers on the facade. Temple N is smaller and less well built than Temple A. Andrae suggests that it might have belonged to a goddess. This structure seems not to have survived into the Parthian period.[73] The foundations and the pavements of Temple A were built of reused bricks, most of which probably came from the ruins of the Assur temple, many of them bear-

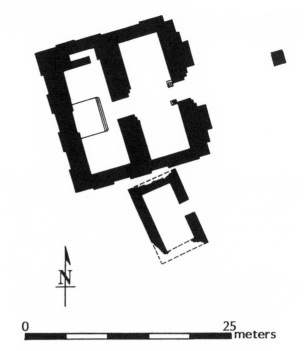

66. Assur, Temples A and N, post-Assyrian period, plan.

ing stamps of Shalmaneser I; but the builder of Temple A did not leave an inscription commemorating his work. The excavators attribute the construction to the Neo-Babylonian conquerors of Assur on the basis of the similarity of its plan to those of the small Neo-Babylonian temples in the city of Babylon and in Babylonia; thus it would represent the intrusion of a foreign type into Assur.[74] Schlumberger leaves open the possibility that the temple might have been built originally in the Parthian period.[75]

Temple A is almost square, 18 meters wide x 19 meters deep, and is oriented slightly to the north of due east. The outer door is set within a niche and flanked by prominent towers; between the tower and each corner is a second, less prominent projection. The other three walls are also decorated with relatively shallow projections. This articulation of

---

[67] Andrae, *Partherstadt Assur*, 6.

[68] Walter Andrae, *Der Anu-Adad-Tempel in Assur* (10. *WVDOG*) (Leipzig, 1909), 84-95.

[69] Andrae, *Partherstadt Assur*, 8 f., pls. 2, 3; idem, *Wiedererstandene Assur*, 163; compare the maps in *Wiedererstandene Assur* and Haller, *Heiligtümer*, final plate.

[70] P. Jensen, "Aramäische Inschriften aus Assur und Hatra aus der Partherzeit," *MDOG* 60 (July 1920), 33.

[71] Andrae, *Wiedererstandene Assur*, 172 (2d ed., 249).

[72] Andrae, *Partherstadt Assur*, 6 f.; idem, *Wiedererstandene Assur*, 176-78 (2d ed., 249, 255-57).

[73] Haller, *Heiligtümer*, 81, pls. 4, 5; Andrae, *Wiedererstandene Assur*, 166 (2d ed., 238 f.).

[74] Andrae, *Partherstadt Assur*, 71, pl. 24; idem, *Wiedererstandene Assur*, 164-66 (2d ed., 237-39, fig. 216); Haller, *Heiligtümer*, 81. Heinrich agrees that these structures represent the intrusion of a foreign type into Assur but argues that since they differ from Babylonian temples in being independent rooms, they should be characterized as cult rooms rather than as Babylonian temples (*Tempel und Heiligtümer*, 217 f., 296).

[75] Schlumberger, *L'Orient hellénisé*, 114 f.

the outer wall, which is characteristic of Babylonian sacred architecture,[76] but which does not seem to appear in the religious architecture of Parthian Mesopotamia, even that under strong Babylonian influence,[77] supports the dating of the original building of Temple A to the Neo-Babylonian period. The interior consists of an antecella and a cella of the same width, with the door between the two rooms, like the outer door, set within a niche. In the rear wall of the cella is a shallow niche with a base for a cult statue in front of it, as is usual in Babylonian temples. The base is preceded by two shallow steps. In the forecourt of the temple, on the axis of the entrance, is a small brick altar. If the temple was built by the Babylonian conquerors, it is unlikely to have been dedicated to the overthrown god Assur. Andrae suggests that the area may well have remained holy to the local inhabitants, however, and that in their eyes the god honored would have been Assur in any case. The evidence from the Parthian period suggests, as Andrae states, that the old religion and the old holy places endured.[78]

If the Neo-Babylonian dating of Temple A is accepted, it seems likely that both the temple's form and its location within the forecourt of the old Assur temple indicate that it was intended to supplant the worship of the old gods and thus that it was perhaps dedicated to a Babylonian deity. On the other hand, the fact that the festival house built for the god Assur by Sennacherib has a cult room of Babylonian form has been interpreted in an opposite fashion, as an adoption of Babylonian forms by an Assyrian conqueror of Babylon.[79] The festival house does demonstrate, in any case, that cult rooms of Babylonian form were known in Assur before the fall of the city.

The non-Assyrian form of Temple A and the long gap between the destruction of the Assur temple of the Assyrian period and the building of a new temple of different form on the old site suggests that the appearance of the old religion in the Parthian period represents a revival, not a survival.

Builders in the Parthian period used the partially standing walls of Temple A as the foundations for a new building that followed the same plan (fig. 67). Of the three building phases apparently distinguishable within the Parthian period, very little re-

mains of the oldest phase, but it is clear that the plan remained the same throughout the period. Though the dimensions varied slightly from those of the earlier building, the temple retained its roughly square shape and two-room plan. The main door, on the east, was flanked by towers as before, but those of the Parthian period were simpler and apparently smaller (2.60 meters wide, 0.77 meters deep) than in the earlier building, and the door was no longer set in a niche. The other three walls were not decorated with projections and recesses, as were the walls of the earlier temple. The two rooms of the temple of the Parthian period were still approximately the same size (antecella, 12 x 4.28 meters; cella, 12.15 x 4.77 meters), though the entrance room was somewhat smaller than the corresponding room in the earlier building. The statue base in the cella lay 1.30 meters above the earlier one, but it was no longer approached by steps, and it occupied the whole depth of the room rather than only a part of it. Apparently there was no trace of a niche in the back wall. The few remains of architectural decoration consist of two small capitals of half-columns and a small pilaster capital, all Ionicizing, and a few bits of ornamental stuccoes of Parthian character. The temple appears, then, to have followed a Babylonian plan and to have retained the idea of towers flanking the entrance. Apparently decorative elements derived ultimately from the Greco-Roman world, and stuccoes of Parthian type were added, perhaps in the interior. The discovery of a stele of Heracles in the cult room suggests that the temple was dedicated to him.[80] Andrae suggests that the god was Heracles-Melqart, but that seems unlikely. Rather, in this case it seems that a temple of a modified Babylonian form was dedicated to a Greco-Roman god.

Temple A lies just outside of a precinct in front of the old Assur ziggurat, a loosely walled precinct that contains two buildings called by Andrae the "peripteros" and the "Freitreppenbau" (figs. 65, 69). Andrae's identification of this enclosed area as an agora, i.e., an area with a predominantly civil function, is apparently based largely on the clear separation of the Assur precinct from the walled area in front of the ziggurat. This identification both conditions and is to some extent conditioned

[76] Moortgat, *The Art of Ancient Mesopotamia*, 2, 4 f.; Koldewey, *Wieder erstehende Babylon*, 55.

[77] The temples of Dura, for example, often have towers or buttresses flanking the entrance doors, but the other walls are unadorned; see the discussion of Dura. The same is true of the small temples of Hatra; see below.

[78] Haller, *Heiligtümer*, 81, pls. 4, 5; Andrae, *Wiedererstandene Assur*, 164-66, fig. 71, pl. 75b (2d ed., 237-39, figs. 216, 217). Cf. Heinrich, *Tempel und Heiligtümer*, 318.

[79] Andrae, *Wiedererstandene Assur*, 153 (2d ed., 221).

[80] Andrae, *Partherstadt Assur*, 71 f.; idem, *Wiedererstandene Assur*, 174 f. (2d ed., 252).

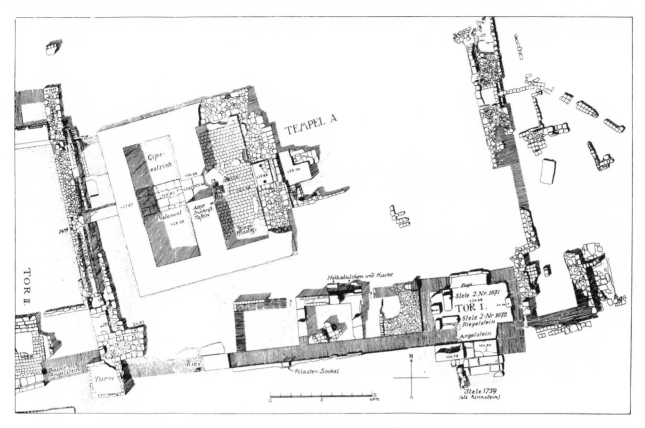

67. Assur, Temple A and surroundings, Parthian period.

by his interpretation of the two buildings enclosed in it, in particular his identification of the "Freitreppenbau" as a tribunal or bouleuterion.[81] Each building also presents considerable problems of reconstruction, since most of the superstructure has vanished, and Andrae's reconstructions (see fig. 69) may not be correct.

PERIPTEROS

The so-called peripteros is a rectangular building divided longitudinally into three rooms and surrounded on three sides by a colonnade (fig 68). The front room is the deepest of the three, 8 meters deep by 9 meters wide; the two rooms behind are identical in size, 5 meters deep by 9 meters wide. The central door opening, whose exceptional width (6.20 meters) led the excavators to consider the front room an iwan, is flanked on the facade by two smaller openings, each one meter wide, with L-shaped spur walls at the corners. Fragments of

column bases and capitals of Ionicizing type have been found, and a number of altars found in the ruins ensure its identification as a temple.

The restoration of this unusual building naturally raises considerable problems. The iwan-like character of the facade has led to the suggestion that it be restored as a triple iwan by analogy with the courtyard facades of the palace at Assur. The restoration (fig. 69) shows a wide central opening flanked by side wings with narrow arched openings in the lowest story and three tiers of engaged columns. This gives a height too great for single columns at the back and sides, however; their true height can be calculated on the basis of the similarity of their proportions to those of the columns in the peristyle of the palace. Thus the excavators have suggested a two-storied colonnade on the back and sides of the building.[82] The result is a rather peculiar building, the facade of which appears unrelated to the structure behind it. The plan of the building, excluding the peristyle, can be in-

[81] Andrae, *Wiedererstandene Assur*, 176-79 (2d ed., 255-58).

[82] Andrae, *Partherstadt Assur*, 64-67, figs. 36, 37; for the palace, see ibid., 25-35, fig. 14, pls. 10-11, 13-14.

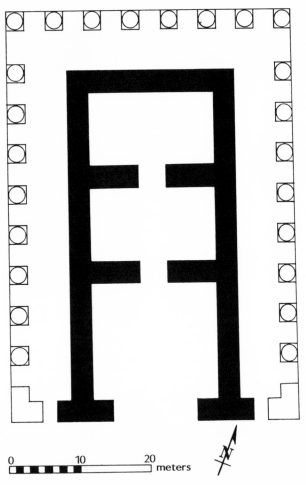

0   10   20 meters

68. Assur, peripteros, restored plan by R. Koldewey.

somewhat like the one in the Jandial temple at Taxila.[84]

"FREITREPPENBAU"

However the components of the plan of the peripteros are interpreted, its form is clearly that of a religious building. The so-called "Freitreppenbau," on the other hand, is not as easily classified, in either form or function. The excavators have called the building a tribunal or bouleuterion[85] without any apparent justification, and Andrae's discussion in *Das Wiedererstandene Assur*[86] is rather subjective. The only concrete basis for his assumption that the "Freitreppenbau" had a civil rather than a religious function appears to be the absence of inscriptions asking that people be remembered before various gods; such inscriptions occur in abundance in the building constructed on the ruins of the old Assur temple. Given the poor state of preservation of the "Freitreppenbau," however, negative evidence should be given very little weight. Furthermore, whatever the form of the building, it is unlike any known Greek bouleuterion, indeed unlike any Greek civic structures.

According to Andrae, the "Freitreppenbau" consisted of three rooms in a row, each accessible only from the outside (fig. 70). Only the central room is preserved in any meaningful fashion, however. All that survives of the room on the south[87] is a portion of the eastern wall with a door, and the northern room has completely disappeared. The central room was approached by a flight of steps, which were originally made of mud brick but were later rebuilt in stone. The door to this central room was 1.75 meters wide, according to Andrae, and the stone floor was 1.50 meters higher than the level of the surrounding area. On three sides of the room the floor was raised slightly, creating a shallow bench or border. The room was approximately 9.50-10 meters deep, and although the width cannot be calculated accurately due to the disappearance of the side walls, it was probably around nine meters across. The east (front) wall can be followed toward the south for approximately 3.50 meters, at which point there is a door with a total width of 1.75 meters and a clear span of slightly more than

terpreted as an antecella and cella of the Babylonian "broad-room" type, preceded by an iwan-like room, thus as a combination of an old Babylonian form with a new, apparently Parthian form, the iwan. The colonnade is obviously based ultimately on Greek architectural forms, but the peripteros has a superficially Greek character in plan only; the fact that the colonnade runs around three sides of the building rather than four, and that the facade is pierced by three openings, gives it a non-Greek character, however it is to be restored.[83] If the restoration is approximately correct, the colonnade might in effect have become rather like a corridor,

[83] Andrae, *Wiedererstandene Assur*, 179, fig. 77 (2d ed., 258 f., fig. 237); H. Lenzen, "Architektur der Partherzeit in Mesopotamien und ihre Brückenstellung zwischen der Architektur des Westens und des Ostens," *Festschrift für Carl Weickert* (Berlin, 1955), 126; Schlumberger, *L'Orient hellénisé*, 114.

[84] Sir John Marshall, *Taxila* (Cambridge, 1951) I, 220-29; III, pl.

44; Colledge, *Parthian Art*, 45, fig. 16e.

[85] Andrae, *Partherstadt Assur*, 67; Andrae, in Haller, *Heiligtümer*, 4.

[86] Andrae, *Wiedererstandene Assur*, 176-79 (2d ed., 255-58).

[87] According to Ghirshman, *Terrasses sacrées*, 217 f., on the north.

69. Assur, "Freitreppenbau" and peripteros, restored view with ziggurat in background.

one meter. There can have been no direct access between the central and the side rooms, given the difference in level. Fragments of architectural decoration, including engaged columns and an architrave with a series of engaged pilasters alternating with engaged columns, which were found on and near the stairs, may come from the upper part of this building (fig. 71).[88]

As can be seen from the above description, the restoration of the "Freitreppenbau" as a two-storied, triple-iwan building (fig. 69, left) rests on very little evidence. Moreover, although the difference in width between the central and the side openings, as given by Andrae in his text, is less than that between the central and the side openings of

the peripteros, Andrae's own restoration drawing does not appear to be based on the measurements given in the text. Finally, even if the restoration of the "Freitreppenbau" as a triple-iwan structure is accepted, its form is not only unlike that of the usual Greek bouleuterion, but it also seems unsuited for such a purpose. The bouleuteria of Miletus and Priene, for example, are large, roofed buildings with theater-like seats and a speakers' platform at the front of the building.[89] The central room of the Assur building is rather small to house an assembly, and there are no traces of seats or of arrangements for installing them.

Ghirshman has questioned both the restoration and the interpretation of the building as a bouleu-

[88] Andrae, *Partherstadt Assur*, 67-70, pls. 27a and b, 35. For the restoration of the building, see fig. 37; Andrae, *Wiedererstandene Assur*, 176-78, figs. 74, 76 (2d ed., 256-58, figs. 234, 236).

[89] D. S. Robertson, *Greek and Roman Architecture*, 2d ed. (Cambridge, 1969), 176-80, figs. 76-80.

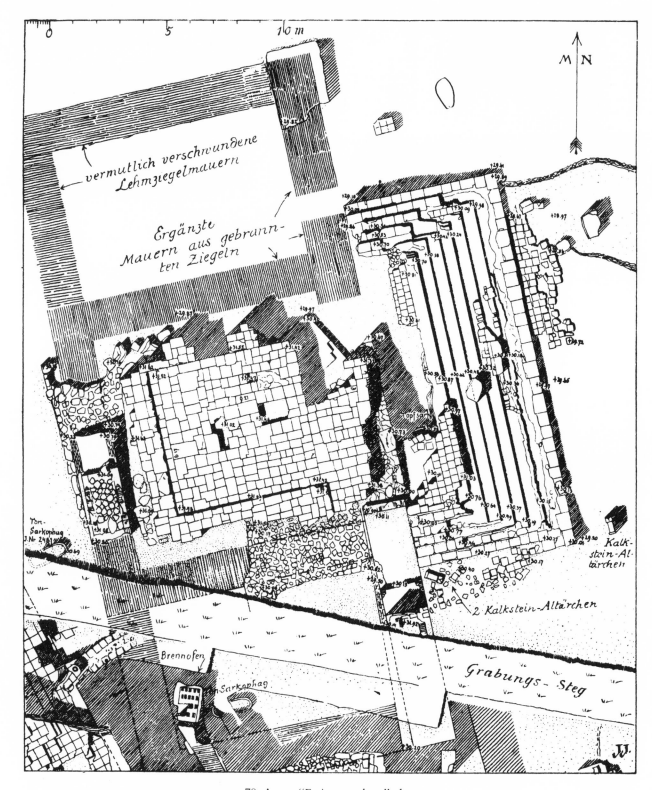

vermutlich verschwundene
Lehmziegelmauern

Ergänzte
Mauern aus gebrann-
ten Ziegeln

M N

Ton-
Sarkophag
J.Nr 2481

Topf

Kalk-
stein-Al-
tärchen

2 Kalkstein-Altärchen

Brennofen

Sarkophag

Grabungs- Steg

70. Assur, "Freitreppenbau," plan.

154

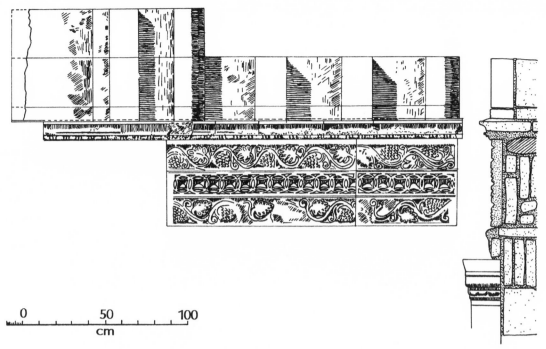

0   50   100
cm

71. Assur, "Freitreppenbau," fragments of architectural decoration.

terion. He notes that its inclusion in a temenos with the peripteros and in particular the fact that it almost backs onto the Assur ziggurat suggest that it must have had a religious purpose. What remains of the central "room," Ghirshman points out, is a seven-stepped staircase leading to a platform paved with stones. Little remains of one of the two flanking rooms, and the other is wholly restored. Ghirshman suggests, therefore, that this construction was a podium for open-air worship, a sacred terrace like those at Masjid-i Solaiman and Bard-è Néchandeh, and that the attached room (his "north room," the excavators' "south room") could be an *ātašgah*. He further states that comparison with Masjid-i Solaiman suggests that the podium was reserved for the cult of Ahuramazda, and the peripteros for that of the divine couple Anahita-Mithras; Verethragna-Heracles would have been worshipped in Temple A.[90] The lack of evidence for Iranian religion at Assur[91] makes especially the last part of this suggestion unlikely; for the same reason, it seems unlikely that the north (or south) room was an *ātašgah*. In addition, there is no con-

vincing parallel in Parthian Mesopotamia for an open-air podium approached by steps and used for worship, though a newly excavated structure in the forecourt of the precinct of Shamash at Hatra (fig. 75, H), if correctly interpreted as a platform for open-air worship, would provide an instance of the adoption of this form in Mesopotamia; the restoration of the Hatran structure is, however, not certain either (see under Hatra).

An understanding of the function of the ruins of the Enlil-Assur ziggurat at Assur in the Parthian period is crucial for the interpretation of the "Freitreppenbau." Andrae believes that the remains of this early ziggurat, the only one of the three ziggurats of the Assyrian city to have survived into the Parthian period, were used as a citadel, and that the area in front of it functioned as an agora. His interpretation appears to have been conditioned by two factors: 1) the opinion of the excavators of Uruk that the ziggurats there had lost their religious function and become watchtowers after the Greek conquest; and 2) the physical separation of the enclosed area in front of the ziggurat at Assur from the tem-

90 Ghirshman, *Terrasses sacrées*, 217 f. Ghirshman suggests in n. 6 that the orientation of the rooms given in Andrae, *Partherstadt Assur*, 67 and pl. 24c (my fig. 67) is mistaken, and that what Andrae called the "south room" should be the north room and vice versa.

Andrae's description seems clear, however.
91 P. Jensen, "Aramäische Inschriften aus Assur," *MDOG* 60 (July 1920), 28 f.

ple of the god Assur.[92] It is now known that not only was the Anu ziggurat at Uruk rebuilt, but the ziggurat in E-anna also continued to function as part of a sanctuary. At Assur, even in Assyrian times the Assur temple was separated from the ziggurat by some distance; since the area between the two was thoroughly cleared in Parthian times, it is impossible to say what lay there, but Andrae suggests that there might have been a separate stair leading to the high temple on the ziggurat.[93] In the Parthian period, the distance between the ziggurat and the Assur temple was increased, and the physical separation was emphasized by the building of a wall to the east of the ziggurat; this wall formed the eastern boundary of a loosely organized precinct that included the ziggurat, the peripteros, and the "Freitreppenbau," but excluded the Assur temple (see fig. 65).

The placement of the "Freitreppenbau" just in front of the ziggurat, although on a slightly different orientation, would appear to suggest that it might be a temple connected with the ziggurat; its position recalls that of the temple built against the ziggurat at Kar Tukulti Ninurta by Tukulti Ninurta in the thirteenth century B.C.[94] Unfortunately, it appears that not enough remains to allow a reasonable reconstruction of the "Freitreppenbau." From the plan, however, it seems clear that it did not have a Babylonian character, unless possibly the supposed central room could be interpreted as a one-room temple like the post-Assyrian Temple N. What is retained here, if the interpretation of the "Freitreppenbau" as a religious structure is correct, is the earlier Mesopotamian idea of a close connection between a temple on ground level and a ziggurat.[95]

"ASSUR TEMPLE"

The last of the great structures on the eastern plateau in the Parthian period is a group of iwans constructed over the ruins of the old Assur temple. The building is so badly destroyed that reconstruction is difficult, but two phases of construction are discernible. In both, the building consists of adjoining iwans set at the back of a walled courtyard. In the first, early Parthian phase (fig. 72) there were two adjoining iwans, the northeastern one raised considerably above the level of the courtyard and approached by a flight of steps. The walls of these rooms were used as the foundations for the later building, and in this second period a third iwan was added to the northeast (fig. 73). This third room provides evidence that in the second period, and therefore probably also earlier, the building was dedicated to Assur and his consort Scherua. Along the walls are benches that were probably used by an assembly of worshippers; and in the plaster of the floor and of the benches are scratched the names of worshippers and of deities. Some of the inscriptions bear dates ranging between 511 and 539, i.e., between A.D. 199/200 and 277/28, assuming that the Seleucid era is used. Most of the personal names are derived from names of Babylonian-Assyrian divinities, and Assur and Scherua are mentioned far more frequently than others.[96] Jensen notes that members of one family, one of whom bears the name Esarhaddon, appear with particular frequency in the inscriptions. He suggests that they might have been a priestly family attached to the temple and that the name Esarhaddon might have been a sign of regard for the great past.[97]

The form of the superstructure of the building remains quite uncertain, but details of the reconstruction do not concern this study, since the iwan plan seems fairly certain.[98] Here, then, a building in a new, "Parthian" form, quite different from the Assyrian temple that it replaced,[99] was built on the site of one of the most important temples of the Assyrian city and dedicated to the old gods. In this, it contrasts strikingly both with Temple A, which uses a Babylonian form but was apparently dedicated to Heracles in the Parthian period, and with the festival house, which followed the Assyrian plan closely.

FESTIVAL HOUSE (BIT AKITU)

The festival house of Assur was built by Sennacherib north of the Gurguri gate between the Tigris

[92] Andrae, *Partherstadt Assur*, 6 f.; idem, *Wiedererstandene Assur*, 176-78 (2d ed., 255-58). Cf. Wetzel, *Das Babylon der Spätzeit*, 31.

[93] Andrae, in Haller, *Heiligtümer*, 3 f.

[94] Ibid., 4; Andrae, *Wiedererstandene Assur*, 92, fig. 42 (2d ed., 134-37, figs. 116, 117); Tilman Eickhoff, *Kār Tukulti Ninurta, Eine mittelassyrische Kult- und Residenzstadt (Abhandlung der Deutschen Orient-Gesellschaft* 21) (Berlin, 1985), 27-35, figs. 8, 9; pl. 17; plan 3.

[95] Interestingly, Schlumberger, *L'Orient hellénisé*, 115, simply calls the building a temple, while accepting its iwan form.

[96] Andrae and Jensen, "Aramäische Inschriften aus Assur," *MDOG* 60 (July 1920), 2-4, 11-34.

[97] Ibid., 42 f.

[98] Andrae, *Partherstadt Assur*, 73-88, fig. 42, pls. 28, 29; idem, *Wiedererstandene Assur*, 173-76, fig. 73 (2d ed., 250-52, fig. 228); Schlumberger, *L'Orient hellénisé*, 115; Colledge, *Parthian Art*, 47 f., fig. 18.

[99] Haller, *Heiligtümer*, 6-73.

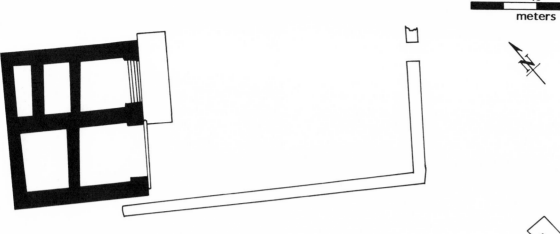

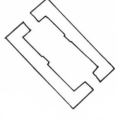

72. Assur, early Parthian buildings over the Assur temple, plan.

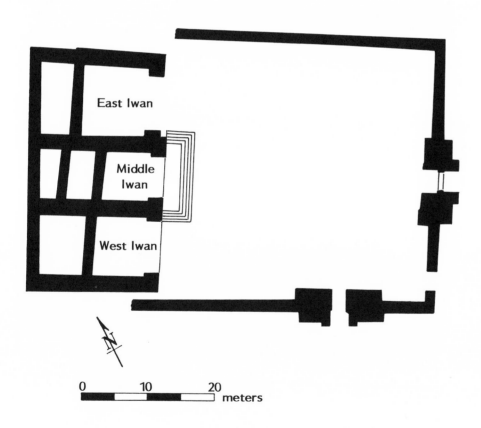

East Iwan

Middle Iwan

West Iwan

0   10   20 meters

73. Assur, late Parthian buildings over the Assur temple, plan.

157

and the road coming from the north. It lay within a garden, and during the first phase of the building, the court was also planted. The first phase apparently did not last long; in fact, Andrae suggests that the rebuilding was ordered by Sennacherib himself.[100] In the second Assyrian phase the plan remained essentially the same as the first, though the new building was moved some ten meters to the southeast along its northwest-southeast axis (fig. 74). The building is nearly square (67 x 60 meters in its final Assyrian phase) and has a large central courtyard. At the rear is a broad cult room of Babylonian type, with three doors rather than the usual one leading into it. No traces remain of a cult niche in the back wall of the earliest building, though Andrae suggests that some large stones decorated with fluting that were found in this area and that can be attributed to the period of Sennacherib could be part of the frame of a niche.[101] In the second Assyrian building a stone pathway led up to the middle door; presumably the image was taken along this pathway to the cella. In the Parthian period a base stood in the center of the cella, just in front of the back wall;[102] it is not entirely clear whether this base had an Assyrian predecessor, though it seems likely that it did.[103] The courtyard of the Assyrian building is lined on the northeast and southwest sides with a row of seven pillars, providing on each side eight openings in which divine images could have been housed during festivals.[104]

After the fall of Assur, the ruins of the festival house apparently served as a stone quarry, so that very little of the structure remained in the Parthian period. Nonetheless, if the scanty remains of the Parthian period are interpreted correctly, the later festival house followed the plan of the Assyrian one closely (fig. 74). Little remains of the cult chamber. A statue base decorated with moldings of Greek type stands in front of the center of the back wall. The base is approached by two steps that Andrae suggested might have belonged to the base of the Assyrian period, which is otherwise lost. Rectangular pillars with engaged columns replaced the simple rectangular pillars that lined the court in the Assyrian period—a clear sign of Greco-Roman in-

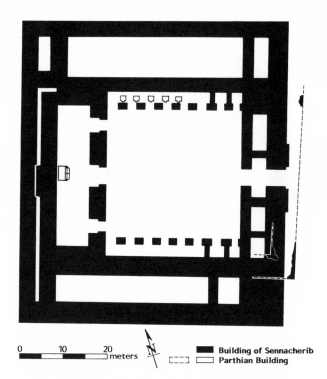

74. Assur, festival house (Bit Akitu), schematic plan.

fluence. Small parts of the entrance wall also survive.[105] Thus it appears that during the Parthian period the inhabitants rebuilt the festival house in essentially its Assyrian form with the addition of a few architectural details of Greco-Roman inspiration. Jensen suggests that the fact that the month Nisan, the first month of the year, is named most often in the inscriptions from the Parthian Assur temple provides evidence for the celebration of the New Year's festival during the Parthian period.[106] Heinrich, on the other hand, feels that it is dubious that the building still served as a festival hall during the Parthian period.[107] The new Assur temple, with its non-Assyrian form, and the more conservative festival house are both manifestations of the revival of Assyrian religion in the Parthian period.

The religious architecture of Parthian Assur is extraordinarily varied, as illustrated by the divergent forms of the Assur temple and the festival

[100] Andrae, *Wiedererstandene Assur*, 152 (2d ed., 219).

[101] Haller, *Heiligtümer*, 74, pl. 64a; 77, pl. 66a.

[102] Andrae, *Partherstadt Assur*, 89 f.

[103] Haller, *Heiligtümer*, 78 f., does not mention a base in his description, but Andrae, (*Heiligtümer*, 74) assumes that there was one. In discussing the second Assyrian building in *Wiedererstandene Assur*, 152 f. (2d ed., 219-21), Andrae mentions a flat niche in the rear wall of the cella, with a low base in front, but the base illustrated in pl. 70b (2d ed., fig. 200) belongs to the Parthian period.

[104] Andrae, *Wiedererstandene Assur*, 151-53, figs. 19 and 20 on p. 40 (2d ed., 219-24, figs. 199-200); Haller, *Heiligtümer*, 74-79, pls. 13-15, 64-71.

[105] Andrae, *Partherstadt Assur*, 89 f., fig. 43, pl. 42; idem, *Wiedererstandene Assur*, 176 (2d ed., 249); Haller, *Heiligtümer*, 78-80, pl. 69a.

[106] Jensen, "Aramäische Inschriften aus Assur," *MDOG* 60 (July 1920), 43-45.

[107] Heinrich, *Tempel und Heiligtümer*, 276.

house and as seen in the other temples. Temple A of the Parthian period retained the Babylonian plan and entrance towers of its predecessor but lacked the articulated walls and cult niche that characterized Babylonian temples. Furthermore, it was apparently dedicated to Heracles. The peripteros can perhaps be considered a temple of the Babylonian "broad-room" type fronted by an iwan and enclosed on three sides by a colonnade. Both the form and the function of the "Freitreppenbau" are doubtful, but its position in front of the ziggurat would suggest that it was the "low temple" of the ziggurat. In form, it is unlikely to have resembled either Assyrian or Babylonian temples. The sacred architecture of Parthian Assur seems to have combined religious conservatism with an experimentation in architectural forms, often combining traditional Mesopotamian elements with forms drawn from the Greco-Roman world, and utilizing also a new Parthian form, the iwan.

Hatra

THOUGH there is apparently some evidence of Assyrian occupation at Hatra, the city as we know it was probably founded in the late first century B.C. It seems to have been ruled, under loose Parthian control, by semi-independent vassal kings.[108] The inscriptions are in Aramaic, except for a few in Latin, and the population seems to have been largely Arab. The Romans tried unsuccessfully to take the city, once under Trajan and twice under Septimius Severus. Apparently later in the third century A.D. Hatra formed an alliance with Rome against the Sasanians,[109] but in spite of this, the city fell to the Sasanians in 240/41.[110] The reasons for its location are not entirely clear. It does not lie on a main caravan route, but does seem to have been on the route of the nomads.[111] The strong fortifications show that the builders felt a need for protection, and the large number of temples led Schlumberger to suggest that Hatra was primarily a holy city, a site of pilgrimage in honor of Shamash and other deities.[112] This idea is plausible, if not provable.

As in Assur, the religious architecture of Hatra exhibits considerable variety. The temple plans and the architectural decoration draw on both Near Eastern and Greco-Roman sources. It is difficult to evaluate the forms of religious architecture, however, largely because of the incomplete excavation and the even more incomplete publication. Especially to be regretted is the lack of publication of the buildings that apparently preceded the imposing structures now visible. Lenzen, for example, remarks that each of the small temples had a predecessor, usually in mud brick but occasionally in stone.[113] Oates states that "recent excavations there [i.e., Hatra] have shown that the great Parthian shrines were preceded by temples of purely Hellenistic aspect."[114] The following analysis must be regarded as tentative and based only on information that is currently available.

Although many of the smaller temples of Hatra follow a plan that appears to have been based on the Babylonian "broad-room" type or on the standard Assyrian antecella-cella arrangement, many other temples employ plans that are unrelated to earlier Mesopotamian traditions. One major temple type, consisting of a series of juxtaposed iwans with a number of subsidiary rooms, is most dramatically exemplified by the great Temple of Shamash (fig. 75). This temple was under construction in A.D. 112, as is shown by an inscription, and was probably completed in the 170s A.D. The architects and sculptors recorded in the graffiti from the complex have Aramaean names.[115] Although the origins of the iwan are controversial, the type does not appear in the architecture of Mesopotamia before the Parthian period, and it seems probable, on the basis of the existing evidence, that the iwan was developed in Mesopotamia no earlier than the first century B.C.[116] The facade and interior of the Temple of Shamash bear elaborate architectural and sculptural decoration. Much of this decoration, notably the Corinthian capitals of the columns and some of the moldings, is derived from Greco-Roman sources, but the elements are often used in non-Roman ways and combined with other decorative elements of different origins.[117]

The square temple behind the iwans is a later ad-

[108] Cf. Fuad Safar, "The Lords and Kings of Hatra," *Sumer* XXIX (1973), 87-98.

[109] André Maricq, "Classica et Orientalia 2. Les dernières années de Hatra: l'alliance romaine," *Syria* XXXIV (1967), 288-96.

[110] Milik, *Dédicaces*, 355.

[111] J. Teixidor, "Notes Hatréenes," *Syria* XLI (1964), 282-84.

[112] Schlumberger, *L'Orient hellénisé*, 123 f.

[113] Lenzen, "Ausgrabungen in Hatra," 361.

[114] Oates, *Studies*, 62; in n. 2 he says that this information is based on conversations with Fuad Safar and Mohammed Ali Mustapha.

[115] Milik, *Dédicaces*, 360, 393, inscription no. 108; 388, inscription no. 106; 390 f., inscriptions no. 1, 46; J. Teixidor, "Aramaic Inscriptions of Hatra," *Sumer* XX (1964), 78.

[116] Schlumberger, *L'Orient hellénisé*, 186-88; Colledge, *Parthian Art*, 47 f., 63 f.

[117] Lenzen, "Architektur der Partherzeit und ihre Brückenstel-

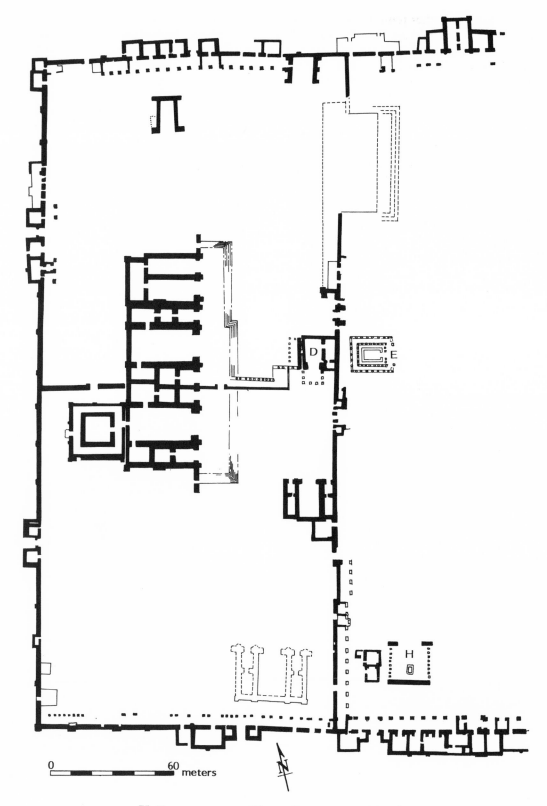

75. Hatra, sanctuary of Shamash, western portion, plan.

dition. Its central space, which was apparently vaulted, is surrounded on all four sides by vaulted corridors, which would allow for circumambulation. The entrance into this temple from the south iwan of the Temple of Shamash lies on a different axis from the door leading from the corridor into the central room, which suggests that the room was reserved for some sort of rite that not all visitors to the main temple were allowed to see. A blocked-up door in the rear wall of the iwan does lie on the axis of the door into the central chamber, however. Either this door predates the addition of the square chamber and was blocked up when it was built, or an originally direct access into the rear sanctuary was later changed.[118] The function of the building is uncertain. Though the plan is strikingly similar to those of many Iranian fire temples, the lack of evidence for Iranian religion at Hatra makes it unlikely that the building was a fire temple, as some scholars have thought.[119] Ghirshman calls this temple and one of the square structures at Seleucia on the Tigris the only examples of architecture "à plan parthe proprement dit."[120]

The scheme of juxtaposed iwans is also used for two other major temples in Hatra. One of these is attributed to the triad that headed the pantheon of Hatra, Maran, Martan, and Bar Maren (Our Lord, Our Lady, and the Son of Our Lords), the other to the goddess Allât. Both of the temples are elaborately decorated with relief sculpture. The sculptures of the "Temple of Allât" included images of dedicants and worshippers.[121] Another temple, located just inside the courtyard wall of the sanctuary of Shamash, consists of a wide central iwan and two narrow flanking rooms.[122] Though the iwan form is new, the fact that access to the roof is provided in the Temples of Shamash, the triad, and Allât might represent a survival of earlier Mesopotamian practices.

Other temples at Hatra are strongly related to

Greco-Roman forms in plan and to some extent in architectural decoration. For example, the little peripteral temple in the outer courtyard of the sanctuary of Shamash, which was perhaps dedicated to Bar Maren (fig. 75, E), is closely related to the Romanized temples of Syria.[123] Even if some of the details of the restoration are not correct, the plan sets it apart from Mesopotamian traditions—a high podium, a simple cella with no cult niche and no antecella, a surrounding colonnade of Corinthian columns and perhaps a second colonnade at the level of the forecourt pavement. The decorative details are derived from Roman forms, though transformed and combined in unorthodox ways. The most closely similar temple in Parthian Mesopotamia, the Temple of Gareus at Uruk (figs. 59-61), combines a plan based on Babylonian prototypes with architectural decoration derived from the Roman world.[124] The Hatra temple cannot be dated, but it probably belongs to the second century A.D. at the earliest, since that is the city's most flourishing period.

The Temple of Shahru (Temple D) (fig. 75), located just to the north of the entrance gate on the inside of the inner eastern courtyard wall of the sanctuary of Shamash, is a peculiar structure both in plan and in elevation. It consists of a long vaulted cella fronted by a porch with Corinthian columns. East of and accessible from the cella is a narrow vaulted space subdivided into two rooms; access to the roof is possible by a stair beginning in the cella. Oddly, the colonnaded porch does not extend in front of this side, giving the facade a disjointed appearance. On the west side of the building is a colonnade, perhaps two stories high.[125] This temple is clearly derived from a Roman prototype. The form of the roof access suggests that it might belong to the type of Romanized *"temples à escaliers"* of Syria discussed by Amy.[126]

Another temple (H) in the outer courtyard of the

lung zwischen der Architektur des Westens und des Ostens," *Festschrift für Carl Weickert* (Berlin, 1955), 126-31; idem, "Gedanken über den grossen Tempel in Hatra," *Sumer* XI (1955), 93-106.

[118] Andrae, *Hatra* II (21. *WVDOG*) (Leipzig, 1912), 126; Schippmann, *Feuerheiligtümer*, 491.

[119] Kurt Erdmann, *Das iranischen Feuerheiligtum* (Leipzig, 1941), 25; Ghirshman, *Iran* (London, 1954), 276; Gullini, *Architettura iranica*, 318; Schippmann, *Feuerheiligtümer*, 489-92, summarizes the problems. Against the idea that the building was a fire temple: H. Lenzen, "Der Altar auf der Westseite des sogenannten Feuerheiligtums in Hatra," *Vorderasiatische Archäologie* (Berlin, 1964), 136-38.

[120] Ghirshman, *Terrasses sacrées*, 216.

[121] A brief note on the excavation of the temple tentatively attrib-

uted to the triad is given by Isa Salman in *Sumer* XXIX (1973), f, g; pls. 6a and b (the plates are in the Arabic section). A rough preliminary plan is shown on the map in Safar and Mustapha, *Hatra*, 328-29, building A (fig. 75). The three large reliefs that are the basis for the attribution of the temple to the Triad are shown on pp. 113-15 figs. 88-90. For the Temple of Allât, see Isa Salman, *Sumer* XXX (1974), d-g, pls. 2-6 (the plates are in the Arabic section); Safar and Mustapha, *Hatra*, 95, fig. 15.

[122] Safar and Mustapha, *Hatra*, 328 f., building C.

[123] Ibid., 16, 374, 380-82, 388, 392 f.

[124] Above, pp. 137-43.

[125] Colledge, *The Parthians* (New York and Washington, 1967), 131-33, fig. 37; Safar and Mustapha, *Hatra*, 338-40.

[126] R. Amy, "Temples à escaliers," *Syria* XXVI (1950), 82-136.

precinct of Shamash appears to be unique among Hatra temples, if it is rightly interpreted as hypaethral. It consists of a roughly square podium approached by stairs in the north corners of the east and west sides and by a third stair at the back; a colonnade runs along the east side. A small, square structure, presumably an altar, rests on the podium (fig. 75).[127] This structure might have been a podium for open-air worship. As such, it would provide an analogy for Ghirshman's interpretation of the "Freitreppenbau" at Assur[128] and would provide a parallel, on a smaller scale, for the unroofed podium at Aï Khanoum.[129]

Thus only some of the many temples of Hatra are based on plans of Mesopotamian type, and even those differ more from their ancient Babylonian predecessors than do the Seleucid temples of Uruk or the Parthian temples of Dura-Europos. At least twelve temples that exhibit variations of a Mesopotamian type of plan have been discovered at Hatra.

Few of the temples can be dated, though most of the stone structures that remain probably belong to the second century A.D., the period of Hatra's greatest prosperity. This is known in the case of Temple VIII, which is dated by an inscription to A.D. 108/109.[130] Inscriptions dated to A.D. 165 and 187 give a *terminus ante quem* for Temple IX.[131] That the temple was still functioning at the time of the fall of the city is shown by three Latin inscriptions, one dated to A.D. 235, the others simply to the reign of Gordian III (A.D. 238-44).[132] The evidence for dating other temples is less certain. An inscription on the lintel of the entrance to the cult chamber of Temple X names NSRW MRY' (or MDY').[133] Safar identifies this Nasru as one of the lords of Hatra, and he dates his rule to A.D. 115-35.[134] These dates, if accepted, give a *terminus ante quem* for this shrine. The evidence for the date of Temple V is more

complex. A door lintel found in the debris is decorated with a relief of a reclining man in the presence of two small, standing men and two Nikai bearing wreaths. Two names, Wologaš and Nasru, are inscribed on the lintel. Milik identifies the reclining figure as Wologaš and one of the standing figures as his son Nasru.[135] Safar, on the other hand, identifies the reclining figure as Nasru and the small standing figure as a young man, Wologaš. Presumably he would suggest that the temple was built during the years of Nasru's lordship, i.e., A.D. 115-35. A Wologaš, who was first lord and later king at Hatra, with the title "king of the Arabs," is mentioned in a number of inscriptions. Safar dates his rule both as lord and as king to the years A.D. 155-65,[136] whereas Milik suggests that he was installed either ca. A.D. 150 or ca. A.D. 200, in the latter case by Septimius Severus. Temple V, then, would date to either the first or the second half of the second century A.D., depending on which interpretation of the relief is accepted.

The multiplicity of divine images and inscriptions in the small temples frequently makes identification of the chief deity difficult. A number of temples are attributed to Nergal or to Heracles-Nergal (I, VII, X, XI), though the evidence for Temples I and XI is quite shaky.[137] Temple II was probably dedicated to Baalshamin,[138] and IV is attributed to Atargatis on the basis of a statue and inscriptions found there.[139] An inscription from Temple V names Assurbel or Iššarbel ("the joy of Bel"); the latter has been interpreted as the epithet of a goddess, either Atargatis or Allât.[140] Temple VIII seems to have been dedicated to the seven planetary deities.[141] In Temple IX a Roman military tribune of the time of Gordian III (A.D. 238-44) dedicated two statues, one to the sun god (Sol Invictus), the other to Hercules. Safar and Mustapha suggest that the temple was originally dedicated to

---

[127] A rough plan is found in Safar and Mustapha, *Hatra*, 328-29, building I. The building, as it was being restored in 1979, did not include the staircase shown along the north (front) side or the colonnade on the east.

[128] Above, pp. 153-155.

[129] Above, p. 75.

[130] Milik, *Dédicaces*, 167, 360, inscription no. 214. Safar and Mustapha, *Hatra*, 360, translate the date as A.D. 98, but the year 419 should correspond to A.D. 108/109.

[131] Milik, *Dédicaces*, 360, inscriptions no. 62, 65; A. Caquot, "Nouvelles inscriptions araméennes de Hatra," *Syria* XXXII (1955), 264-66.

[132] David Oates, "A Note on Three Latin Inscriptions from Hatra," *Sumer* XI (1955), 39 f., figs. 1-3; A. Maricq, "Les dernières années de Hatra: l'alliance romaine," *Syria* XXXIV (1957), 288-90.

[133] Caquot, *Syria* XXXII (1955), 267, no. 67.

[134] Safar, *Sumer* XXIX (1973), 89 f., 98.

[135] Milik, *Dédicaces*, 363 f.

[136] Safar, *Sumer* XXIX (1973), 88-90, 92 f., 98.

[137] Safar and Mustapha, *Hatra*, 350, 359, 364, 366. For Temple X, see Caquot, *Syria* XXXII (1955), 267-69, inscriptions no. 70, 71, 73.

[138] Safar, "Hatra and the First Season of Excavations," *Sumer* VIII (1952), 13; Safar and Mustapha, *Hatra*, 354.

[139] Safar and Mustapha, *Hatra*, 354.

[140] Safar, "Inscriptions of Hatra," *Sumer* IX (1953), 18 f., no. 35; Safar and Mustapha, *Hatra*, 366; Milik, *Dédicaces*, 338-41, 352 f., 364; Wathiq Ismail, "The Worship of Allat at Hatra," *Sumer* XXXII (1976), 178 f.

[141] Safar and Mustapha, *Hatra*, 361.

the sun god and that the worship of Hercules was added later.[142]

The basic scheme of this group of temples has been described by Lenzen as a reversed T (figs. 76-87).[143] The sanctuary consists of a long narrow room with an entrance on one of the long sides and a cult chamber or niche in the rear wall opposite the door. The front room often has benches along the walls. The cult chamber is oriented perpendicularly to the long axis of the front room, and it usually projects beyond the back wall (Temples I, II, III, IV, V, IX, X, XI). It may be a room (Temples I, II, III, IV, V, IX, X, XI), a small aedicula (VI, VII, VIII [later sanctuary], and one of the recently excavated, unpublished temples), or at times simply a niche (VIII [early sanctuary] and the smaller cult room in the unpublished temple mentioned above).

There are a number of variations on this basic scheme. Some of the temples are essentially rectangular, and the description as a reversed T seems inappropriate. The aediculae of Temples VI, VII, and the later complex of Temple VIII (figs. 82-84) barely project beyond the rear walls of the main room, and the niche in the older sanctuary in Temple VIII is taken entirely out of the foreroom. Likewise, both of the cult rooms in one of the unpublished sanctuaries are rectangular. In the larger, northward facing unit a large aedicula forms the holy of holies, and in the rear wall of the single-roomed sanctuary that faces east there is a small semicircular niche.

In the larger temples the broad entrance room is flanked by two rooms on either side, which open onto it (Temples VI, VIII [later complex], one of the newly excavated temples). In Temple V (fig. 80) there is only one smaller room, on the south side of the broad room and opening onto it. Although most temples have only one entrance from the outside, Temples V, IX, and X (figs. 80, 85, 86) have three doors. In Temple VI (fig. 82) one of the side rooms opens to the outside as well as to the broad entrance room, and both of the flanking rooms in the larger unit in Temple VIII (fig. 84) and one of the newly excavated temples are accessible from the outside. In temples with more than one entrance, the main door is distinguished by flank-

ing buttresses or pilasters. Doors in the other temples are also flanked by heavy pilasters (Temples III, IV, VI, VIII [later complex], IX, X, XI, larger unit in unpublished temple), probably a survival of the entrance towers of Babylonian and Assyrian temples. In three temples (I, IV, and V) lions guard the entrances as well.[144] In some temples staircases lead up to the roofs, probably also a survival of Babylonian practices (Temples VI, VII, VIII [later complex], IX, XI, larger unit in unpublished temple).

In some temples additional rooms were built on later. An iwan was added to the front of Temple I (fig. 76) so that the main room no longer opened directly onto the street.[145] In both Temples III and X (figs. 78, 86), two chambers were built onto one side of the broad entrance room, and in Temple X a room was added beside the cult chamber as well. According to Safar and Mustapha, two rooms were added flanking the cult chamber of Temple II (fig. 77), giving the appearance of a naos and two sacristies, as in a number of Dura temples.[146] Lenzen gives a diametrically opposed interpretation of these two rooms, stating that the arched niches in the walls of the cult chamber were originally doors opening into the side chambers.[147] A room built on to the north side of Temple IV was apparently used to store furniture, and a small subsidiary cella was probably built after the fall of the city, according to Safar and Mustapha.[148]

The orientation of the shrines also varies. Nine of the sanctuaries face east (III, IV, V, VI, VIII [earlier unit], IX, X, smaller sanctuary unit in unpublished temple), and five face north (I, II, VII, VIII [later unit], larger sanctuary unit in unpublished temple). Only Temple XI faces south. The reasons for this variation are not clear. Many of the temples are located near the large Temple of Shamash, however, and it is possible that in some cases the orientation was due to a desire to have the sanctuary unit face that temple.

Many of these small temples opened directly onto a street. This was true of Temple I (fig. 76) in its early phase, as well as of Temples II, III, and IV (figs. 77, 78, 79).[149] Some of the sanctuary units were set within or at the back of a court. Temple V (fig. 80), for instance, consists of a free-standing unit within a court. The main entrance to the court-

---

[142] Oates, *Sumer* XI (1955), 39-43; Maricq, *Syria* XXXIV (1957), 288-96; Downey, *Heracles Sculpture*, 93-95; Safar and Mustapha, *Hatra*, 362.

[143] Lenzen, "Ausgrabungen in Hatra," 351 f.

[144] Safar and Mustapha, *Hatra*, 350, 354, 356.

[145] Lenzen, "Ausgrabungen in Hatra," 351; Safar and Mustapha, *Hatra*, 350.

[146] Safar and Mustapha, *Hatra*, 352, 354, 364.

[147] Lenzen, "Ausgrabungen in Hatra," 352.

[148] Safar and Mustapha, *Hatra*, 354 f.

[149] Lenzen, "Ausgrabungen in Hatra," 351-54; Safar and Mustapha, *Hatra*, 350 f., 354.

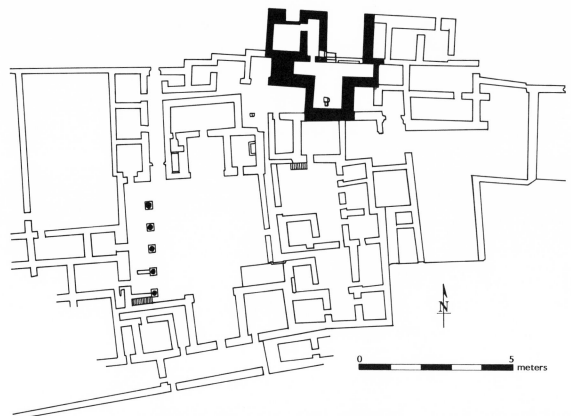

76. Hatra, Temple I and adjacent buildings, plan.

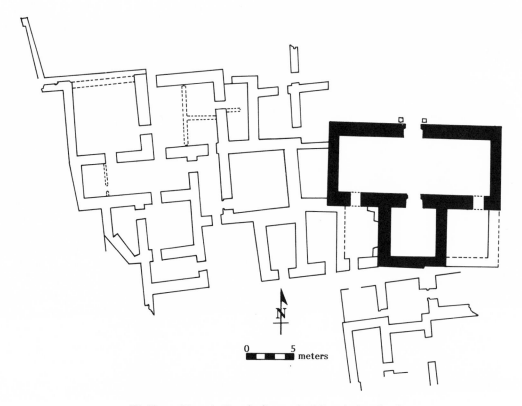

77. Hatra, Temple II and adjacent building (palace?), plan.

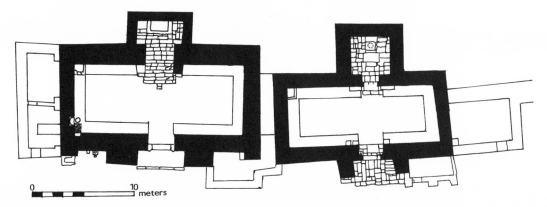

78. Hatra, Temples III and IV, plan.

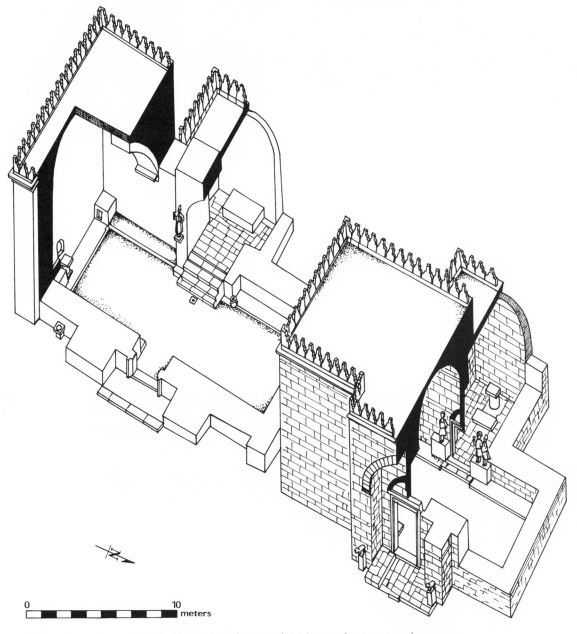

79. Hatra, Temples III and IV, isometric reconstruction.

165

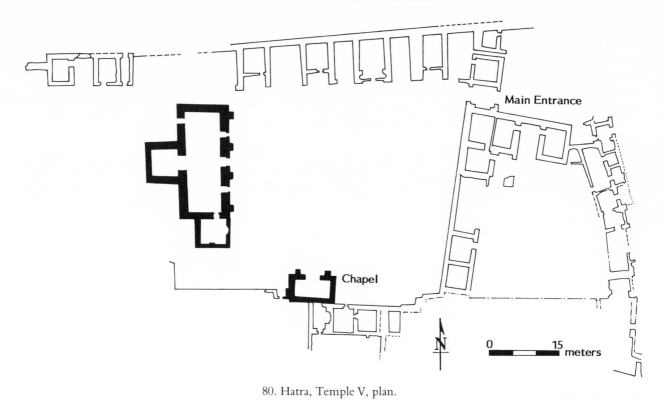

80. Hatra, Temple V, plan.

81. Hatra, Temple V, reconstructed facade.

yard, on the east side, lies off the axis of the entrance to the sanctuary unit. The rooms lining the court may form part of a sacred precinct. The north side is lined with a row of iwans, and the fact that incense burners were found there suggests that they served religious purposes. A single room on the south side of the court was probably a chapel, since six statues were found there. A large structure on the east side, however, was probably a separate building, unconnected with the shrine. If so, the sacred precinct is not set clearly apart from the surrounding houses.[150] A sanctuary excavated during 1979-80 and apparently dedicated to Heracles has a similar arrangement, according to the description. Rooms along the facade facing the street were perhaps shops, and small rooms lined the inside of the north and south enclosure walls. There were two wells within the courtyard.[151]

Temple VIII (fig. 84) includes two sanctuary units facing onto a courtyard, the older and simpler one facing east, the other with its entrance on the north.[152] There were apparently no rooms on the interior of the court, unlike the arrangement in the temples of Dura, and the area outside the court has not been fully excavated, but a number of houses adjoined it. A house placed between the two sanctuary units is accessible from the court by a narrow passage, and a staircase running along its facade leads to the roof. The close connection of the house with the temple court and the discovery of cooking utensils there suggest that it might have been a priests' house, an arrangement very like that of the priests' house between the Temples of Artemis and Atargatis at Dura.[153] The placement of two sanctuary units around one courtyard also recalls the multiple sanctuary units of some of the Dura temples (e.g., Azzanathkona, Adonis, Zeus Megistos).

A similar arrangement exists in a recently excavated sanctuary area in the northwest quadrant of the city. A relatively large shrine, with four side rooms, an entrance marked by pilasters, and an impressive cult aedicula, lies at the back of a court; and a smaller, one-room shrine with merely a cult niche is set against one of the side walls. As with Temple

VIII, stairs leading up to the roof of the larger shrine run along the facade of some rooms that lie outside the court; since they are not fully excavated, it is not clear whether or not they formed part of the sanctuary complex.[154]

Other sanctuaries at Hatra stand at the back of open spaces or courtyards, accessible from several streets and surrounded by houses. In some cases the open spaces are ill defined, however, and it is not clear that these sanctuaries should be considered court temples. Temple IX, for example, lies at the back of an open space approached by streets (fig. 85). Some of the surrounding buildings are houses, but Safar and Mustapha suggest that a room on the south side of the open space might have been an early oratory abandoned during the later periods of the temple's existence.[155] Temple XI (fig. 87) is similarly fronted by an irregularly shaped courtyard surrounded by houses, some of which probably belonged to the temple personnel. The finding of a fire altar and a bust of a nude woman in a building on the south side of the court suggests that it might have had a religious purpose.[156] Temple II (fig. 77) faces an open space connected to a street beside the great temple. The shrine is closely linked with residential buildings, one of which is considered by Safar and Mustapha a possible royal palace.[157] The sanctuary units of Temples VI and VII (figs. 82, 83) lie at the back of courtyards, but there is no indication of subsidiary rooms within the court. It is not clear whether the court in front of Temple VI belongs to the temple or whether, instead, its walls are simply formed by houses that have no connection with the temple.[158] The court in front of Temple VII is unexcavated, and only two of the rooms around the court in front of Temple X (fig. 86) have been excavated.[159]

Although it seems apparent that the plans of these temples are derived from earlier Mesopotamian traditions, there are striking differences. The main distinction lies in the greater simplicity of the Hatran temples. The temples in which the cult chamber is a room oriented at right angles to the long axis of the cella could perhaps be viewed as

[150] Safar and Mustapha, *Hatra*, 356 f., plans 14, 15; Lenzen, "Ausgrabungen in Hatra," 354.

[151] "Excavations in Iraq 1979-80," *Iraq* XLIII (1981), 179.

[152] Safar and Mustapha, *Hatra*, 360 f., plan 18. Lenzen, "Ausgrabungen in Hatra," 356-59, fig. 8, calls the larger sanctuary unit Temple VII and the smaller one Temple VIII.

[153] A. Naudy, *Dura Report* III, 25-27, pl. IV.

[154] I saw this unpublished and only partially excavated complex on a visit to Hatra in April 1979. I wish to thank the State Organi-

zation of Antiquities of the Republic of Iraq for its cooperation and cordial hospitality during my visit.

[155] Lenzen, "Ausgrabungen in Hatra," 359 f.; Safar and Mustapha, *Hatra*, 362.

[156] Safar and Mustapha, *Hatra*, 366.

[157] Ibid., 352.

[158] Lenzen, "Ausgrabungen in Hatra," 354 f.

[159] Safar and Mustapha, *Hatra*, 359, 364.

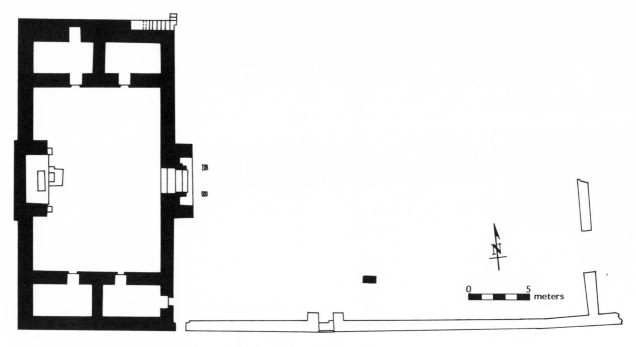

82. Hatra, Temple VI, plan.

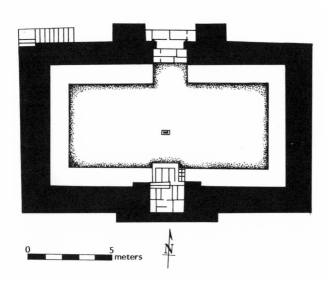

83. Hatra, Temple VII, plan.

court. In this and later Assyrian temples, the ante-cella-cella units form part of a larger complex, including a court and other subsidiary rooms. In the Neo-Assyrian Sin-Shamash Temple built by Assurnasirpal II, the orientation of the building was changed, and the two antecella-cella complexes were set side by side. The principle of a broad antecella and a long, narrow cella was retained, and there was now a cult niche in the rear wall of the cella.[160] The Anu-Hadad Temple at Assur built by Aššurrišiši and finished by Tiglathpilesar also has two shrines of this form side by side, and the basic scheme was apparently retained in the rebuilding by Shalmaneser II. Andrae points out that the three temples on the citadel at Khorsabad also have a wide antecella and a long narrow cella, in this case with a third adyton-like room at the back.[161] The temples at Assur were apparently so ruined by the Parthian period that it is not clear whether they could have served as models for later buildings.

Also in the Neo-Babylonian temples of Babylon and the Seleucid temples of Uruk, the sanctuary units form part of large complexes. The antecella-cella unit is usually set at the back of a courtyard or courtyards; these courts are, in turn, surrounded by a multitude of subsidiary rooms. At Hatra, on the

simplified versions of the usual Assyrian scheme, in which the antecella-cella unit consists of a wide antecella with a narrow, deep cella behind it. This scheme seems to appear for the first time in the Sin-Shamash Temple of Assurnirari I (1516-1491 B.C.) at Assur (fig. 88), where two such units flank a

[160] Haller, *Heiligtümer*, 82-86, fig. 24, pls. 16-18; 89-92, fig. 26.

[161] Andrae, *Der Anu-Adad-Tempel in Assur*, (10. *WVDOG*) (Leipzig, 1909), 7-78, pls. IV, V, VIII, IX; 82-84, fig. 76.

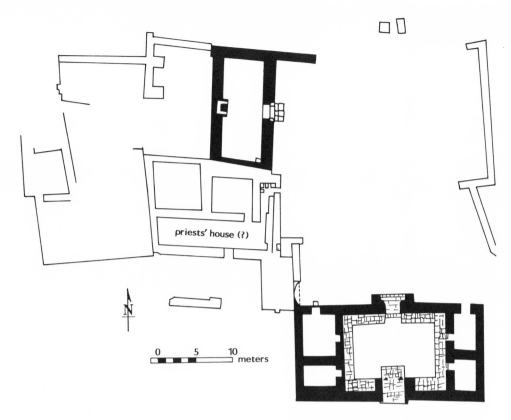

priests' house (?)

N

0   5   10
meters

84. Hatra, Temple VIII, plan.

other hand, many of the temples open directly onto the street; this is true of Temple I in its early phase, as well as of Temples II, III, and IV. In these cases the cult niche and whatever sculpture it contained would have been visible from the street when the temple doors were open. Those temples at Hatra which are set into or at the back of a court with surrounding rooms might belong to the Babylonian court type, although in a very modified form. Temple V (fig. 80), and probably Temples VI and VII as well (figs. 82, 83), are set within precincts that separate the sacred from the secular area fairly clearly. In Temples V and VIII (figs. 80, 84), and probably in one of the newly excavated temples too, the sanctuary included subsidiary rooms around the court. In other cases at Hatra, where the temples are set in courts or in open spaces surrounded by houses, it is not clear that the houses have any connection with the temple, nor is the sacred precinct clearly defined; these should probably not be considered court temples (Temples IX, X, XI; figs. 85-88).

In addition to the similarities in plan, some practices in the small temples of Hatra suggest Mesopotamian origin. It seems probable, for instance, that each shrine was dedicated primarily to one deity, but images of and dedications to numerous deities were placed in each shrine.[162] This sharing of a temple with many deities follows Babylonian practice; for example, a number of deities had seats in the Bit rēš and Irigal sanctuaries at Uruk. The Hatra temples differ from the Uruk shrines, however, in that separate cellae are not provided for subsidiary deities. Also at Dura and especially in the sanctuaries of the steppe area northwest of Palmyra, numerous deities crowd the sanctuaries; in the Palmyrène it is often difficult to determine who is the chief deity.[163] In addition, the custom that is so prevalent at Hatra of dedicating in the shrines statues of the nobility in prayerful attitudes is probably derived from much earlier Mesopotamian practice.[164]

Many statues and reliefs, as well as a number of cult installations and furnishings, were found in

[162] Downey, *Heracles Sculpture*, 84.
[163] Schlumberger, *La Palmyrène du Nord-Ouest*, 114.

[164] Downey, *Stone and Plaster Sculpture*, 289.

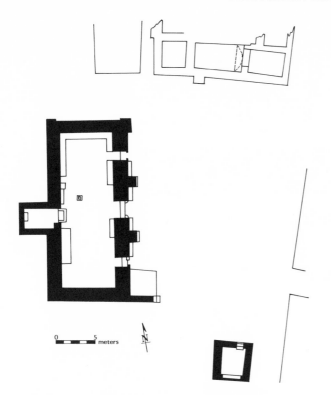

85. Hatra, Temple IX, plan.

86. Hatra, Temple X, plan.

most of the temples at Hatra, and the types and location of these objects can provide some evidence about the forms of worship in the sanctuaries. The statues and reliefs that filled the temples were sometimes found *in situ* but had frequently been displaced, either in a reorganization of the sanctuary or as a consequence of the destruction that accompanied the fall of the city. Thus the finding places of images, basins, or offering boxes are not necessarily a guide to their original placement and therefore to their function within the shrine.

The cult chamber or niche generally had provisions for the installation of one or more statues or cult reliefs, often with an altar or incense burner in front of them. For example, the so-called Cerberus relief was found in the cult chamber of Temple I, with an incense altar in front of it.[165] In the cult chamber of Temple II three niches were provided for reliefs. Statues of a seated god and goddess

stood on bases in the front part of the cult niche in Temple VI, near the main altar, and a statue of Hercules and one of a seated goddess were found in the cult rooms of Temples VII and IX.[166] In other shrines, bases or steps suggest the presence of images that are now missing (II, III, IV, V(?), VIII, IX).[167] In many cases, images of deities were found in the outer room as well, which perhaps suggests that the cult chamber was reserved for the chief deity or deities. No images of either deities or mortals were found in either the foreroom or the cult chamber of Temple V; rather, the sculpture was found in the small room to the south of the cult room, to which Safar and Mustapha suggest that it had been removed.[168]

Cult furniture of various types survives. The cella or cult niche normally contains an altar, either a large, fixed altar or a smaller incense altar. Some temples contained sizeable built-in boxes, perhaps for storage (III, IV, X).[169] In Temple IX a box is set into the floor in front of an altar, perhaps to hold the debris of offerings.[170] Offering boxes, the lids pierced with slots, were also placed in a number of shrines (III, VII, X, XI),[171] a practice attested in Babylon during the Arsacid period. Two cunei-

[165] Harald Ingholt, *Parthian Sculptures from Hatra* (*Memoirs of the Connecticut Academy of Arts and Sciences*, XII) (New Haven, 1954), 32; Safar and Mustapha, *Hatra*, 350 and plan 25.

[166] Lenzen, "Ausgrabungen in Hatra," 352, 355 f.; Safar and Mustapha, *Hatra*, 358, 359, 366.

[167] Safar and Mustapha, *Hatra*, 354, 356, 361, 364; Lenzen, "Ausgrabungen in Hatra," 356, 359.

[168] Safar and Mustapha, *Hatra*, 356.

[169] Ibid., 354, 364, fig. 341.

[170] Lenzen, "Ausgrabungen in Hatra," 359 f.

[171] Safar and Mustapha, *Hatra*, 354, 359, 364, 366, figs. 260, 302, 318; Downey, "Cult Banks from Hatra," *Berytus* XVI (1966), 97-109.

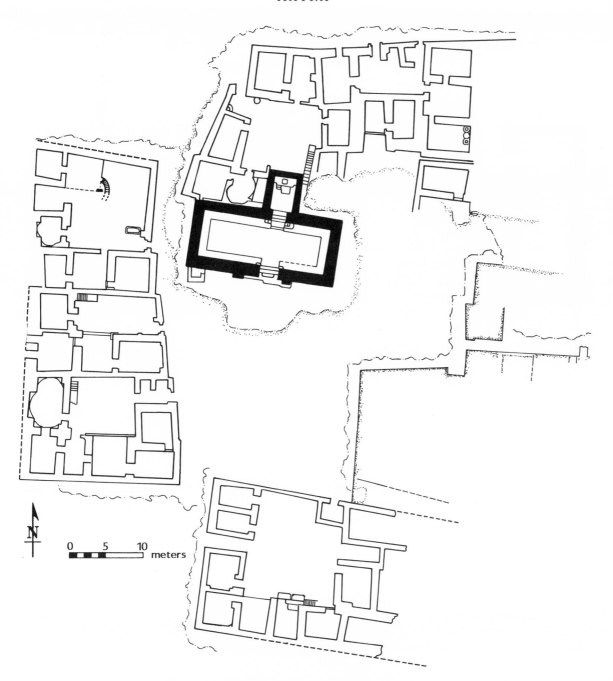

87. Hatra, Temple XI, plan.

form texts from that city mention the income of the offering box (*quppu*) of Esabad, the temple of the goddess Gula.[172] Basins found in some shrines at Hatra suggest that water or another liquid, such as wine, was used in some rituals (III, VII, VIII, X,

XI).[173] The published reports do not mention installations for ritual dining comparable to those in the oikoi of the Dura temples or in the small sanctuaries of the rural area around Palmyra. The discovery of cooking utensils in a house adjoining

[172] McEwan, "Arsacid Temple Records," *Iraq* XLVIII (1981), 134, line 2 and commentary; 142, line 1. The first text dates to the

year 219 of the Arsacid era (28/27 B.C.), the second to the year 218.
[173] Safar and Mustapha, *Hatra*, 354, 359, 364, 366, fig. 317.

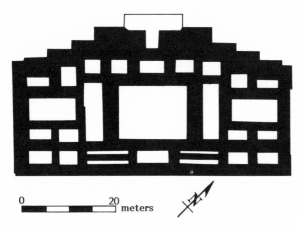

88. Assur, Sin-Shamash Temple of Assurnirari I.

Temple VIII led Lenzen to suggest that it might have been a priests' house,[174] but the reports do not mention a dining room, either in the house or in the sanctuary. Most of the outer rooms in the small shrines do have benches along the walls, but the rooms seem too large and accessible for ritual dining by small groups like those recorded at Dura. Milik finds evidence for associations for ritual dining in a number of inscriptions, but in several cases the evidence seems shaky. This is especially true of his assertion that a college of noble women met for ritual meals in Temple V.[175]

Statues of citizens of Hatra—members of the royal and noble families, priests and priestesses—stood in the outer rooms of many of the small temples (III, IV, V, VI, IX, X, XI). The nobles and members of the royal family are normally shown in prayerful attitudes, often with one hand raised and sometimes holding a leaf, while priests often offer incense.[176] The royal family built or rebuilt a number of shrines, most notably the chief Temple of Shamash, but their activity is evident also in the smaller shrines, particularly Temple V.[177] The close connection of the ruling house with the religious structure of the city is further suggested by the tentative identification of a large dwelling adjacent to

Temple II as the palace of Sanatruq and his family.[178]

The placement of statues of people in the outer room, with the cult niche generally reserved for images of divinities, combines with the evidence of size to suggest that most of the rituals must have taken place in the foreroom. In some shrines, indeed, the holy of holies is merely an aedicula, with no room for priests or worshippers (VI, VII, VIII, and unpublished shrine). The cult chambers in Temples I, II, V, and apparently also III and IV, are relatively big, so that perhaps part of the temple ritual could have been performed there. The cult niches of Temples IX, X, and XI fall between the two types.

Inscriptions giving the titles of a number of temple officials and servants can also provide clues about the organization of worship. Unfortunately, some of these inscriptions present difficulties of interpretation. It does appear, however, that at least some of the deities were served by fairly complex organizations. Whether by chance or because Bar Maren (the "son of Our Lords") had particularly elaborate temple organization, a number of inscriptions mention officials of Bar Maren.

In the inscriptions as well as in sculpture, priests occur more frequently than priestesses, and goddesses as well as gods were served by priests. The goddess Iššarbel was perhaps served in Temple V by a college of priestesses, one of whom, Martabu, dedicated a statue of herself. Even in that temple, however, a priest, Badda, served as well.[179] The title "RB" or "RBYT'," translated by Milik and Caquot as "master of the house (or temple)," occurs often, though the duties attached to this title are not specified. In some cases the inscriptions specify the deity whom the official served; masters of the temples of Our Lord (Shamash) and of Bar Maren are named.[180] Elsewhere, the simple title "RBYT' " is given; in these cases it is probably reasonable to assume that the temple or house is the one in which the inscription occurs.[181]

Milik suggests that one inscription designates a

---

[174] Lenzen, "Ausgrabungen in Hatra," 356-59, fig. 8.

[175] Milik, *Dédicaces*, 372-74, 391 f. Teixidor and Milik interpret inscriptions found along a wall behind the great iwan and in a small room built against this wall as referring to religious associations. The inscriptions name a man and his comrades. Teixidor and Milik suggest that the room was used for ritual dining, though there are no traces of benches, so participants would have had to sit either on wooden benches or on cushions. (Teixidor, *Sumer* XX [1964], 77-81, inscriptions no. 207-213; Milik, *Dédicaces*, 391 f.). Although this interpretation is possible, the inscriptions, unlike those of Dura, do not mention the dedication of a room, and there are no

definite indications of arrangements for dining.

[176] E.g., Safar and Mustapha, *Hatra*, pls. 197-99, 211, 240-45, 252; Ghirshman, *Persian Art*, 89, fig. 100; 93-95, figs. 105-106.

[177] Safar, *Sumer* XXIX (1973), 87-98; Milik, *Dédicaces*, 363 f.

[178] Safar and Mustapha, *Hatra*, 352.

[179] Milik, *Dédicaces*, 372-74; Caquot, "Nouvelles inscriptions araméennes de Hatra," *Syria* XXX (1953), 293 f., inscription no. 34; Safar and Mustapha, *Hatra*, 253, no. 244.

[180] Caquot, "Nouvelles inscriptions araméennes de Hatra," *Syria* XLI (1964), 253, no. 109, with a reference to no. 94; 269, no. 95.

[181] Ibid., 255, no. 116; 260, no. 144. Milik, *Dédicaces*, 372, reads

council to administer the temple property,[182] but Teixidor translates the line in question as "property of Shamash."[183] Both Safar and Caquot interpret an inscription on a statue from Temple V as referring to a treasurer of Bar Maren.[184] Milik challenges that reading, preferring "la maisonée," which he interprets as the residents and servants of Bar Maren.[185] In any case, some official must have had charge of the temple revenues, and an inscription from Temple III refers to the accountant of the Temple of Baalshamin.[186] Another inscription names the scribe of Bar Maren.[187] Milik also reads the title *qaššiš*, "elder" ("presbytre"), in several inscriptions, but these are interpreted differently by other editors, so it is not certain that such an official existed.[188] Milik and Caquot also interpret an inscription on an altar as referring to a porter or porters, and Milik suggests that they are porters of the goddess Šalma.[189]

Music and dance apparently played a role in temple ritual, though the evidence is somewhat weak. A statue from Temple V depicts a woman, Qaimei, carrying a small lyre,[190] and another shows a woman with a tambourine.[191] Caquot suggests that an inscription on a fire altar from the Temple of Shamash should be read *rb qynt'*, probably "master of song" but possibly "master of the forge."[192] Another problematical inscription, also on an altar, is interpreted by Teixidor as referring to a person who performed religious dances in honor of Maran,[193] while Milik interprets the words as a generic term, "fonctionnaire sacré."[194]

At Hatra there is a clear distinction between the religious structures inside the wall delimiting the precinct of the great Temple of Shamash and those outside. The temples outside the enclosure wall are relatively small and are based on Mesopotamian plans. Only occasional columns and moldings betray influence from the Greco-Roman world. The sacred structures within the precinct of Shamash are much more varied in form—juxtaposed iwans, temples of Roman provincial type, possibly a raised platform. Especially the architectural decoration shows strong Roman influence. Chronological considerations cannot explain this difference, since the Temple of Shamash is roughly contemporary with some of the smaller temples. The royal family of Hatra was involved with at least some of the small shrines, as well as playing an important role in the Temple of Shamash, and the nobility of the city worshipped in both. If Schlumberger's theory that Hatra was primarily a holy city, a place of pilgrimage,[195] is correct, perhaps the small temples served primarily the inhabitants, while the more imposing precinct of Shamash served both as a pilgrimage center and as a place of worship for the local population. The idea of the smaller shrines as centers of worship for the inhabitants of Hatra is supported by the fact that many are located in residential neighborhoods. The eclectic style of the precinct of Shamash may have been deemed appropriately impressive for a center of worship drawing people from a wide area, the more traditional forms suitable for the local population.

RBYT' in inscription no. 41 from Temple V, which he interprets as referring to an official of another temple; Caquot, *Syria* XXX (1953), 244, reads DBYT' (untranslated) instead. Teixidor suggests that the RBYT' might be an officer of the royal court with a religious function: "The Altars Found at Hatra," *Sumer* XXI (1965), 88. For interpretations of the title, see Downey, *Heracles Sculpture*, 86 and n. 6.

[182] Milik, *Dédicaces*, 386, referring to inscription no. 107.

[183] Teixidor, *Sumer* XXI (1965), 87, pl. III.1.

[184] Caquot, *Syria* XXX (1953), 240 f., inscription no. 35.

[185] Milik, *Dédicaces*, 353, 366.

[186] Caquot, *Syria* XXXII (1955), 54, no. 49; Milik, *Dédicaces*, 400.

[187] Caquot, *Syria* XXX (1953), 240, inscription no. 35.

[188] Milik, *Dédicaces*, 368, reinterpreting Teixidor, *Sumer* XXI (1965), 86 f., pl. II.1; idem, *Dédicaces*, 337, 372, restoring a missing portion of inscription no. 38, for which see Caquot, *Syria* XXX (1953), 243.

[189] Caquot, *Syria* XLI (1964), 271, no. 9; Milik, *Dédicaces*, 386 f. This interpretation seems more reasonable than Teixidor's translation as "gate" (*Sumer* XXI [1965], 87, pl. II.4).

[190] Safar and Mustapha, *Hatra*, 252, fig. 243; Caquot, *Syria* XXX (1953), 240 f., inscription no. 35.

[191] Safar and Mustapha, *Hatra*, 171, fig. 174.

[192] Caquot, *Syria* XLI (1964), 271, no. 3.

[193] Teixidor, *Sumer* XXI (1965), 87, pl. II.2.

[194] Milik, *Dédicaces*, 272.

[195] Schlumberger, *L'Orient hellénisé*, 123 f.

5

THE MESOPOTAMIAN TRADITION IN RELIGIOUS ARCHITECTURE

MESOPOTAMIAN traditions of religious architecture remained vital during the period of Seleucid and Parthian rule, and the evidence from Aï Khanoum suggests that Greek rulers even exported Mesopotamian temple forms to the eastern part of their realm. The great variety in architecture from one city to another shows that the revival of Mesopotamian temple forms was not merely an antiquarian venture but rather that the architecture was still viable, subject to development and change to fit local needs.

In two of the major centers of southern Mesopotamia, Uruk and Babylon, the traditional religion remained vital or was revived during the period of Seleucid rule. At Babylon, cuneiform records show that Seleucid rulers followed the example of Alexander the Great by clearing debris from and at least beginning to rebuild Esagila, the temple of Marduk. Kings at least occasionally made offerings in the temple. On the other hand, the Seleucid royal cult was established in Esagila, an indication that the Greek rulers used the old religion to help consolidate their rule. The assembly at Esagila continued to function, though only to decide temple affairs, but a Greek community, with Greek civic institutions, was also formed. In the nearby city of Borsippa, Antiochos I began to

lay the foundations of Ezida, the temple of Nabu, and texts show that the temple continued to function, perhaps largely in connection with rituals involving processions between it and Esagila.

At Uruk, on the other hand, there is only indirect evidence of royal support of the temples dedicated to the old divinities. Two members of an old family at Uruk who were also city officials built enormous temples to Anu (the Bit rēš) and Ishtar (the Irigal). There is also slight archaeological evidence for work in E-anna, the original temple of Inanna, during the Seleucid period. The only indication of royal support for these building projects is the fact that Anu-uballit-Nikarchos states that King Antiochos gave him his second name. The sheer size of the buildings, however, might suggest that the projects were beyond the capacity of individual citizens, however wealthy. As at Babylon, the Seleucid royal cult was established in the temples at Uruk, but there is no evidence of the kings offering sacrifices there. It is possible, as McEwan suggests, that active royal support for the temples was limited to the Babylon area.[1] The civic organization of Hellenistic Uruk is not well understood. Two systems of record keeping—one in Greek, with the transactions recorded being subject to government tax; the other in Akkadian, with the transactions

---

[1] McEwan, *Priest and Temple*, 193-96.

free of taxation—existed side by side, and records of both types were housed in the Bit rēš. The fact that transactions involving temple income were free from government tax might suggest that the government at least granted privileges to the temples and the people associated with them, though it seems doubtful that a "civic and temple" society of the sort envisaged by Sarkisian was established.[2] There is no evidence for the establishment at Uruk of a Greek community comparable to that at Babylon.

Slight textual evidence suggests royal interest in Egišnugal, the temple of Sin at Ur, where Antiochos I as crown prince perhaps reestablished worship. The date of the large late temple built over the ruins of the Temple of Inanna at Nippur is controversial. Coin evidence suggests a Parthian date, but Heinrich and Oelsner consider the building Seleucid on the basis of its similarity to the Seleucid temples of Uruk.[3] Otherwise, the old centers of southern Mesopotamia apparently fell into decay during the period of Greek rule. Future excavations and textual finds or new interpretations of known texts may alter this picture to some extent, but it now appears that the large-scale revival of traditional temples was largely limited to Uruk and Babylon.

The revival of traditional culture was apparently confined to southern Mesopotamia. In northern Mesopotamia, there is no evidence that Assur was occupied during the period of Greek rule, and at Nimrud houses were built over the ruins of Ezida, the temple of Nabu, which must therefore have ceased to function. At Nineveh, Greek civic institutions are attested only from the Parthian period, but might have been established earlier. The only other late evidence is a statue of Hermes found in a temple of roughly Assyrian form, which might belong to any time after the Greek conquest. A small structure at Arslan Tash, similar in form to the heroon at Aï Khanoum, might have had a religious function.

In the Greek colonies of Seleucia on the Tigris and Dura-Europos, architects were perhaps trying to create new forms of religious architecture by manipulating traditional elements. Tell ʿUmar at Seleucia, which may go back to the Seleucid period, bears a superficial resemblance to a ziggurat and was probably based on the ziggurat form. If Invernizzi's suggestion that the archives building was enclosed in a precinct that also included Tell ʿUmar[4] is correct, then government officials appear to have followed a policy similar to that at Uruk of keeping official records in a temple precinct. The Seleucid religious architecture of Dura-Europos, poorly known as it is, seems to show a mixture of Greek and other traditions. The early form of the Temple of Artemis resembles open-air precincts in the Greek world, and the first Temple of Zeus Megistos (perhaps dedicated to Zeus Olympios) combines a Greek exterior with an un-Greek plan, which was perhaps derived from Babylonian traditions.

The area between Mesopotamia and Afghanistan is largely unknown in the Seleucid period, though if Ghirshman is correct in assigning a first phase of the Temple of Heracles and of the Great Temple at Masjid-i Solaiman to the Seleucid period, and if the largely unknown first phase of the latter building resembled the one of the Parthian period, then a temple based on Babylonian forms was built in Elymais. On the basis of the excavations at Masjid-i Solaiman, Bernard suggests that Seleucid Iran served as an intermediate step in the transmission of architectural forms from Mesopotamia to Bactria.[5] The uncertainty about the Seleucid date and the form of the first phase of the Great Temple at Masjid-i Solaiman suggests that evidence from this site must be used with caution. The two temples so far discovered at Aï Khanoum are based quite closely on Babylonian forms, though the high podia on which they stand reflect Achaemenid traditions. The extramural temple bears a superficial resemblance to the Seleucid Temple of Zeus Megistos at Dura. An open-air podium at Aï Khanoum is probably based on Achaemenid places of worship.

Thus the religious architecture of the three Greek colonies in the east that are at all well known varies considerably. The form of Tell ʿUmar probably results from a decision to echo the ziggurat of nearby Babylon. Since the city was founded in an attempt to draw off the population of Babylon, perhaps Tell ʿUmar represents an attempt to create a place of worship for a mixed Babylonian and Greek population by using a modified version of traditional forms. At Dura the decision to clothe the non-Greek plan of the Temple of Zeus Megistos in externally Greek architecture may represent an attempt to maintain the Greek appearance of the

---

[2] For a summary of Sarkisian's ideas, see Sarkisian, "City Land in Seleucid Babylonia," in I. M. Diakonoff, ed., *Ancient Mesopotamia* (Moscow, 1969), 313 f.

[3] Heinrich, *Tempel und Heiligtümer*, 303, 334 f., fig. 424; Oelsner,

"Kontinuität und Wandel," 104. See the discussion under Nippur.

[4] Invernizzi, *Mesopotamia* III-IV (1968/69), 75 f.

[5] Bernard, "Traditions orientales," 266-70.

colony. At Aï Khanoum, on the other hand, the architecture in general is very mixed. The Mesopotamian forms of the temples may have been chosen as appropriate to syncretistic deities worshipped by a mixed population, though in the absence of concrete evidence about the divinities and their worshippers, it is difficult to draw conclusions.[6]

Seleucid rule of Mesopotamia and Iran was brought to an end by the Parthian conquest of 141 B.C., but the effects of this conquest are not always easy to determine. The Arsacids do not seem to have imposed a new form of government, as shown by extensive evidence from Dura-Europos and by the survival of some Greek institutions at Babylon and apparently at Nineveh. Cuneiform documents show that some of the temples at Babylon, probably including Esagila, continued to function into the first century B.C. Significantly, one of these texts also implies that the Akitu festival continued to be celebrated.[7] There is no archaeological evidence for Arsacid work on the temples.

At Uruk, both the Bit rēš and the Irigal were destroyed by fire, perhaps during the Parthian conquest, and after this destruction, the areas lost their sacred character and rather poor houses were built over the ruins.[8] A village also grew up in the ruins of E-anna.[9] At Uruk, in fact, the Parthian conquest apparently resulted in a fundamental change. According to Lenzen, the non-Babylonian burial customs suggest that the inhabitants of the villages that grew up in the ruins of the great sanctuaries might have been foreigners. Coin evidence suggests that there was a hiatus of about 130 years between the last activity in the large Seleucid sanctuaries and the reemergence of the town in the last years of the first century B.C.[10] Another fortified settlement was established on a mound to the southeast of the former sanctuaries, probably to house a foreign population, possibly the Dollamēnoi of the inscription of A.D. 111.[11]

A drastic change in the forms of religious architecture followed the destruction and abandonment of the Seleucid sanctuaries and the resettlement of the area. The small temple built against the southeast wall of the Seleucid Anu-Antum temple probably served the population of the village that grew

up in the ruins of the Bit rēš. It took its square shape and cult niche in the rear wall from Babylonian tradition, but the engaged columns and pilasters that decorated the exterior were derived from Hellenistic-Roman architecture. The temple of the otherwise unknown god Gareus was probably built by a small group of foreigners resident in Uruk, the Dollamēnoi of the inscription. The foreign nature of the cult is emphasized by the use of Greek for the inscription and the fact that most of the rituals mentioned follow Greek rather than Babylonian practices.[12] The temple itself is a hybrid: the interior, with its cult niche in the rear wall, reflects Babylonian traditions, but the elaborate articulation of the exterior is based on Hellenistic-Roman architecture, probably at a considerable remove. The columns are hybrid, with Ionic bases and capitals but Doric flutes, and the engaged pilasters are topped with moldings of Greek type, above which are strange monsters perhaps derived from the Babylonian fashion of fantastic animals in molded brick. The relationship between the row of columns in front of the temple and the building proper remains unexplained.

The closest parallels to the Temple of Gareus are found in the Parthian architecture of northern Mesopotamia. The combination of moldings based on Greco-Roman forms with hybrid creatures is seen also in the little peripteral temple in the precinct of Shamash at Hatra (the so-called Temple of Bar Maren), and there also a colonnade stands without a clear relationship to the building proper.[13] The same is true of the peripteros at Assur.

If the Parthian dating of the large temple built over the ruins of the temple of Inanna at Nippur is correct,[14] Nippur would provide the unique instance in southern Mesopotamia of a Parthian rebuilding of a long-destroyed temple following a Babylonian scheme.

The Great Temple of the Parthian period at Masjid-i Solaiman has a highly original plan. The core of the building follows a Babylonian bent-axis scheme, with a long antecella-cella unit behind a court, but this core is encased in a circumambulatory corridor, a feature not found in Babylonian temples and perhaps based on Iranian traditions.

[6] Ibid., 266-74.
[7] McEwan, *Iraq* XLVII (1981), 132-42. The Akitu festival is mentioned in pp. 132-35, lines 13 f.
[8] Falkenstein, *Topographie*, 9, 34; H. Schmid, *UVB* XVI, 20-22.
[9] Lenzen, *UVB* XII/XIII, 19, 31.
[10] Lenzen, *UVB* XV, 24; Robert McC. Adams and Hans J. Nissen, *The Uruk Countryside* (Chicago and London, 1972), 57 f.

[11] J. Schmidt, *BaM* V (1970), 89-91; idem, *UVB* XXVI/XXVII, 57-59, 61.
[12] Meier, *BaM* I (1960), 104-114.
[13] For the temple, see Safar and Mustapha, *Hatra*, 16, 374, 380-82, 388, 392 f.
[14] Keall, *Late Parthian Nippur*, 55 f. and n. 2. The date is discussed in the chapter on Nippur.

The portico on the entrance facade, if correctly restored, could be based loosely on Greco-Roman forms. This temple represents the easternmost example presently known of a temple belonging to the Parthian period that is based in part on Babylonian forms. Elymais can be regarded geographically as an extension of Mesopotamia. Our present evidence, then, suggests that during the Parthian period, temples of Babylonian type were confined to Mesopotamia and the adjacent regions (Elymais in the east and Dura-Europos in Parapotamia in the west).

In northern Mesopotamia, the city of Assur revived probably during the first century B.C., and Hatra flourished from the first century B.C. through about the middle of the third century A.D. The religious architecture of the Parthian period in these two cities exhibits a great deal of variety. At Assur, the only religious structure of the Assyrian period to be rebuilt following the old plan was the festival house. The fact that the building was rebuilt would seem to imply that the Akitu festival was still celebrated. The god Assur continued to be worshipped as well, judging from the graffiti to Assur and his consort Scherua found on the benches of the iwans that were built over the ruins of the Assyrian Assur temple. Though the temple of the Parthian period was built in the old precinct, the iwan was a new form, probably developed in Mesopotamia.[15]

Temple A, built in the courtyard of the old Assur precinct and apparently dedicated to Heracles, followed the form of its Neo-Babylonian predecessor. The peripteros, however it is restored, shows an unusual combination of forms. Its plan can possibly be interpreted as an antecella-cella complex of the Babylonian "broad room" type, preceded by an iwan-like room, the whole encased on three sides in a colonnade of Greek inspiration. The eclectic character of this building recalls the Temple of Gareus at Uruk and the so-called Temple of Bar Maren at Hatra. The "Freitreppenbau" at Assur is extremely difficult to interpret. If it was a religious building, its relationship to the ziggurat behind it recalls the arrangement of some Assyrian temples. If it was essentially an open-air platform, as seems possible, then Iranian influence might be suggested. The main characteristic of the religious architecture of Parthian date in Assur seems to be eclecticism.

Hatra, unlike Assur, was not a major center before the Parthian period, though apparently there are some traces of Assyrian occupation on the site. Only some of the temples followed Mesopotamian traditions. The type consisting of juxtaposed iwans, seen at Assur in the buildings above the old Assur temple, is particularly highly developed at Hatra. Roman influence is stronger at Hatra than at the other sites in the area, and is seen, for example, in the architectural decoration of the Temple of Shamash. The temples within the precinct of Shamash are either juxtaposed iwans or can be regarded as variations on Roman provincial temple types.

Many of the small temples in Hatra that were built outside the precinct of Shamash follow Mesopotamian prototypes, however. The basic scheme, described by Lenzen as a reversed T, has a long narrow sanctuary room entered on one of the long sides, with a cult chamber or niche in the rear wall opposite the door. Some of the temples open directly onto a street, but in others the sanctuary unit is set at the back of a court. This plan can perhaps be viewed as a simplified version of a frequent Assyrian temple type, in which the antecella-cella unit consists of a wide antecella with a deep narrow cella behind it. The scheme seems to appear for the first time in the Sin-Shamash Temple of Assurnirari I at Assur, where two such units flank a court, and it was also used for the Anu-Hadad Temple at Assur.[16] In the temples of the Assyrian period the antecella-cella units form part of a larger complex, including a court (seen in some of the Hatran temples) and other subsidiary rooms. It seems possible, then, that the Hatra temples imitated Assyrian prototypes, though apparently the temples of Assur were so ruined by the Parthian period that it is not clear whether they could have served as models. In any case, it is interesting that the sanctuary unit appears to be based on Assyrian rather than Babylonian schemes. Other elements, such as the access to the roof provided in some temples, may be derived from Babylonia.

The impact of the Parthian conquest on Seleucia on the Tigris is difficult to assess, since the remains of the city are so poorly known. The better preserved of the two possible temples of the Parthian period consists of an unroofed square enclosure surrounded by a covered portico, with a small theater to one side. This somewhat unusual building

---

[15] Colledge, *Parthian Art,* 47 f., 63 f.; Schlumberger, *L'Orient hellénisé*, 186–88.

[16] Haller, *Heiligtümer*, 82–86, fig. 24, pls. 16–18; Andrae, *Der*

Anu-Adad-Tempel in Assur (10. *WVDOG*) (Leipzig, 1909), 7–78, pls. IV, V, VIII, IX.

has analogies with some Sasanian temples (e.g., Bishapur) but also with Syrian sanctuaries like that of Baalshamin at Sîʾ in the Hauran. Theatral areas are a common feature of temples to goddesses at Dura, but otherwise the Seleucia building is very different from the temples of Dura. The incorporation of a theatral area into a sacred precinct seems to be a feature of Syrian cults. In the Parthian period, then, two former Greek colonies, one in Mesopotamia, the other in Parapotamia, share common elements with Syrian sanctuaries.

At Dura-Europos no new temples were built in the years immediately following the Parthian capture of the city in 113 B.C.[17] This period of stagnation was followed by two bursts of temple construction: one lasting from about the middle of the first century B.C. to about the middle of the first century A.D., and another in about the middle of the second century A.D.[18] Perhaps this gap in temple construction should be explained as the result of a period of relative poverty and stagnation following the Parthian conquest, though the fact that changes were made in the agora area in the late second century B.C. shows that building in the city did not altogether stop.[19]

The temples that were built in Dura after the Parthian conquest differ drastically from the two temples of the Seleucid era. With very few exceptions, the temples built during the periods of Parthian and Roman control follow the Babylonian court plan. The forms of the two temples that go back to the Seleucid period were changed completely by the rebuildings of the middle of the first century B.C. The thorough destruction of the first Temple of Zeus Megistos (perhaps originally Zeus Olympios) might have been the result of the Parthian conquest, but there is no evidence of similar destruction in the precinct of Artemis. In the precinct of Artemis, a Doric *naiskos* that was being constructed in place of the earlier structure was apparently pulled down before completion to be replaced by the court temple of 40–32 B.C.[20] In the Temple of Zeus Megistos also, the elements derived from Greek architecture—principally the Doric propylon—disappeared in the new structure, which had the form of a free-standing sanctuary unit set in a court.

The later Dura temples are original creations

based on the principles of Babylonian architecture. Some features characteristic of earlier Babylonian temples are omitted—the cult niche, the decoration of the exterior walls with recesses and projections—but other features that do not appear in earlier Mesopotamian religious architecture are added. The most notable of these is the *salle aux gradins*, apparently an element of Syrian cults. Although the majority of the deities to whom these temples are dedicated are Semitic, the Babylonian temple type appears to have been suitable for the worship of a variety of divinities, including the Greek Artemis and the Anatolian Jupiter Dolichenus.

The dramatic change in temple type in Dura does not appear to have been a direct result of the Parthian conquest, for the new temples followed the capture of the city by some seventy-five years. The Parthians did not displace the Greek civic structure, nor, apparently, did they change the religious structure. A papyrus of A.D. 180 that is dated by the eponymous priests of the Seleucid dynastic cults alongside the official Roman dating shows that these cults survived the period of Parthian rule.[21] Artemis continued to be worshipped in her new temple by members of the Macedonian aristocracy. There is no evidence for a sudden large influx of a new, non-Greek population. In fact, the Macedonian aristocracy continued to dominate the city. Perhaps this aristocracy began to feel distanced from their Greek heritage and more open to local traditions. The evidence from the agora area suggests that the transition from Greek agora to oriental bazaar began in the last quarter of the second century B.C., at the time of the transition from Greek to Parthian political control. Brown suggests that the end of Greek political control led to the "abandonment of the Greek conception of the agora as the characteristic expression of the economic life of the city."[22] The sudden burst of temple building is at any rate evidence of increased prosperity, perhaps as a result of increased trade. A greater openness to foreign elements in about the middle of the first century B.C. is perhaps suggested by the building of the Necropolis Temple by Palmyrenes in 33 B.C. and the erection within the city of a small chapel in the area that was later occupied by a temple built by Palmyrenes in honor of the Gaddé of Dura and Palmyra.[23] The Necropolis

---

[17] For the date of the Parthian conquest of Dura, see A. R. Bellinger, *Final Report VI: The Coins* (New Haven, 1949), 199-201.

[18] Brown, *Dura Report* VII/VIII, 195.

[19] Brown, *Dura Report* IX.1, 28-43.

[20] Brown, *Dura Report* VII/VIII, 407-411, does not discuss the date of or reasons for the destruction of the first precinct.

[21] Welles, *Final Report V: Part I: The Parchments and Papyri* (New Haven, 1959), 6 f., 128-31; idem, *Dura Report* VI, 430 f.

[22] Brown, *Dura Report* IX.1, 43.

[23] Torrey, *Dura Report* VII/VIII, 318-20, no. 916; Brown, *Dura Report* VII/VIII, 226 f., 256 f., 324 f.

temple follows a Babylonian rather than a Palmyrene temple type.

In both Dura-Europos and Uruk the temples built after the Parthian conquest are very different from those built during the period of Seleucid control, but the effects of the Parthian conquest on the two cities were otherwise very different. The Parthian conquest of Uruk apparently brought wholesale destruction of the city and with it of the traditional culture; and the inhabitants of the villages that grew up in the ruins of the Seleucid sanctuaries do not appear to have been Babylonians. The two temples of the Parthian period, then, represent a foreign intrusion, though the fact that the interior arrangements utilize some elements derived from Babylonian architecture shows an awareness of local tradition. Roman influence is very strong in the exterior details. At Dura, on the other hand, there does not seem to be evidence of widespread destruction as a result of the Parthian conquest, nor did the population change drastically. Yet a gradual orientalization of the city's architecture followed the Parthian conquest, beginning perhaps with changes in the agora area in the late second century B.C. and dramatically manifested in the Babylonian form of the temples.

It is not possible easily to explain the different developments at Uruk and at Dura. It is somewhat paradoxical that cities that are more distant from the Roman world—Uruk and Hatra—show stronger influence from Roman architecture than does Dura-Europos, which ultimately fell under Roman administration. The variety of forms of religious architecture in the cities of the Parthian period—Uruk, Hatra, Assur, Masjid-i Solaiman and Bard-è Néchandeh, perhaps Nippur and Seleucia, and Dura-Europos—demonstrates the vitality of Mesopotamian traditions and the strength of local control.

APPENDIX

List of Seleucid Kings

After Colledge, *Parthian Art*, p. 166, with the kind permission of Professor Colledge.

Seleukos I, king	312-281 B.C.
(Antiochos I, son of Seleukos, co-ruler of the eastern satrapies	294/293-281 B.C.)
Antiochos I, king	281-261 B.C.
(Seleukos, son of Antiochos I, co-ruler in east	279-268 B.C.)
(Antiochos II, son of Antiochos I, co-ruler in east	268-261 B.C.)
Antiochos II Theos, king	261-246 B.C.
Seleukos II Kallinikos	246-226 B.C.
Seleukos III Sōtēr Keraunos, son of Seleukos II	226-223 B.C.
Antiochos III "the Great," son of Seleukos II	223-187 B.C.
(Seleukos IV, son of Antiochos III, co-ruler	189-187 B.C.)
Seleukos IV Philopator	187-175 B.C.
Antiochos IV Epiphanēs, son of Antiochos III	175-164/163 B.C.
Antiochos V, son of Antiochos IV	164/163-162 B.C.
Demetrios I, son of Seleukos IV	162-151/150 B.C.
Alexander I Balas	153/152-145 B.C.
Antiochos VI, son of Alexander I Balas	144 B.C.
Diodotos Tryphon	142/141-137 B.C.
(Demetrios II Nikatōr, son of Demetrios I, co-ruler	ca. 153/152-147 B.C.)
Demetrios II Nikatōr, king	147-140/139 B.C.
Antiochos VII Sidetes, son of Demetrios I	138-129 B.C.
Demetrios II Nikatōr, again	129-126/125 B.C.
Alexander II Zabinas (usurper)	ca. 132-123 B.C.
Seleukos V, son of Demetrios II	126 B.C.
Antiochos VIII Grypos, son of Demetrios II	126-96 B.C.
Antiochos IX Cyzicenos, son of Antiochos VII	113-95 B.C.
Seleukos VI, son of Antiochos VIII	95 B.C.
Antiochos X, son of Antiochos IX	ca. 95 B.C.
Antiochos XI, son of Antiochos VIII	ca. 95 B.C.
Demetrios III, son of Antiochos VIII	ca. 95-88 B.C.
Philip I, son of Antiochos VIII	ca. 95-84/83 B.C.
Antiochos XII, son of Antiochos VIII	87 B.C.
Philip II, son of Philip I	84/83-ca. 67 B.C.
Antiochos XIII Asiaticus, son of Antiochos X?	ca. 83 B.C.
(kingdom taken over by Tigranes the Great of Armenia	83-ca. 69 B.C.)
Antiochos XIII (again)	ca. 69-64 B.C.

GLOSSARY

AEDICULA: a small construction, often with the form of a temple facade

AGORA: marketplace (in a Greek city)

ANDRŌN: literally "men's apartment"; the term is used of one of the chambers of the Temple of Aphlad at Dura

ANTA: square pilaster at either side of door or on the corners of a building

ANTECELLA: room in front of the cult room (q.v. *cella*) of a temple

BIT AKITU: house for the New Year's festival in Babylonian religion

BOULĒ: council, senate

BOULEUTAI: councillors, senators

BOULEUTERION: council chamber, senate house

BULLA: clay pellet used to seal a document on parchment or papyrus

CELLA: cult room of a temple

CHREOPHYLAX: registrar

CHTHONIC: of the earth

EPHEBE: a youth eighteen years of age

EPHĒBEION: an association of youths eighteen years of age

EPISTATĒS: "president"; a title of civic office often held concurrently with that of *stratēgos*

EPONYMOUS: used to designate persons or deities after whom a city is named

HEROON: shrine of a hero, often a founder of a city

HYPAETHRAL: unroofed, open to the sky

IWAN: a large rectangular room, with an arched entrance and normally roofed with a barrel vault

KISU: a bench or low terrace wall applied against the exterior wall of buildings

LECTISTERNIUM: a feast offered to deities, in which their images were placed on couches

NAISKOS: small temple or cult chamber

NAOS: cult chamber, cella

ODEON: a public hall, generally for musical performances

OIKODOMĒ: structure; in the Dura inscriptions, it seems to mean room

OIKOS: house, or part of a house; room; in the Dura inscriptions, it seems to mean room

PAREDROS: associate, consort

PATERA: a vessel used for liquid offerings

PERIPTEROS: building surrounded by columns

PERISTYLE: surrounding colonnade

PODIUM: a high platform, serving *inter alia* as a base for a temple

POLIS: city. Used here to designate city organization of a Greek type

PRONAOS: room in front of the naos or cult chamber

PROPYLON: entrance gate

SALLE AUX GRADINS: room with stairs, of ritual use

STOA: a columnar portico

STRATĒGOS: literally "general"; title of a civic office often held concurrently with that of *epistatēs*, "president"

SYNNAOS THEOS: a deity sharing a temple with another deity

TEMENOS: walled precinct, of religious character

TEMPLE À REDANS: temple with niches, at Aï Khanoum

THYMIATĒRION: incense burner

INDEX OF
LITERARY SOURCES

GENERAL INDEX

BUILDINGS are normally indexed under the cities in which they are located. Nouns are given in the singular, except those nouns which appear in the text only in the plural. All Greek is transliterated. Persons who are known only from inscriptions and not from historical sources are identified by profession (if known) and the city in which their name appears.

Abbas Abou (at Dura-Europos), 105
Abbaui, priest (at Dura-Europos), 109
ʿAbdšalmâ (at Dura-Europos), 110
Abeismachchinos, priest of Artemis (at Dura-Europos), 92
ʿAbgal, 112
Abidnerglos (at Dura-Europos), 78, 92
ablutions, 58, 110
acanthus leaf, 134
access to roof, 114, 125, 161. *See also* stair (staircase) to roof
Achaemenid architectural elements, 3, 86; architecture, 3, 84-85; period, 15, 43, 64-65, 75, 84, 131, 134, 136, 147; rule, 15, 34; traditions, 65, 85, 134, 176. *See also* terrace: Achaemenid
Achaemenids, 33-34, 47, 84
acolyte, 129
acrolithic, 60, 71
acrometallic, 60
acropolis, 48, 64, 76, 148
Adadiabos, son of Zabdibolos, son of Siiloi (at Dura-Europos), 112, 130
Adad-nadin-akhé (at Girsu), 48
Adad-nirari II, 48
Addaru (month of), 15
Adeos (at Dura-Europos), 114
Adōn[aiōi ("lord"), 104n
Adonis, 104, 120-22. *See also* Dura-Europos: Temple of Adonis
adyton, 168
aedicula, 89, 97, 107-8, 110, 113, 116, 118, 120, 122, 128, 139, 163, 167
Afghanistan, 3, 63, 73, 176
ʿAglibol, 107-8, 118
agora, 14, 63, 78, 83, 129, 148, 150, 155. *See also* Babylon; Dura-Europos; Seleucia on the Tigris
Ahuramazda, 155
Aḫʾutu (family at Uruk), 44
Aï Khanoum, 3-4, 50, 63-76, 78, 85-86, 132-34, 176; administrative quarter, *see* palace; extramural temple, 73-75, 76, 85, 85n, 142, 176; fountain, 3, 65; gymna-

sium, 65; heroon of Kinéas, 50, 59, 62, 65, 72, 98, 176; mausoleum, 65; palace, 64-65, 86; podium, 75-76, 162, 176; propylaea, 64-65; squatter occupation, 64, 72; temple à redans, 64-76, 85-86, 132; temple à redans phase V, 65-68; theater, 63, 65
Akitu: festival, 13, 27, 177-78; house, 35, 37, 98; of Anu, 35, 37; of Ishtar, 35, 37; temple, 13
Akkad, 7
Akkadian, 18, 28, 32, 42-45, 175
Akra (Jerusalem), 88
alabastron, 130
Albinus (at Dura-Europos), 96
Alexander, son of Epinicus (at Dura-Europos), 115
Alexander the Great, 3, 7, 9, 10-13, 48, 63; successors of, *see* Diadochs
Alexander II, 10
Alexander III, 10
Alexander IV, 9
Alexandria, 120
Allât, 161-62
allotments, 43, 46. *See also* prebend
altar: at Aï Khanoum, 67, 69, 73; at Assur, 150-51; at Babylon, 40; at Dura-Europos, 62, 78-79, 82, 89-90, 92, 95, 97, 99-102, 107-10, 112, 114-16, 119-20, 122, 125-30; fire, 167, 173; at Hatra, 162, 170, 173; horned, 120; incense, 103, 108, 110, 113, 170; at Masjid-i Solaiman, 132, 134; monumental, 82, 89-90, 92-93, 95, 97, 99, 103, 105, 107-8, 110, 113-16, 120-22, 124-25, 127-28; at Nimrud, 48; at Seleucia, 52, 59-60; at Uruk, 22, 25, 32, 142
Altyn, 65
Ammonios, son of Apollophanes (at Dura-Europos), 102, 104-5
amphora, 120, 127; handles, 48
Amu Darya. *See* Oxus
amulet, 116
Anahita, 73, 134-36, 155
Anath, 99, 110, 112, 125
Anatolian, 179
ancestor, 42-43

186

LIBRARY OF CONGRESS CATALOGING-IN-PUBLICATION DATA

Downey, Susan B., 1938–
Mesopotamian religious architecture.

Bibliography: p.   Includes index.
1. Middle East—Civilization—To 622. 2. Middle East—Religion.
3. Architecture—Middle East. 4. Middle East—Antiquities. I. Title.
DS57.D68 1988   939'.4   87-3336
ISBN 0-691-03589-X (alk. paper)